Leipzig Studies on International, European and Foreign Public Law

Edited by
Prof. Dr. Markus Kotzur
Prof. Dr. Stephanie Schiedermair
Prof. Dr. Dominik Steiger
Prof. Dr. Mattias Wendel, Maître en droit

Institute for International Law, European Law and Foreign Public law at the University of Leipzig

Volume 23

Catharina Hübner

The Legitimacy of the Afghan Amnesty Law under International Law

Nomos

The Deutsche Nationalbibliothek lists this publication in the Deutsche Nationalbibliografie; detailed bibliographic data are available on the Internet at http://dnb.d-nb.de

a.t.: Leipzig, Univ., Diss., 2020

ISBN 978-3-8487-7910-9 (Print)
978-3-7489-2237-7 (ePDF)

British Library Cataloguing-in-Publication Data
A catalogue record for this book is available from the British Library.

ISBN 978-3-8487-7910-9 (Print)
978-3-7489-2237-7 (ePDF)

Library of Congress Cataloging-in-Publication Data
Hübner, Catharina
The Legitimacy of the Afghan Amnesty Law under International Law
Catharina Hübner
339 pp.
Includes bibliographic references.

ISBN 978-3-8487-7910-9 (Print)
978-3-7489-2237-7 (ePDF)

Onlineversion
Nomos eLibrary

1st Edition 2020

Preface

This doctoral thesis was undertaken after the completion of my LL.M. in European and International Law at the Department of European, International and Public Law at the University of Leipzig (Germany).

I was inspired to write this thesis after observing contradictory developments in international (criminal) law and discussing these topics with my doctoral supervisor Prof. Dr. Markus Kotzur, LL.M. (Duke Univ.). For these insightful discussions and for Prof. Dr. Kotzur's continual support, suggestions for further thinking, and unwavering confidence in me and my dissertation, I am especially grateful.

At the beginning of my doctoral studies, exchange with various scientists from the Max Planck Institute for the Study of Crime, Security and Law (formerly Max Planck Institute for Foreign and International Criminal Law) and the Max Planck Institute for Comparative Public Law and International Law was also of great importance to me and my work. Especially valuable was the expert opinion of Prof. Dr. Anja Seibert-Fohr, LL.M. (GWU), at the time a research assistant at the Max Planck Institute for Comparative Public Law and International Law, who I would like to thank for her input. The staff from the Rule of Law Unit at the United Nations Assistance Mission in Afghanistan (UNAMA) was also extremely helpful. I would like to take this opportunity to thank them for their willingness to support my work.

I would also like to thank Prof. Dr. Stephanie Schiedermair for providing the second opinion on my dissertation and for her helpful and pleasant support in the final phase of the doctorate.

I am also grateful for the financial support provided by the Free State of Saxony in the form of a scholarship.

My special thanks go to my family and friends. Without their support, their encouragement, their constructive criticism and above all their faith in this project I would not have been able to finish it so successfully.

Berlin, August 20th, 2020 *Catharina Hübner*

Table of Contents

1 Introduction

> *"Every day our children, brothers, and relatives are being killed...Our wives become widows and our children orphans...Everyone wants peace. People are tired of wars and want it to end at any cost."*[1]

Suffering from four decades of war, Afghanistan is still deeply rooted in conflict. The instability has recently increased[2] and, according to the United Nations, about half of the country's provinces are at a high or extreme threat level.[3] Violations of human rights are still a daily reality in many parts of Afghanistan.[4] These pressing problems apart, the country has to tackle a legacy of severe violations of international human rights and humanitarian law, such as torture, rape, disappearances, looting, arbitrary detention, mass executions and bombings that targeted civilians.[5] A survey by the Afghan Independent Human Rights Commission (AIHRC)

---

1 Male, 58, Tajik, Behsud, Nangarhar, Afghanistan. Interview by AREU, *see* Echavez, Chona R., Pilongo, Leah Wilfreda RE, A. Jayakody, Noorzai, Ahmad Saboor Hamza, M. Markova and S. Narasimhaiah, *Transitional Justice: Views from the Ground on How Afghanistan Fares*. https://areu.org.af/wp-content/uploads/2016/12/1622E-Transitional-Justice-Views-from-the-Ground-on-How-Afghanistan-Fares.pdf (30 November 2017), p. 23.

2 Human Rights Watch, *World Report 2016: Afghanistan*. https://www.hrw.org/world-report/2016/country-chapters/afghanistan (28.01.16); Human Rights Watch, *World Report 2015: Afghanistan*. https://www.hrw.org/world-report/2015/country-chapters/afghanistan (04.08.16); B. R. Rubin, 'The Transformation of the Afghan State' in A. J. Thier (ed.), *The Future of Aghanistan* (Washington D.C., 2009), pp. 13–21, at pp. 13–7.

3 Human Rights Watch Human Rights Watch, *World Report 2016: Afghanistan*. https://www.hrw.org/world-report/2016/country-chapters/afghanistan.

4 Human Rights Watch, *Afghanistan: Little Progress on Rights*. http://www.hrw.org/news/2012/01/23/afghanistan-little-progress-rights (18 January 2016), p. 2.

5 Afghanistan Independent Human Rights Commission (AIHRC), *A Call for Justice: A National Consultation on past Human Rights Violations in Afghanistan*. http://www.refworld.org/pdfid/47fdfad50.pdf (11 January 2017), p. 4; E. Winterbotham, *The State of Transitional Justice in Afghanistan: Actors, Approaches and Challenges*. http://www.areu.org.af/Uploads/EditionPdfs/1009E-The%20State%20of%20Transitional%20Justice%20in%20Afghanistan%20-%20Actors,%20Approaches%20and%20Challenges%20DP%202010%20Final%20Web.pdf (18 January 2016), p. 3; A. Jackson, *The Cost of War: Afghan Experiences of Conflict, 1978 – 2009*. http://www.oxfam.org/sites/www.oxfam.org/files/afghanistan-the-cost-of-war.pdf (18 January 2016), p. 4.

revealed that almost all Afghans have in some way experienced the effects of the violence committed by all sides of the conflicts.[6]

As long as these conflicts have troubled Afghanistan various attempts have been made to reconcile the parties in conflict and negotiate a political settlement or peace agreement – unfortunately without success.[7] In 2010, the Afghan government announced the entry into force of a blanket amnesty[8].[9] Relying only on the wording of the controversial Afghan Amnesty Law[10], the motivations seemed indeed to be the promotion of peace and reconciliation as well as the alleviation of internal unrest. However, the real reasons for the amnesty were obscured. Moreover, it encompassed a blanket amnesty not only for perpetrators of past crimes but also for those who ended violence only after the enforcement of the Amnesty Law.[11] This approach surpassed many other amnesty regulations from around the world insofar as in most cases, the crimes concerned must be perpetrated before the amnesty law is enacted.[12]

In September 2016, Ashraf Ghani, current President of Afghanistan and Gulbuddin Hekmatyar, leader of the insurgent group Hezb-e Islami signed

---

6 Afghanistan Independent Human Rights Commission (AIHRC), *A Call for Justice*, p. 8.

7 International Crisis Group, *Talking About Talks: Toward a Political Settlement in Afghanistan*. http://www.crisisgroup.org/~/media/Files/asia/south-asia/afghanistan/221-talking-about-talks-toward-a-political-settlement-in-afghanistan (19 January 2016), p. 5.

8 The term 'amnesty' means the impossibility of bringing perpetrators to account – whether in criminal or in civil proceedings (a form of providing impunity), *see* UN Office of the High Commissioner for Human Rights, *Rule-of-Law Tools for Post-Conflict States: Amnesties*, HR/PUB/09/1. http://www.ohchr.org/Documents/Publications/Amnesties_en.pdf (07 January 2016), p. 5; United Nations Commission on Human Rights, *Report of the Independent Expert to Update the Set of Principles to Combat Impunity, Diane Orentlicher, Addendum: Updated Set of Principles for the Protection and Promotion of Human Rights Through Action to Combat Impunity*, E/CN.4/2005/102/Add.1, p. 6.

9 S. Salahuddin, *Afghanistan Must Not Repeal Amnesty Law* (Kabul: Reuters, 2010).

10 „National Reconciliation, General Amnesty, and National Stability Law", Official Gazette, dated: 13 Qaus 1387 Serial No: (965) (unofficial English translation), in: S. Kouvo, *After Two Years in Legal Limbo: A first Glance at the Approved 'Amnesty law'*. http://aan-afghanistan.com/index.asp?id=665 (13 January 2016).

11 *See* Article 3 (1) and (2) of the National Reconciliation, General Amnesty, and National Stability Law.

12 M. Freeman, *Necessary Evils: Amnesties and the Search for Justice* (Cambridge, UK, New York: Cambridge University Press, 2009), p. 16.

a peace deal.[13] The agreement *inter alia* grants in its Article 9 amnesty to Hekmatyar, "one of Afghanistan's most notorious war crimes suspects"[14], and other members of Hezb-e Islami for alleged international crimes committed during the Afghan civil war in the 1990s.[15] The legal basis for the impunity provision is to be found in the Afghan Amnesty Law of 2010.[16] The declared aim of the deal was to bring peace to Afghanistan.[17] Whether this aim can be achieved through such a broad amnesty is a tough question.

1.1 Purpose of the Study

How does this very broad and unconditional amnesty for serious international crimes fit into the presumed "age of accountability"? Or in other words, are the regulations of the Afghan Amnesty Law compatible with Afghanistan's obligations under international law?[18]

In the view of human rights scholars and activists, as well as many victims, Afghanistan's blanket amnesty stands for lawlessness, the satisfaction of personal interests and entrenched impunity.[19] They would possibly

---

13 S. Bengali and S. Faizy, 'Afghanistan Takes a Step Toward Peace With Notorious Ex-Warlord', Los Angeles Times, 22 September 2016; B. Osman, *Peace With Hekmatyar: What Does It Mean for Battlefield and Politics?* https://www.afghanistan-analysts.org/peace-with-hekmatyar-what-does-it-mean-for-battlefield-and-politics/ (10 October 2016), p. 1.

14 P. Gossman, *Afghanistan War Crimes Suspect Comes Home: Hekmatyar Deal an Affront to Victims of Grave Abuses*. https://www.hrw.org/print/294431 (12 October 2016).

15 Article nine of the agreement says that the government "provides guarantee for the judicial immunity of the leader and members of Hezb-e Islami concerning the party's past political and military actions.", *see* Osman, *Peace With Hekmatyar*, p. 4.

16 Ibid., pp. 10–1.

17 Bengali and Faizy, 'Afghanistan Takes a Step Toward Peace With Notorious Ex-Warlord'.

18 M. Freeman and M. Pensky, 'The Amnesty Controversy in International Law' in F. Lessa and L. A. Payne (eds.), *Amnesty in the Age of Human Rights Accountability: Comparative and International Perspectives* (Cambridge, New York: Cambridge University Press, 2012), pp. 42–65, at pp. 46–8; Afghanistan Independent Human Rights Commission (AIHRC), *Discussion Paper on the Legality of Amnesties*. http://www.aihrc.org.af/media/files/Reports/Thematic%20reports/Amnesties_paper_23_Feb_2010.pdf (25 January 2016).

19 L. Mallinder (2008), p. 1.

deem it illegal without need for further verification.[20] However, it is not as simple as that. In order to reach a conclusion in this matter it is necessary to fully examine relevant international law, while taking into account the specific situation in Afghanistan and the exact details of the Afghan Amnesty Law. An analysis in this sense encompasses different stages of legal examination. In the event that the results of the examination reveal that there is indeed a trend towards outlawing blanket amnesties for serious international crimes, Afghanistan must abrogate or amend its Amnesty Law to remove the blanket amnesty provision and to act in accordance with international law.

In that case, it would be expedient to make proposals with respect to a transitional justice process in Afghanistan to pave the way for lasting peace and reconciliation, for justice and respect for the rule of law. In this context, it is necessary to adequately integrate the specific political, social and cultural circumstances of the country in order to meet the needs of victims and Afghan society. To accomplish this mission, different judicial and non-judicial mechanisms come into consideration. The basic mechanisms of so-called transitional justice[21] are now well established[22] and range from an amnesty, which must however be legitimate under international law, to criminal investigations, trials, and prosecutions by national, international or hybrid courts. In this way perpetrators deemed to be the most responsible for human rights violations shall be brought to justice. Apart from amnesties and prosecutions, the remaining transitional justice mechanisms encompass truth commissions[23], reparation pro-

---

20 *See* W. Schabas, *Unimaginable Atrocities: Justice, Politics, and Rights at the War Crimes Tribunals*, 1st edn. (Oxford: Oxford University Press, 2012), p. 173.

21 United Nations, *What is Transitional Justice? A Backgrounder*. https://www.un.org/en/peacebuilding/pdf/doc_wgll/justice_times_transition/26_02_2008_background_note.pdf (07 January 2016).

22 D. Tolbert, *Address by David Tolbert to the National Forum on Launching the Dialogue on Transitional Justice in Tunisia*. http://ictj.org/news/address-david-tolbert-national-forum-launching-dialogue-transitional-justice-tunisia (07 January 2016).

23 Truth Commissions are temporary bodies officially sanctioned by the state or an international governmental organization to investigate a pattern of past abuses and issue a report, *see* T. D. Olsen, L. A. Payne and A. G. Reiter, *Transitional Justice in Balance: Comparing Processes, Weighing Efficacy* (Washington, D.C: U.S. Institute of Peace Press, 2010), p. 34; United Nations, *What is Transitional Justice? A Backgrounder*, pp. 3–4; International Center for Transitional Justice (ICTJ), *What is Transitional Justice?* http://ictj.org/about/transitional-justice (07 January 2016).

grams[24], lustration policies and institutional reforms[25].[26] Other important elements are the construction of memory projects[27] as well as traditional justice initiatives.[28] Crucial for success of the transitional justice process is a holistic approach. Such an approach includes several transitional justice mechanisms that complement and reinforce each other.[29] This means that, for example truth commissions, reparation programs, institutional reforms and criminal prosecutions should be combined. Single mechanisms, such as truth commissions in isolation from reparation programs and institutional reforms should be avoided since they are inadequate to achieve the objective of justice, reconciliation and respect for the rule of law.[30]

---

24 Reparation programs are state-sponsored initiatives that aim to contribute to repairing the material and moral consequences of past abuses experienced by victims, *see* United Nations, *What is Transitional Justice? A Backgrounder*, pp. 3–4; International Center for Transitional Justice (ICTJ), *What is Transitional Justice?*; International Center for Transitional Justice (ICTJ), *What is Transitional Justice?*.

25 E.g., vetting, the creation of new constitutions, judicial and security sector reforms.

26 G. Werle and F. Jessberger, *Principles of International Criminal Law*, 3rd edn. (Oxford: Oxford University Press, 2014), pp. 84–7; Olsen, Payne and Reiter, *Transitional Justice in Balance*, p. 1; A. Boraine, 'Transitional Justice' in S. Chesterman, M. Ignatieff and R. C. Thakur (eds.), *Making States Work: State Failure and the Crisis of Governance* (Tokyo, New York, Paris: United Nations University Press, 2005), pp. 318–38, at p. 319; United Nations Security Council, *The Rule of Law and Transitional Justice in Conflict and Post-Conflict Societies, Report of the Secretary-General*, S/2004/616. http://daccess-dds-ny.un.org/doc/UNDOC/GEN/N04/395/29/PDF/N0439529.pdf?OpenElement (08 January 2016), p. 4.

27 E.g., museums and memorials, history textbooks.

28 International Center for Transitional Justice (ICTJ), *What is Transitional Justice?*; P. de Greiff, *Transitional Justice, Security, and Development: Security and Justice Thematic Paper*, World Development Report 2011 Background Paper. http://web.worldbank.org/archive/website01306/web/pdf/wdr%20background%20paper_de%20greiff_0.pdf (08 January 2016), p. 2; S. Buckley-Zistel, 'Einleitung: Nach Krieg, Gewalt und Repression' in S. Buckley-Zistel and T. Kater (eds.), *Nach Krieg, Gewalt und Repression: Vom schwierigen Umgang mit der Vergangenheit*, 1st edn. (Baden-Baden: Nomos, 2011), pp. 7–20, at pp. 9–10.

29 United Nations, *What is Transitional Justice? A Backgrounder*, pp. 3–4.

30 T. D. Olsen, L. A. Payne and A. G. Reiter, 'The Justice Balance: When Transitional Justice Improves Human Rights and Democracy', *Human Rights Quarterly* 32 (2010), 980–1007, at 1004–5; United Nations, *What is Transitional Justice? A Backgrounder*, pp. 3–4.

1.2 Methodology and Interdisciplinarity

This theoretical study will analyse international statutes, conventions and documents as well as select case law, state practice, the practice of the United Nations and the academic debate regarding amnesties. This will be followed by a comparison of the findings attained.

The comparative approach used here includes analytical methods and thereby also looks at the political and social problems which raise the amnesty question. Of particular interest is the way these problems are solved in different legal systems and which international standards are applied.[31] In this way detailed information on the legitimacy of the Afghan Amnesty Law under international law will provided.

It is not intended to consider the national laws of Afghanistan, tribal or Sharia law or the legal order of the Taliban. This means that the potential national legal basis for an amnesty law is not taken into account, as only the legitimacy of an Afghan amnesty under international law will be dealt with. However, in addition to aspects of international law, the political, social and cultural circumstances in Afghanistan also play a significant role in the design and successful implementation of an amnesty law.[32]

This dissertation project combines the disciplines of international law and international relations as well as international criminal law. Not only is the relationship between international criminal law and amnesties part of the study, but also the question of whether and how the international legal order should and can establish binding rules on amnesties.

---

31 Adams M., Husa J. and Oderkerk M. (eds.), *Comparative Law Methodology*, The international library of comparative law (Cheltenham, UK, Northampton, MA, USA: Edward Elgar Publishing, 2017), vol. 3; M. van Hoecke, 'Methodology of Comparative Legal Research', *Law and Method* (2015).

32 United Nations Security Council, *The Rule of Law and Transitional Justice in Conflict and Post-Conflict Societies, Report of the Secretary-General*, p. 1; A. J. Thier, 'Introduction: Building Bridges' in A. J. Thier (ed.), *The Future of Aghanistan* (Washington D.C., 2009), pp. 1–11, at pp. 1–2; L. A. Dickinson, 'Transitional Justice in Afghanistan: The Promise of Mixed Tribunals', *Denver Journal of International Law and Policy* 31 (2002–2003), 23–42, at 33; Mallinder, *Amnesty, Human Rights and Political Transitions:*, p. 10.

1.3 Outline of the Chapters

The study is divided into five main parts:

Part 1 (Introduction) contains this chapter and is an introduction to the thesis, including the nature and scope of the research subject, the research questions and the purpose of the study as well as the methodology.

Part 2 (Amnesties in the Age of Accountability) deals with the development of amnesties and especially with their strained relationship to criminal proceedings. The term "amnesty" is defined in order to provide a brief overview of the possible design of amnesty laws, and at the same time to provide examples of the diverse practice of states when it comes to the amnesty question. Subsequently, the example of Afghanistan and the design of its amnesty law are of great interest for this survey. In order to illustrate the development of the Afghan Amnesty Law, a quick glance at the history of conflict and conflict resolution in Afghanistan is taken. The detailed history of the drafting of the amnesty law from the first draft until it entered into force in 2010 as well as the exact content of that law is dealt with in the last chapter of Part 2.

Part 3 (The Legitimacy of the Afghan Amnesty Law under International Law) concerns itself with the crucial question of whether the regulations of the Afghan Amnesty Law are compatible with Afghanistan's obligations under international law. Therefore Part 3 contains an analysis of current international and in part also national trends concerning amnesties. In doing so, the focus always remains on the case of Afghanistan and the compatibility of its amnesty law with international law. Following the sources of international law, as contained in Article 38 (1) of the Statute of the International Court of Justice, the compatibility of the Afghan Amnesty Law with international conventions, international custom, the general principles of law as well as judicial decisions and the teachings of the most highly qualified publicists is looked at.[33] At the end, the

---

33 *See* Statute of the International Court of Justice, Article 38:
"(1) The Court, whose function is to decide in accordance with international law such disputes as are submitted to it, shall apply:
a. international conventions, whether general or particular, establishing rules expressly recognized by the contesting states;
b. international custom, as evidence of a general practice accepted as law;
c. the general principles of law recognized by civilized nations;
d. subject to the provisions of Article 59, judicial decisions and the teachings of the most highly qualified publicists of the various nations, as subsidiary means for the determination of rules of law.",

results of the different stages of the legal examination are compared and a well-founded conclusion can be drawn.

Part 4 (Determination of the Conditions under which an Afghan Amnesty Law would be Legitimate under International Law) makes proposals with respect to a transitional justice process in Afghanistan. This process may include an amnesty which must, however, be legitimate under international law, i.e. an amnesty that is conditional and individualised. Furthermore, the specific political, social and cultural circumstances of the country must be adequately taken into account. Particular aspects of a legitimate Afghan amnesty law are described in detail in this part of the study.

In Part 5 (Final Remarks and Future Prospects) the findings of the study are considered. In this context, the question of whether, and if so, how rules determining the legitimacy of (proposed) amnesty provisions should be codified as binding law within the international legal order are raised. The considerations focus on central issues in the context of further establishing amnesty guidelines, without exploring this matter in depth.

United Nations, *Statute of the International Court of Justice*, 18 April 1946, http://www.refworld.org/docid/3deb4b9c0.html (08 February 2016).

2 Amnesties in the Age of Accountability

Not only countries with a violent or repressive past, but also those with ongoing conflicts seek to pave the way for lasting peace and reconciliation, for justice and respect for the rule of law. To accomplish this mission, different judicial and non-judicial mechanisms come into consideration. The basic mechanisms of the so-called transitional justice[34] are now well established.[35]

At one end of the spectrum stand amnesties, a form of providing impunity. They disable the possibility of bringing the perpetrators to account – whether in criminal or in civil proceedings.[36] In the next chapter *(2.1)* the term "amnesty" will be further analysed. At the other end, there are criminal investigations, trials and prosecutions by national, international or hybrid courts. In this way perpetrators deemed to be the most responsible for human rights violations shall be brought to justice.

Depending on the body of scholarship, amnesty for human rights violation is either out of the question or it offers an opportunity to tackle the transition process. Human rights scholarship[37], with a strong focus on the protection and realisation of human rights, rejects the granting of any kind of amnesty for human rights violations. According to them, accountability, not impunity, will achieve the transition from violent conflict to a more democratic regime and justice.[38] In the view of international relations scholars[39], however, prosecutions would hamper peace negotiations and hence impede regime stability. Therefore, amnesties are a necessary

34 United Nations, *What is Transitional Justice? A Backgrounder.*

35 Tolbert, *Address by David Tolbert to the National Forum on Launching the Dialogue on Transitional Justice in Tunisia.*

36 UN Office of the High Commissioner for Human Rights, *Rule-of-Law Tools for Post-Conflict States*, p. 5; United Nations Commission on Human Rights, *Report of the Independent Expert to Update the Set of Principles to Combat Impunity, Diane Orentlicher, Addendum*, p. 6.

37 Scholars like Naomi Roht-Arriaza, Kathryn Sikkink and Carrie Booth Walling, and NGOs such as The International Center for Transitional Justice, Amnesty International and Human Rights Watch.

38 A. Dayal, *The Institutional Returns of Amnesty?: Evaluating Security Sector Reform in Post-Conflict Cases*. http://citation.allacademic.com/meta/p413445_index.html (07 January 2016), p. 2.

39 Scholars like Jack Snyder and Leslie Vinjamuri, Andreas O'Shea.

and powerful tool to appease perpetrators, bring all conflict parties to the negotiation table and finally achieve peace.[40] As a consequence of these different priorities, different transitional justice definitions, including amnesties[41] or excluding them[42], arise.

How can this controversy be explained? What are the underlying causes for the development of the aforementioned contrary opinions? The answer is that amnesties, as well as international criminal law, have experienced a certain development.

For centuries the granting of amnesties was mainly located in the sphere of the sovereign state. In recent decades, however, amnesties are increasingly measured by applying international law. With the growth and further development of international human rights, humanitarian and criminal law a focus on individual accountability can be recorded[43], with the consequence that several scholars speak about the "age of accountability"[44] or a "justice cascade"[45]. Following this justice-oriented appraisal, there seems to be no longer room for amnesties, especially those relating to genocide, crimes against humanity, war crimes and other serious violations

---

40 Joint report by the Advisory Council on International Affairs (AIV) and the Advisory Committee on Issues of Public International Law (CAVV), *Transitional Justice: Justice and Peace in Situations of Transition*. http://aiv-advies.nl/6cf/publications/advisory-reports/transitional-justice-justice-and-peace-in-situations-of-transition (07 January 2016), p. 9; Dayal, *The Institutional Returns of Amnesty?*, p. 2.

41 See, e.g.,Freeman, *Necessary Evils*, p. 19; Boraine, 'Transitional Justice', 335–6; J. Snyder and L. Vinjamuri, 'Trials and Errors: Principle and Pragmatism in Strategies of International Justice', *International Security* 28 (Winter 2003), 5–44, at 5–6; A. O'Shea, *Amnesty for Crime in International Law and Practice* (The Hague: Kluwer Law International, 2002), pp. 34–5.

42 See, e.g., International Center for Transitional Justice (ICTJ), *What is Transitional Justice?*; United Nations, *What is Transitional Justice? A Backgrounder*, pp. 3–4; Roht-Arriaza N. and Mariezcurrena J. (eds.), *Transitional Justice in the Twenty-First Century: Beyond Truth versus Justice* (Cambridge, UK, New York: Cambridge University Press, 2006).

43 Mallinder, *Amnesty, Human Rights and Political Transitions:*, p. 247; R. C. Slye, 'The Legitimacy of Amnesties Under International Law and General Principles of Anglo-American Law: Is a Legitimate Amnesty Possible?', *Virginia Journal of International Law* 43 (2002), 173–247, at 179–81.

44 K. Sikkink, 'The Age of Accountability: The Global Rise of Individual Criminal Accountability' in F. Lessa and L. A. Payne (eds.), *Amnesty in the Age of Human Rights Accountability: Comparative and International Perspectives* (Cambridge, New York: Cambridge University Press, 2012), pp. 19–41.

45 Ibid., 21–2; E. Lutz and K. Sikkink, 'The Justice Cascade: The Evolution and Impact of Foreign Human Rights Trials in Latin America', *Chicago Journal of International Law* 2 (2001).

of international humanitarian law.[46] Other authors, by contrast, consider that international law does not contain an absolute duty to prosecute, and thus does not completely ban amnesties.[47]

Apart from that, it must be admitted that those responsible for atrocious crimes are almost never sentenced.[48] Several (powerful) states ignore the need to investigate and prosecute perpetrators of human rights violations, mainly for their own political interests. The persistent war in Syria with countless victims of abhorrent violence is only one example of the inability of the international community to stop these crimes and to bring the perpetrators to account.[49]

Also, the International Criminal Court (ICC) is undergoing a major crisis, since it must struggle with diminished support from several African countries such as Burundi and South Africa, who were full members but are now withdrawing from the Court.[50] In addition, Kenya plans to termi-

---

46 F. Lessa and L. A. Payne, 'Introduction' in F. Lessa and L. A. Payne (eds.), *Amnesty in the Age of Human Rights Accountability: Comparative and International Perspectives* (Cambridge, New York: Cambridge University Press, 2012), pp. 1–16, at pp. 5–7; C. Bell, *The 'New Law' of Transitional Justice*, Building a Future on Peace and Justice, "Workshop 1 – From Mediation to Sustainable Peace" (Nuremberg, 2007), p. 14; N. Roht-Arriaza, *Transitional Justice and Peace Agreements*, Peace Agreements: The Role of Human Rights in Negotiations (Belfast, 2005), p. 15; Human Security Network, *Annual Ministerial Meeting: Statement by Ms. Patricia O'Brien, Under-Secretary-General for Legal Affairs, The Legal Counsel.* http://legal.un.org/ola/media/info_from_lc/POB-keynote.pdf (08 January 2016), p. 6.

47 W. N. Ferdinandusse, *Direct Application of International Criminal Law in National Courts* (The Hague, West Nyack, NY: TMC Asser Press; Cambridge University Press, 2006), pp. 182–3; R. Cryer, *Prosecuting International Crimes: Selectivity and the International Criminal Law Regime*, Cambridge studies in international and comparative law (Cambridge, New York: Cambridge University Press, 2005), p. 110; R. O'Keefe, *International Criminal law*, 1st edn. (Oxford: Oxford University Press, 2015), p. 476.

48 M. C. Bassiouni, *Introduction to International Criminal Law*, Second revised edition (Leiden, Boston: Martinus Nijhoff Publishers, 2013), pp. 996–7; W. Kaleck, *Mit zweierlei Maß: Der Westen und das Völkerstrafrecht* (Berlin: Klaus Wagenbach, 2012), p. 116; Greiff, *Transitional Justice, Security, and Development*, p. 4.

49 D. Tolbert, *A Wrong Turn for Human Rights*. http://www.project-syndicate.org/commentary/david-tolbert-warns-that-the-gains-made-since-the-end-of-the-cold-war-are-at-risk (13 January 2016).

50 Human Rights Watch, *Burundi: ICC Withdrawal Major Loss to Victims*. https://www.hrw.org/news/2016/10/27/burundi-icc-withdrawal-major-loss-victims (30 October 2017).

nate its membership.[51] Russia, which signed the Rome Statute in 2000 but had not ratified it, has recently revoked its signature.[52]

Referring to amnesties in particular, it can be seen that states continue to introduce them, also for violations of human rights. They act in this way in the hope of facilitating the transition from violent conflict to lasting peace. Various studies[53] have demonstrated that achievements in international law are not necessarily mirrored in the practice of societies employing amnesties. In fact, the number of amnesties increased or has remained constant even during the proclaimed "age of accountability".[54] This reflects the fact that, despite all the euphoria about international criminal law and international human rights law, the political interests of the affected state cannot be ignored.[55] From a different point of view, it is assumed that amnesties are enacted mainly for legal reasons. That is, for fear of trials and prosecutions perpetrators may claim more guarantees against their individual criminal accountability. In this way it is argued, governments adopt amnesties as a response to the "age of accountability".[56] Another argument for the persistence of amnesties is, as Chapter *3.2.2* shows in detail, that states and international actors politically and/or financially support the amnesty laws of other states. Thus, the value of

---

51 Reuters, *Gambia Withdraws From ICC, Accuses World Body of Bias Against Africans*. http://thewire.in/76049/gambia-withdraws-from-the-icc-accuses-it-of-ignoring-the-war-crimes-of-the-west/ (02.11.16).

52 S. Walker and O. Bowcott, 'Russia Withdraws Signature from International Criminal Court Statute', The Guardian, 16 November 2016.

53 See, e.g.,Mallinder, pp. 18–9; Olsen, Payne and Reiter, *Transitional Justice in Balance*, p. 6.

54 L. Mallinder, 'Amnesties' Challenge to the Global Accountability Norm? Interpreting Regional and International Trends in Amnesty Enactment' in F. Lessa and L. A. Payne (eds.), *Amnesty in the Age of Human Rights Accountability: Comparative and International Perspectives* (Cambridge, New York: Cambridge University Press, 2012), pp. 69–96, at pp. 95–6; Bassiouni, *Introduction to International Criminal Law*, pp. 996–7; Olsen, Payne and Reiter, *Transitional Justice in Balance*, p. 39; Freeman, *Necessary Evils*, p. 4.

55 M. C. Bassiouni, 'Reflections on Contemporary Developments in International Criminal Justice' in B. S. Brown (ed.), *Research Handbook on International Criminal Law*, Research handbooks in international law (Cheltenham, UK, Northampton, MA: Edward Elgar, 2011), pp. 409–17, at pp. 416–7.

56 Sikkink, 'The Age of Accountability:', 21 Mallinder in F. Lessa and L. A. Payne (eds.), *Amnesty in the Age of Human Rights Accountability: Comparative and International Perspectives* (Cambridge, New York: Cambridge University Press, 2012), at p. 90; Slye, 'The Legitimacy of Amnesties Under International Law and General Principles of Anglo-American Law', 175.

amnesties during transitions is implicitly acknowledged.[57]As the above considerations show, both criminal prosecutions and amnesties are relevant mechanisms in coping with a violent past, despite how contrary they are.

Apart from amnesties and prosecutions, the remaining transitional justice mechanisms are almost undisputed. They encompass truth commissions[58], reparation programs[59], lustration policies and institutional reforms[60].[61] Other important elements are the construction of memory projects[62] as well as traditional justice initiatives.[63] Crucial for success of the transitional justice process is a holistic approach. This means that, depending on the unique circumstances in the particular (post-) conflict country different mechanisms that complement and reinforce each other need to be combined.[64] Single mechanisms should be avoided since they are inadequate to achieve the objective of justice, reconciliation and respect for the rule of law.[65]

The continuing relevance of amnesties as a transitional justice mechanism is clearly illustrated by the example of Afghanistan. Therefore,

---

57 Mallinder in F. Lessa and L. A. Payne (eds.), *Amnesty in the Age of Human Rights Accountability: Comparative and International Perspectives* (Cambridge, New York: Cambridge University Press, 2012), at pp. 92–3.

58 Truth Commissions are temporary bodies officially sanctioned by the state or an international governmental organization to investigate a pattern of past abuses and issue a report, *see* Olsen, Payne and Reiter, *Transitional Justice in Balance*, p. 34; United Nations, *What is Transitional Justice? A Backgrounder*, pp. 3–4; International Center for Transitional Justice (ICTJ), *What is Transitional Justice?*.

59 Reparation programs are state-sponsored initiatives that aim to contribute to repairing the material and moral consequences of past abuses experienced by victims, *see* United Nations, *What is Transitional Justice? A Backgrounder*, pp. 3–4; International Center for Transitional Justice (ICTJ), *What is Transitional Justice?*; International Center for Transitional Justice (ICTJ), *What is Transitional Justice?*.

60 E.g., vetting, the creation of new constitutions, judicial and security sector reforms.

61 Werle and Jessberger, *Principles of International Criminal Law*, pp. 84–7; Olsen, Payne and Reiter, *Transitional Justice in Balance*, p. 1; Boraine, 'Transitional Justice', 319; United Nations Security Council, *The Rule of Law and Transitional Justice in Conflict and Post-Conflict Societies, Report of the Secretary-General*, p. 4.

62 E.g., museums and memorials, history textbooks.

63 International Center for Transitional Justice (ICTJ), *What is Transitional Justice?*; Greiff, *Transitional Justice, Security, and Development*, p. 2; Buckley-Zistel, 'Einleitung', 9–10.

64 United Nations, *What is Transitional Justice? A Backgrounder*, pp. 3–4.

65 Olsen, Payne and Reiter, 'The Justice Balance', 1004–5; United Nations, *What is Transitional Justice? A Backgrounder*, pp. 3–4.

the main part of this study will comprehensively deal with the Afghan amnesty law[66]. In the next chapter *(2.1)* the term "amnesty" will be further defined. Subsequently, the Afghan Amnesty Law in particular is of great interest for this survey.

2.1 Amnesties in General

The term "amnesty" stems from the Greek word "*amnéstia*" meaning "forgetfulness" or "oblivion".[67] Used since ancient times, amnesties are, as mentioned above, the most important form of providing impunity. Well-known amnesty laws are those established in Latin America as well as in South Africa. Amnesties must be distinguished from other forms of impunity, such as pardon and official immunity. Unlike an amnesty, which forgoes criminal prosecution and punishment, a pardon forgoes the (full) enforcement of the sentence, without affecting the underlying conviction.[68] Official immunities, such as Head of State and diplomatic immunities prevent officials from being accountable for their wrong-doing, unless international crimes are concerned.[69] These, and other forms of impunity apart from amnesties, do not fall within the scope of this study. Hence, the following descriptions refer to amnesties only.

To start with, the reasons for enacting an amnesty law are manifold, for example to promote peace and reconciliation or to alleviate internal unrest. Also, international pressure can play a crucial role in regard to amnesties. Furthermore, it is not unusual for amnesties to be introduced to protect state agents from criminal investigations, so-called "self-amnesties". These objectives can overlap and co-exist. It may also happen that the real reasons for an amnesty are concealed.[70] For example, perpetrators still in position of power may publicly proclaim an amnesty to foster peace and reconciliation, but in fact they primarily want to protect themselves from prosecution.

66 „National Reconciliation, General Amnesty, and National Stability Law", Official Gazette, published: 13 Qaus 1387 Serial No: (965) (unofficial English translation), in: Kouvo, *After Two Years in Legal Limbo*).

67 Mallinder (2008), p. 4.

68 Roht-Arriaza, *Transitional Justice and Peace Agreements*, p. 9.

69 UN Office of the High Commissioner for Human Rights, *Rule-of-Law Tools for Post-Conflict States*, pp. 5–6.

70 Mallinder (2008), pp. 37–73.

Methods by which amnesties are established range from executive decrees or parliamentary legislation to public consultations and negotiated peace agreements.[71] If the amnesty law is associated with an armed conflict, it will probably apply for the period from the start of the conflict until its end. In any case, the crimes concerned must have been committed before the amnesty law is enacted.[72]

With regard to the personal scope of amnesties, specific categories of beneficiaries come into question. One possibility is to grant amnesty to all perpetrators for all kinds of crimes. Another way is to treat them differently. That is, to grant amnesty only to members of certain groups, for example, state agents, members of rebel forces, or exiles.[73] It can further be distinguished according to the rank of the offender, for example, lower-ranking perpetrators may be amnestied, but higher-ranking officials are excluded from the amnesty.[74] Also the material scope can be extremely broad or more narrowly determined. An amnesty law may encompass even serious human rights violations or, in contrast, exclude precisely those crimes and cover for example political offences.[75]

The meaning of amnesty varies depending on the legal, cultural and political background of the (post-) conflict society affected. Not only blanket or unconditional amnesties, but also qualified or conditional amnesties, self-amnesties and *de facto* amnesties are possible.[76] According to the Office of the High Commissioner for Human Rights *"blanket amnesties exempt broad categories of serious human rights offenders from prosecution and/or civil liability without the beneficiaries' having to satisfy preconditions ..."*[77], whereas *"conditional amnesties exempt an individual from prosecution if he or she applies for amnesty and satisfies several conditions, such as full disclosure of the*

---

71 UN Office of the High Commissioner for Human Rights, *Rule-of-Law Tools for Post-Conflict States*, p. 7; Mallinder (2008), pp. 29–36.

72 M. P. Scharf, 'Trading Justice for Peace: The Contemporary Law and Policy Debate' in E. Hughes, W. A. Schabas and R. C. Thakur (eds.), *Atrocities and International Accountability: Beyond Transitional Justice* (New York: United Nations University Press, 2007), pp. 246–74, at p. 263; UN Office of the High Commissioner for Human Rights, *Rule-of-Law Tools for Post-Conflict States*, pp. 6–7.

73 UN Office of the High Commissioner for Human Rights, *Rule-of-Law Tools for Post-Conflict States*, pp. 6–7.

74 Mallinder (2008), pp. 75–115.

75 Mallinder, *Amnesty, Human Rights and Political Transitions:*, pp. 117–51.

76 Ibid., pp. 5–7.

77 UN Office of the High Commissioner for Human Rights, *Rule-of-Law Tools for Post-Conflict States*, p. 8.

facts about the violations committed."[78] *De facto* or pseudo-amnesties are laws or regulations which, just like *de jure* amnesties, aim to shield perpetrators from prosecution. The only difference is that the term "amnesty" remains deliberately unmentioned.

All these characteristics of amnesties are presented without any evaluation of their legitimacy. Rather, the explanations are intended to provide a brief overview of the possible design of amnesty laws, while at the same time providing examples of the diverse practice of states when it comes to the amnesty question. As already announced, the example of Afghanistan and the design of its amnesty law are the subject of this study. In this particular case, the legality of the amnesty is comprehensively examined. In order to illustrate the development of the Afghan amnesty law, a quick glance at the history of conflict and conflict resolution in Afghanistan is taken.

2.2 *The Case of Afghanistan – History of Conflicts*

Suffering from almost four decades of war, Afghanistan is still deeply rooted in conflict. The instability recently increased, not least because of the controversial presidential election in 2014, the escalating armed conflict between the Taliban insurgents and government forces in 2015 as well as interference by other countries.[79] According to the United Nations about half of the country's provinces are at a high or extreme threat level.[80] As a consequence, violations of human rights are still a daily reality in many parts of Afghanistan.[81] The desire for peace, reconciliation and stability seems to be retreating into the far distance. These pressing problems apart, the country has to tackle a legacy of severe violations of international human rights and humanitarian law, such as torture, rape, disappearances, looting, arbitrary detention, mass executions and bombings that targeted

---

78 Ibid., p. 43.

79 Human Rights Watch, *World Report 2016: Afghanistan*; Human Rights Watch, *World Report 2015: Afghanistan*; Rubin, 'The Transformation of the Afghan State', 13–7.

80 Human Rights Watch Human Rights Watch, *World Report 2016: Afghanistan*. https://www.hrw.org/world-report/2016/country-chapters/afghanistan.

81 Human Rights Watch, *Afghanistan:*, p. 2.

civilians.[82] A survey by the Afghan Independent Human Rights Commission (AIHRC) revealed that almost all Afghans have in some way experienced the effects of the violence committed by all sides of the conflict.[83] The impact on them ranges from financial losses to the loss of loved ones as well as mental and physical diseases. Afghanistan has further to cope with the physical, social, and cultural destruction of its country and its people.

This horrible legacy must be attributed to the different phases and actors of the unique Afghan conflict. Unique, because of its complexity with regard both to the nature of the conflict, where some periods were of national and others of international character, and to the various regimes with their respective protagonists.[84] Different foreign actors, as the former Soviet Union (now Russia), the United States, Pakistan, India as well as Saudi Arabia and Iran have played and are still playing a significant role in the modern conflict in Afghanistan.[85] Leaving aside earlier internal and external tensions and conflicts[86], the recent history of conflict in Afghanistan can be divided in four phases[87]:

The first phase started with the Communist Revolution and People's Democratic Party of Afghanistan (PDPA) government in 1978, which was followed by the Soviet occupation and rule of Afghanistan from 1979 to 1989.[88] This period was characterized by systematic violations of human rights, such as arbitrary detentions, forced disappearance, mass executions, torture, indiscriminate bombardments against civilians, the destruction of

82 Afghanistan Independent Human Rights Commission (AIHRC), *A Call for Justice*, p. 4; Winterbotham, *The State of Transitional Justice in Afghanistan*, p. 3; Jackson, *The Cost of War*, p. 4.

83 Afghanistan Independent Human Rights Commission (AIHRC), *A Call for Justice*, p. 8.

84 C. D. Maass, 'National Reconciliation in Afghanistan.: Conflict History and the Search for an Afghan Approach', *Internationales Asienforum* 37 (2006), 5–36, at 35.

85 Rubin, 'The Transformation of the Afghan State', 13.

86 For example: internal tensions between the central government and regional movements and forces since independence in 1919; external conflicts with Pakistan and during the Cold War, *See* International Center for Transitional Justice (ICTJ), *Afghanistan: Addressing the Past*. http://ictj.org/sites/default/files/ICTJ-Afghanistan-Addressing-Past-2005-English.pdf (19 January 2016), p. 2.

87 E. Winterbotham, *Wartime Suffering: Patterns of Violations in Afghanistan*. http://www.areu.org.af/Uploads/EditionPdfs/1123E%20-%20Legacies%20of%20Conflict%20-%20Wartime%20Suffering%202011.pdf (19 January 2016), p. 1.

88 Ibid., p. 1.

cultivated fields, and forced displacement.[89] The second phase was the fall of the Najibullah government and the subsequent civil war from 1989 to 1996.[90] Armed mujahidin forces committed incredible atrocities such as massacres, mass rapes, bombardments, torture, and mass executions.[91] From 1996 onwards, the hard-line Taliban regime brutally ruled the country by perpetrating massacres, torture, burnings, and deliberate destruction.[92] The basic rights and freedoms of Afghans, especially of Afghan women, were severely limited or even abolished.[93] This third phase lasted until 2001, when the United States and its allies invaded and defeated the Taliban regime. The following fourth – post-Taliban – transitional phase is still ongoing. Despite great hope and proclamations that the violence is over, serious human rights violations and a bloody conflict between the Afghan government and its international supporters on the one hand and the Taliban fighters on the other are still reality.[94] Aerial bombardments, suicide attacks, torture and enforced disappearances are still carried out in several parts of the country.[95]

As long as these conflicts have troubled Afghanistan, various attempts have been made to reconcile the parties in conflict and negotiate a political settlement or peace agreement – unfortunately without success.[96]

89 The Afghanistan Justice Project, *Casting Shadows: War Crimes and Crimes against Humanity:*, 1978–2001. http://reliefweb.int/sites/reliefweb.int/files/resources/B7C09154CD3E144EC12570430049F76A-ajp-afg-18jul.pdf (19 January 2016), p. 2; A. N. Nadery, 'Afghans Struggle to Restore Justice in their Country: How Can Afghans Redress Past Abuses Without Creating New Injustices?' in *Bonn International Center for Conversion – Confronting Afghanistan's Security Dilemma* brief 28, pp. 49–53, at pp. 52–3.

90 Winterbotham, *Wartime Suffering*, p. 1.

91 P. Gossman, *Afghanistan: The Past as a Prologue: Leveraging the Coming Transition to Break the Cycle of Abuse in Afghanistan*. http://ictj.org/sites/default/files/ICTJ-Afghanistan-Briefing-English-%202012.pdf?utm_source=International+Center+for+Transitional+Justice+Newsletter&utm_campaign=98396109c7-PR_Afghanistan_Briefing_24-July-2012&utm_medium=email (19 January 2016), pp. 2–3.

92 Nadery, 'Afghans Struggle to Restore Justice in their Country', brief 28, 52–3; A. N. Khan, 'Afghanistan: War Crimes, ICC and NGOs', *IPRI (Islamabad Policy Research Institute) Journal* XII (2012), 88–118, at 90–1.

93 Nadery, 'Afghans Struggle to Restore Justice in their Country', brief 28, 52–3.

94 Jackson, *The Cost of War*, pp. 3–4.

95 E. Winterbotham, *Healing the Legacies of Conflict in Afghanistan: Community Voices on Justice, Peace and Reconciliation*. http://www.areu.org.af/Uploads/EditionPdfs/1201E-Healing%20the%20Legacies%20of%20Conflict%20in%20Afghanistan%20SP%202011.pdf (19 January 2016), p. 36; The Afghanistan Justice Project, *Casting Shadows:*, pp. 155–6.

96 International Crisis Group, *Talking About Talks*, p. 5.

The reasons for failure are manifold and include, for example, the rapid regime changes with the consequence that the time to reach compromises has been insufficient. Another constant problem has been that issues such as accountability and culpability for breaches of the conditions of a settlement were not on the agenda of the negotiations. Furthermore, the international community failed to appease the country, not least because of their own interests in the region.[97]

The first chance to reconcile the warring parties and to reach a stable peace agreement arose in the 1980s, following the Soviet intervention. Since support for the anti-Soviet mujahidin fighters steadily grew after the intervention, a political solution was required.[98] In the end, two approaches were introduced. In 1981 counter-revolutionaries received a general amnesty under the condition that they stop fighting. This and further efforts to pacify the parties in conflict, however, eventually failed. One reason for this is that no disarmament and demobilization strategy existed and hence the fighting continued.[99] The second approach took place in Geneva. After negotiations between Afghanistan, Pakistan, the United States and the Soviet Union, the Geneva Accords were settled in 1988. They contained *inter alia* the withdrawal of Soviet forces and the cessation of aid to the Afghan mujahidin. But what was missing was the provision of an enforcement mechanism. Moreover, provisions to ensure lasting stability of a post-Soviet Afghan government were not established.[100] According to a senior Afghan official, the reasons for repeated failed reconciliation efforts in Afghanistan must be traced back to the Geneva negotiations: "*Reconciliation is, in effect, the undone job of the 1980s*".[101]

In the following years of civil war, various fruitless attempts were made to broker power-sharing and interim government arrangements to appease the competing mujahidin factions.[102]

A renewed effort to bring peace to Afghanistan was made in the late 1990s, when the United Nations strived for an agreement between the Taliban and the Northern Alliance. However, the resulting 1999 "Tashkent

97 Ibid., p. 5.
98 Ibid., pp. 7–8.
99 Ibid., pp. 7–8.
100 Ibid., pp. 5–7.
101 *See* Crisis Group Interview, New York, 25 May 2011, in: ibid., pp. 5–7.
102 E.g., the Peshawar Accord (April 1992), the Islamabad Accord (March 1993), the Mahiper Accord (May 1995), *see* ibid., pp. 8–9.

Declaration on Fundamental Principles for a Peaceful Settlement of the Conflict" was once again without success as the conflict continued.[103]

Once the Taliban regime was overthrown by the United States and its allies, a new round of talks and negotiations was held in Bonn in 2001. Participants of the UN convened meeting were *inter alia* selected Afghan factions with exception of the Taliban. The negotiations culminated in the "*Agreement on Provisional Arrangements in Afghanistan Pending the Re-establishment of Permanent Government Institutions*" – the so-called "Bonn Agreement".[104] The stated aims were "*to end the tragic conflict in Afghanistan and promote national reconciliation, lasting peace, stability and respect for human rights in the country,*"[105] as well as to establish a transitional government.[106] Furthermore: "*The Interim Administration shall, with the assistance of the United Nations, establish an independent Human Rights Commission, whose responsibilities will include human rights monitoring, investigation of violations of human rights, and development of domestic human rights institutions.*"

However, what is striking is that the agreement does not go further and grapples with issues such as accountability for serious human rights violations or the removal of perpetrators from official positions. Rather, an amnesty for past abuses was debated and a draft provision prohibiting amnesty for war crimes and crimes against humanity has not been successful.[107] It is interesting to note in this context that former mujahidin fighters and thus alleged perpetrators of serious international crimes were even praised for their actions.[108] These critical shortcomings of the Bonn Agreement laid, as will be seen below, the foundation for a failed transitional justice policy in the years that followed.

---

103 Ibid., pp. 8–9.

104 United Nations Security Council, *Agreement on Provisional Arrangements in Afghanistan Pending the Re-Establishment of Permanent Government Institutions: "Bonn Agreement"*, S/2001/1154. http://www.unhcr.org/refworld/docid/3f48f4754.html (20 January 2016).

105 Ibid.

106 Ibid.

107 N. Niland, 'Impunity and Insurgency: a Deadly Combination in Afghanistan', *International Review of the Red Cross* 92 (2010), 931–50, at 936.

108 *See* "Bonn Agreement" United Nations Security Council, *Agreement on Provisional Arrangements in Afghanistan Pending the Re-Establishment of Permanent Government Institutions*: *„Expressing their appreciation to the Afghan mujahidin who, over the years, have defended the independence, territorial integrity and national unity of the country and have played a major role in the struggle against terrorism and oppression, and whose sacrifice has now made them both heroes of jihad and champions of peace, stability and reconstruction of their beloved homeland, Afghanistan,"*.

The amnesty question came up not only in Bonn but also in Kabul. In 2003, the transitional government of Hamid Karzai for the first time decided to announce an amnesty for Taliban fighters in order to stop the still ongoing conflict.[109] The amnesty offer was reiterated in 2004 and 2005.[110] Whether or not war crimes and crimes against humanity were excluded from the amnesty remains unclear. Various official declarations concerning this matter have been contradictory.[111]

In parallel with these amnesty offers, a diametrical development can be recorded. In 2005, the Afghan Independent Human Rights Commission (AIHRC)[112] – established in accordance with the Bonn Agreement – published its first report[113] and advocated for the prosecution of perpetrators of serious crimes as well as the removal of criminals from positions of power. As a consequence, the Afghan government, with support from the AIHRC and the United Nations Assistance Mission in Afghanistan (UNAMA), adopted the Action Plan for Peace, Reconciliation and Justice (APPRJ)[114] in the same year. The Action Plan contains five key areas: acknowledgement of the suffering of the Afghan people; ensuring credible and accountable state institutions; truth-seeking and documentation; reconciliation and national unity as well as the establishment of effective and reasonable accountability mechanisms.[115] The government reiterated that the many cases of human rights violations need to be seriously dealt with. Hence, the objective of key action five reads as follows: *"In order to end impunity in Afghanistan and ensure that there will be no amnesty for war crimes, crimes against humanity and other gross human rights violations, the*

---

109 S. Irving, *Talking With Taliban: A Political Solution to a Political Problem*. http://atlismta.org/online-journals/0809-journal-intervention/talking-with-taliban/ (21 January 2016).

110 L. Mallinder, 'Amnesties' in M. C. Bassiouni (ed.), *The Pursuit of International Criminal Justice: A World Study on Conflicts, Victimization, and Post-Conflict Justice* (Antwerp, Oxford, Portland: Intersentia, 2010), pp. 793–922, at pp. 850–3.

111 *See* ibid., 850–3; C. Gall, 'Afghanistan Offers Amnesty to Wanted Taliban Rebels', The New York Times, 09 May 2005; R. Synovitz, *Afghanistan: Karzai Confirms Amnesty Offer Is for All Willing Afghans*. http://www.rferl.org/content/article/1058802.html (21 January 2016).

112 *Afghanistan Independent Human Rights Commission*. http://www.aihrc.org.af/ (22.01.16).

113 Afghanistan Independent Human Rights Commission (AIHRC), *A Call for Justice*.

114 Government of the Islamic Republic of Afghanistan, *Action Plan on Peace, Reconciliation and Justice in Afghanistan*. http://www.aihrc.org.af/media/files/Reports/Thematic%20reports/Action_Pln_Gov_Af.pdf (22 January 2016).

115 Ibid.

conditions for fair and effective justice procedures are established in accordance with the principles of the sacred religion of Islam, international law and transitional justice."[116].

It is not surprising that former perpetrators and then members of parliament and government protested against the focus on criminal accountability in the Action Plan.[117] But that was not all: it became apparent that the promise to end impunity was nothing more than lip service. The Afghan government disregarded the Action Plan[118] and radically undermined its provisions by introducing a controversial blanket amnesty law in 2007.

The detailed history of the drafting of the amnesty law from the first draft until it entered into force in 2010 as well as the exact content of the law will be dealt with in the following chapter.

2.3 The Afghan Amnesty Law of 2010

The legislative process of the Afghan Amnesty Law started in January 2007 with the hasty approval of the "*National Stability and Reconciliation Resolution*" by the lower and then the upper houses of parliament (Wolesi Jirga and Meshrano Jirga, respectively).[119] This was preceded by a Human Rights Watch (HRW) publication demanding accountability for several named Afghan officials suspected of having committed serious international crimes.[120] Furthermore, the execution of Saddam Hussein in Iraq

---

116 Ibid., p. 11.

117 A. Wardak, D. Saba and H. Kazem, *Afghanistan Human Development Report 2007: Bridging Modernity and Tradition: Rule of Law and the Search for Justice*. http://hdr.undp.org/sites/default/files/nhdr2007.pdf (22 January 2016), pp. 76–7.

118 M. E. Hartmann and A. Klonowiecka-Milart, *Impunity Prevails in Afghanistan*. http://www.rawa.org/temp/runews/2010/12/01/impunity-prevails-in-afghanistan.html (22 January 2016).

119 P. Gossman and S. Kouvo, *Tell Us How This Ends: Transitional Justice and Prospects for Peace in Afghanistan*. http://www.afghanistan-analysts.org/wp-content/uploads/2013/06/2013-06_AAN_TransitionalJustice2.pdf (26 January 2016), p. 30; A. Hakimi and A. Suhrke, 'A Poisonous Chalice: The Struggle for Human Rights and Accountability in Afghanistan', *Nordic Journal of Human Rights* 31 (2013), 201–23, at 211–2; Winterbotham, *The State of Transitional Justice in Afghanistan*, pp. 7–10; Khan, 'Afghanistan: War Crimes, ICC and NGOs', 104–6.

120 Human Rights Watch, *Afghanistan: Justice for War Criminals Essential to Peace*. https://www.hrw.org/news/2006/12/12/afghanistan-justice-war-criminals-essential-peace (22 January 2016).

resulted in a generalized fear among Afghan warlords still in positions of power.[121] The Amnesty Law contained a blanket amnesty for all warring political wings and hostile parties, and all kinds of crimes committed before the formation of the Interim Administration.[122] It was initially rejected by President Karzai, who criticised the resulting impunity for war criminals as well as the elimination of individual rights of victims to demand justice.[123]

In spite of some amendments the revised version still encompasses a blanket amnesty as Article 3 (1) of the then *"National Reconciliation, General Amnesty, and National Stability Law"* (The "Amnesty Law")[124] provides:

> *"**All political factions and hostile parties who were involved in a way or another in hostilities before establishing of the Interim Administration shall be included in the reconciliation and general amnesty program** for the purpose of reconciliation among different segments of society, strengthening of peace and stability and starting of new life in the contemporary political history of Afghanistan, **and enjoy all their legal rights and shall not be legally and judicially prosecuted.**"* (emphasis added)

The provision goes even further, stating in its second paragraph that:

> *"**Those individuals and groups who are still in opposition** to the Islamic Republic of Afghanistan **and cease enmity after the enforcement of this resolution** and join the process of national reconciliation, and respect the Constitution and other laws and abide them **shall enjoy the benefits of this resolution.**"* (emphasis added)

This means that not only the perpetrators of past crimes are possible beneficiaries of the amnesty, but also those who end violence only after the enforcement of the Amnesty Law. This is nothing other than an invitation to commit serious crimes, then join the reconciliation process and simply go unpunished.[125] This approach surpasses many other amnesty

121 Kouvo, *After Two Years in Legal Limbo.*

122 Asian Centre for Human Rights, *Afghan Charter of Impunity: President Karzai as the Lame Duck.* http://www.achrweb.org/Review/2007/155-07.htm (25 January 2016).

123 Winterbotham, *The State of Transitional Justice in Afghanistan*, pp. 7–10.

124 „National Reconciliation, General Amnesty, and National Stability Law", Official Gazette, published: 13 Qaus 1387 Serial No: (965) (unofficial English translation), in: Kouvo, *After Two Years in Legal Limbo.*

125 Khan, 'Afghanistan: War Crimes, ICC and NGOs', 105.

regulations from around the world insofar as, in most cases, the crimes concerned must be perpetrated before the amnesty law is enacted (see *2.1 Amnesties in General*).

In addition, although the revised version contains an individual right of victims to bring charges against individual perpetrators[126], this is unrealistic for many reasons. For example, many victims are intimidated by the superiority of warlords, also in relation to any potential trial. Apart from that, no investigative procedure exists to enforce the codified victim rights – this makes them meaningless.[127]

The reasons given for such a broad amnesty can be read in Article 1 of the Amnesty Law:

"This law is adopted for the purpose of strengthening the reconciliation and national stability, ensuring the supreme interests of the country, ending rivalries and building confidence among the belligerent parties ..." Relying only on the wording of this article the motivations seem to be the promotion of peace and reconciliation as well as the alleviation of internal unrest. However, as mentioned above (see *2.1 Amnesties in General*), it may be that the real reasons for an amnesty are obscured. This is precisely what has occurred in the case of Afghanistan. When members of parliament and government, who at the same time are alleged perpetrators of serious human rights violations[128], introduce a blanket amnesty, anyone might reasonable conclude that they primarily want to protect themselves from criminal investigation and punishment.[129] Therefore, the Afghan Amnesty Law can be qualified as a so-called self-amnesty.[130]

---

126 *See* Art. 3 (3) of the Amnesty Law: *"The provisions set forth in clause (1) and (2) of this article shall not affect the claims of individuals against individuals based up on Haqullabd (rights of people) and criminal offences in respect of individual crimes."*.

127 Hartmann and Klonowiecka-Milart, *Impunity Prevails in Afghanistan*.

128 Among them were, for example, Muhammad Muhaqiq, Abdul Rasul Sayyaf and Burhanuddin Rabbani, *See* The Afghanistan Justice Project, *Amnesty Would Jeopardize National Reconciliation and Security*. http://www.afghanistanjusticep roject.org/ (10 July 2012); S. Mühlmann, 'Afghanistan erteilt Massenmördern einen Freibrief', WELT ONLINE, 18 March 2010.

129 N. Khan, 'Justice to the Extent Possible: The Prospects for Accountability in Afghanistan', *Temple Int'l & Comp.L.J.* 23 (2009), 1–34, at 18–9; I. Wolkowa, 'Generalpardon für "heilige Krieger": Afghanisches Parlament beschloss Amnestie/Kämpfer der letzten 25 Jahre bleiben straffrei', Neues Deutschland, 03 February 2007.

130 Afghanistan Independent Human Rights Commission (AIHRC), *Discussion Paper on the Legality of Amnesties*, p. 9.

On March 10, 2007, the revised Amnesty Law was approved by parliament.[131] After that, the law was again presented to former President Karzai for his signature, but due to international pressure he did not sign the law.[132] According to an Afghan official, Karzai's signature was not mandatory since a two-thirds majority of the parliament had approved the law.[133] However, the legislative process in Afghanistan as well as the Amnesty Law itself[134] demands furthermore publication in an official gazette.[135] This essential step took almost two years. After an unusually long time, Karzai finally transmitted the law to the Ministry of Justice[136] and on December 3, 2008 the Amnesty Law was quietly published in the official gazette.[137] But according to some authors, this is insufficient for the amnesty to acquire legal force. Rather, printed copies need to be handed out and an electronic version must be placed on the website of the Ministry of Justice.[138] It is for this reason that these authors say the law was not published before January 2010, when hard copies were distributed.[139] This

131 Gossman and Kouvo, *Tell Us How This Ends*, p. 30.

132 H. Georg, 'Kolonialisten kommen zurück – NATO-Staaten inclusive Deutschland setzen auf afghanische Warlords', Neue Rheinische Zeitung, 31 March 2010.

133 J. Leopold, *Afghanistan Enacts Law That Gives War Criminals Blanket Immunity*. http://globalresearch.ca/index.php?context=va&aid=18216 (25 January 2016); K. Iliopoulos, *Afghan Amnesty Law a Setback for Peace*. http://www.crimesofwar.org/commentary/afghan-amnesty-law-a-setback-for-peace/ (26 January 2016).

134 *See* Art. 6 of the Amnesty Law: *"This law shall be enforce from the date of endorsement and published in the official gazette."*.

135 Leopold, *Afghanistan Enacts Law That Gives War Criminals Blanket Immunity*; A. Mojumdar, *Afghanistan: Amnesty Law Fuels Debate on Reconciliation Process*. http://www.eurasianet.org/departments/insight/articles/eav031510.shtml (26 January 2016).

136 Hakimi and Suhrke, 'A Poisonous Chalice', 214.

137 „National Reconciliation, General Amnesty, and National Stability Law", Official Gazette, publishing date: 13 Qaus 1387 Serial No: (965), *See:* Afghanistan Research and Evaluation Unit (AREU), *Afghanistan Research Newsletter Number 24, January/February 2010*. http://www.areu.org.af/Uploads/EditionPdfs/1006E-Afghanistan%20Research%20Newsletter%2024%20Jan-Feb%202010.pdf (26 January 2016), p. 22.

138 J. Boone, *Afghanistan Quietly Brings into Force Taliban Amnesty Law*. http://www.guardian.co.uk/world/2010/feb/11/taliban-amnesty-law-enacted (27 January 2016).

139 Human Rights Watch, *Afghanistan: Repeal Amnesty Law*. http://www.hrw.org/en/news/2010/03/10/afghanistan-repeal-amnesty-law (26 January 2016).

view is supported by the fact that the Afghan government announced the entry into force of a blanket amnesty only in January 2010.[140]

To summarise, it can be concluded that during the period between March 2007 and January 2010 the Afghan Amnesty Law was in legal limbo and thus not an official law.[141] But why did it take such a long time until the Amnesty Law was gazetted and more than another year until the Afghan government publicly confirmed the enactment?

A possible explanation may be that the strong criticism from Karzai's international partners and human rights activists led him to postpone the publication of the law. It might also be possible that Karzai wanted to wait until the presidential election in 2009, in order to gain support from powerful warlords and the beneficiaries of an amnesty.[142] However, as time passed, and the international community became more and more silent, the moment to gazette the Amnesty Law was right.[143] From this moment in December 2008 until January 2010 the government was again extraordinarily reluctant with regard to the Amnesty Law. The unexpected announcement of the law in early 2010 can be associated with the worsening security situation in the country and Karzai's efforts to talk to the Taliban.[144] In this sense, the prospect of obtaining amnesty was expected to support the reconciliation and reintegration of the Taliban.[145] This is in accordance with the proclamation of the "*Afghanistan Peace and Reintegration Programme*" at the London Conference in January 2010.[146] This programme includes various initiatives for Taliban insurgents, such as offering work, education, land and pensions on condition that they renounce violence.[147] From today's perspective it should be noted that the Taliban are still not interested in any peace negotiations.[148] Apart from this, it is worth mentioning that Ashraf Ghani, current President of Afghanistan,

140 Salahuddin, *Afghanistan Must Not Repeal Amnesty Law*.

141 Hakimi and Suhrke, 'A Poisonous Chalice', 214.

142 Ibid., p. 214.

143 Leopold, *Afghanistan Enacts Law That Gives War Criminals Blanket Immunity*.

144 Human Rights Watch, *Afghanistan: Repeal Amnesty Law*.

145 Human Rights Watch, *World Report 2011: Afghanistan*. http://www.hrw.org/world-report-2011/afghanistan (26 January 2016), pp. 3–4.

146 UNDP in Afghanistan, *Afghanistan Peace and Reintegration Programme (APRP)*. http://www.af.undp.org/content/afghanistan/en/home/operations/projects/crisis_prevention_and_recovery/aprp.html (27 January 2016).

147 Winterbotham, *The State of Transitional Justice in Afghanistan*, pp. 9–10.

148 Al Jazeera, *Afghan Official: No Plans to Revive Taliban Peace Talks*. http://www.aljazeera.com/news/2016/07/afghan-official-plans-revive-taliban-peace-talks-160714083916947.html (11 October 2016).

and Gulbuddin Hekmatyar, leader of the insurgent group Hezb-e Islami, signed a peace deal in September 2016.[149] The agreement *inter alia* grants in its Article 9 amnesty to Hekmatyar, "one of Afghanistan's most notorious war crimes suspects"[150], and other members of Hezb-e Islami for alleged international crimes committed during the Afghan civil war in the 1990s.[151] The legal basis for the impunity provision is to be found in the Afghan Amnesty Law of 2010.[152] Besides granting amnesty, the peace deal also contains regulations on financial resources, security and moreover an honorary status for Hekmatyar in recognition of his endeavours "for peace and freedom of Afghanistan".[153] In return for these huge concessions and privileges for Hekmatyar and his followers, Hezb-e Islami commits itself merely to renounce violence, respect the Afghan Constitution and "stop all military movements and activities and dismantle its military structures"[154].[155] The declared aim of the peace deal is to bring peace to Afghanistan.[156] Whether this aim can be achieved through such a broad amnesty is a tough question. What should not be denied, however, is the fact that the significance of Hezb-e Islami on the battlefield is severely diminished compared to the civil war era.[157] This means that a peace deal with Hezb-e Islami will not be sufficient on its own to reach the aspired to goal. There is therefore also the hope of encouraging other – more powerful – insurgent groups, such as the Taliban, to join the peace negotiations.[158] This is, in fact, highly doubtful since military action is still the Taliban's method of choice and nothing indicates that this will

149 Bengali and Faizy, 'Afghanistan Takes a Step Toward Peace With Notorious Ex-Warlord'; Osman, *Peace With Hekmatyar*, p. 1.

150 Gossman, *Afghanistan War Crimes Suspect Comes Home*.

151 Article nine of the agreement says that the government "provides guarantee for the judicial immunity of the leader and members of Hezb-e Islami concerning the party's past political and military actions.", *see* Osman, *Peace With Hekmatyar*, p. 4.

152 Ibid., pp. 10–1.

153 *See* Article 18 of the Peace Agreement, ibid., pp. 4–5.

154 *See* Article 19 of the Peace Agreement, ibid., pp. 4–5.

155 Ibid., pp. 4–5; Bengali and Faizy, 'Afghanistan Takes a Step Toward Peace With Notorious Ex-Warlord'.

156 Bengali and Faizy, 'Afghanistan Takes a Step Toward Peace With Notorious Ex-Warlord'.

157 Ibid; Osman, *Peace With Hekmatyar*, p. 1.

158 Bengali and Faizy, 'Afghanistan Takes a Step Toward Peace With Notorious Ex-Warlord'; S. Snow, 'Ghani's Deal With the Devil: Hekmatyar and Transitional Justice', The Diplomat, 22 September 2016.

change in the near future.[159] Apart from this, the fundamental question to be answered is whether the peace agreement may contain an amnesty for serious international crimes. Given that the legal foundation for the impunity provision of the peace agreement is to be found in the Afghan Amnesty Law of 2010, it is advisable to precisely examine this law. How does this very broad and unconditional amnesty fit into the presumed "age of accountability"? Or in other words, are the regulations of the Afghan Amnesty Law compatible with Afghanistan's obligations under international law? What is noteworthy in this context is that during the whole legislative process no one was interested in this question.[160] Therefore the following chapters contain an analysis of current international and in part also national trends concerning amnesties. In doing so, the focus remains on the case of Afghanistan and the compatibility of its Amnesty Law with international law.

159 Osman, *Peace With Hekmatyar*, 10.
160 Gossman and Kouvo, *Tell Us How This Ends*, p. 31.

3 The Legitimacy of the Afghan Amnesty Law under International Law

As noted above (see 2. *Amnesties in the Age of Accountability*), the granting of amnesties is no longer located in the sphere of a sovereign state only. Rather, national amnesties must be evaluated in the context of international law. That is, in which way (post-) conflict states deal with past injustices is not only at their discretion, but needs to be considered as an international affair as well.[161] In this sense, the legitimacy of the Afghan Amnesty Law under international law is discussed in the following.[162]

In the view of human rights scholars and activists as well as many victims, Afghanistan's blanket amnesty stands for lawlessness, the satisfaction of personal interests and entrenched impunity.[163] They would possibly deem it illegal without need for further verification.[164] However, it is not as simple as that. In order to reach a conclusion in this matter it is necessary to fully examine the relevant international law while taking into account the specific situation in Afghanistan and the exact details of the Afghan Amnesty Law. An analysis in this sense encompasses different stages of legal examination. Following the sources of international law, as contained in Article 38 (1) of the Statute of the International Court of Justice, the compatibility of the Afghan Amnesty Law with international conventions, international custom, the general principles of law as well as judicial decisions and the teachings of the most highly qualified publicists is looked at.[165]

---

161 N. Roht-Arriaza and L. Gibson, 'The Developing Jurisprudence on Amnesty', *Human Rights Quarterly* 20 (1998), 843–85, at 843–4.

162 The legitimacy of the Afghan Amnesty Law will be examined with regard only to international law. The compatibility of the Amnesty Law with Afghanistan's domestic legislation as well as the question of whether other countries are bound by the Afghan Amnesty Law is not of interest for this study.

163 Mallinder (2008), p. 1.

164 *See* Schabas, *Unimaginable Atrocities*, p. 173.

165 *See* Statute of the International Court of Justice, Article 38:
"(1) The Court, whose function is to decide in accordance with international law such disputes as are submitted to it, shall apply:
a. international conventions, whether general or particular, establishing rules expressly recognized by the contesting states;
b. international custom, as evidence of a general practice accepted as law;

Accordingly, this part of the study is divided into corresponding chapters: It starts with the question of whether the Afghan Amnesty Law violates relevant international treaty law. This is followed by an analysis of customary international law with regard to the prohibition of amnesties in certain cases. The outcome indicates whether or not the Afghan Amnesty Law is in accordance with the practice of states and other subjects of international law. The next chapter deals only briefly with the general principles of law and amnesties. It finds out whether various national legal systems have a common legal principle in relation to the applicability of amnesties.[166] Finally, the subsidiary sources of international law are consulted.[167] In this regard the decisions of international courts on amnesty regulations from around the world are of great value for the assessment of the Afghan Amnesty Law. Further, the standards and guidelines on amnesties developed by scholars are very useful for determining the legitimacy of the Afghan Amnesty Law. In the end, the results of the different stages of the legal examination are compared and a well-founded conclusion is drawn.

3.1 *Is the Afghan Amnesty Law Consistent with Relevant International Treaties?*

In order to answer the first question of whether or not the Afghan Amnesty Law is in accordance with international treaty law, it is essential to know the exact international obligations by which Afghanistan is bound. Only these specific obligations form the statutory framework within which the legality of the Amnesty Law has to be examined. According to the International Law Commission, this means that *"each State has its own range of international obligations and its own correlative responsibili-*

---

c. the general principles of law recognized by civilized nations;
d. subject to the provisions of Article 59, judicial decisions and the teachings of the most highly qualified publicists of the various nations, as subsidiary means for the determination of rules of law.",
United Nations, *Statute of the International Court of Justice*, 18 April 1946, http://www.refworld.org/docid/3deb4b9c0.html (08 February 2016).

166 H. Thirlway, 'The Sources of International Law' in M. D. Evans (ed.), *International Law*, 3rd edn. (Oxford, New York: Oxford University Press, 2010), pp. 95–121, at p. 109.

167 G. Werle, *Völkerstrafrecht*, 3rd edn. (Tübingen: Mohr Siebeck, 2012), p. 69.

ties"[168]. Thus, to begin with, the relevant international treaties applicable in the case of Afghanistan must be identified.

Any international treaty needs to pass various phases to become a binding legal obligation upon the States concerned.[169] Without going into this matter any further, the essential steps in the process are outlined hereinafter. Depending on the relevant regulations within a treaty several possibilities regarding its recognition by States may arise. The usual act by which a State becomes a party to a multilateral treaty is "accession"[170]. That is, a State acknowledges that it is legally bound by the provisions of a treaty which has already been negotiated and signed by other States.[171] An act of signature by the acceding State is not necessary in this case. Another way is consent by "signature"[172]. This act does not lead to a binding obligation. However, signing implies not only the intent to ratify the particular treaty[173] but also that the State must refrain from acts that would defeat the object and purpose of the treaty[174]. A quite popular and historically well-established method to become a party to an international treaty is the act of "ratification" by the authorities of the State.[175] In this way, the respective State indicates that it is legally bound by the provisions of the treaty.

In consideration of these procedures Afghanistan has become a party to different international treaties. Of particular interest for this study are those treaties with respect to international humanitarian, human rights and criminal law. Therefore, applicable treaties with reference to these subject matters are listed below. The enumeration is not exhaustive, since only those treaties with connection to the research question are quoted.

---

168 United Nations, *Yearbook of the International Law Commission 2001: Volume II, Part Two*, A/CN.4/SER.A/2001/Add.1 (Part 2). http://legal.un.org/ilc/publications/yearbooks/english/ilc_2001_v2_p2.pdf (09 February 2016), p. 64.

169 *See* United Nations, *Vienna Convention on the Law of Treaties*, 23 May 1969, United Nations, Treaty Series, vol. 1155, http://www.refworld.org/docid/3ae6b3a10.html (09 February 2016); M. N. Shaw, *International Law*, 5. ed. (Cambridge: Cambridge Univ. Press, 2006), p. 816.

170 *See* Art. 15 Vienna Convention on the Law of Treaties.

171 United Nations, *United Nations Treaty Collection: Glossary of Terms Relating to Treaty Actions*. https://treaties.un.org/Pages/Overview.aspx?path=overview/glossary/page1_en.xml (10 February 2016).

172 *See* Art. 12 Vienna Convention on the Law of Treaties.

173 Shaw, *International Law*, p. 818.

174 *See* Art. 18 Vienna Convention on the Law of Treaties.

175 Shaw, *International Law*, p. 816; *See* Art. 14 Vienna Convention on the Law of Treaties.

To start with, the pertinent international humanitarian law treaties by which Afghanistan is bound are the Geneva Conventions of 1949 and the 1977 Additional Protocols thereto:

- Geneva Convention (I) for the Amelioration of the Condition of the Wounded and Sick in Armed Forces in the Field (12 August 1949): Afghanistan Signature 08 December 1949, Ratification 26 September 1956[176];
- Geneva Convention (II) for the Amelioration of the Condition of Wounded, Sick and Shipwrecked Members of Armed Forces at Sea (12 August 1949): Afghanistan Signature 08 December 1949, Ratification 26 September 1956[177];
- Geneva Convention (III) relative to the Treatment of Prisoners of War (12 August 1949): Afghanistan Signature 08 December 1949, Ratification 26 September 1956[178];
- Geneva Convention (IV) relative to the Protection of Civilian Persons in Time of War (12 August 1949): Afghanistan Signature 08 December 1949, Ratification 26 September 1956[179];
- Protocol Additional to the Geneva Conventions of 12 August 1949, and Relating to the Protection of Victims of International Armed Conflicts (Additional Protocol I) (08 June 1977): Afghanistan Accession 24 June 2009[180];
- Protocol Additional to the Geneva Conventions of 12 August 1949, and Relating to the Protection of Victims of Non-International Armed Conflicts (Additional Protocol II) (08 June 1977): Afghanistan Accession 24 June 2009[181].

176 University of Minnesota – Human Rights Library, *Ratification of International Human Rights Treaties – Afghanistan*. http://www1.umn.edu/humanrts/research/ratification-afghanistan1.html (11 February 2016).

177 Ibid.

178 Ibid.

179 Ibid.

180 International Committee of the Red Cross (ICRC), *Afghanistan Accedes to Additional Protocols I and II in Historic Step to Limit Wartime Suffering*. https://www.icrc.org/eng/resources/documents/news-release/2009-and-earlier/afganistan-news-240609.htm (11.02.16).

181 Ibid.

With regard to international human rights treaties, Afghanistan acceded or signed and ratified the following:

- Convention against Torture and Other Cruel, Inhuman or Degrading Treatment or Punishment (CAT) (10 December 1984): Afghanistan Signature 04 February 1985, Ratification 01 April 1987[182];
- International Covenant on Civil and Political Rights (ICCPR) (16 December 1966): Afghanistan Accession 24 January 1983[183].

It should be mentioned, that Afghanistan is not yet a member of the 2006 International Convention for the Protection of All Persons from Enforced Disappearance.[184]

Relevant international criminal law treaties applicable in the case of Afghanistan are as follows:

- Convention on the Prevention and Punishment of the Crime of Genocide (09 December 1948): Afghanistan Accession 22 March 1956[185];
- Convention on the Non-Applicability of Statutory Limitations to War Crimes and Crimes against Humanity (26 November 1968): Afghanistan Accession 22 July 1983[186];
- Rome Statute of the International Criminal Court (17 July 1998): Afghanistan Accession 10 February 2003[187].

In general terms, it can be said that the rules of international human rights law come into play both in times of peace and during armed conflict. International humanitarian law, on the other hand, applies in times of armed conflict only, but then constitutes a *lex specialis* in relation to international human rights law.[188] This means that in certain situations, for example, in cases were an enemy combatant is killed in the course of a lawful act during an armed conflict, human rights law cannot be invoked in

182 University of Minnesota – Human Rights Library, *Ratification of International Human Rights Treaties – Afghanistan*.

183 Ibid.

184 Ibid.

185 Ibid.

186 Ibid.

187 Ibid; The Coalition for the International Criminal Court (CICC), *Afghanistan Signs Up for the International Criminal Court: War Crimes in Afghanistan May Now Be Tried Before the ICC*. http://www.iccnow.org/documents/02.10.2003-Afghanistan.pdf (11 February 2016), p. 1.

188 United Nations Assistance Mission in Afghanistan (UNAMA), *Afghanistan Midyear Report 2011: Protection of Civilians in Armed Conflict*. https://unama.unmissions.org/sites/default/files/2011_midyear_poc.pdf (11 February 2016), pp. iii–iv.

an absolute way.[189] Prosecution of the perpetrator is precluded. However, human rights law complements and reinforces the safeguards provided by international humanitarian law.[190] In other words, the application of human rights law does not end in case of an armed conflict.[191]

In relation to the nature of armed conflicts a further distinction has to be made. That is, armed conflicts or phases of such conflicts may have an international, an internal or even a hybrid character. This distinction is important insofar as different rules of international humanitarian law come into consideration.[192] Thus an international armed conflict is governed by the four Geneva Conventions and the Protocol Additional to the Geneva Conventions of 1949, and Relating to the Protection of Victims of International Armed Conflicts (Additional Protocol I). In domestic armed hostilities, however, Article 3 common to the four Geneva Conventions (Common Article 3) as well as the Protocol Additional to the Geneva Conventions of 12 August 1949, and Relating to the Protection of Victims of Non-International Armed Conflicts (Additional Protocol II) contain the relevant standards.[193] In addition, the regulations of customary international humanitarian law are applicable to all types of armed conflict.[194]

As already mentioned, the longstanding armed conflict in Afghanistan is highly complex because of its different phases and nature. The first period from 1978 till 1989, comprising the Communist Revolution and PDPA government as well as the Soviet occupation, was an international armed conflict. The subsequent civil war from 1989 until 1996 can be

---

189 H.-J. Heintze, 'On the Relationship Between Human Rights Law Protection and International Humanitarian Law', *International Review of the Red Cross* 86 (2004), 789–814, at 796–8.

190 International Committee of the Red Cross (ICRC), *IHL and human rights law*. https://www.icrc.org/en/doc/war-and-law/ihl-other-legal-regmies/ihl-human-rights/overview-ihl-and-human-rights.htm (20 December 2018); Heintze, 'On the Relationship Between Human Rights Law Protection and International Humanitarian Law', 796–8.

191 International Court of Justice, *Legal Consequences of the Construction of a Wall in the Occupied Palestinian Territory*. https://www.icj-cij.org/files/case-related/131/1677.pdf (20 December 2018), paras.102 – 113.

192 P. G. Danchin, 'Transitional Justice in Afghanistan: Confronting Violations of International Humanitarian and Human Rights Law', *Yearbook of International Humanitarian Law* 4 (2001), 3–51, at 18–24.

193 A. Bellal, G. Giacca and S. Casey-Maslen, 'International Law and Armed Non-State Actors in Afghanistan', *International Review of the Red Cross* 93 (2011), 47–79, at 52–3.

194 J. Pejic, 'The Protective Scope of Common Article 3: More than Meets the Eye', *International Review of the Red Cross* 93 (2011), 189–225, at 196.

designated as an internal armed conflict. More difficult to assess is the third phase, the Taliban regime from 1996 onwards. In principle, this armed conflict was also of an internal nature. But due to foreign involvement, for example of the US, Russia and Pakistan[195], the conflict may have become internationalised.[196] When the United States and its allies invaded and defeated the Taliban regime in 2001, the hostilities turned again into a pure international conflict.[197] Yet since June 2002, when the transitional government was set up, it has in principle been an internal conflict. Since the government combats non-state armed groups it is no international armed conflict between two or more States.[198] However, international military forces are still involved in the ongoing conflict and fight with the consent and in support of the Afghan government.[199] The latter precludes an international conflict, but could nevertheless constitute an internationalised conflict.

As has been shown, the armed conflict in Afghanistan has been in part an international, a non-international or an internationalised character. However, the classification is not always easy. Hence, it is also not always easy to determine which rules of international humanitarian law are applicable to the different phases. Notwithstanding these difficulties, developments in the field of customary international humanitarian law could prove very useful in this regard. This means that, according to the customary rules, almost all of the regulations governing international armed conflicts are equally applicable to non-international armed conflicts.[200] Thus, in cases like Afghanistan, the difficulties in distinguishing between internal and international armed hostilities as well as the challenge of determining the respective provisions of international humanitarian law can be overcome by the application of customary international humanitarian law.

As described at the beginning of this chapter, the determination of the exact international treaty obligations by which Afghanistan is bound is

---

195 International Center for Transitional Justice (ICTJ), *Afghanistan: Addressing the Past*, pp. 2–3.

196 Danchin, 'Transitional Justice in Afghanistan', 22–4.

197 Pejic, 'The Protective Scope of Common Article 3', 196.

198 Ibid., p. 196.

199 Pejic, 'The Protective Scope of Common Article 3', 196; United Nations Assistance Mission in Afghanistan (UNAMA), *Afghanistan Midyear Report 2011*.

200 State Library of New South Wales, *Non-International Armed Conflict*. http://www.legalanswers.sl.nsw.gov.au/guides/hot_topics/intnl_humanitarian_law/non_intl_armed_conflict.html (12 February 2016).

the necessary first step in order to examine the legitimacy of the Afghan Amnesty Law. Since the abovementioned applicable international treaties are subject to Article 27 of the Vienna Convention on the Law of Treaties, Afghanistan *"may not invoke the provisions of its internal law as justification for its failure to perform a treaty."*[201] That is, the domestic law of Afghanistan cannot be used as justification for breaches of international treaty law. Rather, all Afghan laws, including the Amnesty Law, need to be in compliance with the international treaties and conventions to which Afghanistan is a party.[202] Therefore the next step is to analyse whether the applicable international treaties contain explicit provisions on amnesties. If this is the case, the Afghan Amnesty Law will be assessed for its compatibility with those provisions.

3.1.1 Does the Afghan Amnesty Law Violate Explicit Statutory Provisions on Amnesties?

Notwithstanding the rise of international criminal, human rights and humanitarian law in recent decades, no international treaty explicitly prohibits or discourages the granting of amnesty for international crimes.[203] Although the amnesty question has been regularly posed during multilateral treaty negotiations, as during the negotiations of the ICC Rome Statute, the Convention on the Non-Applicability of Statutory Limitations to War Crimes and Crimes against Humanity or the International Convention for the Protection of All Persons from Enforced Disappearance[204], the parties were unable to agree on this matter.[205] A reason may be that States still believe in amnesties as a powerful bargaining tool and thus do not

201 *See* Art. 27 Vienna Convention on the Law of Treaties; Since the provisions of the Vienna Convention are recognised as customary international law, they are binding on all States. Hence, although Afghanistan is not a party to the Vienna Convention, it is bound by the provisions via customary international law. *See* M. Knust Rassekh Afshar, *Max Planck Manual on Afghan Constitutional Law, Volume Two: Constitutional Practice and Human Rights*. http://www.mpil.de/shared/data/pdf/mpil_hr_engl_1st.pdf (04 October 2012), pp. 7–9.

202 Ibid., pp. 7–9.

203 O'Keefe, *International Criminal law*, p. 468; Freeman, *Necessary Evils*, pp. 32–3; Schabas, *Unimaginable Atrocities*, p. 182.

204 A. Seibert-Fohr, *Prosecuting Serious Human Rights Violations* (Oxford, New York: Oxford University Press, 2009), 171–172, 181–183.

205 Freeman, *Necessary Evils*, pp. 32–3.

want to be bound by any treaty that eliminates this option.[206] As a consequence, the Afghan Amnesty Law cannot violate an explicit international prohibition of certain amnesties, as no such prohibition exists so far.[207]

Even though international treaty law does not contain an explicit prohibition on amnesties, it does contain an explicit encouragement to enact them. Article 6 (5) of Additional Protocol II to the Geneva Conventions, relating to the protection of victims of non-international armed conflicts, provides that: *"At the end of hostilities, the authorities in power shall endeavour to grant the broadest possible amnesty to persons who have participated in the armed conflict, or those deprived of their liberty for reasons related to the armed conflict, whether they are interned or detained."*

Does this mean that international crimes can be amnestied, or what was the intention of this provision? It is clear from the wording of this article that States are authorised to grant wide-ranging amnesties. There is no restriction in terms of the underlying offence. According to the Commentary on Article 6 (5) of Additional Protocol II to the Geneva Conventions the intention was *"to encourage gestures of reconciliation which can contribute to re-establishing normal relations in the life of a nation which has been divided"*.[208] If one follows the argument of the International Committee of the Red Cross (ICRC)[209] relying on the preparatory works and the context of Article 6 (5), then an amnesty only comes into consideration for crimes in connection with sole participation in armed conflicts.[210] That is, an amnesty for killing enemy combatants, rebellion, sedition and treason or other national crimes would be possible, whereas an amnesty for violations

206 Freeman and Pensky, 'The Amnesty Controversy in International Law', 44.

207 *See The Case of the S.S. Lotus* (Permanent Court of International Justice, 07 September 1927).

208 Sandoz Y., Swinarski C. and Zimmermann B. (eds.), *Commentary on the Additional Protocols of 8 June 1977 to the Geneva Conventions of 12 August 1949* (Geneva, Norwell, MA, USA: International Committee of the Red Cross; Martinus Nijhoff Publishers; Distributors for the United States and Canada, Kluwer Academic Publishers, 1987), p. 1402.

209 The International Committee of the Red Cross is the authoritative interpretative body under the Geneva Conventions. *See* Slye, 'The Legitimacy of Amnesties Under International Law and General Principles of Anglo-American Law', 178.

210 Henckaerts J.-M. and Doswald-Beck L. (eds.), *Customary International Humanitarian Law: Volume II: Practice – Part 1 and 2* (Cambridge, UK: Cambridge University Press, 2005), p. 4043.

of international (humanitarian) law is out of the question.[211] In line with this view the United Nations emphasised that it is not acceptable to grant amnesties for serious international crimes perpetrated in non-international conflicts.[212] However, it is worth mentioning that the proposal of the former Soviet Union to explicitly exclude war crimes and crimes against humanity from the scope of Article 6 (5) was not successful.[213]

The question of whether or not the Afghan Amnesty Law is compatible with the only explicit international provision on amnesties, namely Article 6 (5) of Additional Protocol II to the Geneva Conventions, can be answered on the basis of the above interpretation. Since Article 6 (5) does not contain a prohibition or obligation with regard to the enactment of amnesties, the Afghan Amnesty Law cannot violate this provision. Rather, this norm encourages the granting of amnesties to a certain degree. Even if it is not clear from the wording of Article 6 (5) that amnesties for international crimes are exempted, the interpretation and application of the provision indicate it. This means that an unconditional amnesty for serious violations of human rights is certainly not permitted. Consequently, the blanket Afghan Amnesty Law, which grants impunity to all kinds of perpetrators and crimes, goes beyond the scope of Article 6 (5) and thus is not legitimised by this regulation.

Since explicit provisions on amnesties are rare, the assessment of the legality of amnesty laws frequently focuses on obligations under international treaties to prosecute perpetrators of serious international crimes.[214] These obligations could preclude the issuing of amnesties for the crimes in question. Therefore, the next step is to find out whether or not other statutory provisions are opposed to the Afghan Amnesty law.

---

211 Ibid., p. 4043; Slye, 'The Legitimacy of Amnesties Under International Law and General Principles of Anglo-American Law', 178; UN Office of the High Commissioner for Human Rights, *Rule-of-Law Tools for Post-Conflict States*, p. 16.

212 United Nations Commission on Human Rights, *Report of the Special Rapporteur on the Independence of Judges and Lawyers, Leandro Despouy*, E/CN.4/2005/60. http://daccess-dds-ny.un.org/doc/UNDOC/GEN/G05/104/13/PDF/G0510413.pdf ?OpenElement (23 February 2016), p. 16.

213 Federal Political Department, *Official Records of the Diplomatic Conference on the Reaffirmation and Development of International Humanitarian Law Applicable in Armed Conflicts: Volume IX*. http://www.loc.gov/rr/frd/Military_Law/pdf/RC-records_Vol-9.pdf (23.02.16), p. 319; Y. Naqvi, *Impediments to Exercising Jurisdiction over International Crimes* (The Hague: T.M.C. Asser Press, 2010), p. 122.

214 L. Mallinder, 'Amnesties' in W. A. Schabas and N. Bernaz (eds.), *Routledge Handbook of International Criminal Law* (London and New York: Routledge, 2011), pp. 419–34, at p. 420.

3.1.2 Does the Afghan Amnesty Law Violate Other Statutory Provisions?

In order to evaluate the compatibility of the Afghan Amnesty Law with other explicit statutory provisions relating to amnesties, it is initially necessary to determine those provisions implicitly relating to amnesties. As amnesty means impunity, relevant treaty sources must contain provisions which require the investigation and prosecution of international crimes. Only then may an amnesty be incompatible with international treaty law.[215] International law provides various regulations which establish a legal obligation on States to prosecute those individuals responsible for serious crimes. Depending on the specific international treaty, the exact scope of the duty to prosecute varies.[216] This means that some provisions include an unambiguous duty to carry out criminal proceedings, whereas other conventions are rather vague in this regard. The following explanations do not only refer to statutory provisions which entail the obligation to hold offenders accountable for their atrocities and which are binding on Afghanistan, but also to the arguments for and against an absolute duty to prosecute those atrocities. In this context the question of whether and, if so, under what circumstances a violation of the international obligation to prosecute could be justified, will be answered.

The International Obligation to Prosecute

The relevant regulations of international humanitarian law are the following: according to the four Geneva Conventions of 1949[217] and the Additional Protocol I of 1977[218] relating to international armed conflicts, the High Contracting Parties are obliged to *"enact any legislation necessary to provide effective penal sanctions for persons committing, or ordering to be committed, any of the grave breaches"* of the Conventions. Furthermore, the High Contracting Parties shall bring alleged perpetrators of grave breaches before its own courts, or extradite them. These provisions entail a clearly defined duty to prosecute.[219] Grave breaches of the conventions are serious war crimes committed during an international armed conflict.

215 Freeman and Pensky, 'The Amnesty Controversy in International Law', 45–6.

216 Ibid., 46–8.

217 *See* Art. 49 Geneva Convention I, Art. 50 Geneva Convention II, Art. 129 Geneva Convention III, Art. 146 Geneva Convention IV.

218 *See* Art. 85 of Additional Protocol I to the Geneva Conventions.

219 R. Cryer, 'International Criminal Law' in M. D. Evans (ed.), *International Law*, 3rd edn. (Oxford, New York: Oxford University Press, 2010), pp. 752–83, at p. 778; M. Scharf, 'The Letter of the Law: The Scope of the International Legal

The specific crimes are enumerated in the respective convention[220] and encompass for example wilful killing, torture or inhuman treatment, wilfully causing great suffering or serious injury to body or health. In conflicts of a non-international character, governed by Common Article 3 of the Geneva Conventions of 1949 and Additional Protocol II of 1977, an explicit obligation to prosecute perpetrators of serious crimes does not exist. Rather, as mentioned above, Article 6 (5) of Additional Protocol II expressly encourages amnesties. However, in the case of war crimes, as listed in Common Article 3 of the Geneva Conventions, perpetrators shall be prosecuted, according to the ICRC.[221] This view has been confirmed by the ICC Rome Statute[222] and the jurisprudence of the *ad hoc* tribunals[223], such as the International Criminal Tribunal for Rwanda (ICTR)[224] and the International Criminal Tribunal for the former Yugoslavia (ICTY)[225].

Next, provisions of international human rights law are of interest in this context. Article 4 of the Convention against Torture and Other Cruel, Inhuman or Degrading Treatment or Punishment (CAT) provides that "*1. Each State Party shall ensure that all acts of torture are offences under its criminal law. .... 2. Each State Party shall make these offences punishable by appropriate penalties which take into account their grave nature.*" Article 7 (1) adds that the State Party "*shall...if it does not extradite him, submit the case to its competent authorities for the purpose of prosecution.*" Even though

---

Obligation to Prosecute Human Rights Crimes', *Law and Contemporary Problems* 59 (1996), 41–62, at 44.

220 *See* Art. 50 Geneva Convention I, Art. 51 Geneva Convention II, Art. 130 Geneva Convention III, Art. 147 Geneva Convention IV and Art. 85 Additional Protocol I to the Geneva Conventions.

221 Henckaerts J.-M. and Doswald-Beck L. (eds.), *Customary International Humanitarian Law: Volume I: Rules*, 3rd edn. (Cambridge, UK: Cambridge University Press, 2009), p. 611.

222 *See* Article 8 (2) (c) Rome Statute of the International Criminal Court, *Rome Statute of the International Criminal Court*, A/CONF.183/9. https://www.icc-cpi.int/nr/rdonlyres/ea9aeff7-5752-4f84-be94-0a655eb30e16/0/rome_statute_english.pdf (30 July 2016).

223 Mallinder, *Amnesty, Human Rights and Political Transitions:*, p. 126.

224 Human Rights Watch, *Selling Justice Short: Why Accountability Matters for Peace*. http://www.hrw.org/sites/default/files/reports/ij0709webwcover_3.pdf (29 February 2016), p. 11.

225 *See* Prosecutor v. Zejnil Delalic, Zdavko Mucic, Hazim Delic and Esad Landžo (Elebici case), ICTY, Case No. IT-96–21-A, Judgment (Appeals Chamber), February 20, 2001, paras. 163–73; Prosecutor v. Dusko Tadic, ICTY, Case No. IT-94–1-AR72, Decision on the Defence Motion for Interlocutory Appeal on Jurisdiction (Appeals Chamber), October 2, 1995, para. 143.

this wording indicates that the "competent authorities" are in a position to eventually decide whether or not to prosecute the alleged perpetrators of torture[226], the duty to prosecute is derived from the fact that the Convention against Torture under no circumstances allows for derogations from the postulated obligations[227]. However, it is not excluded that this duty to initiate criminal proceedings can be satisfied by prosecuting only a certain number of alleged perpetrators. This means that the "competent authorities" may exercise prosecutorial discretion and develop selective prosecution strategies.[228] Another human rights treaty, the International Covenant on Civil and Political Rights (ICCPR), affirms various rights and freedoms, such as the inherent right to life[229] and the prohibition of torture or cruel, inhuman or degrading treatment or punishment[230]. The covenant does not explicitly establish a duty to investigate and prosecute serious human rights violations. Nevertheless, Article 2 (3) ICCPR determines that State Parties must ensure *"that any person whose rights or freedoms as herein recognized are violated shall have an effective remedy*", and further *„that any person claiming such a remedy shall have his right thereto determined by competent judicial, administrative or legislative authorities, or by any other competent authority*". This right to an effective remedy has been interpreted by authorised bodies to imply a duty to investigate and prosecute.[231] The Human Rights Committee, for example, concluded that State Parties have to make reparations in the case of violations of covenant rights. These reparations *inter alia* involve bringing to justice the perpetrators of human rights violations.[232] Additionally, the Human Rights Committee stated: *"Where the investigations ... reveal violations of certain Covenant rights, States Parties must ensure that those responsible are brought to justice. As with failure to investigate, failure to bring to justice perpetrators*

226 Mallinder, *Amnesty, Human Rights and Political Transitions:*, pp. 127–9.

227 Seibert-Fohr, *Prosecuting Serious Human Rights Violations*, pp. 164–7.

228 U. o. U. Transitional Justice Institute, *The Belfast Guidelines on Amnesty and Accountability*. http://www.ulster.ac.uk/__data/assets/pdf_file/0005/57839/TheBelfastGuidelinesFINAL_000.pdf (24 March 2016), p. 11.

229 *See* Art. 6 of the International Covenant on Civil and Political Rights.

230 *See* Art. 7 of the International Covenant on Civil and Political Rights.

231 Afghanistan Independent Human Rights Commission (AIHRC), *Discussion Paper on the Legality of Amnesties*, pp. 2–3; Seibert-Fohr, *Prosecuting Serious Human Rights Violations*, p. 12; Bell, *The 'New Law' of Transitional Justice*, pp. 4–5.

232 United Nations Human Rights Committee, *General Comment No. 31: The Nature of the General Legal Obligation Imposed on States Parties to the Covenant*, CCPR/C/21/Rev.1/Add.13. https://www1.umn.edu/humanrts/gencomm/hrcom31.html (29.02.16), 16.

of such violations could in and of itself give rise to a separate breach of the Covenant. ..."[233]

Another relevant source which may require the investigation and prosecution of international crimes is the general obligation of State Parties to ensure respect for human rights protected under general human rights treaties.[234] This means that, although most of these treaties do not entail a specific obligation to hold offenders accountable for their human rights violations, they entail other protective obligations, which could encompass the duty to prosecute.[235]

Of course, international criminal law also contains provisions relating to the duty to prosecute. Article 1 of the 1948 Convention on the Prevention and Punishment of the Crime of Genocide states: "*The Contracting Parties confirm that genocide, whether committed in time of peace or in time of war, is a crime under international law which they undertake to prevent and to punish*". According to Article 6, persons charged with genocide shall be tried either before a national or an international court. These provisions entail a clearly defined duty to prosecute.[236] Special mention must be made of crimes against humanity, since the duty to prosecute these crimes cannot be found in a specific international treaty similar to the Genocide Convention.[237] Apart from that, crimes against humanity are explicitly acknowledged in the Rome Statute of the ICC[238] and, moreover, the ICCPR has been interpreted by the Human Rights Committee to entail the obligation to bring to justice perpetrators of crimes against

233 Ibid., 18.

234 O'Shea, *Amnesty for Crime in International Law and Practice*, p. 161; M. Kotzur, '(Internationales) Strafrecht im Dienste des effektiven Menschenrechtsschutzes' in K. Gaede, H. Goerlich, M. Kahlo and B. Zabel (eds.), *Im Zweifel für die Freiheit: Gedächtnisschrift für Manfred Seebode* (Berlin: BWV Berliner Wissenschafts-Verlag, 2015), pp. 287–99.

235 O'Shea, *Amnesty for Crime in International Law and Practice*, p. 161; Kotzur, '(Internationales) Strafrecht im Dienste des effektiven Menschenrechtsschutzes', 296.

236 E. B. Ludwin King, 'Amnesties in a Time of Transition', *George Washington International Law Review* 41 (2010), 571–618, at 603; Cryer, 'International Criminal Law', 778; Mallinder, *Amnesty, Human Rights and Political Transitions:*, pp. 124–7.

237 UN Office of the High Commissioner for Human Rights, *Rule-of-Law Tools for Post-Conflict States*, pp. 13–4.

238 *See e.g.*, Articles 5 and 7 Rome Statute of the International Criminal Court.

humanity.[239] The committee defines crimes against humanity as violations of the covenant committed as part of a widespread or systematic attack on a civilian population.[240] The most comprehensive legal framework with regard to the fight against impunity is the Rome Statute of the ICC. Because of its particular relevance, it will be dealt with in a separate chapter below.

To sum up, it can be concluded that the four Geneva Conventions and Additional Protocol I relating to international armed conflicts as well as the Convention against Torture and the Genocide Convention entail an explicit duty to prosecute the respective crimes. Common Article 3 and Additional Protocol II relating to non-international armed conflicts as well as the ICCPR have been interpreted by authorised bodies as establishing an obligation to conduct criminal proceedings. Furthermore, the general responsibility to protect human rights may imply the obligation to bring to justice perpetrators of human rights violations.

Does the Afghan Amnesty Law Violate the International Obligation to Prosecute?

After determining the statutory provisions which require the investigation and prosecution of international crimes, such as genocide, torture, rape and other war crimes, the next step is to examine whether the Afghan Amnesty Law violates these specific obligations. Since the Afghan authorities are bound by the aforementioned treaties, they must actually ensure that criminal proceedings are carried out against the alleged perpetrators of these international crimes. Notwithstanding this, Article 3 (1) of the Amnesty Law clearly states that *"All political factions and hostile parties ... shall not be legally and judicially prosecuted."* The law does not contain an exemption for certain crimes, such as war crimes or other serious human rights violations. That is, Afghanistan grants impunity for crimes for which the duty to investigate and prosecute exists and thus violates its international treaty obligations.[241] Even though Article 3 (3) of the Amnesty Law contains an individual right of victims to bring charges

239 United Nations Human Rights Committee, *General Comment No. 31*, 18; UN Office of the High Commissioner for Human Rights, *Rule-of-Law Tools for Post-Conflict States*, pp. 13–4.

240 United Nations Human Rights Committee, *General Comment No. 31*, 18.

241 Afghanistan Independent Human Rights Commission (AIHRC), *Discussion Paper on the Legality of Amnesties*, pp. 5–6; UN Office of the High Commissioner for Human Rights, *Rule-of-Law Tools for Post-Conflict States*, p. 11.

against individual perpetrators[242], this still does nothing to alter the fact that Afghanistan contravenes international conventions.[243] That is to say, it is extremely unlikely that individuals are in a position to conduct criminal investigations against powerful warlords.[244] Moreover, the responsibility to investigate and prosecute serious criminal offences lies with the Afghan State and not with private individuals.[245] Hence, as mentioned at the beginning of this chapter, it seems reasonable to presume that the Afghan amnesty meaning impunity is incompatible with international treaty law requiring the investigation and prosecution of international crimes. This is especially the case where serious war crimes committed in international armed conflicts as well as torture is concerned and the connected duty to prosecute these crimes is of an explicit nature.

Is the International Obligation to Prosecute Absolute?

A number of authors infer from this that the granting of amnesty to perpetrators of such atrocities is entirely prohibited.[246] In order to corroborate this view, some commentators refer to the *jus cogens* character of certain international crimes. This means that the prohibition of these crimes is peremptory and no derogation is permitted. The principle of *jus cogens* applies unrestrictedly and stands above all other sources of international law. International crimes falling into this category are *inter alia* war crimes,

---

242 *See* Art. 3 (3) of the Amnesty Law: "*The provisions set forth in clause (1) and (2) of this article shall not affect the claims of individuals against individuals based up on Haqullabd (rights of people) and criminal offences in respect of individual crimes.*".

243 Mojumdar, *Afghanistan: Amnesty Law Fuels Debate on Reconciliation Process*.

244 *See* 2.3 The Afghan Amnesty Law of 2010.

245 Human Rights Watch, *Afghanistan: Repeal Amnesty Law*.

246 L. N. Sadat, 'The Effect of Amnesties Before Domestic and International Tribunals: Morality, Law and Politics' in E. Hughes, W. A. Schabas and R. C. Thakur (eds.), *Atrocities and International Accountability: Beyond Transitional Justice* (New York: United Nations University Press, 2007), pp. 225–45, at p. 234; M. C. Bassiouni, 'Proposed Guiding Principles for Combating Impunity for International Crimes' in M. C. Bassiouni (ed.), *Post-Conflict Justice* (Ardsley, New York: Transnational Publishers, 2002), pp. 255–82, at p. 258; N. J. Kritz, 'Progress and Humility: The Ongoing Search for Post-Conflict Justice' in M. C. Bassiouni (ed.), *Post-Conflict Justice* (Ardsley, New York: Transnational Publishers, 2002), pp. 55–87, at p. 56; W. W. Burke-White, 'Reframing Impunity: Applying Liberal International Law Theory to an Analysis of Amnesty Legislation', *Harvard International Law.Journal* 42 (2001), 467–533, at 478–9; Seibert-Fohr, *Prosecuting Serious Human Rights Violations*, pp. 164–7 *(in the case of torture); Scharf, 'The Letter of the Law', 44 (in the case of serious war crimes).*

torture, genocide and crimes against humanity.[247] These commentators and human rights activists conclude from the status of *jus cogens* an absolute obligation to prosecute the perpetrators of the crimes concerned and consequently, an absolute obligation not to issue amnesties in those cases.[248] In their view, the peremptory prohibition of the worst international crimes and the resulting illegality of any treaty or agreement allowing such crimes would be meaningless without the prohibition of granting impunity for perpetrators who have committed those atrocities classified as *jus cogens*.[249] However, this is not true. Although the effective realisation of the prohibition of international crimes depends on the contribution of States, first and foremost by prosecuting the perpetrators of these crimes, this is certainly not absolutely necessary since the condemnation of international crimes does have meaning without such a duty to prosecute.[250] International law and therefore also international criminal law is based on the mutual benefit to States of ensuring compliance. Enforcement, for example in the form of a duty to prosecute is thus not automatically included in the prohibition of an international crime.[251]

In this sense, some commentators point out that the duty to prosecute *jus cogens* crimes, is not of an absolute nature, but rather permissive inasmuch as States obtain a right to prosecute alleged perpetrators.[252] According to this approach, the peremptory character of the prohibition of certain international crimes does not necessarily lead to a peremptory duty to prosecute those crimes, and thus has no reasonable impact on the legitimacy of respective amnesties.[253] This view is confirmed by the fact that the

---

247 M. C. Bassiouni, 'Accountability for Violations of International Humanitarian Law and Other Serious Violations of Human Rights' in M. C. Bassiouni (ed.), *Post-Conflict Justice* (Ardsley, New York: Transnational Publishers, 2002), pp. 3–54, at p. 19.

248 Ibid., 14; F. Z. Ntoubandi, *Amnesty for Crimes against Humanity under International Law* (Leiden, Boston: Martinus Nijhoff Publishers, 2007), p. 217; Afghanistan Independent Human Rights Commission (AIHRC), *Discussion Paper on the Legality of Amnesties*, pp. 5–6; Burke-White, 'Reframing Impunity', 478–9.

249 *See* Afghanistan Independent Human Rights Commission (AIHRC), *Discussion Paper on the Legality of Amnesties*, pp. 5–6; N. Roht-Arriaza, 'State Responsibility to Investigate and Prosecute Grave Human Rights Violations in International Law', *California Law Review* 78 (1990), 449–513, at 484–8.

250 O'Shea, *Amnesty for Crime in International Law and Practice*, p. 207.

251 Ibid., p. 207 Cryer, *Prosecuting International Crimes*, p. 111.

252 Ferdinandusse, *Direct Application of International Criminal Law in National Courts*, pp. 182–3; Cryer, *Prosecuting International Crimes*, p. 110.

253 O'Keefe, *International Criminal law*, p. 476.

concept of *jus cogens* is related to customary international law. This means that a peremptory duty to prosecute and a subsequent absolute prohibition of amnesties for *jus cogens* international crimes can be determined only if it is "*accepted and recognized by the international community of States as a whole as a norm from which no derogation is permitted ...*" (Article 53 of the Vienna Convention on the Law of Treaties).[254] According to this rule, *jus cogens* norms emerge through widespread State practice and recognition. This is true for the prohibition of the above-mentioned crimes, but with respect to the duty to prosecute those crimes it cannot be assumed that the international community has equally accepted and recognised it as a norm from which no derogation is permitted.[255] State practice in this regard does not support an absolute and non-derogable obligation to prosecute, given that those responsible for atrocious crimes are almost never sentenced (see 2. *Amnesties in the Age of Accountability*).[256] The same applies to the prohibition of amnesties in these cases. States continue to introduce amnesties even for torture and war crimes, as the example of Afghanistan clearly shows and will be analysed further in Chapter 3.2. Even the responsibility to protect human rights does not lead to an absolute obligation to prosecute the perpetrators of severe human rights violations, because this concept itself is still developing.[257] A widespread State practice in this regard can not yet be identified.[258]

Thus, even if the duty to prosecute can be derived from the wording and interpretation of certain international treaties or from the general responsibility to protect human rights, it cannot be said that this duty rises to the level of *jus cogens*. Consequently, the legitimacy of an amnesty has to be evaluated on the basis of the relevant international conventions, but without the need to consider the higher-ranking norms of *jus cogens*.

---

254 Scharf, 'Trading Justice for Peace', 260.

255 Scharf, 'Trading Justice for Peace', 260.

256 Bassiouni, *Introduction to International Criminal Law*, pp. 996–7; A. Cassese and P. Gaeta, *Cassese's International Criminal Law*, 3rd edn. (Oxford: Oxford University Press, 2013), pp. 311–2; Kaleck, *Mit zweierlei Maß*, p. 116; Greiff, *Transitional Justice, Security, and Development*, p. 4.

257 S. Stahl, *Schutzpflichten im Völkerrecht – Ansatz einer Dogmatik: Ein Beitrag zu Grund, Inhalt und Grenzen der völkerrechtlichen Schutzpflichtendogmatik im Bereich konventionell geschützter Menschenrechte*, Zugl.: Hamburg, Univ., Diss., 2010, Beiträge zum ausländischen öffentlichen Recht und Völkerrecht (Berlin: Springer, 2012), vol. 232, pp. 74–6.

258 Kotzur, '(Internationales) Strafrecht im Dienste des effektiven Menschenrechtsschutzes', 297.

Are Amnesties absolutely prohibited?

Nevertheless, the question of whether the violation of the duty to prosecute, and thus the discrepancy between amnesties and international rules governing criminal proceedings, leads to an entire prohibition of amnesties still arises. An argument against this assertion is that the obligation to prosecute must be reconciled with other important and mandatory obligations of States, which could have the effect that an amnesty is necessary in order to prevent further serious human rights violations and to re-establish peace.[259]

It is therefore indispensable to equally take into account the obligation to protect human rights by conducting criminal proceedings on the one hand and the obligation to protect the rights of potential victims by refraining from initiating a prosecution on the other hand. Against this backdrop, the challenge is to solve the conflicting obligations. They have to be applied in balanced manner in order to reach the goal of optimal effectiveness of both these obligations – a sort of "practical concordance"[260].

This aspect has been taken into account by the drafters of the "Princeton Principles on Universal Jurisdiction" inasmuch as Principle 7 states that amnesties are generally inconsistent with the duty of States to prosecute serious crimes under international law, such as *inter alia* war crimes, torture, genocide and crimes against humanity.[261] The wording "*generally inconsistent*" as well as the commentary to Principle 7 indicates that there may be an exception to the duty to prosecute.[262] Another policy paper, "The Belfast Guidelines on Amnesty and Accountability"[263], is even more precise. In Guideline 1a the drafters advocate that where an amnesty leads to different obligations of States coming into conflict, it is essential not

259 Freeman and Pensky, 'The Amnesty Controversy in International Law', 51; R. Cryer, H. Friman, D. Robinson and E. Wilmshurst, *An Introduction to International Criminal Law and Procedure*, 2nd edn. (Cambridge, New York: Cambridge University Press, 2010), p. 564; Schabas, *Unimaginable Atrocities*, p. 182; Mallinder, *Amnesty, Human Rights and Political Transitions:*, p. 124.

260 The principle of „practical concordance" (*praktische Konkordanz*) is a legal concept which stems from German constitutional law. It is applied to solve conflicting rules. K. Hesse, *Grundzüge des Verfassungsrechts der Bundesrepublik Deutschland* (C.F. Müller GmbH, 1999), p. 28.

261 P. U. Program in Law and Public Affairs, *The Princeton Principles on Universal Jurisdiction*. http://lapa.princeton.edu/hosteddocs/unive_jur.pdf (23 March 2016), p. 31.

262 Ibid., p. 52.

263 Transitional Justice Institute, *The Belfast Guidelines on Amnesty and Accountability*.

to lose sight of the overall aim, namely the protection of human rights.[264] What exactly are these other obligations of States, besides the duty to investigate and prosecute serious human rights violations? This question can be answered by those same international treaties which establish the duty to conduct criminal proceedings, since they further entail an obligation to bring to an end to and prevent serious violations of human rights.[265] To cite a few examples: Article 1 of the four Geneva Conventions as well as Article 1 of Additional Protocol I state that the High Contracting Parties commit themselves to respect and to ensure respect for the Conventions and Protocol I in all circumstances. The Convention against Torture affirms in Article 2 (1) the duty of each State Party to take effective measures to prevent acts of torture. Furthermore, Article 2 of the ICCPR demands that the State Parties undertake to respect and to ensure the rights of the covenant. Finally, State Parties to the Convention on the Prevention and Punishment of the Crime of Genocide are obliged to prevent the crime of genocide according to Article 1 of the Convention. From this it follows that the effective protection of human rights, and the prevention of their violation, is mandatory for all States which are party to these international treaties. It may well be that in a particular (post-) conflict setting this desired objective can be best achieved by conducting criminal proceedings. Yet, in some instances it may prove expedient to make use of alternative mechanisms, such as amnesties.[266] In the latter case the different obligations of States – the obligation to prosecute on the one hand, and the obligation to prevent on the other – come into conflict. However, the prevention of international crimes must have the same status as the duty to prosecute these atrocities.[267] That is, an amnesty cannot be said to be implicitly prohibited by the obligation to carry out criminal proceedings in cases such as war crimes, torture, genocide or crimes against humanity, since an amnesty may be deemed necessary to prevent just these crimes. In other words, there might be situations where criminal proceedings would have the effect of prolonging an ongoing conflict and thus prolonging severe human rights violations, as alleged perpetrators would certainly not be willing to halt fighting and negotiate a peace-agreement

264 Ibid., pp. 6–30.

265 Freeman, *Necessary Evils*, pp. 56–7.

266 Seibert-Fohr, *Prosecuting Serious Human Rights Violations*, p. 216.

267 Freeman, *Necessary Evils*, pp. 61–2.

under the threat of prosecution.[268] Instead amnesties, granted in return for stopping an atrocious armed conflict, could make a decisive contribution to protect victims against repeated attacks and future violations of their rights.[269] Of course, refraining from criminal proceedings and enacting broad amnesties shall be used only as measures of last resort and must be justified through exceptional circumstances.[270]

The Justification of Amnesties in Exceptional Circumstances

In order to determine what constitutes exceptional circumstances, the "Draft Articles on Responsibility of States for Internationally Wrongful Acts"[271] provide valuable information.[272] In the context of amnesties Part One, Chapter V and in particular Articles 23, 24 and 25 of the Draft Articles are potentially relevant as they enumerate certain circumstances which preclude "the wrongfulness of an act of a State not in conformity with an international obligation of that State." That is, the violation of Afghanistan's international obligation to prosecute by the enactment of the Afghan Amnesty Law may be justified for the following extraordinary reasons: force majeure, distress or necessity.

By force majeure, Article 23 (1) stipulates *"the occurrence of an irresistible force or of an unforeseen event, beyond the control of the State, making it materially impossible in the circumstances to perform the obligation."* In the case at issue, this means that there must have been a situation in which it was completely impossible for the Afghan authorities to conduct criminal proceedings. In its commentary on Article 23 the International Law Commission emphasises that the possibly justified act of the State – i.e. the

268 M. P. Scharf, 'Justice versus Peace' in S. B. Sewall and C. Kaysen (eds.), *The United States and the International Criminal Court: National Security and International Law* (Lanham, Md, Oxford, England: Rowman & Littlefield Publishers; American Academy of Arts and Sciences, 2000), pp. 179–95, at p. 179.

269 Werle and Jessberger, *Principles of International Criminal Law*, p. 89; Seibert-Fohr, *Prosecuting Serious Human Rights Violations*, p. 227; Freeman, *Necessary Evils*, 109, 181; Slye, 'The Legitimacy of Amnesties Under International Law and General Principles of Anglo-American Law', 198.

270 Werle and Jessberger, *Principles of International Criminal Law*, p. 89; Freeman, *Necessary Evils*, pp. 61–2.

271 International Law Commission, *Draft Articles on Responsibility of States for Internationally Wrongful Acts, with commentaries – 2001*, UN Doc. A/56/10 (2001). http://legal.un.org/ilc/texts/instruments/english/commentaries/9_6_2001.pdf (05 July 2016).

272 The Draft Articles on Responsibility of States for Internationally Wrongful Acts are binding on Afghanistan since they are part of customary international law.

enactment of the Afghan Amnesty Law – must be due to "an irresistible force" or "an unforeseen event". Furthermore, the act in question shall not involve an element of free choice.[273] In other words, the Afghan Amnesty Law must have been adopted involuntarily. None of these conditions is met in the case of Afghanistan. Indeed, a violent conflict between the Afghan government and its international supporters on the one hand and the Taliban fighters on the other had been ongoing for some time. However, as was described in Chapter 2.2, the Afghan government not only drafted an Amnesty Law, but also an Action Plan for Peace, Reconciliation and Justice (APPRJ)[274], which contained, *inter alia*, the establishment of effective and reasonable accountability mechanisms in order to end impunity in Afghanistan and to ensure that there would be no amnesty for war crimes, crimes against humanity and other gross human rights violations. It would therefore appear to be the case that the Afghan authorities, with support from AIHRC and UNAMA, have not considered it impossible to conduct criminal proceedings in this situation. There had been no fundamental changes in the course of the conflict until the date of the entry into force of the Amnesty Law in January 2010, so that the occurrence of "an irresistible force" or "an unforeseen event" cannot be assumed. Moreover, the qualification of the Afghan Amnesty Law as a so-called self-amnesty should not be ignored (see *2.3 The Afghan Amnesty Law 2010*), meaning that former perpetrators of serious human rights violations and then members of parliament and government primarily wanted to protect themselves from criminal investigation and punishment. Thus, the Amnesty Law was voluntarily enacted and it was above all based on selfish motives.

Another possible justification for the Afghan Amnesty Law can be found in Article 24 of the Draft Articles, which postulates that *"The wrongfulness of an act of a State not in conformity with an international obligation of that State is precluded if the author of the act in question has no other reasonable way, in a situation of distress, of saving the author's life or the lives of other persons entrusted to the author's care."* Although this means that it is not absolutely impossible to act in conformity with an international obligation (as it is the case in situations of force majeure), it is nevertheless relatively impossible inasmuch as the author of the act had no other reasonable

273 International Law Commission, *Draft Articles on Responsibility of States for Internationally Wrongful Acts, with commentaries – 2001*, p. 76.

274 Government of the Islamic Republic of Afghanistan, *Action Plan on Peace, Reconciliation and Justice in Afghanistan*.

way of saving life.[275] Hence, the Afghan authorities must have considered the Amnesty Law as the only reasonable way, in a situation of distress, of saving the lives of certain persons. In principle, reference can be made to the findings concerning Article 23 of the Draft Articles. By enacting the Action Plan for Peace, Reconciliation and Justice (APPRJ) the Afghan authorities committed themselves, *inter alia*, to the establishment of accountability mechanisms in order to restore peace for all citizens. Thus, the Amnesty Law has not been considered as the only reasonable way of saving life by the Afghan government. On the contrary, former warlords feared their own prosecution and did not care at all about the lives of the Afghan people. Even if it is assumed that the official aims of the Amnesty Law, namely to strengthen peace and stability as well as ending the war and bloodshed, were trustworthy, Article 24 is nevertheless not relevant. In its commentary, the International Law Commission clarifies that Article 24 encompasses only those cases "where a State agent has acted to save his or her own life or where there exists a special relationship between the State organ or agent and the persons in danger".[276] However, such a special relationship does not exist between the Afghan government und the Afghan people.

More general cases of emergency fall into the category of "necessity" and are dealt with by Article 25 of the Draft Articles.[277] This Article determines that *"1. Necessity may not be invoked by a State as a ground for precluding the wrongfulness of an act not in conformity with an international obligation of that State unless the act: (a) is the only way for the State to safeguard an essential interest against a grave and imminent peril; and (b) does not seriously impair an essential interest of the State or States towards which the obligation exists, or of the international community as a whole."* From this it can be deduced that necessity may only be invoked in exceptional cases and under the narrowly defined conditions of Article 25 (1) (a) and (b). According to the International Law Commission, situations of necessity are marked by the choice "between compliance with international law and other legitimate interests of the State."[278] In the case of Afghanistan, where the act in question, i.e. the Amnesty Law, is not in compliance with the

275 Freeman, *Necessary Evils*, p. 67; International Law Commission, *Draft Articles on Responsibility of States for Internationally Wrongful Acts, with commentaries – 2001*, p. 78.

276 International Law Commission, *Draft Articles on Responsibility of States for Internationally Wrongful Acts, with commentaries – 2001*, p. 80.

277 Ibid., p. 80.

278 Ibid., p. 78.

international obligation to prosecute, a justification might be that it was the only way to safeguard a peaceful transition and end the bloody war. Whether or not an amnesty is the only way to achieve these purposes is a challenging question, since it is a political consideration and anyway an exact estimation cannot be made.[279] It is therefore sufficient that the Afghan government could reasonably expect that without an amnesty a peaceful transition will fail.[280] However, the prerogative of the Afghan government in determining its policy has its limits – namely the human rights of those who are disadvantaged by the Amnesty Law. This means that the interest relied on must be balanced against all other competing interests, whether these are individual or collective.[281]

The political strategy of the Afghan government and its international allies since 2001 has been characterised by the promotion of peace before justice, or in other words by countenancing impunity in the belief of reaching peace.[282] This policy was continued with the entry into force of the Amnesty Law in 2010 and the resulting peace agreement of September 2016. However, the development of, and the present situation in, Afghanistan clearly show that this approach has completely failed.[283]

---

279 A. Cassese, *The Oxford Companion to International Criminal Justice* (Oxford, New York: Oxford University Press, 2009), p. 159; Seibert-Fohr, *Prosecuting Serious Human Rights Violations*, p. 271; O'Shea, *Amnesty for Crime in International Law and Practice*, pp. 82–5.

280 International Law Commission, *Draft Articles on Responsibility of States for Internationally Wrongful Acts, with commentaries – 2001*, p. 83; G. Werle, 'Transitional Justice – Der juristische Rahmen' in H. E. Müller, G. M. Sander and H. Válková (eds.), *Festschrift für Ulrich Eisenberg zum 70. Geburtstag* (München: Beck, 2009), pp. 791–806, at pp. 803–4.

281 International Law Commission, *Draft Articles on Responsibility of States for Internationally Wrongful Acts, with commentaries – 2001*, p. 84.

282 Kouvo, *After Two Years in Legal Limbo*; Niland, 'Impunity and Insurgency: a Deadly Combination in Afghanistan', 936; D. Wisner, 'Is Time Ripe for Transitional Justice in Afghanistan?', *The Fletcher School Online Journal for Southwest Asia and Islamic Civilization* (2008), 1–12, at 1–2; A. N. Nadery, *Peace or Justice?: Transitional Justice in Afghanistan*. https://www.boell.de/sites/default/files/assets/boell.de/images/download_de/worldwide/Peace_or_Justice_Nadery_Oct2007.pdf (28 July 2016), pp. 2–3.

283 International Center for Transitional Justice (ICTJ), *Afghanistan Mapping Report Opportunity to Break Cycles of Abuse*. http://www.ictj.org/news/afghanistan-mapping-report-opportunity-break-cycles-abuse (28 July 2016); P. Gossman, 'Kabul's Stealth Attack on Human Rights', The New York Times, 26 December 2011; Human Rights Watch, *Seductions of "Sequencing": The Risks of Putting Justice Aside for Peace*. http://www.hrw.org/sites/default/files/related_material/Sequencing%20Paper%2012.7.10.pdf (28 July 2016), pp. 4–6; Niland, 'Impunity and

Hence, impunity or the violation of the duty to prosecute is in no way suitable for safeguarding peace and reconciliation in Afghanistan.[284] Apart from this reality, and the fact that the Afghan amnesty served primarily to protect former perpetrators from prosecution, such an extremely broad and also future-orientated Amnesty Law will never be the only way available to safeguard a peaceful transition.[285] Instead, an alternative procedure, for example granting conditional amnesties combined with a truth commission and the prosecution of a certain number of alleged perpetrators, would have been feasible as a less severe, but yet expedient means. Thus, a blanket Amnesty Law surpasses what is "strictly necessary"[286] and consequently cannot be justified by Article 25 of the Draft Articles.[287]

Conclusion

The result of this chapter and the answer to the initial question of whether the Afghan Amnesty Law violates other than explicit statutory provisions on amnesties can be summarised as follows: First of all, Afghanistan is obliged to investigate and prosecute international crimes according to the four Geneva Conventions and their Additional Protocols I and II, as well as the Convention against Torture, the Genocide Convention and the ICCPR. The blanket Afghan Amnesty Law is in violation of these obligations. However, since the duty to prosecute international crimes does not rise to the level of *jus cogens*, the Amnesty Law might be justified in light of further international obligations, in particular the effective protection of human rights and the prevention of their violation. Articles 23, 24 and 25 of the Draft Articles on Responsibility of States for Internationally Wrongful Acts enumerate certain exceptional circumstances which preclude "the wrongfulness of an act of a State not in conformity with an international

Insurgency: a Deadly Combination in Afghanistan', 936–40; Kouvo, *After Two Years in Legal Limbo*; A. N. Nadery, 'A Human Rights Awakening?' in A. J. Thier (ed.), *The Future of Aghanistan* (Washington D.C., 2009), pp. 55–62, at pp. 58–9.

284 Khan, 'Afghanistan: War Crimes, ICC and NGOs', 117.

285 Freeman, *Necessary Evils*, p. 68; P. Hazdra, 'Verurteilen – Vergessen – Versöhnen. Die wichtigsten Ansätze zur Konfliktaufarbeitung im Überblick', *Humanitäres Völkerrecht – Informationsschriften / Journal of International Law of Peace and Armed Conflict* (2006), 156–67, at 156–7; Danchin, 'Transitional Justice in Afghanistan', 45–6; D. F. Orentlicher, 'Settling Accounts: The Duty to Prosecute Human Rights Violations of a Prior Regime', *The Yale Law Journal* 100 (1991), 2537–615, at 2595.

286 International Law Commission, *Draft Articles on Responsibility of States for Internationally Wrongful Acts, with commentaries – 2001*, p. 83.

287 Freeman, *Necessary Evils*, p. 68.

obligation of that State." Yet the Afghan Amnesty Law cannot be justified on these grounds. Article 23 is not relevant as there was no case of *force majeure* "making it materially impossible to perform the obligation" to prosecute. Article 24 is also not applicable, because the Afghan Amnesty Law is not the only reasonable way of saving life in a situation of distress. Finally, the amnesty is not justified by necessity pursuant to Article 25 of the Draft Articles, since such an extremely broad and also future-orientated Amnesty Law will never be the only way available to achieve a peaceful transition in Afghanistan. It goes beyond what is absolutely necessary in order to "safeguard an essential interest against a grave and imminent peril".

3.1.3 The Afghan Amnesty Law and the Rome Statute of the International Criminal Court

As already indicated above, the most comprehensive legal framework with regard to the fight against impunity is the Rome Statute of the International Criminal Court. Since 2003, when Afghanistan became a Party to the Rome Statute, several duties, such as the duty to investigate and prosecute international crimes as well as the duty to implement the Rome Statute into Afghan law[288] and to cooperate fully with the Court[289], have been imposed upon it. Whether or not Afghanistan has fulfilled these duties and what significance is accorded to the Amnesty Law in this context, is discussed in the following.

The Afghan authorities initially proclaimed that they "feel it is in [their] interest to work with the [International Criminal] Court"[290] and some years later they emphasised "the importance of the [Court] in promoting international criminal justice, and addressing the most serious of crimes [...]."[291] In December 2004 a Roundtable on the Implementation of the

288 *See* Preamble of the Rome Statute of the International Criminal Court: „Affirming that the most serious crimes of concern to the international community as a whole must not go unpunished and that their effective prosecution must be ensured by taking measures at the national level and by enhancing international cooperation“ [...] „Recalling that it is the duty of every State to exercise its criminal jurisdiction over those responsible for international crimes“.

289 *See* Article 86 of the Rome Statute of the International Criminal Court.

290 *See* The Coalition for the International Criminal Court (CICC), *Afghanistan Signs Up for the International Criminal Court*, p. 1.

291 Permanent Mission of Afghanistan to the United Nations, *Statement by Dr. Zalmai Rassoul, Minister of Foreign Affairs of the Islamic Republic of Afghanistan at*

Statute of the ICC in Afghanistan's legal order as well as a National Seminar on the Strategies for Implementation of the ICC Statute in Afghanistan were held.[292] The objectives were, *inter alia*, to introduce the regulations of the Rome Statute into the Afghan legal order and to develop Afghanistan's judicial system in order to investigate and prosecute international crimes.[293] For a long time no significant progress was made in this regard. Apart from the above-mentioned announcements no practical steps were taken to criminalise the most atrocious offences or to draft and adopt a cooperation law.[294] More recently, in May 2017, the Afghan parliament however adopted a new Penal Code which now explicitly incorporates Rome Statute crimes.[295]

Notwithstanding this, the Afghan authorities completely ignored the principles contained in the Rome Statute of the ICC in enacting the Amnesty Law in 2010. Most notably Article 3 (2) of the Afghan Amnesty Law, which grants future amnesty to those "who are still in opposition [...] and cease enmity *after* the enforcement of this resolution" (emphasis added), is in contradiction with the duty to investigate and prosecute international crimes committed since the entry into force of the Rome Statute in 2003.[296] Afghanistan may grant amnesties at the domestic level but this does not mean that the ICC must take them into account. In other words, in the event of alleged international crimes the Court has potential jurisdiction, provided that Afghanistan has been "unwilling or unable genuinely to carry out the investigation or prosecution."[297] There-

---

the High-Level Meeting on The Rule of Law at the National and International Levels. http://afghanistan-un.org/2012/09/statement-of-h-e-dr-zalmai-rassoul-minister-of-foreign-affairs-of-the-islamic-republic-of-afghanistan-at-the-high-level-meeting-on-the-rule-of-law/ (31 July 2016).

292 The Coalition for the International Criminal Court (CICC), *Updates on Afghanistan (31 Dec 2005)*. http://www.iccnow.org/?mod=newsdetail&news=1 (31 July 2016).

293 Ibid.

294 H. Moen and A. Z. Mohammadi, *International Criminal Court (ICC) in Afghanistan: A Report on the Consultative Meeting on Obligations of Afghanistan under ICC*. http://www.operationspaix.net/DATA/DOCUMENT/5012~v~International_Criminal_Court__ICC__in_Afghanistan__A_Report_on_the_Consultative_Meeting_on_Obligations_of_Afghanistan_under_ICC.pdf (31 July 2016), p. 4; Khan, 'Afghanistan: War Crimes, ICC and NGOs', 103.

295 International Criminal Court (ICC) – The Office of the Prosecutor, *Situation in the Islamic Republic of Afghanistan*, No. ICC – 02/17. https://www.icc-cpi.int/CourtRecords/CR2017_06891.PDF (05 February 2018), para. 273.

296 Kouvo, *After Two Years in Legal Limbo*.

297 *See* Article 17 (1) (a) (b) Rome Statute of the International Criminal Court.

fore, the crucial questions arising in this connection are: how does the ICC deal with amnesties in general and what are the legal consequences for the Afghan Amnesty Law in particular? This matter is of great practical importance, all the more so because in 2007 the then prosecutor of the ICC, Luis Moreno-Ocampo, initiated preliminary investigations into alleged international crimes occurring in Afghanistan.[298]

As discussed in a previous chapter, no international treaty explicitly prohibits or discourages the granting of amnesty for international crimes (see *3.1.1 Does the Afghan Amnesty Law Violate Explicit Statutory Provisions on Amnesties?*). Neither the Rome Statute of the International Criminal Court nor its Rules of Procedure and Evidence are an exception to this state of affairs.[299] There is absolutely no reference to amnesties in these regulations.[300] Although the amnesty question had been on the agenda during the negotiations over the Rome Statute, the parties were unable to come to agreement on the issue.[301] A reason might be that the Court did not wish to be bound by a rule on amnesties, but rather wanted to have some discretion for the purpose of balancing the interests of a war-torn country and the demands of the international legal order.[302] Be that as it may, in the absence of an explicit provision on amnesties, the Rome Statute has to be interpreted "in accordance with the ordinary meaning to be given to the terms of the treaty in their context and in the light of its object and purpose."[303] According to Article 31 (2) of the Vienna Convention on the Law of Treaties, the context shall comprise, *inter alia*,

---

298 International Criminal Court (ICC), *Preliminary Examination: Afghanistan*. https://www.icc-cpi.int/afghanistan (31 July 2016).

299 *See* L. N. Sadat, 'Individuel Progress in International Law: Considering Amnesty' in R. A. Miller and R. M. Bratspies (eds.), *Progress in International Law* (Leiden, Boston: Martinus Nijhoff Publishers, 2008), pp. 335–56, at p. 355.

300 Freeman, *Necessary Evils*, p. 75.

301 Ibid., pp. 32–3; Mallinder, *Amnesty, Human Rights and Political Transitions:*, pp. 279–80; A. Seibert-Fohr, 'Human Rights as Guiding Principles in the Context of Post Conflict Justice', *Michigan State Journal of International Law* 13 (2005), 179–96, at 181; A. Bos, 'From the International Law Commission to the Rome Conference (1994–1998)' in A. Cassese, P. Gaeta and J. R. W. D. Jones (eds.), *The Rome Statute of the International Criminal Court: A Commentary*, 3 vols. (Oxford, New York: Oxford University Press, 2002), vol. 1, pp. 35–66, at p. 57.

302 M. P. Scharf, 'The Amnesty Exception to the Jurisdiction of the International Criminal Court', *Cornell International Law Journal* 32 (1999), 507–27, at 522; C. Stahn, 'Complementarity, Amnesties and Alternative Forms of Justice: Some Interpretative Guidelines for the International Criminal Court', *Journal of International Criminal Justice* 3 (2005), 695–720, at 718.

303 *See* Art. 31 (1) Vienna Convention on the Law of Treaties.

the text including its preamble. The preamble of the Rome Statute affirms "that the most serious crimes of concern to the international community as a whole must not go unpunished and that their effective prosecution must be ensured [...]." This seems to indicate that granting amnesties for such crimes would be inconsistent with the object and purpose of the Rome Statute.[304] However, having regard to the previous chapter, there may be certain exceptional situations where amnesties are necessary to prevent severe human rights violations and where criminal proceedings would have the effect of prolonging an ongoing conflict and thus prolonging such atrocities. In such periods of transition the ICC is caught between a rock and a hard place. Hence, several provisions of the Rome Statute have taken these considerations into account.[305] For example, Article 16 states that the UN Security Council is allowed to pass a resolution under Chapter VII (Action with Respect to Threats to the Peace, Breaches of the Peace, and Acts of Aggression) of the UN Charter in order to suspend an investigation or prosecution by the ICC for an extendable period of 12 months or more. Good faith amnesties could also be recognised in the course of the principle of complementarity according to Article 17 of the Rome Statute[306] or due to the fact "that an investigation would not serve the interests of justice" (Article 53 of the Rome Statute).

In the case of Afghanistan, the question arises of whether the Amnesty Law should be acknowledged by the International Criminal Court under application of the relevant Articles of the Rome Statute. The legal analysis starts with Article 53 in conjunction with Article 17 of the Rome Statute because these provisions are directly applicable. As already mentioned, the then prosecutor Moreno-Ocampo had been undertaking preliminary investigations since 2007 into alleged international crimes committed by anti-government groups, i.e. the Taliban and other armed groups, as well as by Afghan National Security Forces, US armed forces and Central Intelligence Agency (CIA) in Afghanistan.[307] His successor, Fatou Bensouda,

---

304 Ntoubandi, *Amnesty for Crimes against Humanity under International Law*, p. 204.

305 Ibid., p. 205.

306 A. Seibert-Fohr, 'The Relevance of the Rome Statute of the International Criminal Court for Amnesties and Truth Commissions', *Max Planck Yearbook of United Nations Law* 7 (2003), 553–90, at 590.

307 E. C. Barbour and M. C. Weed, *The International Criminal Court (ICC): Jurisdiction, Extradition, and U.S. Policy*. http://www.amicc.org/docs/R41116_20100316.pdf (01 August 2016), p. 14; International Criminal Court (ICC) – The Office of the Prosecutor, *Situation in Afghanistan: Summary of the Prosecutor's Request for Authorisation of an Investigation Pursuant to Article 15*. https://www.icc-cpi.in

has recently completed the preliminary investigations and requested authorisation from the Court's Judges to open formal investigations.[308] It was the longest-lasting ICC enquiry in this early phase of investigations.[309] According to Article 53 (1) (a) – (c) the preliminary examination consists of considerations by the prosecutor with respect to jurisdiction, admissibility (complementary and gravity) and the interests of justice.[310]

The first formal condition — the jurisdiction of the ICC — was regarded as satisfied since the information gathered have demonstrated that war crimes and crimes against humanity were and continue to be committed in the context of and associated with the armed conflict in Afghanistan.[311] With regard to the admissibility of potential cases, the Office of the Prosecutor analyses whether the requirements for complementarity of Article 17 of the Rome Statute are met, and also the gravity of the cases in question.[312] The principle of complementary entails the assessment of national proceedings and other efforts to ensure justice and accountability.[313] If the prosecutor concludes that the Afghan authorities are "unwilling or unable genuinely to carry out the investigation or prosecution"[314] the final phase of the preliminary examination with a focus on the "interest of

---

t/itemsDocuments/Afghanistan/171120-afgh-art_15-app-summ_ENG.pdf (05 February 2018), para. 14.

308 International Criminal Court (ICC) – The Office of the Prosecutor, *Situation in Afghanistan*.

309 Human Rights Watch, *Afghanistan: ICC Prosecutor Finds Grave Crimes*. http://www.hrw.org/news/2013/12/01/afghanistan-icc-prosecutor-finds-grave-crimes (02 August 2016).

310 International Criminal Court (ICC) – The Office of the Prosecutor, *Report on Preliminary Examination Activities 2016*. https://www.icc-cpi.int/iccdocs/otp/161114-otp-rep-PE_ENG.pdf (16 November 2016), p. 2.

311 *Human Rights Watch, Afghanistan: ICC Prosecutor Finds Grave Crimes; International Criminal Court (ICC) – The Office of the Prosecutor, Report on Preliminary Examination Activities 2014.* https://www.icc-cpi.int/en_menus/icc/structure%20of%20the%20court/office%20of%20the%20prosecutor/comm%20and%20ref/reports/Pages/default.aspx *(02 August 2016), p. 19; International Criminal Court (ICC) – The Office of the Prosecutor, Situation in Afghanistan, para. 7–27.*

312 *See* Article 53 (1) (b) Rome Statute of the International Criminal Court.

313 M. Kersten, *The ICC in Afghanistan: Peace, Justice and Accountability*. http://justiceinconflict.org/2014/01/21/the-icc-in-afghanistan-peace-justice-and-accountability/ (02 August 2016); International Criminal Court (ICC) – The Office of the Prosecutor, *Report on Preliminary Examination Activities 2015*. https://www.icc-cpi.int/en_menus/icc/structure%20of%20the%20court/office%20of%20the%20prosecutor/comm%20and%20ref/reports/Pages/default.aspx (02 August 2016), p. 31.

314 *See* Article 17 (1) (a) (b) Rome Statute of the International Criminal Court.

justice" commences.[315] In the Prosecution's Request seeking authorisation of an investigation from November 2017 it is noticed that no national investigations or prosecutions have been conducted or are ongoing against those who appear most responsible for the crimes allegedly committed by members of the Taliban and affiliated armed groups, members of the Afghan National Security Forces, and members of the US armed forces and the CIA.[316] In the report on Preliminary Examination Activities from November 2016, the Office of the Prosecutor stated that "apart from [...] two individuals[317], no leaders of the principal anti-government armed groups, or other members situated at the highest echelons of responsibility, such as those who ordered, financed or otherwise organized the alleged crimes, have been reportedly investigated or prosecuted."[318] In its previous report on Preliminary Examination Activities from November 2015 the Office of the Prosecutor noted that "those who appear to bear the greatest responsibility for the most serious crimes" have not been detained or prosecuted and that the legal possibility of *in absentia* proceedings has not been exerted.[319] Furthermore, the prosecutor pointed out that the Afghan parliament passed a general amnesty law which grants impunity to all warring factions, "without any temporal limitation to the law's application or any exception for international crimes".[320]

In a policy paper from 2016 the Office of the Prosecutor emphasises the importance of different approaches to combat impunity. This means that not only prosecutions provide a response to international crimes, but also truth seeking, reparations, institutional reform and traditional

---

315 Kersten, *The ICC in Afghanistan*.

316 International Criminal Court (ICC) – The Office of the Prosecutor, *Situation in Afghanistan*, para. 29, 35, 39, 41.

317 "Reportedly two senior members of the Haqqani Network were prosecuted and convicted by a national primary court in August 2016 for an unknown alleged conduct. The Government of Afghanistan is yet to provide information on these proceedings in order for the Prosecution to fully assess the admissibility of these two cases.", *see* International Criminal Court (ICC) – The Office of the Prosecutor, *Report on Preliminary Examination Activities 2016*, p. 48.

318 Ibid., p. 48.

319 International Criminal Court (ICC) – The Office of the Prosecutor, *Report on Preliminary Examination Activities 2015*, pp. 28–9.

320 International Criminal Court (ICC) – The Office of the Prosecutor, *Situation in the Islamic Republic of Afghanistan*, para. 272; International Criminal Court (ICC) – The Office of the Prosecutor, *Report on Preliminary Examination Activities 2016*, p. 48; International Criminal Court (ICC) – The Office of the Prosecutor, *Report on Preliminary Examination Activities 2015*, p. 29.

justice mechanisms can be decisive factors regarding the principle of complementarity.[321] Ultimately, a comprehensive strategy in which all efforts are as complementary to each other as possible is necessary.[322] In practice this means, for example, that the government of a society in transition may prosecute only those perpetrators most responsible for serious human rights violations. Additionally, a truth commission and amnesties for lower-level criminals could be employed in order to satisfy the responsibilities under international law, and to comply with the principle of complementarity.[323] However, in the case of Afghanistan such efforts have not been made. The blanket Afghan Amnesty Law excludes the possibility of any investigation or prosecution, and apart from this the Action Plan for Peace, Reconciliation and Justice has not been realised.[324] Moreover, the release of an 800-page report[325] which contains descriptions of serious violations of international law from 1978 to 2001 in Afghanistan has been prevented by the Afghan Government and the United States.[326] The most recent negative development is the signing of the peace deal between the Government of Afghanistan and Hezb-e Islami's leader Hekmatyar in September 2016. This agreement includes *inter alia* a blanket amnesty for serious international crimes.[327] For all these reasons, Afghanistan could not pass

321 International Criminal Court (ICC) – The Office of the Prosecutor, *Policy Paper on the Interests of Justice*. http://www.icc-cpi.int/nr/rdonlyres/772c95c9-f54d-4321-bf09-73422bb23528/143640/iccotpinterestsofjustice.pdf (03 August 2016), pp. 7–8.

322 Ibid., p. 8.

323 D. Robinson, 'Serving the Interests of Justice: Amnesties, Truth Commissions and the International Criminal Court', *European Journal of International Law* 14 (2003), 481–505, at 500–1; Mallinder, *Amnesty, Human Rights and Political Transitions:*, p. 285; Seibert-Fohr, 'The Relevance of the Rome Statute of the International Criminal Court for Amnesties and Truth Commissions', 588.

324 Human Rights Watch, *Afghanistan: ICC Prosecutor Finds Grave Crimes*.

325 The report is titled "Conflict Mapping in Afghanistan Since 1978", and has been prepared by the "Afghan Independent Human Rights Commission".

326 Human Rights Watch, *Afghanistan: ICC Prosecutor Finds Grave Crimes*; Human Rights Watch, *World Report 2015: Afghanistan*; R. Nordland, 'Top Afghans Tied to '90s Carnage, Researchers Say', The New York Times, 22 July 2012; H. Kazim, 'Kriegsverbrecher-Studie: Massaker-Berichte belasten afghanische Politiker', SPIEGEL ONLINE, 23 July 2012.

327 Osman, *Peace With Hekmatyar*; International Criminal Court (ICC) – The Office of the Prosecutor, *Situation in the Islamic Republic of Afghanistan*, para. 272.

the complementarity test[328] and the prosecutor decided that the conditions for admissibility are satisfied.[329]

Consequently, the final phase of the preliminary examination with a focus on the question of whether there are "substantial reasons to believe that an investigation would not serve the interests of justice"[330] was initiated.[331] Where an investigation would not serve the interests of justice the Office of the Prosecutor will not continue with its endeavours in this regard.[332] In the policy paper mentioned above the concept of the interests of justice is clarified by the Office of the Prosecutor.[333] The prosecutor follows the approach that "only in exceptional circumstances [...] an investigation or a prosecution may not serve the interests of justice"[334], i.e. "there is a presumption in favour of investigation or prosecution"[335].[336] Furthermore, the paper makes clear "that there is a difference between the concepts of the interests of justice and the interests of peace and that the latter falls within the mandate of institutions other than the Office of the Prosecutor."[337] This means that the interests of justice, although

328 Robinson, 'Serving the Interests of Justice', 501; C. Kreß and L. Grover, 'International Criminal Law Restraints in Peace Talks to End Armed Conflicts of a Non-International Character' in M. Bergsmo and P. Kalmanovitz (eds.), *Law in Peace Negotiations*, 2nd edn. (Oslo: Torkel Opsahl Academic EPublisher, 2010), pp. 41–84, at p. 70; Mallinder, *Amnesty, Human Rights and Political Transitions:*, p. 283; Seibert-Fohr, 'The Relevance of the Rome Statute of the International Criminal Court for Amnesties and Truth Commissions', 588; Joint report by the Advisory Council on International Affairs (AIV) and the Advisory Committee on Issues of Public International Law (CAVV), *Transitional Justice*, pp. 20–1.

329 International Criminal Court (ICC) – The Office of the Prosecutor, *Situation in the Islamic Republic of Afghanistan*, paras. 261–363.

330 *See* Article 53 (1) (c) Rome Statute of the International Criminal Court.

331 International Criminal Court (ICC) – The Office of the Prosecutor, *Situation in the Islamic Republic of Afghanistan*, paras. 364–372.

332 International Criminal Court (ICC) – The Office of the Prosecutor, *Policy Paper on the Interests of Justice*, p. 1.

333 Ibid., p. 1.

334 Ibid., p. 3.

335 Ibid., p. 1.

336 International Criminal Court (ICC) – The Office of the Prosecutor, *International Seminar on the Imperatives of the Observance of Human Rights and International Humanitarian Law Norms in International Security Operations: Speech of Mrs Fatou Bensouda – Prosecutor of the International Criminal Court.* https://www.icc-cpi.int/iccdocs/otp/SpeechProsecutor-AbujaNigeriaFra.pdf (07 September 2016), p. 6.

337 International Criminal Court (ICC) – The Office of the Prosecutor, *Policy Paper on the Interests of Justice*, p. 1; International Criminal Court (ICC) – The Office of the Prosecutor, *International Seminar on the Imperatives of the Observance of*

embracing not only criminal justice in the strict sense but also issues of crime prevention and national security, do not relate to "the broader matter of international peace and security".[338] What does such an interpretation mean for amnesty laws in general and the Afghan Amnesty Law in particular? Can an amnesty which leads to national reconciliation and security obstruct investigations by the ICC which by themselves exacerbate the conflict even further and thus are not in the interests of justice since they are not in the interests of national reconciliation and security? The Office of the Prosecutor emphasises that "the interests of victims will generally weigh in favour of prosecution".[339] However, "the Office will listen to the views of all parties concerned."[340] That is, "the Office will give due consideration to the different views of victims, their communities and the broader societies in which it may be required to act."[341] This does not give a concrete indication as to whether the prosecutor would approve amnesty under certain conditions and stop an investigation. Two specific examples illustrate the unclear situation with regard to national peace negotiations including amnesties and their consideration by the ICC. In relation to the Ugandan peace process, which implies an amnesty law and ongoing investigations by the ICC, the former prosecutor, Moreno-Ocampo, had stated "if a solution to end the violence was found, and continuing the investigation did not serve the interests of justice, then the ICC would stop the probe."[342] In the investigations by the International Criminal Court in Libya a different approach can be seen. In an interview published in 2012 Moreno-Ocampo said that the Rome Statute of the ICC does not take into account possible peace negotiations.[343] Ultimately, the Office of the Prosecutor leaves open whether national transitional justice mechanisms including amnesties could affect the choice between investigating or not.[344] However, that the prosecutor or the Court would accept a blanket

---

Human Rights and International Humanitarian Law Norms in International Security Operations, p. 6.

338 International Criminal Court (ICC) – The Office of the Prosecutor, *Policy Paper on the Interests of Justice*, pp. 8–9.

339 Ibid., p. 5.

340 Ibid., p. 5.

341 Ibid., p. 5.

342 *See* IRIN – Humanitarian News and Analysis, *ICC Could Suspend Northern Investigations – Spokesman*. http://www.irinnews.org/report/53945/uganda-icc-could-suspend-northern-investigations-spokesman (15 September 2016).

343 L. Moreno-Ocampo, *"Das Recht darf nicht wegverhandelt werden"* (2012), at p. 7.

344 Mallinder, *Amnesty, Human Rights and Political Transitions:*, p. 290.

amnesty for international crimes is out of the question, since such an amnesty would be absolutely contrary to the object and purpose of the Rome Statute.[345] Hence, the unconditional and comprehensive Afghan Amnesty Law applying to those most responsible for serious human rights violations was disregarded by the Office of the Prosecutor.[346] That is also because the Afghan Amnesty Law has not at all contributed to crime prevention or national security — if this would have been the case the prosecutor might conclude that an investigation would not serve the interests of justice. In other words, if investigations by the ICC would have the effect of prolonging the conflict and thus prolonging severe human rights violations, as alleged perpetrators would not be willing to halt fighting under the threat of prosecution,[347] then they would be detrimental to crime prevention and national reconciliation, and consequently not in the interests of justice.[348] Nevertheless, even in this scenario the amnesty must be restricted to lower-level criminals and accompanied by other transitional justice mechanisms, such as a truth commission. Perpetrators most responsible for international crimes must, in principle, always be prosecuted. Only in a few exceptional cases and under very precise circumstances, may the prosecutor of the ICC acknowledge good faith alternatives to prosecution, provided that these alternative approaches focus on accountability.[349] Since the Afghan Amnesty Law does not make any provision in this regard, it did not receive consideration from the ICC. The current Afghan Amnesty Law is in any case not an appropriate way of stopping the investigations by the Office of the Prosecutor.

To sum up, the legal analysis of Article 53 in conjunction with Article 17 of the Rome Statute revealed that the preliminary examination consisting of considerations by the prosecutor with respect to jurisdiction, admissibility (complementary and gravity) and the interests of justice led to the decision to request the Pre-Trial Chamber to authorise the commencement of a formal investigation.[350]

345 Robinson, 'Serving the Interests of Justice', 484.

346 International Criminal Court (ICC) – The Office of the Prosecutor, *Situation in the Islamic Republic of Afghanistan*, paras. 364–372.

347 Scharf, 'Justice versus Peace', 179.

348 Kreß and Grover, 'International Criminal Law Restraints in Peace Talks to End Armed Conflicts of a Non-International Character', 76–7.

349 Robinson, 'Serving the Interests of Justice', 484.

350 International Criminal Court (ICC) – The Office of the Prosecutor, *Situation in the Islamic Republic of Afghanistan*.

A further possibility of suspending an investigation or prosecution by the ICC is provided by the already mentioned Article 16 of the Rome Statute. The Article states that *"No investigation or prosecution may be commenced or proceeded with under this Statute for a period of 12 months after the Security Council, in a resolution adopted under Chapter VII of the Charter of the United Nations, has requested the Court to that effect; that request may be renewed by the Council under the same conditions."* Given that Chapter VII of the Charter of the United Nations relates to actions in order to maintain or restore international peace and security, Article 16 is not really relevant in the case of national amnesty laws since these laws frequently stem from civil wars which usually have no consequences for international peace and security.[351] This is also true in the case of Afghanistan inasmuch as international peace and security are not in danger. In addition, investigations and prosecutions by the ICC could, at most, have impact on the national peace and security in Afghanistan. Furthermore, Article 16 is intended to support the UN Security Council in its efforts to broker peace by delaying — but not ruling out — ICC investigations and prosecutions which may have destabilizing effects.[352] Amnesties, however, are of a permanent nature and thus, Article 16 would not be suitable to give them full efficacy.[353]

As has been shown in this chapter, it is highly unlikely that the International Criminal Court will consider and approve the broad and unconditional Afghan Amnesty Law.

3.1.4 Conclusion

The initial question whether or not the Afghan Amnesty Law is consistent with international treaty law has been discussed in detail in the previous chapters. In summary it can be said that no international treaty explicitly

351 J. Gavron, 'Amnesties in the Light of Developments in International Law and the Establishment of the International Criminal Court', *The International and Comparative Law Quarterly* 51 (2002), 91–117, at 109.

352 Kreß and Grover, 'International Criminal Law Restraints in Peace Talks to End Armed Conflicts of a Non-International Character', 79–80; Gavron, 'Amnesties in the Light of Developments in International Law and the Establishment of the International Criminal Court', 109.

353 Kreß and Grover, 'International Criminal Law Restraints in Peace Talks to End Armed Conflicts of a Non-International Character', 79–80; Gavron, 'Amnesties in the Light of Developments in International Law and the Establishment of the International Criminal Court', 109.

prohibits or discourages the granting of amnesty for international crimes. As a consequence the Afghan Amnesty Law cannot violate an international prohibition of certain amnesties, as no such prohibition exists so far. But even though international treaty law does not contain an explicit prohibition on amnesties, it does contain an explicit encouragement to enact them, namely Article 6 (5) of Additional Protocol II to the Geneva Conventions, relating to the protection of victims of non-international armed conflicts. Even if it is not clear from the wording of Article 6 (5) that amnesties for international crimes are exempted, the interpretation and application of the provision indicate it.[354] This means that an unconditional amnesty for serious violations of human rights is certainly not permitted. Consequently, the blanket Afghan Amnesty Law, which grants impunity to all kinds of perpetrators and crimes, goes beyond the scope of Article 6 (5) and thus is not legitimised by this regulation.

Since explicit provisions on amnesties are rare, the assessment of the legality of amnesty laws frequently focuses on obligations under international treaties to prosecute perpetrators of serious international crimes.[355] These obligations could preclude the issuing of amnesties for the crimes in question. Afghanistan is obliged to investigate and prosecute international crimes according to the four Geneva Conventions and their Additional Protocols I and II, as well as the Convention against Torture, the Genocide Convention and the ICCPR. The blanket Afghan Amnesty Law is in violation of these obligations. However, since the duty to prosecute international crimes does not rise to the level of *jus cogens*, the Amnesty Law might be justified in light of further international obligations, in particular the effective protection of human rights and the prevention of their violation. Articles 23, 24 and 25 of the Draft Articles on Responsibility of States for Internationally Wrongful Acts enumerate certain exceptional circumstances which preclude "the wrongfulness of an act of a State not in conformity with an international obligation of that State." Yet the Afghan Amnesty Law cannot be justified on these grounds. Article 23 is not relevant as there was no case of *force majeure* "making it materially

354 Henckaerts and Doswald-Beck (eds.), *Customary International Humanitarian Law*, p. 4043; Slye, 'The Legitimacy of Amnesties Under International Law and General Principles of Anglo-American Law', 178; UN Office of the High Commissioner for Human Rights, *Rule-of-Law Tools for Post-Conflict States*, p. 16; United Nations Commission on Human Rights, *Report of the Special Rapporteur on the Independence of Judges and Lawyers, Leandro Despouy*, p. 16; Henckaerts and Doswald-Beck (eds.), *Customary International Humanitarian Law*, p. 4043.

355 Mallinder, 'Amnesties', 420.

impossible to perform the obligation" to prosecute. Article 24 is also not applicable, because the Afghan Amnesty Law is not the only reasonable way of saving life in a situation of distress. Finally, the amnesty is not justified by necessity pursuant to Article 25 of the Draft Articles, since impunity was and is the wrong way to achieve a peaceful transition in Afghanistan. Moreover, such an excessive amnesty goes beyond what is absolutely necessary in order to "safeguard an essential interest against a grave and imminent peril". As a result, even though the Afghan Amnesty Law does not and cannot violate explicit statutory provisions on amnesties, it is nevertheless an unjustified violation of the duty to prosecute perpetrators of serious international crimes.

Since Afghanistan is a State Party to the Rome Statute of the International Criminal Court, the duty to investigate and prosecute international crimes as well as the duty to implement the Rome Statute into Afghan law[356] and the duty to cooperate fully with the Court[357] do arise. For a long time no significant progress was made in this regard.[358] More recently, in May 2017, the Afghan parliament however adopted a new Penal Code which now explicitly incorporates Rome Statute crimes.[359] Notwithstanding this, the Afghan authorities completely ignored the principles contained in the Rome Statute of the ICC in enacting the Amnesty Law in 2010. Yet neither the Rome Statute nor its Rules of Procedure and Evidence explicitly prohibit or discourage the granting of amnesty for international crimes. One reason may be that the Court wants to have some discretion for the purpose of balancing the interests of a war-torn country and the demands of the international legal order.[360] Hence the Rome Statute contains some provisions which can be interpreted as allowing the Court to acknowledge national amnesties under certain circumstances and

356 *See* Preamble of the Rome Statute of the International Criminal Court: "Affirming that the most serious crimes of concern to the international community as a whole must not go unpunished and that their effective prosecution must be ensured by taking measures at the national level and by enhancing international cooperation" [...] "Recalling that it is the duty of every State to exercise its criminal jurisdiction over those responsible for international crimes".

357 *See* Article 86 of the Rome Statute of the International Criminal Court.

358 Moen and Mohammadi, *International Criminal Court (ICC) in Afghanistan*, p. 4; Khan, 'Afghanistan: War Crimes, ICC and NGOs', 103.

359 International Criminal Court (ICC) – The Office of the Prosecutor, *Situation in the Islamic Republic of Afghanistan*, para. 273.

360 Stahn, 'Complementarity, Amnesties and Alternative Forms of Justice', 718; Scharf, 'The Amnesty Exception to the Jurisdiction of the International Criminal Court', 522.

in consequence to stop ongoing investigations. In this light, the Afghan Amnesty Law could play a role in the framework of preliminary examinations into alleged international crimes committed in Afghanistan.[361]

The legal analysis of Article 53 in conjunction with Article 17 of the Rome Statute however revealed that the preliminary investigation consisting of considerations by the prosecutor with respect to jurisdiction, admissibility (complementary and gravity) and the interests of justice led to the decision that the unconditional and comprehensive Afghan Amnesty Law does not justify a closure of the proceeding. A further possibility for suspending an investigation or prosecution by the ICC is included in Article 16 of the Rome Statute. This Article permits the delay — but not the closure — for an extendable period of 12 months provided that it is necessary to maintain or restore international peace and security. Given that the Afghan Amnesty Law is of a permanent nature, Article 16 would not be suitable to give it full efficacy.[362] Furthermore, international peace and security are not in danger, since investigations and prosecutions by the ICC could, at most, have impact on the national peace and security in Afghanistan.

As a conclusion it may be stated that although no international treaty explicitly prohibits or discourages the granting of amnesty for international crimes, the Afghan Amnesty Law is nevertheless inconsistent with international treaty law requiring the investigation and prosecution of serious international crimes. To fully examine whether or not the Afghan Amnesty Law is legitimate under international law, further analysis of international custom, the general principles of law as well as judicial decisions and the teachings of the most highly qualified publicists is needed.[363] The next

---

361 Barbour and Weed, *The International Criminal Court (ICC)*, p. 14.

362 Kreß and Grover, 'International Criminal Law Restraints in Peace Talks to End Armed Conflicts of a Non-International Character', 79–80; Gavron, 'Amnesties in the Light of Developments in International Law and the Establishment of the International Criminal Court', 109.

363 *See* Statute of the International Court of Justice, Article 38:
"(1) The Court, whose function is to decide in accordance with international law such disputes as are submitted to it, shall apply:
a. international conventions, whether general or particular, establishing rules expressly recognized by the contesting states;
b. international custom, as evidence of a general practice accepted as law;
c. the general principles of law recognized by civilized nations;
d. subject to the provisions of Article 59, judicial decisions and the teachings of the most highly qualified publicists of the various nations, as subsidiary means for the determination of rules of law.",

chapter it surveys customary international law with regard to the prohibition of amnesties in certain cases. The outcome will indicate whether or not the Afghan Amnesty Law is in accordance with the practice of States and other subjects of international law.

3.2 Does Customary International Law Preclude the Afghan Amnesty Law?

The unwritten rules of customary international law are an important source of international law since, as has been shown above, without central legislation international treaty law or written international rules are often inadequate and fragmentary, respectively.[364] The Statute of the International Court of Justice defines customary international law in Article 38 (1) (b) as *"evidence of a general practice accepted as law"*.[365] The precise interpretation of these two elements as well as their respective weight in the determination of customary international law is highly disputed.[366] The traditional understanding emphasises the significance of State practice as evidence of a general practice, whereas modern concepts highlight *opinio juris*, i.e. the acceptance as law, as crucial for the formation of customary international law.[367] Ultimately the debate can be neglected, since most

---

United Nations, *Statute of the International Court of Justice*, 18 April 1946, http://www.refworld.org/docid/3deb4b9c0.html (08 February 2016).

364 Werle, *Völkerstrafrecht*, p. 70; N. Petersen, 'Customary Law Without Custom? Rules, Principles, and the Role of State Practice in International Norm Creation', *American University International Law Review* 23 (2007), 275–310, at 276.

365 *See* Statute of the International Court of Justice, United Nations, *Statute of the International Court of Justice*, 18 April 1946, http://www.refworld.org/docid/3deb4b9c0.html (08 February 2016).

366 N. Petersen, *The Role of Consent and Uncertainty in the Formation of Customary International Law*. http://www.coll.mpg.de/pdf_dat/2011_04online.pdf (03 November 2016), p. 1; B. Schlütter, *Developments in Customary International Law: Theory and the Practice of the International Court of Justice and the International Ad Hoc Criminal Tribunals for Rwanda and Yugoslavia*, Developments in international law (Leiden, Boston: Martinus Nijhoff Publishers, 2010), vol. 62, p. 9; R. B. Baker, 'Customary International Law in the 21st Century: Old Challenges and New Debates', *European Journal of International Law* 21 (2010), 173–204, at 173–174, 178; Petersen, 'Customary Law Without Custom? Rules, Principles, and the Role of State Practice in International Norm Creation', 276.

367 Petersen, *The Role of Consent and Uncertainty in the Formation of Customary International Law*, p. 1; G. J. Postema, 'Custom in International Law: A Normative Practice Account' in A. Perreau-Saussine and J. B. Murphy (eds.), *The Nature of Customary Law* (Cambridge: Cambridge University Press, 2009), pp. 279–306,

international scholars assume that both elements are of equal value for the development of customary international law.[368] Thus, a possible working definition of customary international law reads: "*A rule of customary international law is one which emerges from, and is sustained by, the constant and uniform practice of States and other subjects of international law, in their international relations, in circumstances which give rise to a legitimate expectation of similar conduct in the future.*"[369] In other words, "*a customary rule requires the presence of [...] an objective element consisting of a relatively uniform and constant State practice; and a psychological element consisting of the subjective conviction of a State that it is legally bound to behave in a particular way in respect of a particular type of situation.*"[370] These definitions can be traced back to the criteria listed by the International Law Commissions Special Rapporteur M.O. Hudson in 1950[371] as well as the judgements of the International Court of Justice in the North Sea Continental Shelf cases in 1969[372] and the Nicaragua Case in 1986[373]. But what exactly constitutes State practice and *opinio juris*?

Examples of State practice comprise any official act, articulation or other behaviour of a State provided that the State intended thereby to express its acceptance of a rule as customary international law.[374] In this respect, acts of the legislature, the executive as well as the judiciary come into question.[375] Hence, the relevant behaviour might be for example nation-

at pp. 279–81; A. Eichhofer, 'Die Rechtsquellen des Völkerstrafrechts' in H.-H. Kühne, R. Esser and M. Gerding (eds.), *Völkerstrafrecht*, 1st edn. (Osnabrück: Julius Jonscher Verlag, 2007), pp. 1–22, at p. 7; K. Cockburn, *How to Prove a Role of Customary International Criminal Law: Re-imaging a Definition of CIL*. http://www.publiclaw.uct.ac.za/usr/public_law/LLMPapers/cockburn.pdf (03 November 2016), pp. 2–3.

368 Cockburn, *How to Prove a Role of Customary International Criminal Law*, pp. 2–3.

369 M. H. Mendelson, *The Formation of Customary International Law*, Recueil des cours (Leiden: Martinus Nijhoff Publishers, 1998), vol. 272, p. 188.

370 A. Kaczorowska, *Public International Law*, 4th edn. (Abingdon, Oxon [UK], New York: Routledge, 2010), p. 27.

371 M. O. Hudson, 'Working Paper', A/CN.4/16 in United Nations (ed.), *Yearbook of the International Law Commission 1950 Volume II* (1957), pp. 24–33, at p. 26.

372 *North Sea Continental Shelf Cases* ICJ Reports 1969 (International Court of Justice, 20 February 1969).

373 *Case Concerning Military and Paramilitary Activities In and Against Nicaragua* ICJ Reports 1986 (International Court of Justice, 27 June 1986).

374 M. E. Villiger, *Customary International Law and Treaties: A Manual on the Theory and Practice of the Interrelation of Sources*, Developments in international law, 2nd edn. (The Hague [u.a.]: Kluwer Law International, 1997), vol. 28, pp. 16–7.

375 Werle, *Völkerstrafrecht*, pp. 70–3.

al legislation, national court decisions, official governmental statements at international conferences and in diplomatic correspondence, general declarations of foreign or legal policy and opinions of national legal advisors.[376] For the purpose of the present analysis, namely the exploration of customary international law with regard to amnesties, the verbal or written statements of State representatives play a crucial part. This is because it frequently happens that State officials, although theoretically rejecting amnesties for serious international crimes, behave differently in specific situations.[377] The practice of States regarding a certain rule must be "general", i.e. consistent, widespread and also permanent, whereby universal practice is not required.[378] However, a customary rule cannot emerge if States, even though identifying a common issue, do not act in concert to cope with that issue. The consequence is that State practice is too disparate and cannot lead to a general rule.[379] Also the practice of international organisations, most notably of the United Nations, can be pertinent for the development of customary international law.[380] This is because international law usually arises from inter-state exchanges, which often take place under the umbrella of an international organisation.[381] Particularly in the areas of international criminal law as well as human rights protection and human rights enforcement, the decisions and resolutions of international organisations may serve as an important indicator of State practice, and thus may contribute to the creation of customary international law.[382] Non-governmental organisations on the other hand may at most influence State representatives by, for example, publishing reports, surveys or communiqués and in doing so, they may indirectly

---

376 M. B. Hoffman and R. C. Berring, *International Legal Research in a Nutshell*, West nutshell series (St. Paul, MN: Thomson/West, 2008), pp. 80–1; Villiger, *Customary International Law and Treaties*, vol. 28, pp. 16–7; Thirlway, 'The Sources of International Law', 111; K. Ambos, *Internationales Strafrecht: Strafanwendungsrecht, Völkerstrafrecht, Europäisches Strafrecht, Rechtshilfe*, 4th edn. (München: C.H. Beck, 2014), p. 111.

377 *See also*, Werle, *Völkerstrafrecht*, p. 73, with respect to international criminal law and the importance of verbal statements.

378 Ibid., pp. 70–1; Thirlway, 'The Sources of International Law', 105.

379 Villiger, *Customary International Law and Treaties*, vol. 28, p. 30.

380 Mendelson, *The Formation of Customary International Law*, vol. 272, p. 188.

381 O'Shea, *Amnesty for Crime in International Law and Practice*, pp. 213–4.

382 Werle, *Völkerstrafrecht*, pp. 70–1; O'Shea, *Amnesty for Crime in International Law and Practice*, p. 214.

contribute to a particular practice of States.[383] That is why the viewpoint of non-governmental bodies has been considered additionally by international criminal law tribunals when determining customary international law.[384] However, the practice of non-governmental organisations by itself is not relevant for the emergence of customary international law.[385]

As regards the second subjective element of customary international law, *opinio juris* or the acceptance of the general practice as law, *"the [...] conviction of a State that it is legally bound to behave in a particular way in respect of a particular type of situation"*[386] is essential.[387] It should be noted that it might not always be possible clearly to distinguish between the two components of customary international law, state practice and *opinio juris*, since they may overlap.[388] It frequently occurs that a particular behaviour of a State, for example a verbal statement can be considered as practice and at the same time the conviction to be legally bound to behave in that way becomes apparent.[389] Furthermore, in situations where State practice is consistent, widespread and also permanent, *opinio juris* can in principle be presumed.[390] However, as long as State practice is not consistent or widespread, the existence of a rule of customary international law is precluded.[391]

Another very interesting aspect regarding the evaluation of the Afghan Amnesty Law is that of the point in time at which a rule of customary international law must have been developed in order to have an impact on the legitimacy of the Afghan Amnesty Law. More concretely this means: must a rule of customary international law already have been established on the date of the entry into force of the Afghan Amnesty Law in 2010 or does customary international law that only emerged at a later date also

383 Y. Dinstein, *The Interaction between Customary International Law and Treaties*, Recueil des cours (Leiden: Martinus Nijhoff Publishers, 2007), vol. 322, p. 267.

384 R. C. Slye and B. van Schaack, *International Criminal Law: Essentials*, Essentials (Austin, New York, NY: Wolters Kluwer Law & Business; Aspen Publishers, 2009), pp. 104–5.

385 Dinstein, *The Interaction between Customary International Law and Treaties*, vol. 322, p. 267.

386 Kaczorowska, *Public International Law*, p. 27.

387 Villiger, *Customary International Law and Treaties*, vol. 28, 48.

388 Ludwin King, 'Amnesties in a Time of Transition', 604.

389 Werle, *Völkerstrafrecht*, p. 72; Henckaerts and Doswald-Beck (eds.), *Customary International Humanitarian Law*, xlvi.

390 Henckaerts and Doswald-Beck (eds.), *Customary International Humanitarian Law*, xlvi.

391 Ludwin King, 'Amnesties in a Time of Transition', 604.

matter? The retroactive effect of customary international law is a difficult issue and there is no clear-cut answer to this problem. Nevertheless, it is assumed here that in the first instance those rules of customary international law which already existed at the date of the entry into force of the Afghan Amnesty Law in 2010 are decisive for its legal assessment.[392] Where customary international law developed only subsequently, it can at the earliest have an effect from the moment of its formation— this means that a new rule of customary international law would have no influence on all acts adopted on the basis of the Amnesty Law between 2010 and the emergence of this new customary rule.[393] Newly developed customary international law could at most be viewed as an indication within the frame of the decision on the legality of the Afghan Amnesty Law. The situation is quite different when rules of *jus cogens* are affected. This means that if a peremptory norm of general international law needs to be safeguarded, and newly established customary international law serves this purpose, then the Afghan Amnesty Law would become null and void *ab initio* in the event that it is not in accordance with these new rules of international law.[394] A general problem in this context is that it is virtually impossible to identify the precise date at which a rule of customary international law is

---

392 M. Kotzur, 'Intertemporal Law' in R. Wolfrum (ed.), *Max Planck Encyclopedia of Public International Law* at 2, 5; S. Williams, 'Amnesties in International Law: The Experience of the Special Court for Sierra Leone', *Human Rights Law Review* 5 (2005), 271–309, at 302–3.

393 For comparison – In the area of international treaty law the principle of non-retroactivity is firmly anchored: *see* Art. 28 Vienna Convention on the Law of Treaties: *"Non-retroactivity of treaties: Unless a different intention appears from the treaty or is otherwise established, its provisions do not bind a party in relation to any act or fact which took place or any situation which ceased to exist before the date of the entry into force of the treaty with respect to that party."*.

394 For comparison – In the area of international treaty law the Joint Declaration of Judges Shi and Koroma with reference to the 'Case Concerning Application of the Convention on the Prevention and Punishment of the Crime of Genocide' (Bosnia and Herzegovina v. Serbia and Montenegro) (Judgment of 26 February 2007) is worth mentioning: *"Nevertheless, in some respects the interpretation of a treaty's provisions cannot be divorced from developments in the law subsequent to its adoption. Thus, even though a treaty when concluded did not conflict with any rule of jus cogens, it will become void if there subsequently emerges a new rule of jus cogens with which it is in conflict. […]"* (para. 2), *see International Court of Justice, Joint Declaration of Judges Shi and Koroma with reference to the 'Case Concerning Application of the Convention on the Prevention and Punishment of the Crime of Genocide': Judgment of 26 February 2007.* http://www.icj-cij.org/docket/files/91/13695.pdf *(11 November 2016)*; Kotzur, 'Intertemporal Law', 4.

finally established. This is because, in contrast to the enactment of a treaty, customary international law develops over a fairly long period of time and not at a specific date. However, within the scope of this study both past and present State practice is relevant since even currently developed customary international law may have consequences for the Afghan Amnesty Law, as has been shown above. Should it indeed turn out that customary international law regarding the evaluation of amnesties has established and hence the time of origin is of interest, this matter will be adequately dealt with in due course.

Now that the theoretical issues have been clarified as well as possible, the decisive question of whether customary international law with respect to a prohibition of amnesties in cases of serious international crimes has already developed or perhaps is still developing, is examined in the following. In the event that such a norm has developed or is at least "crystallizing", the legitimacy of the Afghan Amnesty Law can be reviewed on that basis. To analyse the entire practice of all States would be very work-intensive given that an extensive survey ought to be performed. However, as the present thesis is not an empirical study, only a reasonable selection of exemplary cases is necessary. The most obvious approach is therefore to survey some of those States which have enacted an amnesty law — these are 'affected' States. Also Afghanistan is of interest in this connection and thus will be mentioned as one of various countries. In addition, those States which — even though they themselves have not enacted an amnesty law — commented on amnesty laws of 'affected' States play an equally important role for the determination of customary international law regarding amnesties.[395] As indicated above, the practice of international organisations, in particular of the United Nations, is also of relevance for the purpose of this study, as their resolutions and decisions may serve as an important indicator of State practice, and thus may contribute to the creation of customary international law.[396] Since the practice of non-governmental organisations by itself is not relevant for the emergence of customary international law[397], no separate chapter is devoted to their attitudes towards amnesties. Nonetheless, due account will be taken of the

---

395 Freeman and Pensky, 'The Amnesty Controversy in International Law', 54–5.

396 Werle, *Völkerstrafrecht*, pp. 70–1; O'Shea, *Amnesty for Crime in International Law and Practice*, p. 214.

397 Dinstein, *The Interaction between Customary International Law and Treaties*, vol. 322, p. 267.

statements and opinions of these organisations since they may influence relevant policy makers and thus, indirectly affect the practice of States.[398]

3.2.1 State Practice Concerning Amnesties

In this context, it is noteworthy, first that the international community of States has signed several declarations rejecting amnesties for serious human rights violations. For example, in 2013, ministers from 113 countries promised to intensify the fight against sexual violence in conflict.[399] The corresponding declaration intends, *inter alia*, that *"all peace, security and conflict mediation processes explicitly recognise the need to prevent, respond to and reduce crimes of sexual violence in conflict and stressed the need to exclude such crimes from amnesty provisions."*[400] In 2010, six Central African States[401] issued a declaration on ending the use of child soldiers.[402], which includes a provision emphasising that *"the crime of recruitment and use of children by armed forces and groups [shall not be] part of any amnesty law and is treated as a war crime."*[403] Furthermore, in 2007, the governments of Finland, Germany and Jordan organised the international conference "Building a Future on Peace and Justice" which was attended by the representatives

398 Ibid., p. 267.

399 Ynetnews, *113 Countries Sign Pledge Against Sexual Violence*. http://www.ynetnews.com/articles/0,7340,L-4433351,00.html (24 January 2017).

400 *A Declaration of Commitment to End Sexual Violence in Conflict*. https://www.gov.uk/government/uploads/system/uploads/attachment_data/file/244849/A_DECLARATION_OF_COMMITMENT_TO_END_SEXUAL_VIOLENCE_IN_CONFLICT__TO_PRINT...pdf (24 January 2017), p. 2; Ynetnews, *113 Countries Sign Pledge Against Sexual Violence*.

401 Chad, the Central African Republic, Sudan, Nigeria, Niger and Cameroon, *see* S. Zulfiqar and H. Calderon, *Chad and Five Other Central African Countries Pledge to End Use of Children in Armed Conflict: 'N'Djaména Declaration' Adopted*. http://www.unicef.org/infobycountry/chad_53966.html (23 January 2017).

402 Ibid.

403 *Ending Recruitment and Use of Children by Armed Forces and Groups: Contributing to Peace, Justice and Development*, N'DJAMENA DECLARATION – N'Djamena, 7–9 June 2010. https://www.unicef.org/protection/files/DDR_Conference_Declarations_de_NDjamena.pdf (23 January 2017), para. 4; Zulfiqar and Calderon, *Chad and Five Other Central African Countries Pledge to End Use of Children in Armed Conflict*.

of over 60 countries.[404] The conference concluded with the "Nuremberg Declaration on Peace and Justice" stating, *inter alia*, that *"[...] amnesties must not be granted to those bearing the greatest responsibility for genocide, crimes against humanity and serious violations of international humanitarian law."*[405] Whereas it seems possible for the international community to agree on a non-binding declaration on amnesties, the same does not apply when it comes to reaching a binding agreement as the negotiations of the ICC Rome Statute, the Convention on the Non-Applicability of Statutory Limitations to War Crimes and Crimes against Humanity or the International Convention for the Protection of All Persons from Enforced Disappearance[406] clearly show.[407] However, whether the non-binding declarative statements of various States remain mere empty words or whether amnesties for serious international crimes are indeed rejected in specific situations, is examined below. As already mentioned, the focus is on those States which have enacted an amnesty law. The practice of these States is of particular importance because it provides evidence whether certain crimes are explicitly excluded from their respective amnesty law. Following a short overview of amnesty laws around the world, a well-founded selection of 'affected' States is more closely considered.

The Amnesty Law Database created by Louise Mallinder, Professor of Human Rights and International Law, provides great insight into diverse amnesty processes in all regions of the world.[408] The database encompasses 537 amnesty laws in 138 countries which were issued between 1945 and 2011.[409] In the period from 1979 (the beginning of the "age of accountability" or "justice cascade") to 2011 a total of 398 amnesty laws were introduced in 115 countries.[410] It is shown that besides political and ordi-

404 German Federal Foreign Office, *Nuremberg Declaration on Peace and Justice*, press release. http://www.auswaertiges-amt.de/EN/Infoservice/Presse/Meldungen/2008/080620-Nuernberger-Erklaerung.html (07 February 2017).

405 *Nuremberg Declaration on Peace and Justice*. http://www.auswaertiges-amt.de/cae/servlet/contentblob/491058/publicationFile/3491/080620-NuernbergerErklaerung-EN.pdf (07 February 2017), Section III para. 2.

406 Seibert-Fohr, *Prosecuting Serious Human Rights Violations*, 171–172, 181–183.

407 A reason may be that States nevertheless believe in amnesties as a powerful bargaining tool and thus do not want to be bound by any treaty that eliminates this option. *See* Chapter 3.1.1.

408 L. Mallinder, *The Amnesty Database*. http://www.incore.ulst.ac.uk/Amnesty/index.html (23 November 2016).

409 Mallinder, 'Amnesties' Challenge to the Global Accountability Norm? Interpreting Regional and International Trends in Amnesty Enactment', 79.

410 Ibid., 79.

nary crimes, serious international crimes are also still being amnestied.[411] What is also noteworthy is that shortly after the entry into force of the Rome Statute of the International Criminal Court in 2003, "the number of amnesty laws enacted [...] amounted to the largest annual total to have been enacted in any year."[412] As discussed at the beginning of this thesis (see 2. *Amnesties in the Age of Accountability*), this may reflect the fact that amnesties are issued mainly for legal reasons. This means that perpetrators could claim more legal guarantees against their individual criminal accountability. They fear trials and prosecutions, for example by the ICC, and want to be protected by an amnesty. Governments thus may adopt amnesties as a negative response to the "age of accountability"[413] with the aim of shielding the perpetrators from criminal proceedings. However, in 2008 and 2009 the number of amnesty laws declined, whereas an increase of newly introduced amnesty laws can be noticed in the period between January 2010 and June 2011.[414] Further study and research regarding the enactment of amnesty laws from 2011 until now would be very instructive. However, it is undeniable that States continue to adopt amnesty laws, as this chapter shows.

In what follows, several amnesty laws from different countries are examined in more detail. The selection of States is based on significant stages in the recent history of amnesty laws.[415] Therefore, the analysis starts with some of the numerous amnesty laws utilised in Latin American States

---

411 Mallinder, *Amnesty, Human Rights and Political Transitions:*, pp. 19–23; Mallinder, *Amnesty, Human Rights and Political Transitions:*, 118, 121–122; Mallinder, 'Amnesties' Challenge to the Global Accountability Norm? Interpreting Regional and International Trends in Amnesty Enactment', 92–3.

412 Mallinder, 'Amnesties' Challenge to the Global Accountability Norm? Interpreting Regional and International Trends in Amnesty Enactment', 81.

413 Sikkink, 'The Age of Accountability:', 21 Mallinder in F. Lessa and L. A. Payne (eds.), *Amnesty in the Age of Human Rights Accountability: Comparative and International Perspectives* (Cambridge, New York: Cambridge University Press, 2012), at p. 90; Slye, 'The Legitimacy of Amnesties Under International Law and General Principles of Anglo-American Law', 175.

414 Mallinder, 'Amnesties' Challenge to the Global Accountability Norm? Interpreting Regional and International Trends in Amnesty Enactment', 92–3.

415 Amnesties have a long history as they are used since ancient times, for example in ancient Greece and in the Byzantine Empire. They were issued mainly on religious grounds. Over the years, amnesties have been used to safeguard political and social peace, for example the Treaty of Westphalia (1648) entailed an amnesty. More recently, amnesties were frequently applied in the context of the military dictatorships in Latin America in the 1980s. *See* Cryer, Friman, Robinson and Wilmshurst, *An Introduction to International Criminal Law and*

during and after the military dictatorships in the 1980s. These States are of great relevance as they have a long tradition of impunity, but are now experiencing a move away from blanket amnesties.[416] This is followed by the well-known South African amnesty of 1995. Finally, the focus is on the post-2000 developments with regard to the enactment of amnesty laws.[417] In doing so, it is envisaged that amnesty laws from all parts of the world are assessed to avoid a one-sided view and also to adequately consider some less famous amnesty laws, such as those from Asian countries. Such an approach is all the more useful, since this region presently has some of the highest rates of newly introduced amnesty laws.[418] But also Europe and the United States provide interesting examples of State practice concerning amnesty.

3.2.1.1 Latin American States

The practice of issuing amnesties during or after military rule in many Latin-American countries in the 1980s and 1990s is an outstanding example of the purported privilege of peace over justice. Even perpetrators of the most serious international crimes have been amnestied automatically without the need for an individual application or fulfilling any noteworthy condition.[419] The countries affected were, *inter alia*, Brazil, Guatemala, El Salvador, Peru, Uruguay, Chile, and Argentina. In the early years of newly established civilian governments and democracies things initially remained the same, i.e. the amnesty laws persisted and there were almost no criminal investigations or prosecutions[420].[421] Only after the civilian governments had become more stable and moreover, the Inter-American

---

Procedure, p. 563; Mallinder, *Amnesty, Human Rights and Political Transitions:*, p. 4.

416 Mallinder, 'Amnesties', 849–50.

417 United Nations Human Rights Council, *Analytical Study on Human Rights and Transitional Justice*, A/HRC/12/18. http://www2.ohchr.org/english/bodies/hrcouncil/docs/12session/A-HRC-12-18_E.pdf (24 November 2016), p. 18.

418 Mallinder, 'Amnesties' Challenge to the Global Accountability Norm? Interpreting Regional and International Trends in Amnesty Enactment', 72.

419 Mallinder, 'Amnesties', 826.

420 An exception to this was, for example, Argentina, which prosecuted members of the military government in 1985. *See N. Roht-Arriaza, 'Amnesty Laws in Latin America: Devalued Currency?', The Canadian Consortium on Human Security 6 (2008), 13–6, at 13.*

421 Ibid., p. 13.

human rights bodies had expressed their strong opposition to the blanket amnesties shielding the old military regime, were most of these amnesty laws annulled or at least severely limited.[422] The longstanding preference for impunity over justice then turned into a policy of criminal investigations and prosecutions in order to cope with the past[423] — in other words, justice has followed peace. This development is also due to the strong and active civil society in many Latin American States.[424] In the following, the development of amnesty laws in some of the Latin American countries is demonstrated in more detail.

The first country in Latin America to confront the problem of impunity and ultimately nullify its amnesty law was ***Argentina***.[425] After decades of political violence, military coups, massacres and guerrilla wars a democratically elected civilian government came into power in December 1983.[426] Shortly before, in September 1983, the outgoing military junta had managed to enact a blanket self-amnesty law[427] to protect itself from prosecution.[428] However, by December 1983 the amnesty law had already been repealed and the newly-elected President Raúl Alfonsín promised criminal proceedings against the former military government.[429] Following the first prosecutions the situation escalated once again in 1986 as the military violently protested against these trials.[430] In their view, the number of criminal investigations was too great as they surpassed all expectations.[431] Furthermore, active armed forces officers argued that they are not bound by judicial decisions of civilian courts.[432] Eventually, the military rejected to cooperate with the prosecution strategy of the government.[433] The debil-

422 Mallinder, 'Amnesties', 849–50.

423 Werle, 'Transitional Justice – Der juristische Rahmen', 793.

424 Mallinder, 'Amnesties', 849.

425 P. Engstrom and G. Pereira, 'From Amnesty to Accountability: The Ebbs and Flows in the Search for Justice in Argentina' in F. Lessa and L. A. Payne (eds.), *Amnesty in the Age of Human Rights Accountability: Comparative and International Perspectives* (Cambridge, New York: Cambridge University Press, 2012), pp. 97–122, at p. 97.

426 Mallinder, 'Amnesties', 826.

427 Ley de Pacificación Nacional (Law of National Pacification), Law No. 22.924 (22 September 1983).

428 Mallinder, Amnesties', 827–8.

429 Mallinder, 'Amnesties', 829; Henckaerts and Doswald-Beck (eds.), *Customary International Humanitarian Law*, pp. 4021–2.

430 Engstrom and Pereira, 'From Amnesty to Accountability', 103–4.

431 Mallinder, 'Amnesties', 830.

432 Engstrom and Pereira, 'From Amnesty to Accountability', 103–4.

433 Ibid., 103.

itated Argentine government reacted by restricting criminal proceedings and issuing the Full Stop Law in December 1986[434] as well as the Due Obedience Law in June 1987[435], which radically undermined the promise to prosecute the former military rulers.[436] In 1989 President Alfonsín was replaced by Carlos Menem, who — like his successors — preferred reconciliation over prosecutions, which has meant that alleged perpetrators of serious international crimes have been left untroubled.[437] During this time Argentinian non-governmental organisations as well as Argentinian courts played a predominant role in the fight against impunity. They investigated and documented violations of human rights and identified the perpetrators.[438] All this work culminated in the challenge to the Full Stop and Due Obedience Laws by a Federal Judge in March 2001 and the subsequent decision that these laws were unconstitutional.[439] It is stated that these laws violate the duty to investigate and punish human rights violations and crimes against humanity.[440] This ruling was upheld by the Argentine Chamber of Appeals in November 2001[441] and the Supreme Court in June 2005[442].[443] The state of impunity was also addressed at a political level. In August 2003, shortly after Néstor Kirchner became President, the Argentine Congress voted in favour of abolishing the amnesty laws.[444] These

434 Ley de Punto Final (Full Stop Law), Law No. 23.492 (23 December 1986).

435 Ley de Obediencia Debida (Due Obedience Law), Law No. 23.521 (04 June 1987).

436 Engstrom and Pereira, From Amnesty to Accountability, 104–5.

437 Engstrom and Pereira, 'From Amnesty to Accountability', 107.

438 Mallinder, 'Amnesties', 832; Y. Sooka, 'The Politics of Transitional Justice' in C. L. Sriram and S. Pillay (eds.), *Peace versus Justice? The Dilemma of Transitional Justice in Africa* (Oxford: James Currey, 2010), pp. 21–43, at p. 27.

439 Resolución del Cavallo, Argentina, Decision of 6 March 2001, *see* Naqvi, *Impediments to Exercising Jurisdiction over International Crimes*, p. 83; Henckaerts and Doswald-Beck (eds.), *Customary International Humanitarian Law*, p. 4027; Engstrom and Pereira, 'From Amnesty to Accountability', 112.

440 Henckaerts and Doswald-Beck (eds.), *Customary International Humanitarian Law*, p. 4027.

441 Cámara Federal en lo Criminal y Correccional [CFCyC], case n. 17889, appeal by Simón, Julio, judgment of 9 Nov. 2001.

442 Corte Suprema de Justicia [CSJN], case n. 17768, "Simón, Julio Héctor y otros s/ privación ilegítima de la libertad, etc.," S. 1767. XXXVIII, 14 June 2005, *see* Naqvi, *Impediments to Exercising Jurisdiction over International Crimes*, p. 83.

443 Engstrom and Pereira, 'From Amnesty to Accountability', 113, 116–117; Mallinder, 'Amnesties', 832–3.

444 „Diputados aprobó la anulación de las leyes de perdón," La Nación, August 12, 2003, *see* Engstrom and Pereira, 'From Amnesty to Accountability', 114–5.

political and legal achievements led to the reopening of numerous cases against those responsible for serious violations of human rights during the military regime.[445] By 2016 the number of convictions amounted to more than 600.[446]

Apart from Argentina, the country that has been most successful in the fight against impunity is ***Chile***.[447] During the military junta, led by General Augusto Pinochet, an unconditional self-amnesty had been issued in 1978[448], applying to *"all persons who have been the authors, accomplices, or accessories of unlawful deeds during the period in which the state of siege was in force, between 11 September 1973 and 10 March 1978, unless they are currently being tried or have been sentenced and to those persons who as of the date that this decree-law took effect have been sentenced by military tribunals since 11 September 1973."*[449] Pinochet's regime lasted until 1990 and his successor Patricio Aylwin was the first democratically elected President after the dictatorship. Even though Aylwin was not able to repeal the amnesty law, his government established the National Commission on Truth and Reconciliation in order to investigate the most serious human rights abuses.[450] However, there were several restrictions on the scope of the commission's mandate, which hampered the process of truth finding.[451] Besides this, some Chilean lower courts ruled against the amnesty law, but did not convince the Supreme Court of Chile which decided in two cases, in 1990[452] and 1995[453], that the amnesty was constitutional and consistent with international law.[454] The judges ruled that the Geneva Conventions do not prohibit amnesty laws. They further argued that the principle of

445 Ibid., 118–119, 121.

446 J. Gilbert, 'Ex-Military Officers Convicted of Human Rights Crimes During Argentina Dictatorship', The New York Times, 25 August 2016; Centro de Estudios Legales y Sociales (CELS), *Estadísticas*. http://www.cels.org.ar/blogs/estadisticas/ (02 December 2016).

447 E. Skaar, *Judicial Independence and Human Rights in Latin America: Violations, Politics, and Prosecution*, 1st edn. (New York: Palgrave Macmillan, 2011), pp. 95–6.

448 Roht-Arriaza and Gibson, 'The Developing Jurisprudence on Amnesty', 847.

449 Chile, Decree-Law on General Amnesty (1978), Article 1, *see* Henckaerts and Doswald-Beck (eds.), *Customary International Humanitarian Law*, p. 4023.

450 Roht-Arriaza and Gibson, 'The Developing Jurisprudence on Amnesty', 848.

451 Ibid., p. 848.

452 Supreme Court of Justice of Chile, Insunza Bascuñán Case, pt. 2, § 4, at 64 (May-August 1990).

453 Supreme Court of Justice of Chile, Romo Mena Case, (26 October 1995).

454 Roht-Arriaza and Gibson, 'The Developing Jurisprudence on Amnesty', 848.

non-retroactivity obstructs the application of several international human rights treaties, such as the Convention against Torture and the ICCPR, since Chile had not ratified these conventions at the time when the crimes in question occurred.[455] However, encouraged by the detention of General Pinochet in London in 1998, Chilean courts increasingly critically assessed the amnesty law. In line with this development, the Supreme Court of Chile decided in 1999 that the amnesty law should not be applied in cases of 'enforced disappearance' as this was an ongoing crime until the death of the victim is proved or the disappearance has been clarified in some other way.[456] In 2006 the Inter-American Court of Human Rights ruled in *Almonacid-Arellano et al. versus Chile* that the Chilean amnesty law had to be abolished, since it granted impunity for serious international crimes. The judges stated that crimes against humanity could not remain unpunished. The non-prosecution of the perpetrators thus was in violation of Articles 8.1 (Right to a Fair Trial) and 25 (Right to Judicial Protection) together with Articles 1.1 (Obligation to Respect Rights) and 2 (Domestic Legal Effects) of the American Convention on Human Rights.[457] In accordance with this decision, the Supreme Court of Chile determined in March 2007 that *"The so-called amnesty law can clearly be defined as an act of exonerating oneself from criminal responsibility for serious human rights violations since it was drafted after these acts took place and by those in power during and after the acts, thereby guaranteeing the impunity of those responsible for these acts. [The amnesty law therefore] violates Article 148 of [the 1949] Geneva Convention IV."*[458] Notwithstanding this and other similar verdicts by Chilean courts[459] and besides the fact that hundreds of military officers

---

455 Amnesty International, *Chile – Transition at the Crossroads: Human Rights Violations under Pinochet Rule Remain the Crux*. https://www.amnesty.org/download/Documents/172000/amr220011996en.pdf (04 January 2019), p. 21.

456 Sooka, 'The Politics of Transitional Justice', 28.

457 *Case of Almonacid-Arellano et al v. Chile* (Inter-American Court of Human Rights, 26 September 2006), para. 114 53–4; Mallinder, 'Amnesties', 836; C. Binder, 'The Prohibition of Amnesties by the Inter-American Court of Human Rights', *German Law Journal* 12 (2011), 1203–30, at 1210–1.

458 Supreme Court of Justice of Chile, Criminal Law Chamber, Víctor Raúl Pinto case, Case No. 3125–04, Decision on Annulment, 13 March 2007, § 24, *see* International Committee of the Red Cross (ICRC), *Practice Relating to Rule 159. Amnesty*. http://www.icrc.org/customary-ihl/eng/docs/v2_rul_rule159 (05 December 2016).

459 In 2010, for example, the Supreme Court of Chile ruled that the amnesty law is inapplicable in cases of crimes against humanity. *See* Supreme Court of Justice of Chile, Case of Claudio Abdón Lecaros Carrasco for the crime of

have already been convicted of serious crimes[460], the amnesty law is still in force.[461] This means that even though the amnesty law has been severely restricted over the years[462], it has not yet been annulled. Furthermore, many Chileans and human rights activists criticize the apparently lenient sentences applied by the courts for serious human rights violations.[463]

In the case of ***Uruguay***, the military dictatorship was followed by a transitional phase encompassing two different amnesty processes, whereby the military's strong role remained almost unchanged.[464] In March 1985, the just-established civilian government enacted the first amnesty law.[465] It included an amnesty for all political offences and criminal and military offences related thereto committed after 1 January 1962.[466] Political offences were described as those perpetrated directly or indirectly for political motives.[467] Beneficiaries of the amnesty were all persons accused of committing these offences as authors, co-authors or accomplices and accessories.[468] The amnesty law excluded acts of inhuman, cruel or degrading treatment as well as certain cases of disappearance from its scope.[469] Therefore criminal proceedings against military and police officers who had committed these human rights violations were initiated. However, due to political tensions and the military's substantial influence — striv-

---

aggravated kidnapping, Rol No. 47.205, Remedy No. 3302/2009, Resolution 16698, Appeals Judgment, and Resolution 16699, Replacement Judgment, of 18 May, 2010, supra note 268.

460 At the end of 2015 more than 1000 people had been convicted, *see* G. Slattery, *Chile Doubles Down on Prosecutions for Pinochet-era Crimes*. http://www.reuters.com/article/us-chile-dictatorship-trials-idUSKCN0SQ2D120151101 (17.12.15); Sooka, 'The Politics of Transitional Justice', 28–9; Roht-Arriaza, 'Amnesty Laws in Latin America', 13.

461 Skaar, *Judicial Independence and Human Rights in Latin America*, p. 117.

462 Roht-Arriaza, 'Amnesty Laws in Latin America', 13.

463 Slattery, *Chile Doubles Down on Prosecutions for Pinochet-era Crimes*; adveniat – Blickpunkt Lateinamerika, *Chile: Schleppende Aufarbeitung von Militärdiktatur*. http://www.blickpunkt-lateinamerika.de/news-details/article/schleppende-aufarbeitung-von-militaerdiktatur.html?no_cache=1&cHash=de4bd055606f8b214b963d9df7809aff (08 January 2015).

464 Mallinder, 'Amnesties', 846.

465 Ley de Pacificación Nacional, Ley No. 15.737, Se aprueba la Ley de amnistía (1985).

466 *See* Henckaerts and Doswald-Beck (eds.), *Customary International Humanitarian Law*, p. 4027.

467 Ibid., p. 4027.

468 Ibid., p. 4027.

469 Ibid., p. 4027.

ing for the termination of the proceedings — a second amnesty law was adopted in December 1986.[470] It benefited military and police personnel who acted for political reasons or in fulfilment of their functions.[471] From that moment on different attempts were made by human rights activists, courts and politicians to eliminate the law.[472] Nevertheless, the Supreme Court of Uruguay pronounced the constitutionality of the amnesty law in a minimum majority decision in May 1988.[473] The judges declared that the law constitutes a sovereign act of clemency which is in accordance with international human rights law since it strives to achieve reconciliation.[474] Nonetheless, as the amnesty caused significant opposition from victims of human rights abuses, their families and human rights activists[475], a referendum on the abolishment of the law was held in 1989. It was, however, not successful.[476] The amnesty question was raised also outside Uruguay. In 1992 the Inter-American Commission on Human Rights stated that Uruguay's amnesty law is inconsistent with Article XVIII (Right to a Fair Trial) of the American Declaration of the Rights and Duties of Man and Articles 1, 8 and 25 (Right to a Fair Trial; Right to Judicial Protection) of the American Convention on Human Rights.[477] The Com-

470 Ley de Caducidad de la Pretensión Punitiva del Estado, Ley No. 15.848 (1986).

471 Ley de Caducidad de la Pretensión Punitiva del Estado, Ley No. 15.848 (1986), Article 1, *see* Henckaerts and Doswald-Beck (eds.), *Customary International Humanitarian Law*, p. 4027.

472 F. Lessa, 'Barriers to Justice: The Ley de Caducidad and Impunity in Uruguay' in F. Lessa and L. A. Payne (eds.), *Amnesty in the Age of Human Rights Accountability: Comparative and International Perspectives* (Cambridge, New York: Cambridge University Press, 2012), pp. 123–51, at p. 130.

473 R. van Eijl, *Dealing with Crimes of the Past: No More Amnesty? An Inquiry into the Lawfulness of Amnesty for Human Rights Atrocities Under International Law* (Utrecht: Kennispunt Recht, Economie, Bestuur en Organisatie, Universiteit Utrecht, 2009), p. 15; Lessa, 'Barriers to Justice', 132; Roht-Arriaza, 'Amnesty Laws in Latin America', 14.

474 United Nations Human Rights Committee, *Rodríguez v. Uruguay, Communication No. 322/1988: U.N. Doc. CCPR/C/51/D/322/1988 (1994)*. http://hrlibrary.umn.edu/undocs/html/vws322.htm (07 December 2016), para. 8.2.

475 Mallinder, 'Amnesties', 848.

476 R. van Eijl, *Dealing with Crimes of the Past: No More Amnesty? An Inquiry into the Lawfulness of Amnesty for Human Rights Atrocities Under International Law* (Utrecht: Kennispunt Recht, Economie, Bestuur en Organisatie, Universiteit Utrecht, 2009), p. 15; Lessa, 'Barriers to Justice', 132; Roht-Arriaza, 'Amnesty Laws in Latin America', 14.

477 Inter-American Commission on Human Rights, *Report № 29/92: Cases 10.029, 10.036, 10.145, 10.305, 10.372, 10.373, 10.374 and 10.375 Uruguay*. https://www.cidh.oas.org/annualrep/92eng/Uruguay10.029.htm (04 February 2019).

mission stipulated, *inter alia*, that „*The law in question has the intended effect of dismissing all criminal proceedings involving past human rights violations. With that, the law eliminates any judicial possibility of a serious and impartial investigation designed to establish the crimes denounced and to identify their authors, accomplices, and accessories after the fact.*"[478] Thus, the Uruguayan authorities had to investigate human rights violations. However, the Commission had not explicitly demanded that the amnesty law be abolished.[479] In comments in 1993[480], 1994[481] and 1998 another human rights body, the UN Human Rights Committee, found that the Uruguayan amnesty law violated Article 7, in connection with Article 2, Paragraph 3 of the ICCPR.[482] The Committee noted „*with deep concern that the adoption of this law effectively excludes in a number of cases the possibility of investigation into past human rights abuses and thereby prevents the State party from discharging its responsibility to provide effective remedies to the victims of those abuses. Moreover, the Committee is concerned that, in adopting this law, the State party has contributed to an atmosphere of impunity which may undermine the democratic order and give rise to further grave human rights violations.*"[483] Despite this reiterated criticism of the amnesty law, it took some time until the Uruguayan authorities shifted their attention from impunity to accountability. In the course of this, reparations laws were adopted in 2006 and 2009[484] and although the nullification of the amnesty law failed by a narrow margin in a second referendum in October 2009 the resistance against it gained momentum.[485] Also in October 2009, the Supreme Court of Justice decided that the amnesty law contradicted the Uruguayan constitution as well as several international human rights conventions.[486] The Court ruled, that the separation of powers as well as the independence

---

478 Ibid., para.35.

479 Ibid.; Lessa, 'Barriers to Justice', 132–3.

480 United Nations Human Rights Committee, *Concluding Observations of the UN Human Rights Committee: Uruguay: CCPR/C/79/Add.19*. http://tbinternet.ohchr.org/_layouts/treatybodyexternal/Download.aspx?symbolno=CCPR%2FC%2F79%2FAdd.19&Lang=en (07 December 2016), para.7.

481 United Nations Human Rights Committee, *Rodríguez v. Uruguay, Communication No. 322/1988*, para. 12.4.

482 Lessa, 'Barriers to Justice', 133.

483 United Nations Human Rights Committee, *Rodríguez v. Uruguay, Communication No. 322/1988*, para.12.4.

484 Lessa, 'Barriers to Justice', 135–6.

485 Ibid., 138.

486 Supreme Court of Uruguay, Unconstitutionality Sentence No. 365 (19 October 2009), *see* ibid., 139.

of the judiciary had been violated, because the executive branch had the power to decide whether a particular crime or episode fell within the scope of the amnesty. Furthermore, the judges found that the law interfered with the rights of victims to truth and to judicial process.[487] Subsequently trials against military officials were initiated from October 2010 onward.[488] Following the decision of the Inter-American Court of Human Rights in February 2011 that the Uruguayan amnesty law violated the American Convention on Human Rights and the Inter-American Convention on Forced Disappearance of Persons[489], the Uruguayan parliament annulled the amnesty law in October 2011.[490] This led to criminal proceedings in numerous new cases.[491] However, in February 2013 the Supreme Court of Uruguay ruled that the 2011 law annulling the amnesty was unconstitutional because of its retroactive effect.[492] This unequal development in Uruguay over the years exemplifies the challenging task of dealing with amnesties.

As regards ***Peru***, the amnesty process was much more straightforward and started with a highly disputed amnesty law signed by Alberto Fujimori on 14 June 1995[493], in the midst of his presidency. It came after years of violence, repression and human rights abuses committed by the Peruvian forces and guerrilla movements. Most notably, the killings in Barrios Altos in 1991[494] and the La Cantuta Massacre of 1992[495] are well

487 N. Roht-Arriaza, *Uruguay Supreme Court Annuls Amnesty Law, as Accountability Continues in Latin America*. http://www.intlawgrrls.com/2010/11/uruguayan-supreme-court-annuls-amnesty.html (04 February 2019).

488 Lessa, 'Barriers to Justice', 139.

489 Inter-American Court of Human Rights, Case Gelman v. Uruguay, Judgement of February 24, 2011 (Merits and Reparations), para. 312.11, *see* ibid., 140.

490 Ibid., 142, 149–150.

491 Ibid., 150.

492 M. Slater, *Uruguay High Court Declares Dictatorship Trials Unconstitutional*. http://jurist.org/paperchase/2013/02/uruguay-high-court-declares-dictatorship-trials-unconstitutional.php (08 December 2016); 'Uruguay: Justice or Democracy?', The Economist, 23 March 2013.

493 Law No. 26479 (15 June 1995), *see* Roht-Arriaza and Gibson, 'The Developing Jurisprudence on Amnesty', 855.

494 In the Barrios Altos neighborhood fifteen people were killed by paramilitaries and four others suffered severe injuries. *See* C. Josi, 'Nach fast 20 Jahren: Gerechtigkeit für die Opfer von Barrios Altos und La Cantuta in Peru', *TRIAL Zeitschrift* (2010), 9–12, at 9.

495 The incident took place at the La Cantuta University, where a university professor and nine students were abducted and subsequently executed by paramilitaries. *See* ibid., p. 9.

known atrocities perpetrated by the Fujimori regime.[496] The amnesty law granted impunity to police, military personnel, and civilian officials for any human rights abuses or other criminal acts committed between May 1980 and 15 June 1995 *"in relation to all events derived or originated from, or a consequence of, the fight against terrorism"*.[497] This law was followed by further similar amnesty laws, namely the Law on Amnesty for Retired Officers of the Armed Forces and the Law on Amnesty for Military and Civil Personnel, both issued in 1996.[498] As a result of this, criminal proceedings already initiated were halted and absolute impunity prevailed in Peru.[499] This led to the mobilisation of the Inter-American Court of Human Rights by victims and/or their relatives. In March 2001, the Court decided in the Barrios Altos case that Peru's amnesty laws *"prevented the victims' next of kin and the surviving victims in this case from being heard by a judge, as established in Article 8(1) of the Convention; they violated the right to judicial protection embodied in Article 25 of the Convention; they prevented the investigation, capture, prosecution and conviction of those responsible for the events that occurred in Barrios Altos, thus failing to comply with Article 1(1) of the Convention, and they obstructed clarification of the facts of this case."*[500] The Inter-American Court further stated that *"Self-amnesty laws lead to the defencelessness of victims and perpetuate impunity; therefore, they are manifestly incompatible with the aims and spirit of the Convention. This type of law precludes the identification of the individuals who are responsible for human rights violations, because it obstructs the investigation and access to justice and prevents the victims and their next of kin from knowing the truth and receiving the corresponding reparation."*[501] This ground-breaking verdict prompted the subsequent annulment of the amnesty law in 2002[502] and previously

---

496 Ibid., pp. 9–10.

497 Law No. 26479 (15 June 1995), Art. 1, *see* Roht-Arriaza and Gibson, 'The Developing Jurisprudence on Amnesty', 855.

498 Henckaerts and Doswald-Beck (eds.), *Customary International Humanitarian Law*, p. 4025.

499 Josi, 'Nach fast 20 Jahren', 10; Roht-Arriaza and Gibson, 'The Developing Jurisprudence on Amnesty', 855–6.

500 *Case of Barrios Altos v. Peru* (Inter-American Court of Human Rights, 14 March 2001), para. 42.

501 Ibid., para. 43.

502 The automatic annulment of the amnesty law is a consequence of Peruvian constitutional law which determines that international human rights law and the judgements of the Inter-American Court of Human Rights are part of Peru's domestic law. Therefore, it was not necessary to formally abolish the amnesty law. *See* L. Mallinder, 'The End of Amnesty or Regional Overreach?:

halted cases were reopened.[503] In accordance with this development the Constitutional Court of Peru ruled in March 2007 that an amnesty *"cannot be enacted if contrary to international obligations arising from international human rights treaties ratified by the state of Peru."*[504] In April 2009 the Supreme Court of Peru condemned former President Alberto Fujimori for ordering the paramilitaries to conduct the Barrios Altos and La Cantuta massacres and sentenced him to 25 years in prison.[505] It was an historic decision as never before had a democratically elected Latin-American President been convicted in his own country for international crimes.[506]

It was only recently — in July 2016 — that the Supreme Court of ***El Salvador*** overruled the country's blanket Amnesty Law[507], which was passed in 1993 following more than ten years of civil war. The violent war ended with peace negotiations between the guerrilla and the military in 1992.[508] During the transitional phase various peace accords, which included, *inter alia*, the establishment of a truth commission and of an *ad hoc* commission to investigate the military forces, had been brokered.[509] Furthermore, the Salvadoran government enacted a restricted amnesty, excluding perpetrators of serious human rights violations to be identified

Interpreting the Erosion of South America's Amnesty Laws', *International and Comparative Law Quarterly (ICLQ)* 65 (2016), 645–80, at 653.

503 Josi, 'Nach fast 20 Jahren', 10.

504 Peru, Constitutional Court, Santiago Enrique Martin Rivas case, Case No. 679–2550-PA/TC, Judgement of 2 March 2007, §§ 28 and 30, *see* International Committee of the Red Cross (ICRC), *Practice Relating to Rule 159. Amnesty.*

505 A. C. Sain, *Latin American Amnesty Laws Annulled; the Struggle Against Impunity Continues.* http://www.peacepalacelibrary.nl/2011/01/latin-american-amnesty-laws-annulled-the-struggle-against-impunity-continues/ (09 December 2016); Josi, 'Nach fast 20 Jahren', 9.

506 T. Cespedes and T. Wade, *Peru's Fujimori Gets 25 Years Prison for Massacres.* http://www.reuters.com/article/us-peru-fujimori-idUSTRE5363RH20090407 (09 December 2016).

507 International Center for Transitional Justice (ICTJ), *With Amnesty Law Overturned in El Salvador, Prosecutors Must Work with Victims to Investigate Civil War Atrocities.* https://www.ictj.org/news/amnesty-el-salvador-civil-war (29 November 2016).

508 Roht-Arriaza and Gibson, 'The Developing Jurisprudence on Amnesty', 850; R. van Eijl, *Dealing with Crimes of the Past: No More Amnesty? An Inquiry into the Lawfulness of Amnesty for Human Rights Atrocities Under International Law* (Utrecht: Kennispunt Recht, Economie, Bestuur en Organisatie, Universiteit Utrecht, 2009), p. 15; Mallinder, 'Amnesties', 840.

509 Roht-Arriaza and Gibson, 'The Developing Jurisprudence on Amnesty', 850; Mallinder, 'Amnesties', 840.

in the report expected from the truth commission.[510] In March 1993 the truth commission finished its work, naming a number of high-ranking officials responsible for serious crimes.[511] In response to pressure from the military and in order to protect the named offenders from prosecution the government issued a further — blanket — amnesty law[512].[513] The new law determined that *"a broad, absolute and unconditional amnesty is granted in favour of all those who in one way or another participated in political crimes, crimes with political ramifications, or common crimes committed by no less than twenty people, before January 1st 1992, regardless of whether proceedings against them for the perpetration of these crimes have commenced or not, or whether they have received a sentence as a consequence."*[514] In the years that followed, the Supreme Court of El Salvador had to deal with the amnesty law on several occasions. In 1993, the Court decided that in general it is for the legislature to enact an amnesty law[515] but, where human rights are concerned, the application of the amnesty must be evaluated for each individual case.[516] In the years 1995 and 2000, the amnesty law was found by the Supreme Court to be constitutional.[517] Due to criticism this decision was somewhat

510 Law of National Reconciliation, Legislative Decree 147, Official Journal 14, vol. 314 (1992), *see* Mallinder, 'Amnesties', 840.

511 Ibid., 840.

512 Ley de Amnistía General para la Consolidación de la Paz, Decreto No. 486 (20 March 1993).

513 Mallinder, 'Amnesties', 840; Roht-Arriaza and Gibson, 'The Developing Jurisprudence on Amnesty', 850.

514 Ley de Amnistía General para la Consolidación de la Paz, Decreto No. 486 (20 March 1993), Art. 1, *see* Henckaerts and Doswald-Beck (eds.), *Customary International Humanitarian Law*, p. 4024; van Eijl, *Dealing with Crimes of the Past: No More Amnesty? An Inquiry into the Lawfulness of Amnesty for Human Rights Atrocities Under International Law*, p. 16.

515 El Salvador: Supreme Court of Justice, Decision on the Amnesty Law, Proceedings No. 10–93 (20 May, 1993); O'Shea, *Amnesty for Crime in International Law and Practice*, p. 62.

516 E. Braid and N. Roht-Arriaza, 'De Facto and De Jure Amnesty Laws: The Central American Case' in F. Lessa and L. A. Payne (eds.), *Amnesty in the Age of Human Rights Accountability: Comparative and International Perspectives* (Cambridge, New York: Cambridge University Press, 2012), pp. 182–209, at p. 199.

517 Van Eijl, *Dealing with Crimes of the Past: No More Amnesty? An Inquiry into the Lawfulness of Amnesty for Human Rights Atrocities Under International Law*, p. 13; Braid and Roht-Arriaza, 'De Facto and De Jure Amnesty Laws', 199.

limited in rulings in 2000[518] and 2003[519] as the Supreme Court allowed the lower courts to decide on a case-by-case basis whether or not to make use of the amnesty. In cases were fundamental rights are concerned the amnesty shall not apply.[520] The government of El Salvador unabatedly advocated the amnesty law, for example in a 2007 report, by stating that the amnesty is a contribution to national reconciliation.[521] In the international arena the amnesty law was looked at more critically. In 2009, the UN Committee against Torture called on the Salvadoran government to abolish the law.[522] The Inter-American Court of Human Rights decided in 2004 in the Serrano-Cruz case[523] and in 2012 in the El Mozote case[524] that the state of El Salvador has an obligation to investigate and that the amnesty law shall not present an obstacle for the investigations.[525] The judges stated that the amnesty prevents *"the survivors and the victims' next of kin from being heard by a judge, in keeping with the provisions of Article 8(1) of the American Convention and receiving judicial protection, in keeping with the right established in Article 25 of this instrument."*[526] On the other hand, they declared that *"the Law of General Amnesty for the Consolidation of Peace has resulted in the installation and perpetuation of a situation of impunity owing the absence of investigation, pursuit, capture, prosecution and punishment*

---

518 Acción de inconstitucionalidad contra los artículos 1 y 4 del Decreto Legislativo No. 486, Sala de lo Constitucional, Corte Suprema de Justicia, 27 September 2000, *see* Braid and Roht-Arriaza, 'De Facto and De Jure Amnesty Laws', 199.

519 Proceso de Amparo promovido por Juan Antonio Ellacuría Beascoechea y otros, Sala de lo Constitucional, Corte Suprema de Justicia, 23 December 2003, *see* ibid., 199.

520 Ibid., 199.

521 Mallinder, 'Amnesties', 840–1.

522 UN Committee Against Torture (CAT), *Concluding Observations of the Committee Against Torture: El Salvador: CAT/C/SLV/CO/2.* http://tbinternet.ohchr.org/_layouts/treatybodyexternal/Download.aspx?symbolno=CAT/C/SLV/CO/2&Lang=En (12 December 2016), para 15.

523 *Case of the Serrano-Cruz Sisters v. El Salvador* (Inter-American Court of Human Rights, Judgement of 23 November 2004, (Preliminary Objections)), *see* Braid and Roht-Arriaza, 'De Facto and De Jure Amnesty Laws', 202.

524 *Case of the Massacres of el Mozote and Nearby Places v. El Salvador* (Inter-American Court of Human Rights, 25 October 2012).

525 Tico Times, *Human Rights Court Condemns El Salvador for El Mozote Massacre.* http://www.ticotimes.net/More-news/News-Briefs/Human-rights-court-condemns-El-Salvador-for-El-Mozote-massacre_Tuesday-December-11-2012 (12 December 2016); Braid and Roht-Arriaza, 'De Facto and De Jure Amnesty Laws', 202–3.

526 *Case of the Massacre's of El Mozote and Nearby Places v. El Salvador* (Inter-American Court of Human Rights, 25 October 2012), para.295.

of those responsible for the facts, thus failing to comply with Articles 1(1) and 2 of the Convention; the latter in relation to the obligation to adapt its domestic law to the provisions of the Convention."[527] Due to the political change in El Salvador's government, an increasingly negative attitude towards the amnesty law emerged from 2010 onward.[528] Although it had taken time and represented only the first step, the then President Mauricio Funes recognised the responsibility of the military for serious human rights violations during the civil war and publicly apologized for the El Mozote massacre.[529] However, this did not necessarily mean that a similar change occurred on the legal front as no perpetrators had yet been prosecuted.[530] It was only in 2014 that the Salvadoran Supreme Court induced the investigation of civil war massacres and contemplated the annulment of the country's amnesty law.[531] Finally, in July 2016, the same court repealed the amnesty law, declaring that its provisions violate the constitution as well as El Salvador's obligations under international law.[532] The judges reasoned, *inter alia*, that Article 6 (5) of Additional Protocol II „*is not absolute and unconditional, since it must be construed in light of other international provisions embodying obligations to respect and safeguard fundamental rights, which therefore restrict the scope and effects of amnesties declared in post-conflict situations. Hence this provision must be interpreted restrictively and confined to acts of war of the parties to the conflict and not encompass grave and systematic violations of constitutional rules and international law, such as crimes against humanity and war crimes.*"[533]The Court further argued that the amnesty law „*[...] is contrary to the right to judicial and non-judicial protection (Article*

527 Ibid., para.296.

528 Braid and Roht-Arriaza, 'De Facto and De Jure Amnesty Laws', 206–7.

529 Ibid., 206; International Center for Transitional Justice (ICTJ), *Twenty Years Later, A Chance for Accountability in El Salvador*. http://ictj.org/news/twenty-years-later-chance-accountability-el-salvador (13 December 2016).

530 International Center for Transitional Justice (ICTJ), *Twenty Years Later, A Chance for Accountability in El Salvador*.

531 N. Renteria, *El Salvador Top Court Orders Probe of Civil War Massacre*. http://www.reuters.com/article/2014/02/06/us-elsalvador-justice-idUSBREA1506K20140206 (13 December 2016).

532 International Center for Transitional Justice (ICTJ), *With Amnesty Law Overturned in El Salvador, Prosecutors Must Work with Victims to Investigate Civil War Atrocities*.

533 *Sala de lo Constitucional de la Corte Suprema de Justicia: Incostitucionalidad 44–2013/145–2013, San Salvador*, (unofficial translation, footnotes omitted). http://www.jurisprudencia.gob.sv/VisorMLX/PDF/44-2013AC.PDF (04 February 2019), para.8.

2, paragraph 1, and Article 144, paragraph 2, of the Constitution, read with Articles 1, paragraph 1, and 2 of the American Convention on Human Rights, Article 2, paragraph 2, of the International Covenant on Civil and Political Rights and Article 4 of Additional Protocol II), because it prevents compliance with the State's obligations to prevent, investigate, prosecute, punish and redress serious breaches of fundamental rights. "[534]

In ***Guatemala*** the civil war lasted for over 30 years and was characterised, on the one hand, by killings which reached the dimension of genocide and, on the other hand, by the enactment of numerous blanket amnesty laws which, however, did not help in stopping the war.[535] In 1996, after several years of peace negotiations, the final peace agreement was approved.[536] It contained a limited amnesty[537], excluding some, but not all, crimes under international law from its scope.[538] The crimes of genocide, torture and forced disappearance were not covered by the amnesty law.[539] Nonetheless, this did not lead to extensive prosecutions of those responsible for these crimes.[540] Furthermore, crimes against humanity, war crimes and other serious violations of human rights had not been excluded from the scope of the amnesty.[541] Nevertheless, the deliberate choice of precluding the granting of amnesty in certain cases of international crimes was an absolute novelty in Latin-America at that time.[542] Shortly after the amnesty law was implemented, it was challenged by human rights activists on the grounds that it was unconstitutional, as it violated internal law.[543] In 1997 the Guatemalan Constitutional Court decided, however, that the amnesty law was in accordance with the constitution as it could be interpreted and applied in a way consistent with international law.[544] Moreover, in 2001 in the Dos Erres massacre case, the

534 Ibid., p. 16.
535 Mallinder, 'Amnesties', 841.
536 Ibid., 842.
537 Ley de Reconciliación Nacional, Decree 145–96.
538 UN Office of the High Commissioner for Human Rights, *Rule-of-Law Tools for Post-Conflict States*, p. 39.
539 Ley de Reconciliación Nacional, Decree 145–96, Art. 8, *see* Henckaerts and Doswald-Beck (eds.), *Customary International Humanitarian Law*, pp. 4024–5.
540 Mallinder, 'Amnesties', 843.
541 UN Office of the High Commissioner for Human Rights, *Rule-of-Law Tools for Post-Conflict States*, p. 39.
542 Mallinder, 'Amnesties', 842.
543 Braid and Roht-Arriaza, 'De Facto and De Jure Amnesty Laws', 186.
544 Guatemalan Constitutional Court Opinion on Amnesty, No. 8–97, 20–97, October 7, 1997, *see* ibid., 186.

same court determined that the amnesty law was applicable to the officers who ordered and carried out the massacre.[545] International human rights bodies, such as the UN Committee against Torture and the Inter-American Court of Human Rights intervened, for example, by condemning the state of impunity and demanding criminal proceedings in cases of serious human rights violations.[546] In November 2009, the Inter-American Court stated that the application of the amnesty law in the Dos Erres massacre case constituted a violation of Articles 8 (Right to a Fair Trial) and 25 (Right to Judicial Protection) of the American Convention on Human Rights.[547] As a result of this judgement, the Guatemalan Supreme Court concluded in February 2010 that amnesty in the Dos Erres case was inapplicable.[548] Consequently, proceedings against those responsible for the massacre were launched and finally, in July 2011 and in March 2012, the perpetrators were convicted and sentenced to long prison terms.[549] Due to the persistent pressure exerted by international human rights bodies, domestic human rights groups and, not least, the former attorney general Claudia Paz y Paz and her legal team the number of prosecutions increased from 2010.[550] Probably the most prominent trial was that of former Guatemalan dictator Efraín Ríos Montt. In May 2013, he was convicted of genocide and crimes against humanity committed during the civil war in the 1980's.[551] Only a few days later, however, Guatemala's

545 Ibid., 191.

546 Ibid., 187, 191; BBC, *Ex-Paramilitaries Jailed for Guatemala Massacre*. http://www.bbc.co.uk/news/world-latin-america-17454434 (14 December 2016).

547 *Case of the Las Dos Erres Massacre v. Guatemala* (Inter-American Court of Human Rights, 24 November 2009), para. 131;Braid and Roht-Arriaza, 'De Facto and De Jure Amnesty Laws', 190–2 Braid and Roht-Arriaza, 'De Facto and De Jure Amnesty Laws', 191.

548 Braid and Roht-Arriaza, 'De Facto and De Jure Amnesty Laws', 191.

549 Ibid., 192; N. Quinones, *6,060 Years in Prison for Former Guatemalan Soldier*. http://edition.cnn.com/2012/03/13/world/americas/guatemala-human-rights-trial/index.html (14 December 2016).

550 Braid and Roht-Arriaza, 'De Facto and De Jure Amnesty Laws', 187–188, 194–196.

551 International Center for Transitional Justice (ICTJ), *Anniversary of Guatemala's Genocide Verdict Marked by Denial and Polarization*. http://ictj.org/multimedia/audio/anniversary-guatemala-genocide-verdict-marked-denial-and-polarization?utm_source=International+Center+for+Transitional+Justice+Newsletter&utm_campaign=5c2da04a39-World_Report_Issue_35_May_2014&utm_medium=email&utm_term=0_2d90950d4d-5c2da04a39-237811229 (14 December 2016); S. Brodzinsky and J. Watts, *Former Guatemalan Dictator Convicted of Genocide and Jailed for 80 Years*. http://www.theguardian.com/world/2013/may/11/guatemala

Constitutional Court annulled the conviction and ordered a retrial because the trial should have been stopped while appeals filed by the defence were resolved.[552] This decision marked the beginning of a change in the judicial and political landscape where conservative forces became stronger.[553] In order to ensure justice, a petition was filed by human rights and victims' organisations before the Inter-American Commission on Human Rights in November 2013 to convict Guatemala for the declaration of impunity in the Ríos Montt case.[554] In May 2014, attorney general Claudia Paz y Paz had to step down, seven months before her term officially ended[555] and 'right-wing' lawyer Thelma Esperanza Aldana Hernández was appointed in her place.[556] This meant that the fight against impunity in Guatemala, vigorously pushed by the former prosecutor Paz y Paz, further lost momentum.[557] What's more, at the same time the Guatemalan Congress adopted a nonbinding resolution denying genocide during the civil war.[558] In addition, the scheduled retrial of Efraín Ríos Montt has repeatedly been suspended for reasons such as the court's busy schedule or an assumed

---

n-dictator-rios-montt-jailed-genocide (14 December 2016); International Center for Transitional Justice (ICTJ), *Conviction of Ríos Montt on Genocide a Victory for Justice in Guatemala, and Everywhere*. http://www.ictj.org/news/ictj-conviction-rios-montt-genocide-victory-justice-guatemala-and-everywhere (14 December 2016).

552 The guardian, *Guatemala Overturns Former Dictator's Genocide Conviction*. http://www.theguardian.com/world/2013/may/21/guatemala-efrain-rios-montt-genocide-conviction (14 December 2016); L. Carasik, *Rios Montt Edges Closer to Escaping Accountability for Genocide*. http://america.aljazeera.com/opinions/2013/11/rios-montt-guatemalagenocidetrial.html.

553 International Center for Transitional Justice (ICTJ), *Lawyers for Guatemala's Ixil Community Take Justice Demands to Inter-American Commission*. http://ictj.org/news/lawyers-ixil-justice-demands (14 December 2016); E. MacLean, *Guatemala Justice Update, January 2014: Rios Montt Trial Faces Continued Challenges as Guatemala Selects New Slate of Judges and Attorney General*. https://www.ijmonitor.org/2014/01/guatemala-justice-update-january-2014/ (14 December 2016).

554 International Center for Transitional Justice (ICTJ), *Lawyers for Guatemala's Ixil Community Take Justice Demands to Inter-American Commission*.

555 S. Perez, *Guatemalan Court Upholds Top Prosecutor's Ouster*. http://bigstory.ap.org/article/guatemalan-court-upholds-top-prosecutors-ouster (14 December 2016).

556 K. Alford-Jones, *Guatemala's New 'Right-wing' Attorney General Raises Questions and Fears*. http://upsidedownworld.org/main/guatemala-archives-33/4851-guatemalas-new-right-wing-attorney-general-raises-questions-and-fears- (15 December 2016).

557 Ibid.

558 International Center for Transitional Justice (ICTJ), *Anniversary of Guatemala's Genocide Verdict Marked by Denial and Polarization*.

conflict of interest on the part of a judge.[559] Because of his poor health and his advanced age it is far from clear whether the trial will ever be finalised.[560] In January 2019 the Guatemalan Congress initiated an amendment of the 1996 National Reconciliation Law.[561] If adopted, the amendment means that perpetrators in jail for enforced disappearances, summary executions, sexual violence and torture, will be released from prison within 24 hours.[562] The UN High Commissioner for Human Rights, Michelle Bachelet said: *"This in effect means complete impunity for all those involved in some truly horrendous violations, including crimes against humanity [...]"*.[563] She highlighted that amnesties for the most serious crimes are *"incompatible with State obligations to prosecute grave violations of human rights."*.[564]

In the case of ***Brazil*** the military dictatorship lasted between 1964 and 1985, but was not as violent as in other Latin-American countries. Instead the military government harassed the local population through economic and social repression.[565] Brazil's transition to democracy began in 1979 with the enactment of an amnesty law[566] by the military rulers.[567] A special feature of the law was that it not only contained an amnesty for political

559 M. Castillo and P. Vasquez, *Guatemala Genocide Trial Hits Hurdles: Rios Montt Accused in Massacres of 1,700 Ixil Mayans in '80s*. http://www.wptz.com/guatemala-genocide-trial-hits-hurdles/30559846 (07 January 2015); S. Beaudoin, *Appeals Court's Decision Suspends Genocide Trial*. http://www.ijmonitor.org/2015/10/appeals-courts-decision-suspends-genocide-trial/ (17 December 2015); S. Beaudoin, *Guatemala Opens a New Court to Hear Cases Related to Grave Crimes*. http://www.ijmonitor.org/2015/11/guatemala-opens-a-new-court-to-hear-cases-related-to-grave-crimes/ (17.12.15); Reuters, *Genocide Trial for Guatemala Ex-Dictator Rios Montt Suspended*. http://www.reuters.com/article/us-guatemala-trial-idUSKCN0UP21F20160111 (29 November 2016).

560 Reuters, *Genocide Trial for Guatemala Ex-Dictator Rios Montt Suspended*; Castillo and Vasquez, *Guatemala Genocide Trial Hits Hurdles*.

561 The European Sting, *Amending Guatemala 'Reconciliation Law' Would Lead to Unjust Amnesty, Warns Bachelet*. https://europeansting.com/2019/01/23/amending-guatemala-reconciliation-law-would-lead-to-unjust-amnesty-warns-bachelet/ (08 February 2019).

562 Ibid.

563 Ibid.

564 Ibid.

565 P. Abrão and M. D. Torelly, 'Resistance to Change: Brazil's Persistent Amnesty and its Alternatives for Truth and Justice' in F. Lessa and L. A. Payne (eds.), *Amnesty in the Age of Human Rights Accountability: Comparative and International Perspectives* (Cambridge, New York: Cambridge University Press, 2012), pp. 152–81, at p. 155.

566 Lei No. 6.683/1979 (28 August 1979).

567 Abrão and Torelly, 'Resistance to Change', 153.

and related crimes[568], but also reparation measures, such as the restitution of political rights and the right to job reinstatement for those who had been removed from their position for political reasons.[569] This is why the Brazilian people supported the adoption of the amnesty law.[570] Nonetheless, due to the amnesty provision, those responsible for human rights violations have not been prosecuted and hence, many victims have been deprived of their right to justice.[571] In response to this situation of impunity, the Brazilian Ministry of Justice organised a public hearing in 2008, to gauge the limits and possibilities of holding the perpetrators accountable for their actions.[572] Following this, the Supreme Court was consulted in order to determine whether or not the amnesty law was in breach of the Brazilian constitution.[573] In April 2010, the Supreme Court justified the application of the amnesty law under the constitution with regard to perpetrators of human rights crimes.[574] The Court recognised the dictatorship as a legitimate rule of law regime and thus, accepted the amnesty law as a political tool.[575] Furthermore, the Court reaffirmed the exclusive competence of the legislative branch to reconsider the law.[576] The Inter-American Court of Human Rights strongly disagreed with this ruling and criticised in *Gomes Lund et al. vs. Brazil* in November 2010[577] the Supreme Court's interpretation of the amnesty law.[578] The Court emphasised that the law violated the American Convention on Human Rights, including the rights to life, liberty, and personal security (Articles 1, 4, and 7), juridical personality (Article 3), humane treatment (Article 5), fair trial (Article 8),

568 *See* Lei No. 6.683/1979 (28 August 1979), Art. 1, *reprinted in Case of Gomes Lund et al. ("Guerrilha do Araguaia") v. Brazil* (Inter-American Court of Human Rights, 24 November 2010), para 134.
569 Abrão and Torelly, 'Resistance to Change', 153.
570 Ibid., 153.
571 Ibid., 164.
572 Ibid., 165.
573 Ibid., 165.
574 Case ADPF 153/ DF–Distrito Federal, Plenary Judgment, 29 April 2010, *see* ibid., 165, 176–178; Sain, *Latin American Amnesty Laws Annulled; the Struggle Against Impunity Continues*.
575 Case ADPF 153/ DF–Distrito Federal, Plenary Judgment, 29 April 2010, *see* Abrão and Torelly, 'Resistance to Change', 177.
576 Ibid., 165.
577 *Case of Gomes Lund et al. ("Guerrilha do Araguaia") v. Brazil* (Inter-American Court of Human Rights, 24 November 2010).
578 *Case of Gomes Lund et al. ("Guerrilha do Araguaia") v. Brazil* (Inter-American Court of Human Rights, 24 November 2010), para. 173, 175; Abrão and Torelly, 'Resistance to Change', 1656.

the right to information (Article 13) and judicial protection (Article 25) by forcibly disappearing the victims and withholding access to truth and information from their families.[579] Moreover, the amnesty law should not be an obstacle to criminal proceedings in cases of serious international crimes.[580] However, for a variety of reasons, the question of impunity has never had priority for the Brazilian authorities. Those reasons are, *inter alia*, the lasting influence by the former military rulers and their adherents, who all benefited from the amnesty provision, as well as a lack of commitment on the part of civil society.[581] Compared to other Latin-American countries, the relatively fragmented social and human rights movements in Brazil do not campaign as strongly for accountability, but instead focus on other — in their view, more pressing — social demands.[582] Although the criminal law approach therefore remains inadequate[583], the National Congress of Brazil at least established a truth commission in November 2011.[584] The commission's mandate was to examine and clarify the severe human rights violations committed between 1946 and 1988.[585] During the course of the truth commission's work, Brazil's Defence Minister authorised investigations into military facilities where human rights abuses had allegedly been perpetrated.[586] In December 2014, Brazil's truth commission published its final report, calling on the judiciary to hold perpetrators of serious human rights violations to account and to disregard the amnesty

579 C. Osberg, *Inter-American Court Invalidates Amnesty Law Enacted during Brazil's Military Dictatorship*. http://hrbrief.org/2011/04/inter-american-court-invalidate s-amnesty-law-enacted-during-brazil-military-dictatorship/ (12 February 2014); Open Society Foundations, *Gomes Lund v. Brazil*. http://www.opensocietyfound ations.org/litigation/gomes-lund-v-brazil (12 February 2014).

580 Ibid., para. 172, 174; Sain, *Latin American Amnesty Laws Annulled; the Struggle Against Impunity Continues.*

581 Abrão and Torelly, 'Resistance to Change', 170–4.

582 Ibid., 174–175, 181.

583 Up to December 2013, only four criminal proceedings regarding serious human rights violation committed during the dictatorship, had been initiated. *See* L. J. Ferreira-Hidaka, *Accountability for Gross Human Rights Violations in Brazil: The Araguaia Case and Its Repercussions*. http://lostintranslationbrazil.wordpress.com/ 2013/12/10/accountability-for-gross-human-rights-violations-in-brazil-the-aragua ia-case-and-its-repercussions/ (19 December 2016); M. Sibaja, 'Brazil Prosecutors: Judge Takes First Junta Case', The Huffington Post, 31 August 2012.

584 Truth Commission Law No. 12,528/2011, *see* Abrão and Torelly, 'Resistance to Change', 178–9.

585 Ibid., 179.

586 'Brazil to Focus on Past Abuses', The New York Times, 01 April 2014.

law, as it contradicts Brazilian and international law.[587] Shortly before this announcement, in September 2014, the Federal Supreme Court of Brazil decided in a case against five military officers that they were protected by the amnesty law of 1979.[588]

Another example of a Latin American country upholding or even extending its amnesty law is ***Suriname***, where a military government under Desiré Bouterse has ruled since 1980. In December 1982, 15 prominent political opponents were abducted and murdered by the military regime.[589] The situation deteriorated further and a civil war lasted between 1986 and 1992. In 1992, the Parliament enacted an amnesty law with retroactive effect, invalidating all proceedings concerning human rights violations perpetrated between 1985 and 1991.[590] Crimes against humanity were exempted from the scope of the amnesty.[591] In April 2008, a military tribunal in Suriname decided to initiate criminal proceedings against those allegedly responsible for the "December killings" of 1982, including former military ruler and current President Bouterse.[592] In response to this accusation the Parliament, controlled by Bouterse's party, passed an amended amnesty law in April 2012, even before the trial against Bouterse could be finalised.[593] The new law extended the period covered by the amnesty from April 1980 to August 1992 and thus granted impunity for the atrocious crimes committed in December 1982.[594] The amended law further stated that amnesty is accorded to those who *"have committed criminal offences*

587 International Center for Transitional Justice (ICTJ), *ICTJ Welcomes the Historic Final Report from Brazil's National Truth Commission*. http://www.ictj.org/news/ictj-welcomes-historic-final-report-brazil%E2%80%99s-national-truth-commission (18 December 2016).

588 A. Richter, V. Aguiar and A. Queiroz, *Supreme Court Halts Proceedings Against Military Accused of Dictatorship Crimes*. http://agenciabrasil.ebc.com.br/en/politica/noticia/2014-09/supreme-court-halts-proceedings-against-military-accused-dictatorship (19 December 2016).

589 Human Rights Watch, *Suriname: Revoke Amnesty Legislation*. http://www.hrw.org/news/2012/04/18/suriname-revoke-amnesty-legislation (20 December 2016).

590 Inter-American Commission on Human Rights, *Aldea de Moiwana v. Suriname: Case 11.821, Report No 26/00*, OEA/Ser.L/V/II.106 Doc. 3 rev. at 278 (1999). http://hrlibrary.umn.edu/cases/26-00.html (20 December 2016), para 7.

591 Ibid., para 7.

592 JURIST Legal News & Research, *Suriname Lawmakers Pass Amnesty Bill Ending President's Trial*. http://jurist.org/paperchase/2012/04/suriname-lawmakers-pass-amnesty-bill-ending-presidents-trial.php (20 December 2016).

593 Mallinder, 'The End of Amnesty or Regional Overreach?', 675.

594 Amnesty International, *Annual Report: Suriname 2013*. http://www.amnestyusa.org/research/reports/annual-report-suriname-2013 (20 December 2016).

and/or are suspected of having done so within the framework of the defence of the State and/or overthrow of the lawful authorities such as the events occurring during December 1982 and the Guerrilla War".[595] This clearly constitutes a self-amnesty for Bouterse and his co-defendants.[596] The law provoked strong criticism from national opponents as well as international human rights bodies, such as the Inter-American Commission on Human Rights and the Office of the UN High Commissioner for Human Rights.[597] In June 2016 a military court declared that the amended amnesty law was in breach of Suriname's constitution[598] and furthermore, violated several international treaties that Suriname had signed.[599] What impact this decision will have on the trial against Bouterse and his co-defendants remains to be seen. At present a local court hears cases against 14 suspects, including Bouterse. In his case the prosecutors have already recommended a 20-year prison sentence.[600]

Apart from the latter examples of Brazil and Suriname, it has been shown that state practice with regard to amnesties in most Latin American countries has developed towards abolishing or at least limiting blanket and unconditional amnesty laws. As indicated at the beginning of this chapter, this development is attributable to various factors. For example, the establishment of well-fortified democracies which are influenced by the resolutions and judgements of international human rights bodies, such as the Inter-American Court of Human Rights, as well as the outstanding engagement of civil society were indispensable conditions for rethinking the blanket amnesty laws which shielded the old military regimes. The change in the approach regarding amnesties in Latin America is very well

595 Ibid.

596 Human Rights Watch, *Suriname: Revoke Amnesty Legislation*.

597 Ibid; Amnesty International, *Annual Report: Suriname 2013*.

598 E.g. Article 131 (3) of the Constitution forbids any interference in the investigation or prosecution of cases, *see International Commission of Jurists, Independent Observation Mission to the Trial of President Desiré Delano Bouterse and Others in Relation to Extrajudicial Executions That Took Place in December 1982 at Fort Zeelandia, Paramaribo, Suriname: Statement on the Importance of Resuming the Trial Without Undue Delay.* https://www.icj.org/wp-content/uploads/2017/05/Suriname-Justice-delayed-Bouterse-case-Advocacy-2017-ENG.pdf *(04 February 2019).*

599 DailyMail – MailOnline, *Court: Murder Trial Against Suriname President Must Continue*. http://www.dailymail.co.uk/wires/ap/article-3634186/Court-Murder-trial-against-Suriname-leader-continue.html (20 December 2016).

600 B. Wilkinson, *Court to Soon Rule in Military Executions Trial in Suriname*. http://amsterdamnews.com/news/2018/nov/08/court-soon-rule-military-executions-trial-suriname/ (04 February 2019).

illustrated by the example of ***Colombia***. In 2012, peace negotiations between the Colombian government and left-wing guerrillas Revolutionary Armed Forces of Colombia – People's Army (FARC-EP) were initiated and a final peace agreement was promulgated in August 2016. The agreement determines, *inter alia*, that Article 6 (5) of Protocol II of the Geneva Conventions will be applied, and that *"the political and related offences committed as part of rebellion by the persons that are part of rebel groups with whom a peace agreement is being signed, will be granted amnesty or pardon. [...] Among the political and related crimes are, for example, rebellion, sedition, military uprising, as well as illegal possession of weapons, death in combat compatible with International Humanitarian Law, agreement to commit an offence to the purpose of rebellion and other related offences."*[601] It further specifies that *"Crimes against humanity, genocide, serious war crimes, hostage taking or another severe deprivation of physical liberty, torture, extrajudicial executions, forced disappearance, violent sexual intercourse and other kinds of sexual violence, child abduction, forced displacement, as well as the recruitment of minors, according to what has been established by the Rome Statute, won't be eligible for amnesty or pardon.*"[602] Instead of amnesty, perpetrators of these serious international crimes will receive 'alternative sanctions' such as community service in order to contribute to reparation, peace and reconciliation, provided they confess their guilt and help to uncover the truth.[603] Many Colombians were dissatisfied with this regulation as it would be much too lenient towards the perpetrators.[604] Hence, the peace agreement was narrowly rejected in a referendum in October 2016.[605] Shortly after the failed referendum, the negotiating parties signed a revised peace deal which was approved by the Colombian Congress on 30 November 2016, without consulting the voters this time.[606] Although the amended peace agreement includes a provision which clarifies the procedure before a special court in the case of serious human rights crimes, it still does not

601 FARC-EP International, *Agreement Victims*. http://farc-epeace.org/peace-process/agreements/agreements/item/939-agreement-victims (22 December 2016), para 37–8.

602 Ibid., para 40.

603 C. Kress, 'Frieden statt Recht?', Süddeutsche Zeitung, 27 August 2016, p. 5; Mallinder, 'The End of Amnesty or Regional Overreach?', 675–6.

604 N. Casey, 'Colombia's Congress Approves Peace Accord With FARC', The New York Times, 30 November 2016.

605 Ibid.

606 Ibid.

allow for prison sentences in these cases.[607] Apart from the crucial question whether the 'alternative sanctions' are sufficient to fulfil the international duty to prosecute serious human rights violations[608], it is notable that Colombia turned away from blanket and unconditional amnesties. Instead it opted for limited amnesties for political and related offences, as well as at least 'alternative sanctions' in exchange for confession and truth in cases of international crimes.[609] In addition to Colombia, the changed approach to amnesties in many Latin American countries seems also to have had impact on the above-mentioned decision of Suriname's military court to condemn the recently enacted amnesty law. Whether or not the regional trend in Latin American countries to abolish or restrict their broad and unconditional amnesty laws of the 1980s and 1990s can also be observed in other parts of the world, is examined in the following.

3.2.1.2 African States

In ***South Africa*** the fight against the apartheid regime, which institutionalised racial discrimination and segregation from 1948 onwards, was very long and in part extremely violent.[610] In the course of peace negotiations which started in 1993, a blanket amnesty, *inter alia* for anti-apartheid activists, had been considered but finally rejected.[611] However, the Interim Constitution of 1993 determined that "*In order to advance such reconciliation and reconstruction, amnesty shall be granted in respect of acts, omissions and offences associated with political objectives and committed in the course of the conflicts of the past. To this end, Parliament under this Constitution shall adopt a law [...] providing for the mechanisms, criteria and procedures, including tribunals, if any, through which such amnesty shall be dealt with at any time after the law has been passed.*"[612] In accordance with this provision, the South African Parliament passed the 'Promotion of National Unity and Reconciliation Act' in 1995.[613] The act entailed the establishment of a Truth and

607 Ibid.

608 Kress, 'Frieden statt Recht?'.

609 Mallinder, 'The End of Amnesty or Regional Overreach?', 675–6.

610 Roht-Arriaza and Gibson, 'The Developing Jurisprudence on Amnesty', 856.

611 Van Eijl, *Dealing with Crimes of the Past: No More Amnesty? An Inquiry into the Lawfulness of Amnesty for Human Rights Atrocities Under International Law*, p. 19.

612 *Constitution of the Republic of South Africa: Act 200 of 1993* (1994).

613 *Promotion of National Unity and Reconciliation Act: Act 34 of 1995* (1995); Roht-Arriaza and Gibson, 'The Developing Jurisprudence on Amnesty', 856.

Reconciliation Commission (TRC) including an Amnesty Committee[614], which was authorised to grant immunity from civil and criminal liability for political crimes, and encompassing international crimes, provided these crimes occurred between March 1960 and May 1994.[615] Additionally, it was necessary for the amnesty applicant to make *"a full disclosure of all relevant facts"*[616] in order to contribute to the process of truth-finding and reconciliation.[617] This last requirement was a novelty at that time and thus makes the South African amnesty particularly noteworthy.[618] Perpetrators who did not apply for amnesty within the prescribed period[619] or those who did not meet the conditions for amnesty would instead be prosecuted.[620] Shortly after the Amnesty Committee had been established, the constitutionality of the amnesty provision was questioned by relatives of victims of the apartheid era, in a case known as *Azanian People's Organisation (AZAPO) and Others vs. the President of the Republic of South Africa* of 1996.[621] The applicants argued that their constitutional right to have disputes settled by a court of law (Section 22 of the Constitution) as well as international law (for example the Geneva Conventions of 1949 which require penal sanction in cases of grave breaches of the conventions) had been violated by the granting of immunity from civil and criminal liability to perpetrators of the crimes concerned.[622] The Constitutional Court of South Africa rejected the arguments of the petitioners. The judges declared the amnesty provision constitutional and held that the epilogue ('National Unity and Reconciliation') to the Constitution sanctioned the limitation

---

614 *Promotion of National Unity and Reconciliation Act: Act 34 of 1995* (1995), Section 16.

615 *Promotion of National Unity and Reconciliation Act: Act 34 of 1995* (1995), Section 20 (1)(b), 20 (2), 20 (7).

616 *Promotion of National Unity and Reconciliation Act: Act 34 of 1995* (1995), Section 20 (1)(c).

617 Van Eijl, *Dealing with Crimes of the Past: No More Amnesty? An Inquiry into the Lawfulness of Amnesty for Human Rights Atrocities Under International Law*, p. 19.

618 Ibid., p. 19.

619 *Promotion of National Unity and Reconciliation Act: Act 34 of 1995* (1995), Section 18 (1).

620 Roht-Arriaza and Gibson, 'The Developing Jurisprudence on Amnesty', 857; Mallinder, 'Amnesties', 891.

621 *Azanian Peoples Organization (AZAPO) and Others v President of the Republic of South Africa and Others* (Constitutional Court of South Africa, 25 July 1996).

622 Ibid., 11, 24.

on the right of access to court.[623] In their view, the granting of amnesty is a necessary incentive for offenders to disclose the truth about past atrocities. This fosters the process of reconciliation and reconstruction.[624] The court, moreover, refused to invoke the rules of international law as they were not relevant to that case.[625] It was argued that "*International conventions and treaties do not become part of the municipal law of our country, enforceable at the instance of private individuals in our courts, until and unless they are incorporated into the municipal law by legislative enactment. […] there is no obligation […] to ensure the prosecution of those who might have performed acts of violence or other acts which would ordinarily be characterised as serious invasions of human rights. On the contrary, article 6(5) of Protocol II to the Geneva Conventions of 1949 provides that "[a]t the end of hostilities, the authorities in power shall endeavour to grant the broadest possible amnesty to persons who participated in the armed conflict, or those deprived of their liberty for reasons related to the armed conflict, whether they are interned or detained.*""[626] In 1998, the Truth and Reconciliation Commission finished its work with the publication of its final report which included testimony from over 22 000 victims and witnesses.[627] The Commission recommended criminal proceedings in more than 300 cases,[628] but, although legally possible, there were hardly any prosecutions of human rights violations.[629] On the contrary, in a presidential pardons process, secret proceedings were held to accomplish 'the unfinished business of the Truth and Reconciliation Commission'[630], that is, to pardon those who had been convicted.[631] Furthermore, in 2005 the National Prosecuting Authority introduced amended

623 *Azanian Peoples Organisation (AZAPO) and Others v President of the Republic of South Africa and others: Case CCT 17/96*, Explanatory Note. http://www.saflii.org/za/cases/ZACC/1996/16media.pdf (05 February 2019).

624 Ibid.

625 Ibid., *Azanian Peoples Organization (AZAPO) and Others v President of the Republic of South Africa and Others*, para 26, 50; Roht-Arriaza and Gibson, 'The Developing Jurisprudence on Amnesty', 872–4.

626 *Azanian Peoples Organization (AZAPO) and Others v President of the Republic of South Africa and Others*, para.26, 30.

627 International Center for Transitional Justice (ICTJ), *South Africa*. https://www.ictj.org/our-work/regions-and-countries/south-africa (04 January 2017).

628 International Center for Transitional Justice (ICTJ), *South Africa: Impunity, Political Interference Emerge Below Veneer of a Celebrated Reconciliation Process*. https://www.ictj.org/multimedia/audio/south-africa-impunity-nokuthula-simelane-justice (05 January 2017).

629 Mallinder, 'Amnesties', 891.

630 International Center for Transitional Justice (ICTJ), *South Africa*.

631 Mallinder, 'Amnesties', 891.

prosecutorial guidelines for past crimes[632], which in fact meant nothing else than impunity for the perpetrators of apartheid-era crimes, who would otherwise have been prosecuted since they had failed to apply for amnesty under the 'Promotion of National Unity and Reconciliation Act (1995)'.[633] In 2008, however, the Pretoria High Court determined that the amended prosecutorial guidelines contradicted the South African constitution, as they resulted in *de facto* amnesties for the perpetrators of past crimes in order to ensure their future political as well as economic support for the government.[634] The granting of amnesties during the TRC process, in contrast, fostered the transition and reconciliation and was thus in accordance with the constitution.[635] In 2010, the Constitutional Court decided that the right of victims to be consulted before political pardons were granted must be respected.[636] Despite these rulings, only a few perpetrators have been prosecuted up to now.[637] It must therefore be concluded that, due to political and legal shortcomings, South Africa's initial innovative approach to transitional justice could not be realised in its entirety. Victims' rights have been disregarded and a policy of impunity for serious human rights violations prevails.[638]

---

632 National Prosecuting Authority of South Africa, *Prosecution Policy and Directives Relating to the Prosecution of Criminal Matters Arising from Conflicts of the Past.* http://pmg-assets.s3-website-eu-west-1.amazonaws.com/docs/2005/060117nel.htm (05 January 2017).

633 Mallinder, 'Amnesties', 891; International Center for Transitional Justice (ICTJ), *South Africa*.

634 *Nkadimeng and Others v National Director of Public Prosecutions and Others* (High Court of South Africa, 12 December 2008); B. Schmolze, *Ein wichtiger Sieg für die Gerechtigkeit: Amnestiepolitik der südafrikanischen Anklagebehörde für verfassungswidrig erklärt.* http://www.gerechtigkeit-heilt.de/texte/suedafrika-amnestiepolitik.html (04 January 2017).

635 *Nkadimeng and Others v National Director of Public Prosecutions and Others* (High Court of South Africa, 12 December 2008); Schmolze, *Ein wichtiger Sieg für die Gerechtigkeit.*

636 International Center for Transitional Justice (ICTJ), *South Africa.*

637 In February 2016, the National Prosecuting Authority launched criminal proceedings against four apartheid-era perpetrators. *See* International Center for Transitional Justice (ICTJ), *South Africa: Impunity, Political Interference Emerge Below Veneer of a Celebrated Reconciliation Process.*

638 International Center for Transitional Justice (ICTJ), *ICTJ Denounces South African Government's Attempt to Exit the International Criminal Court.* https://www.ictj.org/news/ictj-denounces-south-africa-icc-withdrawl (29 November 2016); P. Seils, 'Political Pardons Would Damage the Legacy of South Africa's Truth and Reconciliation Commission', The Huffington Post, 06 March 2015.

A further interesting example of amnesties practice in African States is ***Uganda***. The longstanding and brutal civil war between the Lord's Resistance Army (LRA) and the Ugandan government lasted until 2006. In the course of the war several attempts were made to bring the fighting to an end and to agree on a peace process. The Amnesty Act of 2000, for example, determined that "*An Amnesty is declared in respect of any Ugandan who has at any time since the 26th day of January, 1986 engaged in or is engaging in war or armed rebellion against the government of the Republic of Uganda [...]*"[639]. The Act was amended in 2002 and again in 2006 to clarify the scope of the amnesty. The aim of the 2006 amendment was to exclude the leaders of the rebellion from receiving amnesty. Therefore the Act contained a provision stating that "*[...] a person shall not be eligible for grant of amnesty if he or she is declared not eligible by the Minister by statutory instrument made with the approval of Parliament.*"[640] The Minister of Internal Affairs thus had the power to deny the granting of amnesty in certain cases.[641] In accordance with this changed approach, the Ugandan government requested the ICC in 2003 to investigate the alleged commission of international crimes by the LRA.[642] In the following years the Ugandan authorities took further steps in the pursuit of justice and accountability.[643] This development culminated in the abolishment of the blanket amnesty provision of the Amnesty Act in May 2012.[644] In the view of some civil society organisations and religious and cultural leaders the annulment of the amnesty provision was counterproductive as peace and

639 *The Amnesty Act, 2000*, Uganda, Article 3. P. Girke and M. Kamp, *Norduganda: Frieden versus Gerechtigkeit?* http://www.kas.de/wf/doc/kas_18362-1522-1-30.pdf?091209114909 (05 January 2017), p. 2.

640 *The Amnesty Amendment Act, 2006*, Uganda. http://www.ulii.org/ug/legislation/act/2015/2006 (05 January 2017).

641 Mallinder, *Amnesty, Human Rights and Political Transitions:*, pp. 38–9.

642 Ibid., pp. 38–9.

643 For example: The signing of the ‚Agreement on Accountability and Reconciliation between the Government of the Republic of Uganda and the Lord's Resistance Army‘ in June 2007, which aimed to set up several transitional justice mechanisms, including criminal prosecutions in order to cope with the atrocities of the civil war. See M. Otim and K. S. Kihika, *On the Path to Vindicate Victims' Rights in Uganda: Reflections on the Transitional Justice Process Since Juba*. https://www.ictj.org/sites/default/files/ICTJ-Briefing-Uganda-TJProcess-2015_0.pdf (06.01.17), pp. 3–4.

644 IRIN – Humanitarian News and Analysis, *Uganda: No More Amnesty Certificates for Rebels*. http://www.irinnews.org/report/95569/uganda-no-more-amnesty-certificates-for-rebels (06 January 2017).

reconciliation would be jeopardised.[645] For this reason, they successfully petitioned the Ugandan Parliament to reinstate the amnesty provision in May 2013.[646] As a countermeasure, the government's Transitional Justice Working Group drafted the transitional justice policy in September 2014, which included the rejection of blanket amnesties as well as the encouragement to participate in truth-telling and traditional justice processes.[647] These contradictory processes demonstrate the hesitation by and difficulties of the Ugandan authorities in dealing with impunity for serious human rights violations.[648] Another example of discrepancy is the case of Thomas Kwoyelo, a former mid-level LRA commander, who was arrested and put on trial in 2009.[649] Since then several Ugandan courts have been concerned with his case and as a consequence with the amnesty provision of the Amnesty Act. In September 2011, the Constitutional Court decided that Thomas Kwoyelo had the legal right to amnesty under the Amnesty Act.[650] The Court further emphasised the constitutionality of the Act, since it contributed to peace and reconciliation in Uganda.[651] The compatibility of the amnesty provision with Uganda's international treaty obligations has not been considered by the judges.[652] The appeal hearing before the Supreme Court of Uganda was concluded in April 2015 with the ruling that the case of Thomas Kwoyelo must once again be referred to the International Crimes Division of the High Court of Uganda.[653] The Supreme Court judges deeply analysed international legal practice on amnesties and concluded that in the absence of a uniform standard or practice regarding amnesties, each country determines the approach to deal with its unique

645 K. S. Kihika and Regué Meritxell, *Pursuing Accountability for Serious Crimes in Uganda's Courts: Reflections on the Thomas Kwoyelo Case*. https://www.ictj.org/sites/default/files/ICTJ-Briefing-Uganda-Kwoyelo-2015.pdf (06 January 2017), p. 7.

646 Ibid., p. 7.

647 Otim and Kihika, *On the Path to Vindicate Victims' Rights in Uganda*, p. 5.

648 Ibid., p. 8.

649 S. Kasande, *Kwoyelo and Ongwen Trials Show Progress in Fight Against Impunity*. http://www.monitor.co.ug/OpEd/Commentary/Kwoyelo-and-Ongwen-trials-show-progress-in-fight-against/689364-3308688-pl7jgr/index.html (06 January 2017).

650 *Thomas Kwoyelo alias Latoni v. Uganda UGCC 10* (Constitutional Court of Uganda, 22 September 2011).

651 Ibid.

652 Kihika and Regué Meritxell, *Pursuing Accountability for Serious Crimes in Uganda's Courts*, pp. 5–6.

653 *Uganda versus Thomas Kwoyelo* (Supreme Court of Uganda, 08 April 2015); S. Nakandha, *Supreme Court of Uganda Rules on the Application of the Amnesty Act*. http://www.ijmonitor.org/2015/04/supreme-court-of-uganda-rules-on-the-application-of-the-amnesty-act/ (06 January 2017).

conflict situation.[654] However, they emphasised that serious international crimes cannot be amnestied.[655] Perpetrators of crimes under Article 8 (2) (e) of the Rome Statute and grave breaches under Article 147 of the Fourth Geneva Convention need instead to be prosecuted.[656] Despite these findings, they further stated that the Amnesty Act was not in violation of Uganda's international treaty obligation as the amnesty would not cover all crimes and, in addition, the Minister of Internal Affairs had the power to deny the granting of amnesty in certain cases.[657] The trial before the International Crimes Division of the High Court was however delayed because of a lack of resources and procedural problems.[658] Meanwhile, in June 2015, the Ugandan government extended the Amnesty Act for an additional period of two years.[659]

Another African State under consideration is the ***Democratic Republic of the Congo*** (DRC). The two Congo wars mainly took place in the east and northeast of the country between 1996 and 2003.[660] But even after the official end of the war the hostilities repeatedly flared up.[661] This resulted in the enactment of several amnesty laws, aimed at stopping the fighting and establishing peace. The Presidential Decree of April 2003 granted amnesty for acts of war, political breaches of the law, and crimes of opinion committed between August 1998 and April 2003.[662] The decree excluded genocide, war crimes, and crimes against humanity from its scope.[663] In December 2005 the Congolese transitional parliament issued a new amnesty law in which the period of time had been extended to include crimes committed between August 1996 and June 2003.[664] In order

---

654 Ibid.

655 Ibid.

656 Ibid.

657 Ibid.

658 Kasande, *Kwoyelo and Ongwen Trials Show Progress in Fight Against Impunity*.

659 S. Okiror, *Forgive and Forget? Amnesty Dilemma Haunts Uganda*. http://www.irinnews.org/report/101625/forgive-and-forget-amnesty-dilemma-haunts-uganda (09 January 2017).

660 Amnesty International, *The Time for Justice Is Now: New Strategy Needed in The Democratic Republic of the Congo*, AFR 62/006/2011. https://www.amnesty.org/en/documents/AFR62/006/2011/en/ (09 January 2017), p. 3.

661 International Center for Transitional Justice (ICTJ), *Amnesty Must Not Equal Impunity*. http://ictj.org/sites/default/files/ICTJ-DRC-Amnesty-Facts-2009-English.pdf (09 January 2017).

662 Presidential Decree №03–001 of April 15, 2003, *see* ibid.

663 Ibid.

664 Law №05/023 of December 19, 2005, *see* ibid.

to appease the war-torn country and support national reconciliation President Joseph Kabila implemented a further amnesty law in May 2009.[665] It determined that *"Amnesty is granted to all Congolese [...] for acts of war and insurrection committed in the provinces of North Kivu and South Kivu. [...] The present amnesty does not apply to the crime of genocide, war crimes and crimes against humanity."*[666] The temporal scope of the amnesty encompassed the period from June 2003 to the date of enactment of the amnesty law.[667] Although all the amnesty laws mentioned explicitly exclude genocide, war crimes and crimes against humanity, they have nevertheless prevented the investigation and prosecution of these atrocities.[668] The Congolese Minister of Justice, for example, ordered the Public Prosecutor not to put on trial members of certain armed groups and expressly referred to the Amnesty Law.[669] Those perpetrators of international crimes are instead still powerful and in positions of command.[670] Thus, peace and stability have taken priority over justice and accountability.[671] However, this approach has clearly failed, as former rebels and warlords still continue to commit serious human rights violations.[672] In 2013, a renewed attempt was made to overcome the failed policy of previous years. The Nairobi Declarations, a peace agreement between the DRC army and the M23 rebel group, included, *inter alia*, a proposal for an amnesty.[673] In February 2014, the Congolese Parliament adopted the proposed amnesty law granting impunity for acts of insurgency, acts of war, and political offences

665 Ibid; *Democratic Republic of Congo: Peace Agreement Between the Government and the Congrès National pour la Défense du Peuple (CNDP)*, Goma, March 23, 2009. http://friendsofthecongo.org/images/pdf/cndp_accord.pdf (09 January 2017).

666 *2009 DRC Amnesty Law: Law No. 09/003 of May 7, 2009*. http://content.glin.gov/summary/218412 (09 January 2017), Art. 1, 3, *see* International Center for Transitional Justice (ICTJ), *Amnesty Must Not Equal Impunity*.

667 *2009 DRC Amnesty Law: Law No. 09/003 of May 7, 2009* Art. 5, *see* International Center for Transitional Justice (ICTJ), *Amnesty Must Not Equal Impunity*.

668 Human Rights Watch, *Seductions of "Sequencing"*, 10, 16.

669 Amnesty International, *The Time for Justice Is Now*, 14.

670 Ibid., p. 38.

671 Human Rights Watch, *Seductions of "Sequencing"*, 10, 16.

672 Ibid., 10, 16; Amnesty International, *Democratic Republic Of The Congo: Annual Report 2013*. http://www.amnestyusa.org/research/reports/annual-report-democratic-republic-of-congo-2013?page=show (09 January 2017).

673 International Justice Resource Center, *DR Congo Parliament Approves New Amnesty Law for Insurgency and Other Crimes, as Part of Agreement with M23 Rebel Group*. http://www.ijrcenter.org/2014/02/10/dr-congo-parliament-approves-new-amnesty-law-for-insurgency-and-other-crimes-as-part-of-agreement-with-m23-rebel-group/ (09 January 2017).

dating back to 2006.[674] Crimes against humanity, war crimes and genocide were again excluded from the scope of the amnesty.[675] In this respect, the 2014 amnesty simply reproduces the previously mentioned amnesty laws. But beyond that similarity, the creation of a national reconciliation commission as well as the prosecution of the perpetrators who are most responsible for war crimes, acts of genocide, crimes against humanity, sexual violence and the recruitment of child soldiers had been envisaged.[676] In order to conduct proceedings concerning international crimes, specialised chambers within the Congolese courts should be established.[677] In fact, however, those who committed serious human rights violations are almost never tried[678], not least because of the weak justice system.[679] This contributes to ongoing violence and severe human rights abuses.[680]

Next, two other African States with an amnesty law are presented. They are only mentioned briefly here, as otherwise the scope of this study would be exceeded. In ***Libya*** the "Law on Some Measures Regarding the Transitional Period", enacted in May 2012 by the National Transitional Council,

674 Ibid; International Center for Transitional Justice (ICTJ), *DRC: Refusal to Pardon Serious Crimes Signals Justice Could Be on the Way*. http://ictj.org/news/drc-refusal-pardon-serious-crimes-signals-justice-could-be-way (11 January 2017).

675 International Justice Resource Center, *DR Congo Parliament Approves New Amnesty Law for Insurgency and Other Crimes, as Part of Agreement with M23 Rebel Group*; International Center for Transitional Justice (ICTJ), *DRC: Refusal to Pardon Serious Crimes Signals Justice Could Be on the Way*.

676 International Justice Resource Center, *DR Congo Parliament Approves New Amnesty Law for Insurgency and Other Crimes, as Part of Agreement with M23 Rebel Group*; International Center for Transitional Justice (ICTJ), *Experts Gather in Kinshasa to Discuss the National Judicial Response to Serious Crimes in the DRC*. http://www.ictj.org/news/experts-gather-kinshasa-discuss-national-judicial-response-serious-crimes-drc (11 January 2017).

677 International Justice Resource Center, *DR Congo Parliament Approves New Amnesty Law for Insurgency and Other Crimes, as Part of Agreement with M23 Rebel Group*.

678 M. Raymond-Jetté, *Small Gains on Large Crimes in DR Congo*. http://www.insightonconflict.org/2015/07/small-gains-large-crimes-dr-congo/ (11 January 2017); International Center for Transitional Justice (ICTJ), *Experts Gather in Kinshasa to Discuss the National Judicial Response to Serious Crimes in the DRC*; UN News Centre, *DR Congo: UN Officials Urge Justice for Grave Crimes Committed by M23*. http://www.globalsecurity.org/military/library/news/2014/10/mil-141009-unnews02.htm (11 January 2017).

679 Amnesty International, *Annual Report – Democratic Republic of the Congo 2015/2016*. https://www.amnesty.org/en/countries/africa/democratic-republic-of-the-congo/report-democratic-republic-of-the-congo/ (11 January 2017).

680 Ibid.

the interim legislative body, determined that *"there shall be no penalty for military, security, or civil actions dictated by the February 17 Revolution that were performed by revolutionaries with the goal of promoting or protecting the revolution."*[681] This means that amnesty was granted to fighters opposing Muammar Qaddafi for crimes relating to the February 2011 uprising. According to an UN commission of inquiry, the rebels had committed war crimes and crimes against humanity.[682] In addition, they were suspected of having participated in the extrajudicial killing of Qaddafi.[683] The effect of the amnesty provision has been that armed groups have continued to commit serious crimes on the alleged grounds that these actions are essential to protect the "17 February revolution".[684] Apart from the ICC prosecutor, Fatou Bensouda, who demanded that there should be no amnesty for international crimes in Libya[685], the international community has to a large extent overlooked the amnesty law.[686] Thus, the desire for peace seemed to be more important than the struggle for justice.[687] In ***Algeria***, following thirteen years of civil war between the Algerian army and rebel forces, an amnesty law had been enacted in February 2006[688].[689] The "Charter for Peace and National Reconciliation" granted amnesty to the members of armed groups provided that they were not involved in crimes such as mass

681 Law No 38 of 2012 on Some Measures Regarding the Transitional Period, Art. 4, *see* K. M. Showaia, 'Transitional Justice in Libya: Between Current Challenges and Future Prospects', *Macquarie Law Journal* 13 (2014), 61–78, at 64–5; International Crisis Group, *Trial by Error: Justice in Post-Qadhafi Libya*, Middle East/North Africa Report N°140. https://www.crisisgroup.org/middle-east-north-africa/north-africa/libya/trial-error-justice-post-qadhafi-libya (16 January 2017), pp. 28–9.

682 United Nations Human Rights Council, *Report of the International Commission of Inquiry on Libya: A/HRC/19/68*. http://www.ohchr.org/Documents/HRBodies/HRCouncil/RegularSession/Session19/A.HRC.19.68.pdf (20 January 2017).

683 Human Rights Watch, *Death of a Dictator: Bloody Vengeance in Sirte*. https://www.hrw.org/report/2012/10/16/death-dictator/bloody-vengeance-sirte (20 January 2017).

684 International Crisis Group, *Trial by Error*, pp. 28–9.

685 L. Charbonneau, *Hague Prosecutor Urges Libya Not to Grant Amnesty for War Crimes*. http://www.reuters.com/article/2012/11/07/us-libya-icc-idUSBRE8A629N20121107 (16 January 2017).

686 S. Figgins, *After Libya's Elections, Transitional Justice in the Balance*. http://www.egyptindependent.com/news/after-libya-s-elections-transitional-justice-balance (16 January 2017).

687 Ibid.

688 Charter for Peace and National Reconciliation, 27 February 2006, Ordinance No 06–01.

689 Ludwin King, 'Amnesties in a Time of Transition', 578.

killings, rape or using explosives in public places.[690] The Charter further entails an unconditional amnesty for state agents and denies that they have been responsible for disappearances and other serious crimes.[691] This false assertion[692] as well as the fact that the legal option to prosecute certain serious crimes has not been utilised by the Algerian authorities, has led to widespread impunity in Algeria.[693]

To sum up, legislative authorities as well as courts of several African countries support amnesty as a tool of the process of reconciliation and reconstruction. At the same time, most of them acknowledge that impunity for serious international crimes is increasingly condemned by the international community. In practice, however, investigations and prosecutions of severe human rights violations are not pursued so that *de facto* amnesty prevails.

3.2.1.3 Asian States

In this section, some Asian countries and in particular their practice with regard to amnesties are examined. The first country under consideration is ***Afghanistan***. Although the Afghan Amnesty Law has already been analysed in detail in the previous chapters, it will also be dealt with here because the emphasis is on Afghanistan's contradictory practice regarding accountability and impunity. The development of the still ongoing violent conflict in Afghanistan which has had in part an international character has been thoroughly described in Chapter 2.2.[694] The analysis here therefore focuses on the conduct of the Afghan authorities with respect to the issue of impunity. In March 2002, the then President, Hamid Karzai, stated that *"[A]nother important matter to consider is the question of human*

690 Charter for Peace and National Reconciliation, Art. 10, *see* Mallinder, 'Amnesties', 876.

691 Ibid., 875–6.

692 International human rights organisations have found evidence that security forces committed serious human rights violations, including enforced disappareances. *See inter alia*, Human Rights Watch, *World Report 2008: Algeria*. https://www.hrw.org/world-report/2009/country-chapters/algeria (23 January 2017).

693 Ibid; Mallinder, 'Amnesties', 876–7; Amnesty International, *Annul Report: Algeria 2015/2016*. https://www.amnesty.org/en/countries/middle-east-and-north-africa/algeria/report-algeria/ (23 January 2017).

694 Chapter 2.2 The Case of Afghanistan – History of Conflicts.

rights violations in the past. I cannot say whether the current interim administration has the full authority to address this issue, but it is my hope that the Loya Jirga government will have the authority to establish a truth seeking mechanism and ensure that the people will have justice [...]"[695] However, only a few months later, Karzai emphasised that "*[...] justice becomes a luxury for now. We must not lose peace for that.*"[696] In subsequent years many inconsistencies have characterised policy decisions in Afghanistan. To start with, the mandate of the Afghan Independent Human Rights Commission (AIHRC), the national human rights institution established in 2002, included the investigation of violations of human rights as well as the elaboration of proposals for a national strategy on transitional justice and on addressing the abuses of the past.[697] All national authorities and official institutions were required to fully cooperate with the commission and to facilitate its work.[698] The AIHRC would furthermore publicise and submit reports to local, regional and national authorities.[699] In 2005, the commission published its first report[700] and advocated for the prosecution of perpetrators of serious crimes as well as the removal of criminals from positions of power. As a consequence, the Afghan government adopted the Action Plan for Peace, Reconciliation and Justice (APPRJ)[701] in the same year. The Action Plan contains, *inter alia*, the objective of ending impunity in Afghanistan and ensuring that there will be no amnesty for war crimes, crimes against humanity and other gross human rights violations.[702] However, the subsequent development has not complied with these stipulations at all, as the enactment of the blanket Amnesty Law and further questionable decisions show. As already described in Chapter

695 *See* Afghanistan Independent Human Rights Commission (AIHRC), *A Call for Justice*, p. 5.

696 International Crisis Group, *Afghanistan: Judicial Reform and Transitional Justice*. https://www.crisisgroup.org/asia/south-asia/afghanistan/afghanistan-judicial-reform-and-transitional-justice (11 January 2017), p. 2.

697 *Decree of the Presidency of the Interim Administration of Afghanistan on the Establishment of an Afghan Independent Human Rights Commission* (2002), p. 2, Art. 2, 9.

698 Ibid., p. 2, Art. 8.

699 Ibid., p. 2, Art. 9, 12.

700 Afghanistan Independent Human Rights Commission (AIHRC), *A Call for Justice*.

701 Government of the Islamic Republic of Afghanistan, *Action Plan on Peace, Reconciliation and Justice in Afghanistan*.

702 Ibid., p. 11.

2.3[703], the legislative process of the Afghan Amnesty Law started in January 2007 with the hasty approval of the *"National Stability and Reconciliation Resolution"* by the lower and then upper houses of parliament (Wolesi Jirga and Meshrano Jirga).[704] Following some minor amendments, the *"National Reconciliation, General Amnesty, and National Stability Law"*[705] was drafted. The law contains a blanket amnesty for all political factions and hostile parties and all kinds of crimes. It applies not only to perpetrators of past crimes but also to those who end violence only after the enforcement of the Amnesty Law.[706] On 10th March 2007, the revised Amnesty Law was approved by the parliament.[707] After an unusually long time, the Amnesty Law was quietly published in the official gazette on 3rd December 2008[708], and in January 2010 the Afghan government finally announced the entry into force of the blanket amnesty.[709] The manifestation of impunity for serious human rights violations by the Amnesty Law is in clear contradiction to the aforementioned objectives of the APPRJ.[710] It is therefore not surprising that the then President Karzai denied the extension of the Action Plan which expired in March 2009.[711] Apart from that, none of the objectives of the APPRJ has been fully implemented.[712] The Afghan

---

703 Chapter 2.3 The Afghan Amnesty Law 2010.

704 Gossman and Kouvo, *Tell Us How This Ends*, p. 30; Hakimi and Suhrke, 'A Poisonous Chalice', 211–2; Winterbotham, *The State of Transitional Justice in Afghanistan*, pp. 7–10; Khan, 'Afghanistan: War Crimes, ICC and NGOs', 104–6.

705 „National Reconciliation, General Amnesty, and National Stability Law", Official Gazette, publishing date: 13 Qaus 1387 Serial No: (965) (unofficial English translation), in: Kouvo, *After Two Years in Legal Limbo*.

706 Ibid., Art. 3 (1) (2).

707 Gossman and Kouvo, *Tell Us How This Ends*, p. 30.

708 „National Reconciliation, General Amnesty, and National Stability Law", Official Gazette, publishing date: 13 Qaus 1387 Serial No: (965), *See:* Afghanistan Research and Evaluation Unit (AREU), *Afghanistan Research Newsletter Number 24, January/February 2010*, p. 22.

709 Salahuddin, *Afghanistan Must Not Repeal Amnesty Law*.

710 Iliopoulos, *Afghan Amnesty Law a Setback for Peace*; M. E. Hartmann, 'Casualties of Myopia' in W. Mason (ed.), *The Rule of Law in Afghanistan* (Cambridge: Cambridge University Press, 2011), pp. 172–204, at pp. 183–5; Amnesty International, *Afghanistan: 10-Point Human Rights Agenda for President Karzai*. https://www.amnesty.nl/sites/default/files/public/afghanistan_10point_human_rights_agenda_for_president_karzai.pdf (12 January 2017), p. 4; United Nations, *High Commissioner Expresses Concern Over National Stability Plan Passed by Afghanistan's Lower House*, Press Release (2007).

711 *Afghanistan: Justice Action Plan Heading for Oblivion* (IRIN Asia, 2010).

712 International Center for Transitional Justice (ICTJ), *Challenges to Peace and Justice in Afghanistan*. http://ictj.org/sites/default/files/ICTJ-Afghanistan-Peace-Ju

Government disregarded not only the APPRJ but also the competences of the Afghan Independent Human Rights Commission by preventing the release of an 800-page report which contained serious violations of international law from 1978 to 2001 in Afghanistan.[713] The report is titled „Conflict Mapping in Afghanistan Since 1978" and was prepared by the AIHRC in the performance of its mandate in 2011.[714] All these actions have contributed to a state of impunity for serious human rights abuses in Afghanistan. The latest development in this regard is the signing of a peace deal between Ashraf Ghani, current President of Afghanistan, and Gulbuddin Hekmatyar, leader of the insurgent group Hezb-e Islami, in September 2016.[715] The agreement *inter alia* grants amnesty to Hekmatyar, "one of Afghanistan's most notorious war crimes suspects"[716], and other members of Hezb-e Islami for alleged international crimes committed during the Afghan civil war in the 1990s.[717]

A very recent example of State practice concerning amnesties is the case of ***Yemen***. The country has been plagued by armed conflicts and severe human rights violations for many years.[718] The Yemeni uprising which started in January 2011 aimed, *inter alia*, at the resignation of the then President Ali Abdullah Saleh, who was finally ousted in 2012.[719] The removal from power of Saleh was preceded by a power-transfer deal initiated by the Gulf Cooperation Council (GCC) and negotiated with the

---

stice-2009-English.pdf (12 January 2017), pp. 1–2; E. Winterbotham, *The State of Transitional Justice in Afghanistan*. http://www.areu.org.af/Uploads/EditionPdfs/1014E-The%20State%20of%20Transitional%20Justice%20in%20Afghanistan%20PN%20April%202010.pdf (12 January 2017), p. 2.

713 Nordland, 'Top Afghans Tied to '90s Carnage, Researchers Say'; Kazim, 'Kriegsverbrecher-Studie: Massaker-Berichte belasten afghanische Politiker'; Human Rights Watch, *World Report 2015: Afghanistan*.

714 Nordland, 'Top Afghans Tied to '90s Carnage, Researchers Say'; Kazim, 'Kriegsverbrecher-Studie: Massaker-Berichte belasten afghanische Politiker'.

715 Bengali and Faizy, 'Afghanistan Takes a Step Toward Peace With Notorious Ex-Warlord'; Osman, *Peace With Hekmatyar*, p. 1.

716 Gossman, *Afghanistan War Crimes Suspect Comes Home*.

717 Article 9 of the agreement states that the government "provides guarantee for the judicial immunity of the leader and members of Hezb-e Islami concerning the party's past political and military actions.", *see* Osman, *Peace With Hekmatyar*, p. 4.

718 International Center for Transitional Justice (ICTJ), *Facing a Troubled Past, Yemen Debates Transitional Justice Measures*. https://ictj.org/news/facing-troubled-past-yemen-debates-transitional-justice-measures (15 January 2017).

719 Ibid.

participation of an UN envoy in November 2011.[720] The Gulf Cooperation Council Initiative envisaged a political transition and for this purpose determined that Saleh *"shall tender his resignation"* once a law on safeguards had been adopted.[721] This law on safeguards would grant *"immunity from legal and judicial prosecution to [Saleh] and those who worked with him during his time in office."*[722] In accordance with this provision, Law No. 1 of 2012 "Concerning the Granting of Immunity from Legal and Judicial Prosecution" was enacted by the Yemeni Parliament in January 2012.[723] The law states that *"[...] Saleh, [...], shall hereby be granted complete immunity from legal and judicial prosecution."*[724] It further provided for immunity from criminal prosecution for the officials who have worked under Saleh.[725] Even though the law did not explicitly mention the term 'amnesty', it could nevertheless be assumed that Saleh and his associates received a blanket amnesty, since the immunity provision permanently bars prosecutions.[726] Moreover, as there was no provision defining the crimes which were eligible for immunity, it seemed reasonable to conclude that international crimes were also covered by the law.[727] Both the Gulf Cooperation Council Initiative and the Yemeni immunity law of 2012 violated Yemen's duties under international law.[728] Notwithstanding this, there had been

720 Yemen Times, *Yemen's Immunity Law: Breach of International Obligations.* http://www.yementimes.com/en/1720/report/3013/Yemen%E2%80%99s-immunity-law-Breach-of-international-obligations.htm (15 January 2017).

721 The Gulf Cooperation Council Initiative, UN Translation, *see* International Crisis Group, *Yemen: Enduring Conflicts, Threatened Transition*, Middle East Report N°125. https://www.crisisgroup.org/middle-east-north-africa/gulf-and-arabian-peninsula/yemen/yemen-enduring-conflicts-threatened-transition (15 January 2017), p. 32.

722 The Gulf Cooperation Council Initiative, UN Translation, *see* ibid., p. 32.

723 Law No. 1 of 2012 "Concerning the Granting of Immunity from Legal and Judicial Prosecution", Translation by Amnesty International, *see* Amnesty International, *Yemen's Immunity Law: Breach of International Obligations.* https://doc.es.amnesty.org/cgi-bin/ai/BRSCGI/mde310072012en?CMD=VEROBJ&MLKOB=30564653838 (15 January 2017), pp. 11–2.

724 Law No. 1 of 2012 "Concerning the Granting of Immunity from Legal and Judicial Prosecution", Art. 1.

725 Law No. 1 of 2012 "Concerning the Granting of Immunity from Legal and Judicial Prosecution", Art. 2.

726 Amnesty International, *Yemen's Immunity Law: Breach of International Obligations*, p. 6.

727 Amnesty International, *Yemen's Immunity Law*, p. 6.

728 International Center for Transitional Justice (ICTJ), *Facing a Troubled Past, Yemen Debates Transitional Justice Measures.*

no clear rejection of the immunity provision by the UN[729].[730] It may be for this reason that the UN Security Council insisted on the adoption of a law on transitional justice in June 2012 in order to support national reconciliation.[731] However, the draft of the 'Transitional Justice and National Reconciliation Law' which strives for accountability for past crimes and reparations to victims did not enter into force as the Yemeni Cabinet failed to reach consensus on its enactment.[732] This is also attributed to the persisting influence of former President Saleh and his party, who obviously oppose such a law.[733] Besides that, the situation in Yemen deteriorates steadily and perpetrators of serious human rights violations still act with impunity.[734]

The last Asian country under consideration is ***Nepal***. In February 1996, a violent civil war between Maoist insurgents and the Nepalese army

---

729 The UN Office of the High Commissioner for Human Rights is an exception in this regard, since it rejected from the outsed any power transfer deal including an amnesty for Saleh and his officials. *See* Reuters, *UN Rights Office Against Proposed Saleh Immunity*. http://in.reuters.com/article/2011/10/18/idINIndia-59968420111018 (15 January 2017); The UN Security Council's position, however, has been much more vague. In a resolution of 2011, the Security Council reaffirmed its support for the GCC and its initiatives, while at the same time demanding full accountability. *See* United Nations Security Council, *Resolution 2014 (2011)*, S/RES/2014 (2011). http://www.securitycouncilreport.org/atf/cf/%7B65BFCF9B-6D27-4E9C-8CD3-CF6E4FF96FF9%7D/YEMEN%20S%20RES%202014.pdf (15 January 2017), p. 1.

730 M. Al-Samei, *Derailment of Transitional Justice Law Provokes Exchange of Wild Accusations*. http://www.yementimes.com/en/1592/report/1189/Derailment-of-Transitional-Justice-Law-provokes-exchange-of-wild-accusations.htm (15 January 2017).

731 Ibid; International Center for Transitional Justice (ICTJ), *Facing a Troubled Past, Yemen Debates Transitional Justice Measures*.

732 International Center for Transitional Justice (ICTJ), *Facing a Troubled Past, Yemen Debates Transitional Justice Measures*; A. Saeed, *Armed Men Besiege House of Legal Affairs Minister*. http://www.yementimes.com/en/1796/news/4069/Armed-men-besiege-house-of-legal-affairs-minister.htm (16 January 2017); A. M. al Sharjabi, *Yemen's Revolutionary Ideals Stumble*. http://www.al-monitor.com/pulse/security/2015/01/yemen-revolution-saleh-hadi-garden-public-space-mohsen.html (16 January 2017).

733 A. Madabish, *Yemen Legal Affairs Minister: Former President Saleh Could Be Prosecuted*. http://www.aawsat.net/2014/01/article55326833 (15 January 2017); Saeed, *Armed Men Besiege House of Legal Affairs Minister*.

734 Amnesty International, *Amnesty International Report 2017/18 – Yemen*. https://www.refworld.org/publisher,AMNESTY,ANNUALREPORT,YEM,5a99382fa,0.html (05 February 2019).

erupted.[735] A decade later, in November 2006, the 'Comprehensive Peace Agreement'[736] was signed by the Government of Nepal and the United Communist Party Nepal – Maoist (UCPN-M) in order to end the armed conflict and start a transitional process.[737] The agreement, therefore, envisaged the establishment of a Truth and Reconciliation Commission (TRC) and a procedure to resolve cases of enforced disappearance as well as criminal proceedings in cases of human rights violations and reparations to victims.[738] In addition, the Nepalese Interim Constitution emphasised the responsibility of the State to establish a Commission of Inquiry into disappearances as well as a high-level Truth and Reconciliation Commission.[739] Furthermore, in 2007 the Supreme Court of Nepal ordered the Government to make provision for a Disappearance Commission and to initiate criminal proceedings in the cases concerned.[740] The implementation of these projects took a very long time and, beyond this, has been inadequate. It started in 2007 and 2008 with controversial draft legislation for the establishment of a TRC and a Disappearance Commission.[741] The TRC would be empowered to recommend amnesty for perpetrators of serious human rights violations.[742] In May 2012, after several years of stagnation,

---

735 International Center for Transitional Justice (ICTJ), *No One Above the Law: Vetting the Security Sector in Nepal*. https://ictj.org/news/no-one-above-law-vetting-security-sector-nepal (16 January 2017).

736 *Unofficial Translation of the Comprehensive Peace Agreement concluded between the Government of Nepal and the Communist Party of Nepal (Maoist)*. http://www.usip.org/sites/default/files/file/resources/collections/peace_agreements/nepal_cpa_20061121_en.pdf (16 January 2017).

737 International Center for Transitional Justice (ICTJ), *Briefing Note on the Recent Political Developments in Nepal Leading to a Lack of Access to Justice for Victims of Gross Human Rights Violations and International Humanitarian Law*. http://ictj.org/sites/default/files/Briefing%20Note%20to%20the%20SR%20on%20TJ%2023%2008%202012.pdf (20 January 2014), p. 8.

738 M. Kersten, *Rethinking Amnesty and Accountability*. http://justiceinconflict.org/2014/01/14/rethinking-amnesty-and-accountability/ (16 January 2017); International Center for Transitional Justice (ICTJ), *Briefing Note on the Recent Political Developments in Nepal Leading to a Lack of Access to Justice for Victims of Gross Human Rights Violations and International Humanitarian Law*, p. 8.

739 *The Interim Constitution of Nepal 2063 (2007)*. http://www.wipo.int/edocs/lexdocs/laws/en/np/np006en.pdf (17 January 2017), Part 4, para 33 (q) (s).

740 *Rabindra Prasad Dhakal v Nepal Government, Ministry of Home Affairs and Others* (The Supreme Court of Nepal, 01 June 2007), p. 41.

741 International Center for Transitional Justice (ICTJ), *Briefing Note on the Recent Political Developments in Nepal Leading to a Lack of Access to Justice for Victims of Gross Human Rights Violations and International Humanitarian Law*, p. 8.

742 Ibid., p. 8.

the Nepalese Government decided to revoke the draft bills and to introduce, instead, just one law on transitional justice which would also include a provision regarding amnesty.[743] The 'Ordinance on the Investigation of Disappeared Persons, Truth and Reconciliation Commission' was enacted by the Nepalese President in March 2013.[744] Section 23 determines "*While carrying out investigation pursuant to the ordinance, the Commission may, if deemed reasonable for amnesty to perpetrator, make recommendation to the Government of Nepal explaining sufficient grounds and reasons thereof. Notwithstanding anything contained in Sub Section (1), serious crimes which lack sufficient reasons and grounds for granting amnesty following the investigation of the Commission, including rape, shall not be recommended for amnesty by the Commission.*"[745] Although the Ordinance does not explicitly allow for amnesty in cases of serious human rights violations, it also does not define "*serious crimes*" and thus leaves open the question of which crimes are excluded from the amnesty.[746] Moreover, the wording "*serious crimes which lack sufficient reasons and grounds for granting amnesty*" indicates that, where it is reasonable, even such serious crimes can be amnestied.[747] The vagueness of the ordinance and in particular its openness towards amnesty for serious violations of human rights have been strongly criticised.[748] Following a request from victims' organisations, the Supreme Court of Nepal decided in January 2014 that: "*The provision of amnesty in Section 23 of the Ordinance does not appear to have guaranteed not to recommend amnesty for [serious violations of human rights]. These crimes are made the subject of amnesty, and instead of making participation and consent of victims for the amnesty process primary,*

---

743 Ibid., p. 2; My Republica, *Nepal: Govt Proposes Amnesty to Serious HR Violators*. http://www.myrepublica.com/portal/index.php/thweek/www.cpnm.org/index.php?action=news_details&news_id=40343 (17 January 2017).

744 Kersten, *Rethinking Amnesty and Accountability*.

745 *Ordinance on Investigation of Disappeared Persons, Truth and Reconciliation Commission*, Nepal 2013. http://www.simonrobins.com/missing/wp-content/uploads/2013/02/Nepal-TRC-Ordinance.pdf (17 January 2017), Section 23.

746 UN Office of the High Commissioner for Human Rights, *OHCHR Comments on the Nepal "Commission on Investigation of Disappeared Persons, Truth and Reconciliation Ordinance – 2069 (2013)"*. http://www.ohchr.org/Documents/Countries/NP/OHCHRComments_TRC_Ordinance.docx (18 January 2017); Kersten, *Rethinking Amnesty and Accountability*.

747 UN Office of the High Commissioner for Human Rights, *OHCHR Comments on the Nepal "Commission on Investigation of Disappeared Persons, Truth and Reconciliation Ordinance – 2069 (2013)"*.

748 Ibid; G. Adhikari, *Nepal Inches Towards Truth About War*. http://www.thehindu.com/news/international/south-asia/nepal-inches-towards-truth-about-war/article4526543.ece (18 January 2017).

it has been made secondary. [...] Therefore, this provision needs to be reviewed, reformed and amended accordingly."[749] In order to implement these demands, an expert panel was set up,[750] but their recommendations were, however, ignored by the Nepalese Government and, therefore, the TRC Bill had the same shortcomings as before.[751] In April and May 2014, the new law which provided for the establishment of a TRC and a Commission on Enforced Disappearance was approved by Parliament and Government.[752] It again contained the possibility of granting amnesty for serious crimes, as Section 26 (2) of the Law states that *"[...] the Commission shall not recommend for amnesty to the perpetrators involved in rape and other crimes of serious nature in which the Commission follows the investigation and does not find sufficient reasons and grounds for amnesty."*[753] Furthermore, Section 26 (4) empowered the TRC to recommend amnesties for gross violations of human rights, provided that the perpetrator submitted an application stating the acts committed, accepted repentance, agreed to apologise and committed themselves not to repeat such acts in future.[754] Due to these inadequacies, the new bill was also challenged by victims' organisations before the Supreme Court

---

749 *See* Kersten, *Rethinking Amnesty and Accountability*; UN News Centre, *Nepal: Pillay Welcomes Supreme Court Ruling Against Amnesty for Serious Crimes*. http://www.un.org/apps/news/story.asp?NewsID=46872#.WH9RpH3zz90 (18 January 2017); International Center for Transitional Justice (ICTJ), *ICTJ Urges Nepal to Amend Flawed Bill on Truth Seeking*. http://ictj.org/news/ictj-urges-nepal-amend-flawed-bill-truth-seeking (18 January 2017).

750 International Center for Transitional Justice (ICTJ), *ICTJ Urges Nepal to Amend Flawed Bill on Truth Seeking*.

751 Ibid; International Center for Transitional Justice (ICTJ), *ICTJ Program Report: Nepal*. http://ictj.org/news/ictj-program-report-nepal (18 January 2017).

752 Al Jazeera America, *Nepal Parliament Passes Amnesty Bill*. http://www.aljazeera.com/news/asia/2014/04/nepal-parliament-passes-amnesty-bill-20144271502645838.html (18 January 2017); International Center for Transitional Justice (ICTJ), *ICTJ Program Report: Nepal*.

753 *See* UN Office of the High Commissioner for Human Rights, *The Nepal Act on the Commission on Investigation of Disappeared Persons, Truth and Reconciliation, 2071 (2014) – as Gazetted 21 May 2014*. http://www.ohchr.org/Documents/Countries/NP/OHCHRTechnical_Note_Nepal_CIDP_TRC_Act2014.pdf (18 January 2017); The Himalayan Times Online, *ICJ Finds Faults in TRC Act, Says Amend It*. http://www.thehimalayantimes.com/fullNews.php?headline=ICJ+finds+faults+in+TRC+Act%26sbquo%3B++says+amend+it+&NewsID=416400&a=3 (01 June 2014).

754 UN Office of the High Commissioner for Human Rights, *The Nepal Act on the Commission on Investigation of Disappeared Persons, Truth and Reconciliation, 2071 (2014) – as Gazetted 21 May 2014*.

in June 2014.[755] In February 2015, the Court declared the provision on amnesty invalid, stating that the wording in Section 26 (2) means *"that if the Commission wants it can recommend amnesty even for the perpetrators of serious human rights violations"*.[756] This not only violated the Court's earlier verdicts but also constitutional provisions and international law.[757] The judges further explained that it was the duty of the TRC to identify perpetrators for the purpose of prosecution, but it did not suit the commission to search for reasons and grounds for blanket amnesty.[758] However, the Government has until now disregarded the Supreme Court's verdict to abolish the invalid amnesty provision as no legislative or administrative action has been taken in this respect.[759] Hence, another decade later, Nepal is still struggling for truth, justice and accountability. In conclusion, the examination of some Asian countries revealed that their authorities tend to accept wide-ranging amnesties to gain peace and stability.

3.2.1.4 European States and the US

Among the countries of Europe, ***Spain*** provides an interesting example of State practice regarding an almost forgotten amnesty law. Following the dictatorship of Francisco Franco, an Amnesty Act[760] was ratified in 1977 in order to pave the way for a peaceful transition to democracy. The act grants a blanket amnesty to all perpetrators and all kinds of crimes committed

755 International Center for Transitional Justice (ICTJ), *ICTJ Program Report: Nepal*; D. Rai, *Panel Set to Start TRC Formation*. http://www.ekantipur.com/2014/09/12/top-story/panel-set-to-start-trc-formation/394922.html (07 January 2017).

756 N. Khatiwada, *SC Annuls Discretionary Powers of TRC*. http://www.myrepublica.com/portal/index.php?action=news_details&news_id=93003 (19 January 2017).

757 'Govt's Disregard for Court Order Upsets Victims of Conflict', 16 November 2015.

758 Khatiwada, *SC Annuls Discretionary Powers of TRC*.

759 N. Khatiwada, *No Support to TRC, CIEDP on Present Status: UNOHCHR*. http://admin.myrepublica.com/feature-article/story/38075/no-support-to-trc-ciedp-on-present-status-unohchr.html (19 January 2017); 'Govt's Disregard for Court Order Upsets Victims of Conflict'; BBC, *Nepal to Investigate Civil War Crimes*. http://www.bbc.com/news/world-asia-37118106 (19 January 2017); D. Rai, *Transitional Justice Process Hangs in Balance: Victims Worried About Being Left out in Cold*. http://kathmandupost.ekantipur.com/news/2017-01-19/victims-worried-about-being-left-out-in-cold.html (09 February 2017).

760 Amnesty Act 46/1977 (BOE n. 248, 17 Oct. 1977, 22765), *see* R. Escudero, 'Road to Impunity: The Absence of Transitional Justice Programs in Spain', *Human Rights Quarterly* 36 (2014), 123–46, at 125.

during the dictatorship.[761] Despite the developments concerning amnesties in other countries, most notably in Latin America, the Spanish Amnesty Act was neglected by the population as well as the courts and the government for a long time.[762] But more recently, however, the amnesty provision has become a subject for discussion. In December 2006, victims groups lodged several complaints in relation to cases of enforced disappearance and illegal detentions which took place in Spain during the Franco era, and criticised the 1977 Amnesty Act for hampering investigations.[763] In an important ruling in October 2008, Judge Baltasar Garzón declared his competence to investigate crimes against humanity committed by General Franco and his subordinates.[764] Due to strong opposition and criminal lawsuits by right-wing organisations, Judge Garzón was temporarily suspended from his duties in May 2010 because of his unlawful attempt to open investigations into crimes which were covered by the 1977 Amnesty Act.[765] In March 2012, the Spanish Supreme Court declared that Garzón had not abused his power by investigating crimes against humanity committed during Franco's dictatorship.[766] However, the Court stressed the erroneous interpretation of the Amnesty Law by Judge Garzón, but decided not to consider it a crime of judicial misconduct.[767] Apart from this, the Supreme Court judges affirmed *„the validity of the Amnesty Law of 1977. This Act is part of a process of transition from an authoritarian state to the current democracy. […] It was not a Law passed by the victors, bearers of power to cover up his own crimes, but a law that*

761 Ibid., p. 125; P. Rafael and J. Yardley, 'No Extradition for Franco-Era Police Inspector', The New York Times, 30 April 2014.

762 P. Aguilar, 'The Spanish Amnesty Law of 1977 in Comparative Perspective: From a Law for Democracy to a Law for Impunity' in F. Lessa and L. A. Payne (eds.), *Amnesty in the Age of Human Rights Accountability: Comparative and International Perspectives* (Cambridge, New York: Cambridge University Press, 2012), pp. 315–35, at p. 332.

763 Ibid., 333.

764 Ibid., 333.

765 Ibid., 334.

766 *Tribunal Supremo. 'Manos Limpias' and Association Liberty and Identity against Judge Baltasar Garzón for 'Prevaricación' (Criminal Offence of Breach of Judicial Duty): Summary of the Judgment 101/2012, of 27 February*. http://www.poderjudicial.es/portal/site/cgpj/menuitem.0cb0942ae6fbda1c1ef62232dc432ea0/?vgnextoid=3dc82a011feb5310VgnVCM1000006f48ac0aRCRD&vgnextlocale=en&perfil=2&vgnextfmt=default&lang_choosen=en&vgnextchannel=6d70f20408619210VgnVCM100000cb34e20aRCRD (20 January 2017); J. Easterday.

767 *Tribunal Supremo. 'Manos Limpias' and Association Liberty and Identity against Judge Baltasar Garzón for 'Prevaricación' (Criminal Offence of Breach of Judicial Duty).*

was enacted with the agreement of all political forces acting with a clear sense of reconciliation. For that reason, that is to say, because the "transition" was the will of the Spanish people embodied in a law, no Judge or Tribunal can in any way call into question the legitimacy of such a process. It is a law that may exclusively be repealed by the Parliament."[768] They further argued that international law cannot overrule a national amnesty retroactively.[769] In other words, the possible incompatibility between the Amnesty Law and international law could not be applied with retroactive effect.[770] The Supreme Court, therefore, rejected the opposite approach of the Inter-American Court of Human Rights on amnesties.[771] This verdict is astonishing, not least because Spanish courts have considered themselves competent to deal with international crimes committed in other countries and thereby ignored the national amnesty laws of those countries.[772] Despite repeated requests by international human rights bodies to abolish the Amnesty Act of 1977 and to investigate the crimes of the Franco era, the Spanish authorities have refused to comply with these demands.[773] Ironically, in September 2013, an Argentine judge made an extradition request relating to cases of torture committed by former Spanish police officials during Franco's dictatorship.[774] In doing so, Judge María Romilda Servini de Cubría referred to the principle of universal jurisdiction.[775] In April 2014, the National Court of Spain rejected the extradition of a former police inspector to Argentina as his acts would not qualify as crimes against humanity.[776] Thus, serious human rights abuses of the past remain unsolved and unpunished.

---

768 Ibid.

769 E. González, *Spain Declares Itself Powerless*. https://ictj.org/news/spain-declares-itself-powerless (14 January 2017); Easterday, *Spain: 1977 Amnesty Law "All Tied Up & Well Tied Up"*; N. Roht-Arriaza, 'The Spanish Civil War, Amnesty, and the Trials of Judge Garzón', *The American Society of International Law* 16 (2012).

770 Ibid.

771 Ibid.

772 E.g. in the case against former Chilean Dictator, Augusto Pinochet, *see* J. Easterday, *No Justice Cascade in Spain*. http://www.intlawgrrls.com/2012/03/no-justice-cascade-in-spain.html (14 January 2017).

773 Escudero, 'Road to Impunity', 130.

774 R. Minder, 'Argentine Judge Seeks to Put Franco Officials on Trial', The New York Times, 30 September 2013.

775 Ibid.

776 Rafael and Yardley, 'No Extradition for Franco-Era Police Inspector'.

Impunity for international crimes and an incomplete reconciliation process still cast a shadow over Spain and its institutions.[777]

It was only recently that the ***Ukraine*** intended to issue an amnesty law. Following the Minsk Agreement of February 2015 which called for *„pardon and amnesty by way of enacting a law that forbids persecution and punishment of persons in relation to events that took place in particular departments of Donetsk and Luhansk Oblasts of Ukraine.“*[778], a draft amnesty law was introduced. The „Law on the Exemption from Prosecution and Punishment of Persons Taking Part in Events on the Territory of the Donetsk and Lughansk Obla“ grants amnesty to members of armed groups who committed crimes and/or were involved in the acts by the self-proclaimed authorities of the Donetsk and Lughansk Oblasts, and to those who obstructed anti-terrorist operations.[779] The law did not exclude certain international crimes such as crimes against humanity, war crimes, torture and enforced disappearance from its scope.[780] This is alarming, in particular because there is evidence that war crimes, torture, enforced disappearances and other serious human rights violations have been committed by both Ukrainian forces and pro-Russian separatists.[781] In July 2016, the Ukrainian parliament approved the controversial amnesty law.[782] However, the law has not yet entered into force since it was vetoed by President Petro Poroshenko in August 2016.[783]

The next country under consideration, the ***United States of America***, does not precisely correspond with the chapter heading, as only States with an amnesty law should be examined. In the United States, however, the rules

777 D. Tolbert, *Much Work Ahead for Spain in Facing the Ghosts of the Past.* http://www.huffingtonpost.com/david-tolbert/much-work-ahead-for-spain_b_5965638.html (07 January 2017).

778 The Telegraph, *Minsk Agreement on Ukraine Crisis: Text in Full.* http://www.telegraph.co.uk/news/worldnews/europe/ukraine/11408266/Minsk-agreement-on-Ukraine-crisis-text-in-full.html (23 January 2017).

779 International Partnership for Human Rights, *Making Amnesty Work: Prospects of Granting Amnesty to the Parties of the Conflict in Eastern Ukraine.* http://iphronline.org/wp-content/uploads/2016/01/ENG-Making-amnesty-work-January-2016.pdf (23 January 2017), p. 6.

780 Ibid., p. 9.

781 Human Rights Watch, *World Report 2017: Ukraine.* https://www.hrw.org/world-report/2017/country-chapters/ukraine (24 January 2017); Amnesty International, *Ukraine: Abuses and War Crimes by the Aidar Volunteer Battalion in the North Luhansk Region*, AI Index: EUR 50/040/2014. https://www.amnesty.org/en/documents/EUR50/040/2014/en/ (24 January 2017).

782 Human Rights Watch, *World Report 2017: Ukraine.*

783 Ibid.

which are of interest in the context of this chapter do not explicitly refer to amnesty. But it is quite possible that the impact of these rules is similar to the impact of an amnesty and hence the conditions for a *de-facto* or pseudo amnesty[784] would be met. As a consequence of the September 11th, 2001 attacks the Bush government established harsh interrogation techniques to question terror suspects.[785] These highly controversial practices, including waterboarding, beatings, extended sleep deprivation, religiously degrading treatment and choking systematically violated human rights and thus clearly contradicted international law.[786] For the purpose of shielding the perpetrators of such acts, some legal measures were taken by the Bush administration. The relevant provisions are contained in the „Detainee Treatment Act" of 2005 and the „Military Commissions Act" of 2006 which relate to prisoner abuse committed by U.S. personnel.[787] Section 1004 (a) of the Detainee Treatment Act determines that *„In any civil action or criminal prosecution against an officer, employee, member of the Armed Forces, or other agent of the United States Government who is a United States person, arising out of [...] engaging in specific operational practices, that involve detention and interrogation of aliens who the President or his designees have determined are believed to be engaged in or associated with international terrorist activity [...] that were officially authorized and determined to be lawful at the time that they were conducted, it shall be a defence that such officer, employee, member of the Armed Forces, or other agent did not know that the practices were unlawful and a person of ordinary sense and understanding would not know the practices were unlawful. [...]"*[788] This means that U.S. personnel who participated in unlawful interrogation or detention go unpunished as they are allowed to defend their criminal conduct on the ground that they did not know that

784 *De-facto* or pseudo amnesties are laws or regulations which like *de-jure* amnesties aim to shield perpetrators from prosecution. The only difference is that the term "amnesty" remains deliberately unmentioned.

785 L. Mallinder, 'Power, Pragmatism, and Prisoner Abuse: Amnesty and Accountability in the United States', *Oregon Review of International Law* 14 (2012), 307–76, at 313.

786 C. P. Blum, L. Magarrell and M. Wierda, *Prosecuting Abuses of Detainees in U.S. Counter- terrorism Operations: Criminal Justice for Criminal Policy*. https://www.ictj.org/sites/default/files/ICTJ-USA-Criminal-Justice-2009-English.pdf (25 January 2017); Mallinder, 'Power, Pragmatism, and Prisoner Abuse', 314.

787 Mallinder, 'Power, Pragmatism, and Prisoner Abuse', 322.

788 *Detainee Treatment Act of 2005*, Public Law 109–148 of December 30, 2007, Title X; 119 STAT. 2739. https://www.dni.gov/index.php/about/organization/ic-legal-reference-book/ref-book-detainee-treatment-act-of-2005 (24 January 2017), Sec. 1004 (a).

it was unlawful. Furthermore, the Military Commissions Act stipulates in its Section 5 (a) that "*No person may invoke the Geneva Conventions or any protocols thereto in any habeas corpus or other civil action or proceeding to which the United States, or a current or former officer, employee, member of the Armed Forces, or other agent of the United States is a party as a source of rights in any court of the United States or its States or territories.*"[789] The act thus severely restricts the scope of international law and further entrenches impunity.[790] In none of the rules just mentioned is the term amnesty used. However, it is not unusual that state agents who want to protect themselves from prosecution, but at the same time do not want to reveal this intention, avoid wording such as 'amnesty' or 'immunity' when enacting relevant laws.[791] Nevertheless, the legal consequences of such acts, namely immunity for perpetrators who committed human rights violations, are equivalent to those of an explicit amnesty.[792] For this reason, the provisions of the Detainee Treatment Act and the Military Commissions Act quoted, which provide legislative immunity for state agents who abused prisoners, can be classified as a *de-facto* or pseudo amnesty.[793] Another opportunity to shield U.S. personnel from criminal proceedings has been used by the Government of the United States when it concluded Bilateral Immunity Agreements (BIAs) with many state parties to the ICC Rome Statute.[794] In so doing the U.S. — which is not a member of the ICC — aimed to avoid other countries extraditing U.S. nationals alleged to have committed war crimes, crimes

789 *Military Commissions Act of 2006*, PUBLIC LAW 109–366. https://www.congress.gov/109/plaws/publ366/PLAW-109publ366.pdf (25 January 2017), Sec. 5 (a).

790 Center for Constitutional Rights, *Military Commissions Act of 2006: A Summary of the Law*. http://ccrjustice.org/sites/default/files/assets/files/report_MCA.pdf (26 January 2017), p. 7; Mallinder, 'Power, Pragmatism, and Prisoner Abuse', 323.

791 *See* Chapter 2.1 Amnesties in General; Mallinder, 'Power, Pragmatism, and Prisoner Abuse', 321.

792 Freeman, *Necessary Evils*, p. 13; Mallinder, 'Power, Pragmatism, and Prisoner Abuse', 321–2.

793 Mallinder, 'Power, Pragmatism, and Prisoner Abuse', 322.

794 102 Bilateral Immunity Agreements (BIAs) have been reported since 2004, *see* American Non-Governmental Organizations Coalition for the International Criminal Court (AMICC), *Countries Concluding Bilateral Immunity Agreements*. http://www.amicc.org/usicc/bialist (26 January 2017); The Coalition for the International Criminal Court (CICC), *U.S. Bilateral Immunity Agreements or So-Called "Article 98" Agreements*. http://www.iccnow.org/documents/FS-BIAs_Q&A_current.pdf (27 January 2017).

against humanity or genocide to the ICC.[795] The legal basis for these Bilateral Immunity Agreements is to be found in Article 98 (2) Rome Statute[796] which was drafted in order to give the „sending State" — in this case the U.S. — priority in conducting criminal proceedings in respect of crimes committed by its citizens.[797] However, the BIAs concluded do not entail an obligation on the part of the United States to investigate and prosecute international crimes.[798] Moreover, U.S. officials have announced that perpetrators of the most serious international crimes will only be prosecuted when appropriate, and that the immunity agreements give the United States the safeguards it was seeking.[799] This kind of state practice intends to legitimise impunity for serious violations of international law and can therefore be regarded as fostering amnesty for such crimes.[800]

In conclusion, it has been shown that impunity for serious international crimes also plays a role in European countries and in the United States.

---

795 The Coalition for the International Criminal Court (CICC), *U.S. Bilateral Immunity Agreements or So-Called "Article 98" Agreements*; Barbour and Weed, *The International Criminal Court (ICC)*, p. 2.

796 Bilateral Immunity Agreements or Article 98 Agreements are international agreements concluded on the basis of Art. 98 (2) of the Rome Statute which states that „*The Court may not proceed with a request for surrender which would require the requested State to act inconsistently with its obligations under international agreements pursuant to which the consent of a sending State is required to surrender a person of that State to the Court […].*", *see* Rome Statute of the International Criminal Court, A/CONF.183/9; Barbour and Weed, *The International Criminal Court (ICC)*, pp. 7–10.

797 This corresponds with the Rome Statute's principle of complementarity; The Coalition for the International Criminal Court (CICC), *U.S. Bilateral Immunity Agreements or So-Called "Article 98" Agreements.*

798 Amnesty International, *International Criminal Court: US Efforts to Obtain Impunity for Genocide, Crimes Against Humanity and War Crime*, IOR 40/025/2002. http://www.amicc.org/docs/aiusimpunity.pdf (27 January 2017), pp. 17–8; The Coalition for the International Criminal Court (CICC), *U.S. Bilateral Immunity Agreements or So-Called "Article 98" Agreements.*

799 Amnesty International, *International Criminal Court*, p. 28; C. Marquis, 'U.S. Is Seeking Pledges to Shield Its Peacekeepers From Tribunal', The New York Times, 07 August 2002.

800 Y. Naqvi, 'Amnesty for War Crimes: Defining the Limits of International Recognition', *International Review of the Red Cross* 85 (2003), 583–626, at 585–6; Amnesty International, *International Criminal Court*, p. 28.

3.2.1.5 States on Foreign Amnesties

As mentioned previously, the practice of States which commented on amnesty laws of other States also plays an important role for the determination of customary international law regarding amnesties.[801] In what follows, therefore, the reaction of States to foreign amnesties is examined.

In general, international actors have a wider range of options than the national authorities of States dealing with the transition from an armed conflict to peace.[802] They can reject amnesties for perpetrators of serious human rights violations, broker a peace deal including an amnesty or support the drafting and implementation of an amnesty by financial, logistical or technical contributions.[803] Additionally, States can reinforce their position by means of diplomatic, economic, legal or military pressure.[804] It is not unusual that an individual State does not act consistently when assessing foreign amnesty laws. Depending on its national priorities, a State may condemn or endorse an amnesty by another State.[805] According to a survey conducted by Louise Mallinder, over five times more amnesty processes have been encouraged than condemned.[806] Besides this, in many cases the external community of States does not react at all to amnesty laws covering serious human rights violations[807], which might also be seen as an indicator of State practice.[808] The Afghan Amnesty Law, for example, was strongly criticised by the international community when the Afghan Parliament approved it in 2007[809], but when it entered into force

801 Freeman and Pensky, 'The Amnesty Controversy in International Law', 54–5.

802 D. Cassel, 'Lessons from the Americas: Guidelines for International Response to Amnesties for Atrocities', *Law and Contemporary Problems* 59 (1996), 197–230, at 201–4.

803 Mallinder, 'Power, Pragmatism, and Prisoner Abuse', 331–2; Cassel, 'Lessons from the Americas', 201–4.

804 Mallinder, 'Power, Pragmatism, and Prisoner Abuse', 332.

805 Ibid., p. 332.

806 Mallinder, *Amnesty, Human Rights and Political Transitions:*, p. 329.

807 For example, in the case of the Algerian or the Afghan amnesty. *See* Freeman, *Necessary Evils*, p. 54.

808 Mallinder, *Amnesty, Human Rights and Political Transitions:*, p. 327.

809 In general, European countries (for example Sweden, Denmark and the Netherlands) were more critical than the US. *See* J.-N. Ferrié, 'The Uncertainties of Democratic Promotion in Afghanistan' in Z. Laidi (ed.), *EU Foreign Policy in a Globalized World: Normative Power and Social Preferences*, 1st edn. (Oxon: Routledge, 2008), pp. 134–42, at pp. 140–2; Khan, 'Afghanistan: War Crimes, ICC and NGOs', 117–8; Moen and Mohammadi, *International Criminal Court (ICC) in Afghanistan*, p. 10.

in 2010 only a deafening silence could be heard and not a single word of condemnation has since been said.[810] On the contrary, the 2016 peace deal between the Afghan Government and Hezb-e Islami, which contains a blanket amnesty for alleged international crimes, has been praised by the European Union and the United States as a step forward in bringing the conflict to a peaceful end.[811] Another example of the endorsement of immunity from prosecution for human rights violations is Sierra Leone, where several States showed understanding for the blanket amnesty of the Lomé Peace Agreement[812]: the United States mentioned its commitment "to the pursuit of accountability" but also "recognised the need to allow the Lomé Agreement to bear fruit"[813]; Gabon agreed with the amnesty provision[814], and others, such as Canada or France refrained from commenting on the amnesty[815]. The Netherlands was the only country that explicitly criticised the blanket amnesty.[816] In the case of Uganda, the implementation of the Amnesty Act 2000, which provides for a wide-ranging amnesty, has been supported by financial funds contributed by, *inter alia*, Denmark, Norway, the Netherlands, Sweden and the UK.[817]

810 Human Rights Watch, *Afghanistan: Repeal Amnesty Law*; Salahuddin, *Afghanistan Must Not Repeal Amnesty Law*; Mojumdar, *Afghanistan: Amnesty Law Fuels Debate on Reconciliation Process*; International Crisis Group, *Talking About Talks*, p. 25; Georg, 'Kolonialisten kommen zurück – NATO-Staaten inclusive Deutschland setzen auf afghanische Warlords'; C. Rondeaux and N. Grono, 'Prosecuting Taliban War Criminals', The New York Times, 23 March 2010; Niland, 'Impunity and Insurgency: a Deadly Combination in Afghanistan', 940; Leopold, *Afghanistan Enacts Law That Gives War Criminals Blanket Immunity*.

811 Bengali and Faizy, 'Afghanistan Takes a Step Toward Peace With Notorious Ex-Warlord'; Deutschlandfunk, *Bundesregierung Lobt Friedensabkommen Zwischen Kabul und Hisb-e Islami* (2016).

812 States, such as the UK, the US, Argentina, Gabon and Slovenia. *See* Schabas, *Unimaginable Atrocities*, pp. 180–1.

813 United Nations Security Council, *Sierra Leone*, S/PV.4035. http://www.un.org/en/ga/search/view_doc.asp?symbol=S/PV.4035 (28 February 2017), pp. 13–4.

814 Ibid., p. 8.

815 Ibid., 9,11.

816 Ibid., pp. 12–3.

817 The World Bank, *Uganda – Emergency Demobilization and Reintegration Project*. http://documents.worldbank.org/curated/en/366461468318292528/pdf/dh0Project0Inf1raisal0Stage1updated.pdf (27 February 2017); Mallinder, 'Amnesties' Challenge to the Global Accountability Norm? Interpreting Regional and International Trends in Amnesty Enactment', 92–3.

These examples serve to demonstrate that States tend to support rather than criticise amnesty laws of foreign countries.[818]

3.2.1.6 Conclusion

The objective of this chapter is to explore whether customary international law with respect to a prohibition of amnesties in cases of serious international crimes has already developed or perhaps is still developing. For this purpose, several countries' amnesty laws as well as the reactions of States to foreign amnesties have been examined in more detail.

It has been shown that many Latin American countries tend to abolish or severely restrict their blanket and unconditional amnesty laws which had been enacted during and after the military dictatorships in the 1980s. This change is very well illustrated by the recent example of Colombia. The peace agreement, signed by the Colombian government and FARC-EP in late 2016, determined that perpetrators of serious international crimes will receive 'alternative sanctions' instead of amnesty.[819] There are nevertheless States such as Brazil or Guatemala which uphold their blanket amnesty laws, and other States, for example Chile, where the sentences applied by the courts for serious human rights violations have been criticised as being too lenient.[820]

The analysis of several African countries[821] has demonstrated that their legislative authorities are indeed conscious of the fact that impunity for serious international crimes is increasingly condemned by the international community. Hence, the wording of their amnesty laws to a large extent excludes those atrocities from the scope of the amnesty. In practice, however, investigations and prosecutions of severe human rights violations are not pursued so that *de facto* amnesty also prevails in these cases. The example of South Africa has illustrated that the initial innovative approach to transitional justice, which combines truth telling, amnesty and prosecution, could not be achieved in its entirety. Political and legal shortcomings led to impunity for serious human rights violations and disrespect for victims'

---

818 Ludwin King, 'Amnesties in a Time of Transition', 605; M. J. Osiel, *Making Sense of Mass Atrocity* (Cambridge, UK, New York: Cambridge University Press, 2009), p. 234; Mallinder, *Amnesty, Human Rights and Political Transitions:*, p. 329; Mallinder, 'Power, Pragmatism, and Prisoner Abuse', 333.

819 *See* Chapter 3.2.1.1.

820 Ibid.

821 *See* Chapter 3.2.1.2.

rights.[822] The amnesty laws of the DR Congo explicitly exclude genocide, war crimes and crimes against humanity. Furthermore, the creation of a national reconciliation commission as well as the prosecution of perpetrators who are most responsible for serious human rights violations had been envisaged. In fact, however, peace and stability have had priority over justice and accountability since there have been almost no criminal proceedings for these atrocities.[823] In Algeria the legal option to prosecute certain serious crimes has not been utilised by the authorities, with the result that widespread impunity continues to exist in the country. In Uganda the amnesty provision was abolished in 2012. However, following protests the amnesty was reinstated by the Ugandan Parliament in 2013 and extended for an additional period of two years in 2015. At the same time, a transitional justice policy, which includes the rejection of blanket amnesties as well as encouraging participation in truth telling and traditional justice processes, had been drafted. These contradictory processes demonstrate the hesitation by and difficulties of the Ugandan authorities in dealing with impunity for serious human rights violations.[824] Obviously unimpressed by the increasing call for accountability, Libya presents an exception to the approach of the aforementioned African countries with regard to the design of amnesty laws. In 2012, its interim legislative body introduced a law which granted blanket amnesty to fighters opposing Muammar Qaddafi for, *inter alia*, war crimes and crimes against humanity relating to the February 2011 uprising. Thus, impunity for international crimes has been deliberately formalized by enacting a broad amnesty.[825]

The authorities in Asia tend to accept wide-ranging amnesties to gain peace and stability. In Afghanistan, for example, a blanket amnesty law was enacted although the Afghan Government had committed itself to investigate international crimes, end impunity and ensure that there will be no amnesty for gross human rights violations. The state of impunity was reflected in the recently signed peace deal between Ashraf Ghani and Gulbuddin Hekmatyar, leader of the insurgent group Hezb-e Islami, which encompasses an amnesty for international crimes.[826] A blanket amnesty was also introduced in Yemen. Law No. 1 of 2012 provides for immunity from criminal prosecution for Saleh and his personnel. As there

822 Ibid.
823 Ibid.
824 Ibid.
825 Ibid.
826 *See* Chapter 3.2.1.3.

is no provision defining the crimes which are eligible for immunity, it seems reasonable to conclude that international crimes are also covered by the law. Besides this, the situation in Yemen deteriorates steadily and perpetrators of serious human rights violations still act with impunity.[827] In Nepal after several attempts to establish a TRC and a Commission on Enforced Disappearance, a corresponding law was finally approved in 2014. It empowers the TRC to recommend amnesties for gross violations of human rights. Even though the Supreme Court declared the provision invalid, stating that it violates the constitution and international law, the government has not yet abolished the amnesty and the country is still struggling for truth, justice and accountability.[828]

Impunity for serious international crimes also plays a role in European countries and in the United States. In other words, amnesties are not outlawed in Western democracies as the following examples show. The Spanish Amnesty Act which grants blanket amnesty to all perpetrators and all kinds of crimes committed during the dictatorship dates back to 1977. In 2012, the Spanish Supreme Court affirmed its validity and argued that international law cannot overrule a national amnesty. Despite repeated requests by international human rights bodies to abolish the Amnesty Act and to investigate the crimes of the Franco era, the Spanish authorities have refused to comply with these demands. Thus, serious human rights abuses of the past remain unsolved and unpunished.[829] A relatively recent amnesty law has been drafted in Ukraine, which grants amnesty for acts relating to the armed conflict in the Donbass region. Remarkably, the law does not exclude international crimes such as crimes against humanity, war crimes, torture and enforced disappearance from its scope.[830] In the United States, harsh interrogation techniques have been justified by the Detainee Treatment Act and the Military Commissions Act, which provide legislative immunity for state agents who commit serious human rights violations. The impact of the relevant provisions is similar to the impact of an explicit amnesty and hence, the conditions for a *de-facto* or pseudo amnesty are met. Furthermore, Bilateral Immunity Agreements (BIAs) have been concluded to shield U.S. personnel alleged to have committed war crimes, crimes against humanity or genocide from criminal proceedings before the ICC. This policy legitimises impunity for serious

827 Ibid.
828 Ibid.
829 See Chapter 3.2.1.4.
830 Ibid.

human rights violations and thus disregards the achievements in the area of international criminal law.[831]

The analysis of the practice of various States has demonstrated that amnesties for the most serious international crimes are still being enacted. Even where the term amnesty is not explicitly used or in cases in which the amnesty law excludes severe human rights violations from its scope, the situation is nevertheless characterised by impunity, that is, by *de facto* amnesty. Nonetheless, by circumventing an explicit amnesty for specific international crimes, States in a certain sense admit that these offences should not go unpunished. Latin American countries have made the most progress as many of them have abolished or restricted their comprehensive amnesty laws and additionally endeavour to investigate and prosecute those most responsible for the worst atrocities. It has been shown, however, that this regional trend[832] can neither be transferred to other parts of the world nor does it mean that amnesties are completely rejected.[833]

These findings are consistent with the practice of those States which commented on amnesties of other States. Here, too, it became clear that amnesties even for the most serious crimes are not entirely opposed by the international community.[834] In fact, more amnesty processes have been encouraged than condemned. This means that States tend to support rather than criticise amnesty laws of foreign countries.[835]

Having examined the State practice concerning amnesties, it will be dealt with the practice of the United Nations. Their resolutions and decisions may serve as an important indicator of State practice, and thus may contribute to the creation of customary international law.[836]

831 Ibid.

832 That is, the development with regard to amnesties in South America as described by Louise Mallinder, *see* Mallinder, 'The End of Amnesty or Regional Overreach?', 671.

833 Ibid., 671, 677–678; Freeman, *Necessary Evils*, p. 30.

834 *See* Chapter 3.2.1.5.

835 Ludwin King, 'Amnesties in a Time of Transition', 605; M. J. Osiel, *Making Sense of Mass Atrocity* (Cambridge, UK, New York: Cambridge University Press, 2009), p. 234; Mallinder, *Amnesty, Human Rights and Political Transitions:*, p. 329; Mallinder, 'Power, Pragmatism, and Prisoner Abuse', 333.

836 Werle, *Völkerstrafrecht*, pp. 70–1; O'Shea, *Amnesty for Crime in International Law and Practice*, p. 214.

3.2.2 The United Nations on Amnesties

As mentioned at the beginning of this chapter, the practice of the most important international organisation, namely the United Nations comprising 193 Member States, is also of relevance because its resolutions may serve as a valuable indicator of State practice and/or *opinio juris*.[837] As the UN consists of various organisations and specialised agencies, the determination of which bodies contribute most to the creation of customary international law is necessary. The decisions and resolutions of the UN Security Council and the UN General Assembly are of particular importance since they may reflect *opinio juris* of the participating states.[838] Furthermore, Article 25 of the UN Charter determines that *"the Members of the United Nations agree to accept and carry out the decisions of the Security Council [...]"*, that is, these decisions are binding upon the Member States[839] and in this way contribute to the formation of customary international law.[840] General Assembly resolutions, on the other hand, are merely recommendatory and do not have any legal force.[841] However, in cases where resolutions are widely supported by many states or adopted unanimously, it seems appropriate to attribute to them normative value and thus considerable influence on the development of customary norms.[842] This is all the more true when a resolution uses the wording "shall" instead of "should", as this indicates a legal obligation and not only a recommendation.[843] The resolutions, statements and opinions of other UN bodies, such as the Human Rights Committee, the Human Rights Council, the Office of the High

837 Werle, *Völkerstrafrecht*, pp. 70–1; O'Shea, *Amnesty for Crime in International Law and Practice*, p. 214.

838 Mendelson, *The Formation of Customary International Law*, vol. 272, p. 201; Werle, *Völkerstrafrecht*, p. 78.

839 Thirlway, 'The Sources of International Law', 117.

840 A. Orakhelashvili, 'The Acts of the Security Council: Meaning and Standards of Review' in A. v. Bogdandy, R. Wolfrum and C. E. Philipp (eds.), *Max Planck Yearbook of United Nations Law* (Leiden, Biggleswade: Martinus Nijhoff Publishers/Brill Academic, 2007), pp. 143–95, at p. 145.

841 Slye and van Schaack, *International Criminal Law*, p. 104; Thirlway, 'The Sources of International Law', 117.

842 O'Shea, *Amnesty for Crime in International Law and Practice*, p. 249; Villiger, *Customary International Law and Treaties*, vol. 28, p. 24; *Legality of the Threat or Use of Nuclear Weapons* (International Court of Justice, 08 July 1996), para. 70.

843 Dinstein, *The Interaction between Customary International Law and Treaties*, vol. 322, p. 306; Cryer, *Prosecuting International Crimes*, p. 107; *Legality of the Threat or Use of Nuclear Weapons* (International Court of Justice, 08 July 1996), para. 70.

Commissioner for Human Rights and the Secretary-General do not have any binding force and are all sources of soft law.[844] Notwithstanding this, these UN bodies can significantly impact the development of international law or, more precisely, contribute to the emergence of a new rule of customary international law.[845] In this regard, it is essential that they all adopt the same position on a specific issue.[846]

For the purpose of this study the United Nations approach to amnesties is of great interest. In general it can be said that the UN increasingly opposes amnesties for war crimes, crimes against humanity, genocide and other gross violations of human rights.[847] However, this has not always been the case, but is rather the result of evolution based on significant experience.[848] Before 1999, it was quite possible that UN personnel supported blanket amnesties during peace negotiations, in order to end a violent conflict.[849] From 1999 onwards, UN practice has undergone a change away from broad and unconditional amnesties to new mechanisms for the prosecution of international crimes and accordingly the rejection of amnesties for such offences.[850] There are nevertheless situations in which amnesties even for international crimes are still endorsed by the United Nations, as is shown below.

This gradual development can be corroborated by the following examples, starting with the pre-1999 period. In the aftermath of peace negotiations in El Salvador, which were carried out with the participation of UN mediators, the Salvadoran Government enacted a wide-ranging amnesty law in 1993.[851] The UN Secretary-General's response to the amnesty was rather reluctant.[852] He merely criticised the procedure which led to the enactment of the law, but did not complain about its content, that is,

844 Ludwin King, 'Amnesties in a Time of Transition', 606.

845 Ibid., p. 606.

846 Ibid., p. 606.

847 UN Office of the High Commissioner for Human Rights, *Rule-of-Law Tools for Post-Conflict States*, pp. 1–3.

848 Ibid., p. 2.

849 Ibid., p. 2.

850 C. Stahn, 'United Nations Peace-Building, Amnesties and Alternative Forms of Justice: A Change in Practice?', *International Review of the Red Cross* 84 (2002), 191–206, at 196; Naqvi, *Impediments to Exercising Jurisdiction over International Crimes*, pp. 82–3.

851 *See* Chapter 3.2.1.

852 Stahn, 'United Nations Peace-Building, Amnesties and Alternative Forms of Justice', 192–3.

the blanket amnesty as such.[853] The UN supported further controversial amnesty laws, *inter alia* in the cases of Haiti (1993)[854] and Guatemala (1996)[855].

The first time that an amnesty for serious crimes was called into question by the United Nations was in 1999 when the Government of Sierra Leone and the Revolutionary United Front signed the Lomé Peace Agreement.[856] In this case the Special Representative of the Secretary-General in Sierra Leone made an explicit reservation to his signature, stating that the United Nations did not recognise amnesty for genocide, crimes against humanity, war crimes, and other serious violations of international humanitarian law.[857] In accordance with this statement, the Secretary-General in his report on the establishment of the Special Court for Sierra Leone highlighted that the *„United Nations has consistently maintained the position that amnesty cannot be granted in respect of international crimes"*.[858] Since then, the United Nations policy to reject the unlimited granting of amnesties has been consolidated and expanded. The position taken during the peace negotiations in Sierra Leone was reaffirmed, *inter alia*,

---

853 Ibid., p. 193.

854 The „Governors Island Agreement" of 1993 included a blanket amnesty. *See* Naqvi, *Impediments to Exercising Jurisdiction over International Crimes*, p. 95; Stahn, 'United Nations Peace-Building, Amnesties and Alternative Forms of Justice', 193–4; Scharf, 'Justice versus Peace', 179.

855 The Ley de Reconciliación Nacional contained a limited amnesty, excluding some, but not all, crimes under international law from its scope. *See* Chapter 3.2.1; Stahn, 'United Nations Peace-Building, Amnesties and Alternative Forms of Justice', 194–5.

856 W. A. Schabas, 'National Amnesties, Truth Commissions and International Criminal Tribunals' in B. S. Brown (ed.), *Research Handbook on International Criminal Law*, Research handbooks in international law (Cheltenham, UK, Northampton, MA: Edward Elgar, 2011), pp. 373–90, at pp. 376–7; United Nations Human Rights Council, *Analytical Study on Human Rights and Transitional Justice*, p. 17; Stahn, 'United Nations Peace-Building, Amnesties and Alternative Forms of Justice', 196.

857 *Peace Agreement between the Governement of Sierra Leone and the RUF (Lomé Peace Agreement)*. http://peacemaker.un.org/sierraleone-lome-agreement99 (13 February 2017); United Nations Human Rights Council, *Analytical Study on Human Rights and Transitional Justice*, p. 17; Stahn, 'United Nations Peace-Building, Amnesties and Alternative Forms of Justice', 196.

858 United Nations Security Council, *Report of the Secretary-General on the Establishment of a Special Court for Sierra Leone*, S/2000/915. http://www.rscsl.org/Documents/Establishment/S-2000-915.pdf (16 February 2017), para. 22.

in Angola in 2002[859] and in the Sudan in 2004[860]. In addition to the disapproval of blanket amnesties in peace agreements, ceasefires and other negotiated settlements, the United Nations drafted several sets of principles incorporating existing obligations under international human rights and humanitarian law, as well as the condemnation of amnesties that prevent prosecution of those responsible for serious international crimes.[861]

In 2005, for example, the General Assembly adopted the „Basic Principles and Guidelines on the Right to a Remedy and Reparation for Victims of Gross Violations of International Human Rights Law and Serious Violations of International Humanitarian Law" which emphasised the duty of states to investigate, prosecute and punish crimes under international law.[862] A very recent example of the practice of the General Assembly in relation to the question of whether or not to demand accountability for war crimes and other serious violations of international law is the case of Syria. The divergent suggestions of individual states in that regard range from immunity for Syria's President Baschar al-Assad, allegedly responsible for serious international crimes, in order to force him into exile[863] to a polit-

---

859 The 2002 Luena Memorandum of Understanding between the Angolan Armed Forces and the National Union for the Total Independence of Angola (UNITA) contained a reservation on the rejection of any blanket amnesty by the United Nations. *See* United Nations Human Rights Council, *Analytical Study on Human Rights and Transitional Justice*, p. 17; Naqvi, *Impediments to Exercising Jurisdiction over International Crimes*, pp. 82–3.

860 In 2004, the Sudanese Government withdrew a blanket amnesty provision from the agreement with the Sudan People's Liberation Movement. *See* United Nations Human Rights Council, *Analytical Study on Human Rights and Transitional Justice*, p. 17.

861 UN Office of the High Commissioner for Human Rights, *Rule-of-Law Tools for Post-Conflict States*, pp. 27–9.

862 United Nations General Assembly, *Basic Principles and Guidelines on the Right to a Remedy and Reparation for Victims of Gross Violations of International Human Rights Law and Serious Violations of International Humanitarian Law*, A/RES/60/147.

863 L. Leicht and C. Baldwin, 'In Syrien müssen Kriegsverbrechen geahndet werden', Zeit Online, 03 August 2012; BBC, *David Cameron: Safe Passage for Syria's Assad Acceptable*. http://www.bbc.co.uk/news/world-middle-east-20223759 (16 January 2017); Spiegel Online, *Bürgerkrieg in Syrien: Cameron befürwortet Exil für Assad*. http://www.spiegel.de/politik/ausland/buergerkrieg-in-syrien-cameron-schlaegt-exil-fuer-assad-vor-a-865704.html (16 January 2017); *Westerwelle Recommends Assad the Passage Into Exile*. http://www.zitecode.com/Articles/detail/westerwelle-recommends-assad-the-passage-into-exile.html (21 August 2012).

ical transition with al-Assad as negotiating partner[864] and finally to the deployment of investigators for the purpose of gathering evidence needed for any future criminal trials[865]. Apart from that, the Member States of the General Assembly adopted a resolution in December 2016, which noted *„with concern the impunity for serious violations of international humanitarian law and violations and abuses of human rights law“* and provided for the establishment of an *„international, impartial and independent mechanism to assist in the investigation and prosecution of those responsible for the most serious crimes“* committed in Syria since March 2011.[866] The resolution was approved by a vote of 105 to 15 with 52 abstentions[867]. This is obviously not unanimous, but also not widely supported as 67 Member States could not bring themselves to give their approval.[868] Furthermore, it remains to be seen whether practical steps that foster justice and accountability instead of impunity will indeed be initiated.[869]

In addition to the General Assembly, the Security Council has also dealt with the issue of impunity in different contexts. In a resolution from 2006, for example, the Council insisted on the *"responsibility of States to comply with their relevant obligations to end impunity and to prosecute those responsible*

864 France 24, *Assad Exit not Necessary for Syria Transition, Says Fabius*. http://www.france24.com/en/20151205-assad-exit-not-necessary-syria-transition-france-fabius-islamic-state-group (17.12.15); M. Küntzel, *Westliches Wunschdenken: Keine Anti-Terror-Allianz mit Assad* (2015). http://www.deutschlandradiokultur.de/westliches-wunschdenken-keine-anti-terror-allianz-mit-assad.1005.de.html?dram:article_id=338520 (17.12.15).

865 M. Simons, 'Investigators in Syria Seek Paper Trails that Could Prove War Crimes', The New York Times, 07 October 2014; J. Borger, *Smuggled Syrian Documents Enough to Indict Bashar al-Assad, Say Investigators*. http://www.theguardian.com/world/2015/may/12/smuggled-syrian-documents-indict-assad-investigators (01 June 2015).

866 United Nations General Assembly, *International, Impartial and Independent Mechanism to Assist in the Investigation and Prosecution of Those Responsible for the Most Serious Crimes under International Law Committed in the Syrian Arab Republic since March 2011*, A/71/L.48. http://www.un.org/ga/search/view_doc.asp?symbol=A/71/L.48 (24 February 2017).

867 Deutsche Welle (DW), *UN to Set Up War Crimes Panel for Syria Investigations*. http://www.dw.com/en/un-to-set-up-war-crimes-panel-for-syria-investigations/a-36869596?maca=en-Twitter-sharing (04 February 2017).

868 Dinstein, *The Interaction between Customary International Law and Treaties*, vol. 322, p. 305.

869 Rather sceptical: P. Seils, *In Syria, Little Chance of Justice or Change Without Return of Displaced*. https://www.ictj.org/news/syria-refugees-justice-return-displaced (04 February 2017); A. Zumach, 'Signal gegen Straflosigkeit', taz, 23 December 2016.

for war crimes, genocide, crimes against humanity and serious violations of international humanitarian law".[870] However, it did not explicitly comment on the issue of amnesties for such crimes.[871] Although a general declaration on amnesties has not yet been made by the Security Council, it has clearly expressed its position in the specific case of the 'Agreement between the United Nations and the Lebanese Republic on the Establishment of a Special Tribunal for Lebanon'. Article 16 of the Agreement reads as follows: *"The Government undertakes not to grant amnesty to any person for any crime falling within the jurisdiction of the Special Tribunal. An amnesty already granted in respect of any such persons and crimes shall not be a bar to prosecution."*[872] A more conservative approach has been taken by the Security Council with regard to the Secretary-General's Report on the Rule of Law and Transitional Justice in Conflict and Post-Conflict Societies of 2004. In this report the Secretary-General stated that *"United Nations-endorsed peace agreements can never promise amnesties for genocide, war crimes, crimes against humanity or gross violations of human rights."*[873] During the debate on the report the Security Council could not reach a consensus on this highly disputed statement concerning the rejection of amnesties for the most serious crimes.[874] Several Security Council members refused to accept such a ban on amnesties.[875] In his 2011 Report on the Rule of Law and Transitional Justice in Conflict and Post-Conflict Societies, the Secretary-General reaffirmed his negative stance regarding amnesties for international crimes and encouraged the Security Council to reject any endorsement of such amnesties.[876] In stark contrast to this report, the

870 United Nations Security Council, *Resolution 1674 (2006)*, S/Res/1674 (2006). https://documents-dds-ny.un.org/doc/UNDOC/GEN/N06/331/99/PDF/N0633199.pdf?OpenElement (16 February 2017), para. 8.

871 Freeman, *Necessary Evils*, p. 46.

872 United Nations Security Council, *Resolution 1757 (2007)*, S/RES/1757 (2007). http://daccess-dds-ny.un.org/doc/UNDOC/GEN/N07/363/57/PDF/N0736357.pdf?OpenElement (12 February 2017), p. 10.

873 United Nations Security Council, *The Rule of Law and Transitional Justice in Conflict and Post-Conflict Societies, Report of the Secretary-General*, para. 10.

874 United Nations Security Council, *United Nations Security Council – 5052nd meeting*, S/PV.5052 (Resumption 1). http://www.securitycouncilreport.org/atf/cf/%7B65BFCF9B-6D27-4E9C-8CD3-CF6E4FF96FF9%7D/IJ%20SPV5052%20Res1.pdf (16 February 2017); Scharf, 'Trading Justice for Peace', 258–9.

875 United Nations Security Council, *United Nations Security Council – 5052nd meeting*; Scharf, 'Trading Justice for Peace', 258–9.

876 United Nations Security Council, *The Rule of Law and Transitional Justice in Conflict and Post-Conflict Societies: Report of the Secretary-General*, S/2011/634.

Secretary-General's Special Adviser Jamal Benomar supported the Yemeni power transfer deal which resulted in the 2012 immunity law.[877] The law grants blanket amnesty to former President Saleh and his associates.[878] The position of the Security Council with regard to possible amnesties for international crimes in Yemen remains unclear[879]. The resolution adopted in 2011 on the one hand demanded full accountability and the avoidance of impunity, but on the other hand supported the Gulf Cooperation Council initiative which provided for the granting of immunity from legal and judicial prosecution.[880] The inconsistent approach taken by the Secretary-General and the Security Council is also reflected in the case of Afghanistan. In his 2001 and 2004 reports on the situation in Afghanistan, the Secretary-General reiterated that it is essential to ensure accountability for past abuses as a *"sustainable peace cannot be built on a foundation of impunity"*.[881] Referring to the enactment of the Afghan Amnesty Law in 2010, the Secretary-General found it to be *"in violation of the obligations of Afghanistan under its Constitution and international law."*[882] In addition, the then Special Representative of the Secretary-General and head of the UN Assistance Mission in Afghanistan (UNAMA) Kai Eide stated: *"[...] an Amnesty Law had been gazetted and apparently kept away from the attention of the public [...]. The process itself gives reason for serious concerns. So does*

http://www.securitycouncilreport.org/atf/cf/%7B65BFCF9B-6D27-4E9C-8CD3-CF6E4FF96FF9%7D/ROL%20S2011%20634.pdf (17 February 2017), p. 18.

877 Yemen Times, *Yemen's Immunity Law: Breach of International Obligations*.

878 *See* Chapter 3.2.1.

879 Yemen Times, *Yemen's Immunity Law: Breach of International Obligations*.

880 United Nations Security Council, *Resolution 2014 (2011)*, 1, 2–3; Yemen Times, *Yemen's Immunity Law: Breach of International Obligations*; *See* Chapter 3.2.1.

881 United Nations General Assembly – Security Council, *The Situation in Afghanistan and Its Implications for International Peace and Security: Report of the Secretary-General*, A/56/681–S/2001/1157. http://www.un.org/en/ga/search/view_doc.asp?symbol=S/2001/1157 (20 February 2017), para. 83; United Nations General Assembly – Security Council, *The Situation in Afghanistan and Its Implications for International Peace and Security: Report of the Secretary-General*, A/59/581 – S/2004/925. http://www.securitycouncilreport.org/atf/cf/%7B65BFCF9B-6D27-4E9C-8CD3-CF6E4FF96FF9%7D/Afgh%20S2004%20925.pdf (20 February 2017), para. 39.

882 United Nations General Assembly – Security Council, *The Situation in Afghanistan and Its Implications for International Peace and Security: Report of the Secretary-General*, A/64/705–S/2010/127. http://afghanistan-un.org/wp-content/uploads/2010/11/S20101271.pdf (13 February 2017), para. 36.

the content."[883] In its 2010 Mid-Year Report, UNAMA noticed that the Afghan Government fails in its duty to investigate and punish perpetrators of serious crimes and risks further entrenching the state of impunity by providing amnesty.[884] However, a few years later these perceptions had changed radically. Following the signing of the peace agreement between the Afghan Government and Hezb-e Islami in September 2016, which contained a blanket amnesty for alleged international crimes[885], UNAMA commented that it supported the efforts by the Afghan Government and applauded the peace deal as it demonstrated the preparedness to seek peace with armed anti-government elements.[886] It devoted not a single word to the question of criminal accountability. Instead the Security Council removed the name of Gulbuddin Hekmatyar, leader of Hezb-e Islami and "one of Afghanistan's most notorious war crimes suspects"[887], from its sanctions list.[888]

Of all UN organisations and mechanisms, the UN human rights bodies have made the most progress in the assessment of amnesties. Of particular note in this context are the 'Rule-of-Law Tools for Post-Conflict States: Amnesties' issued by the UN Office of the High Commissioner for Human Rights (UNOHCHR) in 2009.[889] The principles contained should guide United Nations personnel when dealing with amnesties that may contra-

883 Statement by SRSG Kai Eide "Legislation for women," Kabul, 6 March 2010, *see* Winterbotham, *The State of Transitional Justice in Afghanistan*, p. 9; M. J. Sharifzada, *Eide Concerned at Amnesty Law*. http://www.pajhwok.com/ps/node/90839 (20 February 2012).

884 United Nations Assistance Mission in Afghanistan (UNAMA), *Afghanistan Mid Year Report on Protection of Civilians in Armed Conflict 2010*. https://unama.unmissions.org/sites/default/files/August102010_MID-YEAR%20REPORT%202010_Protection%20of%20Civilians%20in%20Armed%20Conflict.pdf (17 February 2017), pp. 11–2.

885 The legal basis for the impunity provision is to be found in the Afghan Amnesty Law of 2010.

886 United Nations Assistance Mission in Afghanistan (UNAMA), *Draft Peace Agreement Between Government and Hezb-i-Islami Gulbuddin*. http://unama.unmissions.org/print/draft-peace-agreement-between-government-and-hezb-i-islami-gulbuddin (11 October 2016); Osman, *Peace With Hekmatyar*, p. 5.

887 Gossman, *Afghanistan War Crimes Suspect Comes Home*.

888 NDTV, *UN Removes Former Afghan Warlord Gulbuddin Hekmatyar From Blacklist*. http://www.ndtv.com/world-news/un-removes-former-afghan-warlord-gulbuddin-hekmatyar-from-blacklist-1655968 (04 February 2017).

889 UN Office of the High Commissioner for Human Rights, *Rule-of-Law Tools for Post-Conflict States*.

dict international law.[890] Even though of a non-binding character, the legal principles of the Rule-of-Law Tools do nevertheless restrict the discretion of states and the United Nations.[891] The tools determine, for example, that "*Under various sources of international law and under United Nations policy, amnesties are impermissible if they: (a) Prevent prosecution of individuals who may be criminally responsible for war crimes, genocide, crimes against humanity or gross violations of human rights, including gender-specific violations; (b) Interfere with victims' right to an effective remedy, including reparation; or (c) Restrict victims' and societies' right to know the truth about violations of human rights and humanitarian law.*"[892] Furthermore, they specify that even when intended to foster peace and reconciliation, amnesties cannot be accepted for serious international crimes.[893] These guidelines have been complied with on several occasions. In 2010, for example, the then Representative of the OHCHR in Afghanistan, Norah Niland, demanded the abolishment of the Afghan Amnesty Law as it greenlit impunity.[894] In 2011, the OHCHR underscored that any power transfer deal in Yemen should avoid an amnesty for then President Saleh.[895] Two years later, in 2013, the former UN High Commissioner for Human Rights Navi Pillay publicly criticised the 2012 Yemeni immunity law and stated that amnesties are not permissible if they prevent the prosecution of individuals who may be responsible for international crimes.[896] In the case of Nepal, Pillay raised serious concerns that the political parties were incorporating a blanket amnesty for serious violations of international human rights and humanitarian law into the bills on transitional justice mechanisms.[897] With a view to the ongoing Syrian civil war, current High Commissioner for Human

890 Ibid., p. 1.
891 Ibid., p. 2.
892 Ibid., p. 11.
893 Ibid., p. 46.
894 United Nations Assistance Mission in Afghanistan (UNAMA), *Transcript of Press Conference in Kabul by Norah Niland, Representative of the UN High Commissioner for Human Rights in Afghanistan*. https://unama.unmissions.org/norah-niland-representative-un-high-commissioner-human-rights-afghanistan-0 (16 February 2017); *Afghanistan: Immunity to Perpetrators of Mass Atrocities Greenlights Impunity* (IRIN, 2010); A.-K. Otto.
895 Reuters, *UN Rights Office Against Proposed Saleh Immunity*.
896 Yemen Times, *Yemen's Immunity Law: Breach of International Obligations*.
897 K. R. Sigdel, *War-Era Crimes: UN Report to Sound Alarm Bell against Nepal's Blanket Amnesty*. http://kathmandupost.ekantipur.com/printedition/news/2012-03-18/war-era-crimes-un-report-to-sound-alarm-bell-against-nepals-blanket-amnesty.html (17 February 2017); *See* Chapter 3.2.1.

Rights Prince Zeid Ra'ad al-Hussein has stressed the need to prosecute war crimes and crimes against humanity.[898] He has further emphasised that these atrocities shall not be covered by any amnesty linked to ending the conflict as amnesties are not permissible in these cases.[899]

Besides the above-mentioned UNOHCHR Rule-of-Law Tools on Amnesties, other UN human rights bodies have drafted documents. The „Updated Set of Principles for the Protection and Promotion of Human Rights through Action to Combat Impunity" submitted by the UN Commission on Human Rights in 2005 provides in its Principle 24 that: "*Even when intended to establish conditions conducive to a peace agreement or to foster national reconciliation, amnesty and other measures of clemency shall be kept within the following bounds: (a) The perpetrators of serious crimes under international law may not benefit from such measures until such time as the State has met the obligations to which principle 19 refers or the perpetrators have been tried before a court with jurisdiction—whether international, internationalized or national—outside the State in question[…].*"[900] In his 2014 Report on the Promotion of Truth, Justice, Reparation and Guarantees of Non-Recurrence, the Special Rapporteur of the UN Human Rights Council[901] expressed grave concern at blanket amnesties that shield perpetrators of even the worst violations from their legal responsibility.[902] The UN Human Rights Committee, the authoritative organ that monitors implementation of the ICCPR, has issued various General Comments and Concluding Observations which have been extremely critical of amnesties for serious crimes.[903] That is, when examining legislation granting amnesty for such crimes in several Latin American states, France, Lebanon, Niger, Senegal, Yemen and elsewhere the committee has repeatedly stressed that

898 Al Jazeera America, *UN Rights Chief: War Crimes Not to Be Part of Any Syria Amnesty Deal*. http://america.aljazeera.com/articles/2016/2/1/un-rights-chief-war-crimes-not-to-be-part-of-any-syria-amnesty-deal.html (08.02.16).

899 Ibid.

900 United Nations Commission on Human Rights, *Report of the Independent Expert to Update the Set of Principles to Combat Impunity, Diane Orentlicher, Addendum*.

901 The UN Human Rights Council replaced the former UN Commission on Human Rights.

902 United Nations Human Rights Council, *Report of the Special Rapporteur on the Promotion of Truth, Justice, Reparation and Guarantees of Non-Recurrence*, A/HRC/27/56. http://www.ohchr.org/EN/HRBodies/HRC/RegularSessions/Session27/Pages/ListReports.aspx (12 January 2017), para. 31.

903 Freeman, *Necessary Evils*, p. 48; Seibert-Fohr, *Prosecuting Serious Human Rights Violations*, pp. 47–9; Mallinder, *Amnesty, Human Rights and Political Transitions:*, pp. 342–4.

impunity for perpetrators of serious human rights violations is contrary to the obligations under the ICCPR.[904]

Thus, although the United Nations has increasingly condemned blanket amnesties for serious human rights violations from 1999 onwards, this approach has so far not been applied consistently. Above all, the UN human rights bodies have made considerable progress in the assessment of amnesties. The 'Rule-of-Law Tools for Post-Conflict States: Amnesties' issued by the UNOHCHR, as well as various reports, General Comments and Concluding Observations drafted by the Human Rights Council and the Human Rights Committee, reject amnesties for atrocious crimes. This policy is mirrored in the condemnation of several amnesty laws, for example in the cases of Afghanistan, Yemen and Nepal. However, other UN organs, especially the Security Council and the Secretary-General have sent conflicting messages regarding amnesties. That is, amnesties for international crimes are even supported to some extent, as the examples of Yemen and Afghanistan show. Furthermore, the Security Council has not yet made a general declaration on amnesties and could not reach a consensus on the rejection of amnesties for the most serious crimes.

3.2.3 The Afghan Amnesty Law and Customary International Law

The purpose of this chapter was to explore whether customary international law with respect to a prohibition of amnesties in cases of international crimes has already developed or perhaps is still developing. If such a norm has developed or is at least "crystallizing", the legitimacy of the Afghan Amnesty Law could be reviewed on that basis.

The result of the analysis of the practice of several states as well as of the United Nations can be summarised as follows: With regard to the state practice it has been determined that although Latin American countries have made significant progress as many of them have abolished or restricted their comprehensive amnesty laws, this regional trend[905] can neither be transferred to other parts of the world nor does this trend mean that

904 United Nations Commission on Human Rights, *Report of the Special Rapporteur on the Independence of Judges and Lawyers, Leandro Despouy*, p. 17; Seibert-Fohr, *Prosecuting Serious Human Rights Violations*, 47–49.

905 That is, the development with regard to amnesties in South America as described by Louise Mallinder, *see* Mallinder, 'The End of Amnesty or Regional Overreach?', 671.

amnesties are completely rejected.[906] In other words, states continue to enact amnesties for international crimes. Even where the term amnesty is not explicitly used, or where an amnesty law excludes severe human rights violations from its scope, the situation is nevertheless characterised by impunity, that is, by *de facto* amnesty. This result can be further substantiated by the fact that those states, which commented on amnesties of other states, also tend to support rather than criticise them.[907] Even in the case of the most serious crimes, amnesties have been encouraged by the international community. The analysis of the practice of the United Nations has demonstrated that on the one hand there is a trend towards outlawing blanket amnesties for serious international crimes as the policy of various UN organs, in particular of the UN human rights bodies, shows. But on the other hand, this approach has so far not been applied consistently. Above all, the Security Council as well as the Secretary-General do not always oppose or even support peace agreements which include amnesties for perpetrators of heinous crimes. Apart from this, a general declaration on amnesties or their rejection in cases of the most serious crimes could not be enforced within the Security Council.

As mentioned previously, the practice of states and the United Nations regarding a prohibition of amnesties for international crimes must be "general", i.e. consistent, widespread and also permanent in order to establish a new rule of customary international law.[908] The result of the study does, however, indicate that the approach to amnesties is not sufficiently uniform and widespread. That is, even though the international community has identified a common issue, it has not acted in concert to cope with that issue. The consequence is that a customary rule has not (yet) emerged and thus amnesties for the most serious crimes are not (yet) prohibited by customary international law.[909] It follows that the Afghan Amnesty

---

906 Ibid., 671, 677–678; Freeman, *Necessary Evils*, p. 30.

907 Ludwin King, 'Amnesties in a Time of Transition', 605; Osiel, *Making Sense of Mass Atrocity*, p. 234; Mallinder, *Amnesty, Human Rights and Political Transitions:*, p. 329; Mallinder, 'Power, Pragmatism, and Prisoner Abuse', 333.

908 Werle, *Völkerstrafrecht*, pp. 70–1; Thirlway, 'The Sources of International Law', 105.

909 Mallinder, 'The End of Amnesty or Regional Overreach?', 671, 677–678; O'Keefe, *International Criminal law*, pp. 468–70; Cassese and Gaeta, *Cassese's International Criminal Law*, pp. 310–2; Ludwin King, 'Amnesties in a Time of Transition', 604–6; Freeman, *Necessary Evils*, p. 33; Seibert-Fohr, *Prosecuting Serious Human Rights Violations*, pp. 285–6; Mallinder, *Amnesty, Human Rights and Political Transitions:*, 9, 122, 135; Scharf, 'Trading Justice for Peace', 258; Freeman and Pensky, 'The Amnesty Controversy in International Law', 57.

Law is not illegitimate according to current customary international law. However, if the trend towards outlawing blanket amnesties for serious international crimes continues and further expands[910], the legitimacy of the Afghan Amnesty Law would have to be judged differently. Due to its extensive scope and unconditional application, the Afghan Amnesty Law would most probably become unlawful.

But this would also be precluded when Afghanistan holds the status of a 'persistent objector'. The persistent objector rule allows a state which persistently objects to an emerging customary international law, to reject being bound by that law.[911] In order to benefit from the persistent objector doctrine a country has to fulfil two conditions: the objection must be pursued "from the early stages of the customary rule onwards, up to its formation, and beyond"[912] and furthermore, the objection must be maintained consistently.[913] Therefore it is not sufficient if a state objects to an emerging rule only occasionally, but applies it at other times.[914] But this is exactly what the Afghan Government has done in recent years. The analysis of the Afghan state practice in Chapter 3.2.1 clearly revealed its contradictory approach regarding accountability and amnesty. The many inconsistencies which characterise policy decisions in Afghanistan range from the adoption of the Action Plan for Peace, Reconciliation and Justice (APPRJ) which contained the aim of ensuring that there will be no amnesty for war crimes, crimes against humanity and other gross human rights violations[915] to the enactment of the blanket Amnesty Law in 2010. Apart from that, the objection is to be made expressly, which means that the Afghan authorities would have to inform other states about the country's rejective stance.[916] This, however, has not yet happened. Thus, Afghanistan does not hold the status of a persistent objector and a possible

910 Ludwin King, 'Amnesties in a Time of Transition', 606; Afghanistan Independent Human Rights Commission (AIHRC), *Discussion Paper on the Legality of Amnesties*, pp. 4–5; Naqvi, *Impediments to Exercising Jurisdiction over International Crimes*, p. 119; Iliopoulos, *Afghan Amnesty Law a Setback for Peace*.

911 *See Fisheries Case (United Kingdom v. Norway)* (International Court of Justice, 18 December 1951); Villiger, *Customary International Law and Treaties*, vol. 28, p. 34; Thirlway, 'The Sources of International Law', 106.

912 Villiger, *Customary International Law and Treaties*, vol. 28, p. 34.

913 Ibid., p. 34; Kaczorowska, *Public International Law*, p. 41.

914 Villiger, *Customary International Law and Treaties*, vol. 28, p. 34; Kaczorowska, *Public International Law*, p. 41.

915 Government of the Islamic Republic of Afghanistan, *Action Plan on Peace, Reconciliation and Justice in Afghanistan*, p. 11.

916 Kaczorowska, *Public International Law*, p. 41.

future customary international law prohibition of amnesties for serious international crimes would be binding on Afghanistan.

As described in the introductory chapter, where customary international law subsequently develops, it can only have an effect at the earliest from the moment of its formation. This means that a new rule of customary international law would have no influence on all acts adopted on the basis of the Amnesty Law between 2010 and the emergence of this new customary rule.[917] The legal situation would be quite different if rules of *jus cogens* are affected. In the event that a peremptory norm of general international law needs to be safeguarded and the newly established customary international law serves this purpose, the Afghan Amnesty Law would become null and void *ab initio*.[918] Yet, since it is *lex ferenda*, i.e. a desirable future law, it cannot be assessed at this stage whether an absolute prohibition on amnesties for international crimes[919], which is safeguarded by customary international law, will ever take shape.[920]

917 For comparison – In international treaty law the principle of non-retroactivity is firmly anchored: see Art. 28 Vienna Convention on the Law of Treaties: *"Non-retroactivity of treaties: Unless a different intention appears from the treaty or is otherwise established, its provisions do not bind a party in relation to any act or fact which took place or any situation which ceased to exist before the date of the entry into force of the treaty with respect to that party."*.

918 For comparison – In international treaty law the Joint Declaration of Judges Shi and Koroma with reference to the 'Case Concerning Application of the Convention on the Prevention and Punishment of the Crime of Genocide' (Bosnia and Herzegovina v. Serbia and Montenegro) (Judgment of 26 February 2007) is worth mentioning: *"Nevertheless, in some respects the interpretation of a treaty's provisions cannot be divorced from developments in the law subsequent to its adoption. Thus, even though a treaty when concluded did not conflict with any rule of jus cogens, it will become void if there subsequently emerges a new rule of jus cogens with which it is in conflict. […]"* (para. 2), *see International Court of Justice, Joint Declaration of Judges Shi and Koroma with reference to the 'Case Concerning Application of the Convention on the Prevention and Punishment of the Crime of Genocide'*; Kotzur, 'Intertemporal Law', 4.

919 An absolute prohibition on issuing amnesties for international crimes cannot be derived from the *jus cogens* prohibition of these crimes, *See* Chapter 3.1.2.

920 Mallinder, *Amnesty, Human Rights and Political Transitions:*, p. 9; Freeman and Pensky, 'The Amnesty Controversy in International Law', 57.

3.3 Do the General Principles of Law Preclude the Afghan Amnesty Law?

Following the analysis of international treaty law as well as customary international law with regard to the legitimacy of the Afghan Amnesty Law, the next step is to examine its compatibility with the "general principles of law recognised by civilised nations" (*see* Article 38 (1) (c) of the Statute of the International Court of Justice)[921]. This step is necessary and possible since both international treaty law and customary international law do not provide for a prohibition of amnesties in cases of serious human rights violations.[922] Hence, the general principles of law, that is, those legal principles which can be derived from national laws of a large number of states[923], can be used to fill the gap.[924] In other words, in the event that international law in the form of treaties or custom has reached its limits, a comparison of the various national legal systems will help to find out whether there exists a common legal principle in relation to the applicability of amnesties, which can establish an internationally accepted standard.[925]

There are similarities between the general principles of law and customary international law as for example certain legal principles contained in the national laws of a state may be seen as evidence for the one and also for the other source of international law.[926] The difference however is that customary international law consists of *opinio juris* and furthermore, that legal principles constituting customary international law have been

921 Basic literature on „general principles of law", e.g.: F. O. Raimondo, *General Principles of Law in the Decisions of International Criminal Courts and Tribunals*, Zugl.: Amsterdam, Univ., Diss., 2007 (Leiden: Nijhoff, 2008); S. Vogenauer and S. Weatherill, *General Principles of Law*, Studies of the Oxford Institute of European and Comparative Law (Oxford UK, Portland, Oregon: Hart Publishing, 2017); G. Del Vecchio, *General Principles of Law* (Littleton, Colo.: F.B. Rothman, 1986, 1956).

922 The general principles of law are a subsidiary source and will only be used when international treaty law as well as international customary law do not provide for relevant provisions. *See* Werle, *Völkerstrafrecht*, p. 69.

923 *See* Art. 21 (1) (c) Rome Statute of the International Criminal Court; Thirlway, 'The Sources of International Law', 109.

924 J. G. Apple, *What are General Principles of International Law?* http://www.judicialmonitor.org/archive_0707/generalprinciples.html (06 March 2017); Werle, *Völkerstrafrecht*, p. 69.

925 Apple, *What are General Principles of International Law?*.

926 Slye and van Schaack, *International Criminal Law*, p. 100.

enacted by states as principles of international law.[927] In the case of legal principles which constitute general principles of law, on the other hand, states have not necessarily relied on them as principles of international law.[928]

With respect to amnesties, not much attention has been paid to the legal principles of national laws.[929] This may be due to the fact that the general principles of law are very rarely applied as a source of international law.[930] But, apart from that, the reluctance to search for legal principles on amnesties in national laws may also be due to the fact that many states have granted amnesties, in part even for the most serious crimes.[931] In considering this state practice, it seems unreasonable to assume that a comparison of the various national legal systems would lead to the conclusion that there exists a common legal principle concerning the prohibition of amnesties for international crimes.[932] A brief glance at constitutions around the world will show whether this presumption can be sustained.

In a comparative analysis on amnesty provisions in constitutions[933] the question of whether and, if so, how states deal with amnesties in their constitutions has been explored. The study revealed that of the 193 UN Member States, 186 refer to amnesty and/or pardon in their constitutions.[934] There are 105 constitutions which contain provisions on both amnesty and pardon, and four constitutions[935] which exclusively deal with amnesties.[936] The material scope of possible amnesties, that is, the determination of crimes which are eligible for amnesty and which are not, can be found in 21 constitutions. Eight countries[937] determine that

---

927 Ibid., p. 100.

928 Ibid., p. 100.

929 Slye, 'The Legitimacy of Amnesties Under International Law and General Principles of Anglo-American Law', 175.

930 Ibid., p. 175.

931 *See* chapter 3.2.1; ibid., pp. 175–6.

932 Ibid., pp. 175–6.

933 The analysis was conducted by Josepha Close in 2015. It is available online at: J. Close, *Amnesty Provisions in the Constitutions of the World: A Comparative Analysis*. https://aninternationallawblog.wordpress.com/2015/01/05/amnesty-provisions-in-the-constitutions-of-the-world-a-comparative-analysis/ (08 March 2017).

934 Ibid.

935 Those of Cambodia, Guatemala, Laos and Montenegro; see ibid.

936 Ibid.

937 Colombia, Costa Rica, the Dominican Republic, Greece, Guatemala, Haiti, Honduras and Panama. *See* ibid.

amnesty may be granted for political crimes or related common crimes.[938] It is, however, not defined what exactly constitutes a political or related common crime.[939] Therefore, it is not clear from the constitutions of these eight countries which crimes are eligible for amnesty. The constitutions of 13 other countries expressly stipulate which crimes are excluded from the scope of a possible amnesty.[940] Seven of them[941] provide for a prohibition on amnesties for all or some international crimes, i.e. genocide, crimes against humanity, war crimes and torture.[942] Thus, only a small minority of the 193 UN Member States make provisions for a ban on amnesties for serious international crimes in their constitutions. The vast majority of countries, on the other hand, do not exclude these crimes from the scope of constitutionally authorised amnesties.[943]

To sum up, the comparison of constitutions from around the world leads to the conclusion that a common legal principle concerning the prohibition of amnesties for international crimes does not exist. This is not surprising in view of the results obtained so far. Amnesties for international crimes are neither prohibited by international treaty law nor by customary international law, as the previous chapters have shown. Since the general principles of law cannot be used to fill the gap[944], the Afghan Amnesty Law cannot be declared unlawful on this basis.

3.4 How Does International Jurisprudence Assess Amnesty Laws?

The next stage in the legal assessment of the Afghan Amnesty Law is to analyse several decisions by international, hybrid and regional human rights courts[945] on amnesty regulations from around the world, in order to evaluate whether or not the Afghan amnesty is in accordance with this jurisprudence. Article 38 (1) (d) of the Statute of the International

---

938 Ibid.
939 Ibid.
940 Ibid.
941 Angola, Brazil, Ecuador, Ethiopia, Iraq, Niger and Venezuela; *see* ibid.
942 Ibid.
943 Ibid.
944 Seibert-Fohr, *Prosecuting Serious Human Rights Violations*, p. 277.
945 The international court system consists of: permanent international courts (ICC, ICJ) and ad hoc international tribunals (ICTY, ICTR); hybrid courts (e.g. SCSL, ECCC); regional human rights courts (e.g. IACtHR, ECHR). *See* Mallinder, *Amnesty, Human Rights and Political Transitions:*, pp. 424–8.

Court of Justice reads: *"[...] judicial decisions [...], as subsidiary means for the determination of rules of law."* This means that 'judicial decisions' on amnesties — in contrast to international treaties, customary international law and general principles of law — do not have the status of a primary source of international law.[946] They can nevertheless contribute to the determination of legal principles, not least because judges provide valuable assessment of the current state of law.[947]

The two permanent international courts, namely the International Court of Justice and the International Criminal Court, have not yet ruled on the legitimacy of a particular amnesty law.[948] Among the *ad hoc* international tribunals and hybrid courts, the International Criminal Tribunal for the former Yugoslavia, the Special Court for Sierra Leone as well as the Extraordinary Chambers in the Courts of Cambodia have been concerned with specific amnesty laws.[949] With regard to regional human rights courts, the Inter-American Court of Human Rights has most notably dealt with Latin American amnesty laws. But the European Court of Human Rights has also addressed the issue of amnesty. These courts have usually drawn on international human rights law to find out whether the state concerned acted in violation of relevant provisions, for example whether the state violated its duty to investigate, to prosecute and punish.[950]

In what follows, a closer look is taken at some meaningful judgements by international, hybrid and regional courts. In order to avoid a one-sided approach, the analysis focuses on decisions from different parts of the world. With this in mind the jurisprudence of the Inter-American Court for Human Rights, the Special Court for Sierra Leone, the European Court for Human Rights, the International Criminal Tribunal for the former Yugoslavia and the Extraordinary Chambers in the Courts of Cambodia is of great interest. The objective of this analysis is to establish whether, despite regional disparities and different circumstances, a common standard for the assessment of amnesties can be defined. If so, the Afghan Amnesty Law could be evaluated according to this standard.

---

946 Freeman, *Necessary Evils*, p. 47.

947 Cassese, *The Oxford Companion to International Criminal Justice*, p. 53; Ambos, *Internationales Strafrecht*, p. 111.

948 Freeman, *Necessary Evils*, p. 48.

949 Ibid., p. 50.

950 Mallinder, *Amnesty, Human Rights and Political Transitions:*, pp. 248–9.

3.4.1 The Inter-American Human Rights System

Inter-American jurisprudence[951] on amnesty laws is manifold[952] and there is a vast amount of academic literature on this topic. To avoid repetition, this chapter does not include a detailed examination of the evolution of decisions on amnesties made by the Inter-American Court of Human Rights and the Inter-American Commission on Human Rights. Instead, the Court's and Commission's general approach towards Latin American amnesty laws as well as some ground-breaking rulings from the recent past is summarised. As several Latin-American countries and their amnesty laws were the focus of Chapter 3.2.1 (*State Practice concerning Amnesties*), the following explanations do not reiterate the circumstances leading to the amnesty laws or any details of these laws. The impact of Inter-American jurisprudence on the respective state practice has also been evaluated in the context of Chapter 3.2.1. Therefore, the present chapter will only deal with the Court's rulings on the amnesty provisions.

The Inter-American human rights treaty bodies have assessed a large number of amnesty laws which were enacted by the military regimes in many Latin American countries.[953] Both the Inter-American Commission and the Inter-American Court have continuously condemned broad and unconditional amnesties.[954] In various decisions issued since 2001, the Inter-American Court has stated that amnesties for serious human rights violations are inadmissible as they violate non-derogable rights protected by international human rights law.[955] The court has furthermore empha-

---

951 The Inter-American human rights system includes the Inter-American Commission on Human Rights and the Inter-American Court of Human Rights, as the main human rights treaty bodies of the Organisation of American States. *See* B. D. Tittemore, 'Ending Impunity in the Americas: The Role of the Inter-American Human Rights System in Advancing Accountability for Serious Crimes under International Law', *Southwestern Journal of Law and Trade in the Americas* 12 (2005–2006), 429–75, at 430.

952 Freeman, *Necessary Evils*, pp. 48–9.

953 Binder, 'The Prohibition of Amnesties by the Inter-American Court of Human Rights', 1208.

954 Tittemore, 'Ending Impunity in the Americas', 448–9; Seibert-Fohr, *Prosecuting Serious Human Rights Violations*, 95–97, 106.

955 United Nations Commission on Human Rights, *Report of the Independent Expert to Update the Set of Principles to Combat Impunity, Diane Orentlicher*, E/CN.4/2005/102. https://documents-dds-ny.un.org/doc/UNDOC/GEN/G05/111/03/PDF/G0511103.pdf?OpenElement (13 March 2017), p. 14; Case of Barrios Altos v. Peru, *Case of Barrios Altos v. Peru*, para. 41.

sised the non-compatibility of such amnesty provisions with the American Convention on Human Rights[956] and consequently demanded that perpetrators of international crimes must be investigated, prosecuted and punished.[957]

The country that has most often been dealt with by the Inter-American Court is Peru.[958] In its landmark judgement in the **Barrios Altos Case**[959] in 2001 the Court made it clear that self-amnesties contradict the American Convention on Human Rights.[960] This means that Peru's amnesty laws *"prevented the victims' next of kin and the surviving victims [...] from being heard by a judge, as established in Article 8(1) of the Convention; they violated the right to judicial protection embodied in Article 25 of the Convention; they prevented the investigation, capture, prosecution and conviction of those responsible for the events that occurred in Barrios Altos, thus failing to comply with Article 1(1) of the Convention, and they obstructed clarification of the facts of this case."*[961] On this note, the Court further declared that it *"considers that all amnesty provisions [...] are inadmissible, because they are intended to prevent the investigation and punishment of those responsible for serious human rights violations such as torture, extrajudicial, summary or arbitrary execution and forced disappearance, all of them prohibited because they violate non-derogable rights recognized by international human rights law."*[962]

956 In the cases of Peru (Barrios Altos), Chile (Almonacid Arellano et al.) and Brazil (Gomes Lund et al.), *See Case Gelman v. Uruguay* (Inter-American Court of Human Rights, 24 February 2011), p. 196.

957 Transitional Justice Institute, *The Belfast Guidelines on Amnesty and Accountability*, p. 44.

958 Twenty-two cases were decided between 1995 and 2007, *see* C. Sandoval, 'The Challenge of Impunity in Peru: The Significance of the Inter-American Court of Human Rights', *Essex Human Rights Review* 5 (2008), 1–20, at 6.

959 In the Barrios Altos neighborhood fifteen people were killed by the Fujimori regime in 1991. The perpetrators were not prosecuted due to amnesty laws passed in 1995 and 1996. *See* Chapter 3.2.1.

960 According to the Court, the amnesty laws „*prevented the investigation, capture, prosecution and conviction of those responsible for the events that occurred in Barrios Altos, thus failing to comply with Article 1(1) of the Convention*", Case of Barrios Altos v. Peru, para. 42*Case of Barrios Altos v. Peru*; Mallinder, *Amnesty, Human Rights and Political Transitions:*, p. 271; Seibert-Fohr, *Prosecuting Serious Human Rights Violations*, pp. 100–1.

961 *Case of Barrios Altos v. Peru* (Inter-American Court of Human Rights, 14 March 2001), para. 42.

962 Case of Barrios Altos v. Peru, *Case of Barrios Altos v. Peru*, para. 41; United Nations Commission on Human Rights, *Report of the Independent Expert to Update the Set of Principles to Combat Impunity, Diane Orentlicher*, p. 14.

In line with this position, the 2006 judgement of the Inter-American Court in the case **Almonacid-Arellano versus Chile**[963] was based on the fundamental premise that *"the States cannot neglect their duty to investigate, identify, and punish those persons responsible for crimes against humanity by enforcing amnesty laws [...]. Consequently, crimes against humanity are crimes which cannot be susceptible of amnesty."*[964] It was further found that *"Amnesty laws [...] leave victims defenseless and perpetuate impunity for crimes against humanity. Therefore, they are overtly incompatible with the wording and the spirit of the American Convention, [...] Consequently, given its nature, Decree Law No.2.191 does not have any legal effects and cannot remain as an obstacle for the investigation of the facts inherent to the instant case, or for the identification and punishment of those responsible therefor."*[965] The court considered that the application of the Chilean amnesty law *„was contrary to the obligations embodied in Article 1(1) of the American Convention and in violation of the rights [...] embodied in Articles 8(1) and 25 of the Convention, for all of which the Chilean State is internationally responsible."*[966] This means that Chile has violated the right to a fair trial and the right to judicial protection.

In 2010, the Court had to deal with the case **Gomes Lund versus Brazil**[967] and decided that the Brazilian Amnesty Law of 1979[968] was contrary to the obligations established in the American Convention and in the Inter-American Court's jurisprudence as it shields perpetrators of serious human rights violations.[969] The Court stated that *"the provisions of the Brazilian Amnesty Law that impedes the investigation and punishment of serious human rights violations lack legal effect. As a consequence, they cannot continue to represent an obstacle in the investigation of the facts in the present*

---

963 The case concerned the Chilean self-amnesty law of 1978 which hindered the prosecution of those responsible for the extrajudicial killing of a professor in 1973. See *Case of Almonacid-Arellano et al v. Chile* (Inter-American Court of Human Rights, 26 September 2006), para. 114Binder, 'The Prohibition of Amnesties by the Inter-American Court of Human Rights', 1210–1.

964 *Case of Almonacid-Arellano et al v. Chile*, para. 114.

965 Ibid., para.119.

966 Ibid., para.128.

967 The case concerned Brazil's 1979 Amnesty Law which hindered the prosecution of those responsible for the disappearance, torture and killings of over 60 students and workers in the early 1970's. *See* Case of Gomes Lund et al.(„Guerrilha do Araguaia") v. Brazil; Freeman and Pensky, 'The Amnesty Controversy in International Law', 58–9.

968 *See* chapter 3.2.1.

969 Case of Gomes Lund et al.(„Guerrilha do Araguaia") v. Brazil.

case, nor for the identification and punishment of those responsible, [...]."[970] The judges argued that the prohibition of enforced disappearance of persons and its related obligation to investigate and punish those responsible has reached a nature of *ius cogens.*[971] In its judgement, the Court explicitly cited various similar rulings of the Inter-American Commission on Human Rights, the organisations of the United Nations, and other universal and regional organisations for the protection of human rights.[972] The judges concluded that all these organisations were convinced of the non-compatibility of amnesty laws related to serious human rights violations with international law and the international obligations of states.[973] It seems reasonable to assume that the Inter-American Court thereby intended to emphasise that a norm for international law on amnesties is crystallizing.[974]

The Court reiterated its view on blanket amnesties in the case **Gelman versus Uruguay**[975] and found that the Uruguayan amnesty law violated the American Convention on Human Rights and the Inter-American Convention on Forced Disappearance of Persons.[976] Moreover, the court determined that "*When a State has ratified an international treaty such as the American Convention, all of its bodies, including its judges, are also subject to such a treaty, and this obligates them to ensure that the effects of the provisions of the Convention are not diminished by the application of norms contrary to its object and purpose.*"[977] Thus, judges in the Inter-American community are bound by international law and must not apply national laws, such as amnesty laws, which are contrary to these international treaties and conventions.[978] The latest judgement by the Inter-American Court concerning a blanket amnesty law was delivered in 2012.

---

970 Case of Gomes Lund et al.(„Guerrilha do Araguaia“) v. Brazil, para. 174.

971 *Case of Gomes Lund et al. ("Guerrilha do Araguaia") v. Brazil*, para.137.

972 Case of Gomes Lund et al.(„Guerrilha do Araguaia“) v. Brazil, paras. 147–170.

973 Case of Gomes Lund et al.(„Guerrilha do Araguaia“) v. Brazil, para. 170.

974 Freeman and Pensky, 'The Amnesty Controversy in International Law', 58–9.

975 The case concerned the enforced disappearance of Maria Claudia Garcia and Uruguay's decision not to investigate and prosecute those responsible. *See* Lessa, 'Barriers to Justice', 140.

976 Inter-American Court of Human Rights, Case Gelman v. Uruguay, Judgement of February 24, 2011 (Merits and Reparations), para. 312.11; *see* chapter 3.2.1.

977 Inter-American Court of Human Rights, Case Gelman v. Uruguay, para. 193.

978 A. Gaudin, *IACHR Rules Against Uruguay in Operacion Condor Case*. http://www.thefreelibrary.com/IACHR+rules+against+Uruguay+in+Operacion+Condor+case.-a0254827283 (12 March 2017).

In the case of **El Mozote versus El Salvador**[979] the Court again decided that the state has an obligation to investigate and that the amnesty law shall not present an obstacle to the identification, prosecution and punishment of those responsible.[980] However, contrary to the cases examined previously the general amnesty law relates to acts committed in the context of an internal armed conflict.[981] Therefore, the Court examined Article 6 (5) of Protocol II Additional to the 1949 Geneva Conventions and found that *„According to the international humanitarian law applicable to these situations, the enactment of amnesty laws on the conclusion of hostilities in non-international armed conflicts are sometimes justified to pave the way to a return to peace. However, this norm is not absolute, because, under international humanitarian law, States also have an obligation to investigate and prosecute war crimes. [...] Consequently, it may be understood that article 6(5) of Additional Protocol II refers to extensive amnesties [...], provided that this does not involve facts, [...] that can be categorized as war crimes, and even crimes against humanity.*"[982]Thus, the Salvadorian amnesty law can not be justified by the application of Article 6 (5) of Additional Protocol II.

To sum up, the Inter-American Court's assessment of various wide-ranging (self-) amnesty laws leads to the conclusion that such laws are illegitimate, since they obstruct the prosecution of perpetrators responsible for serious human rights violations. In the case of Brazil it was argued that the obligation to investigate and punish those responsible for enforced disappearance has reached a nature of *ius cogens.*[983] In almost all cases the judges determined that the respective amnesty laws prevented the victims' next of kin and the surviving victims from being heard by a judge, as established in Article 8(1) of the American Convention on Human Rights. Furthermore, that they violated the right to judicial protection embodied in Article 25 of the Convention and that they prevented the investigation, capture, prosecution and conviction of those responsible, thus failing to comply with Article 1(1) of the Convention. The court took a tough stance in so far as the judges in all but one case did not consider the possibility

979 The case concerned the executions of more than 1000 Salvadorans by the Salvadoran army in 1981 and the failure of El Salvador to investigate and prosecute those responsible for these atrocities. *See* Tico Times, *Human Rights Court Condemns El Salvador for El Mozote Massacre.*

980 *Case of the Massacres of el Mozote and Nearby Places v. El Salvador*, para. 296; *see* Chapter 3.2.1.

981 Ibid., para.284.

982 Ibid., para.285, 286.

983 *Case of Gomes Lund et al. ("Guerrilha do Araguaia") v. Brazil*, para.137.

that an amnesty might be necessary in order to prevent further serious human rights violations and re-establish peace.[984] This may be due to Latin-America's specific history as well as to the particular circumstances in the region.[985] However, in the case of El Salvador the Court examined Article 6 (5) of Protocol II Additional to the 1949 Geneva Conventions and stated that amnesty laws are sometimes justified to pave the way to a return to peace. Nevertheless, the judges found that States also have an obligation to investigate and prosecute war crimes and crimes against humanity and therefore, the Salvadorian amnesty law can not be justified by the application of Article 6 (5) of Additional Protocol II.

3.4.2 The Special Court for Sierra Leone

Following many years of civil war between the Revolutionary United Front (RUF) and the Government of Sierra Leone, the parties in conflict signed a peace accord, the Lomé Agreement, in 1999.[986] Article IX of the Agreement established an *"absolute and free pardon and reprieve to all combatants and collaborators in respect of anything done by them in pursuit of their objectives, up to the time of the signing of the present Agreement."* Thus, no official or judicial action has been taken against those responsible for horrendous crimes. In the final stage of the Lomé peace negotiations, the Special Representative of the UN Secretary-General made an explicit reservation to his signature, stating that the United Nations does not recognise amnesty for genocide, crimes against humanity, war crimes, and other serious violations of international humanitarian law.[987] Since violence continued despite the granting of amnesties, the Sierra Leonean Government refrained from implementing the Lomé accord and instead

---

984 *See* Chapter 3.1.2; Seibert-Fohr, *Prosecuting Serious Human Rights Violations*, 107.

985 Seibert-Fohr, *Prosecuting Serious Human Rights Violations*, 108–109.

986 Peace Agreement between the Governement of Sierra Leone and the RUF (Lomé Peace Agreement); S. M. Meisenberg, 'Legality of Amnesties in International Humanitarian Law: The Lomé Amnesty Decision of the Special Court for Sierra Leone', *International Review of the Red Cross* 86 (2004), 837–51, at 839; *see also*, Chapter 3.2.2.

987 *Peace Agreement between the Governement of Sierra Leone and the RUF (Lomé Peace Agreement)*; United Nations Human Rights Council, *Analytical Study on Human Rights and Transitional Justice*, p. 17; Stahn, 'United Nations Peace-Building, Amnesties and Alternative Forms of Justice', 196; *see* Chapter 3.2.2.

requested the formation of a hybrid tribunal.[988] In 2002, the Special Court for Sierra Leone (SCSL) was created in order *"to prosecute persons who bear the greatest responsibility for serious violations of international humanitarian law and Sierra Leonean law committed in the territory of Sierra Leone since 30 November 1996."*[989] In accordance with his earlier statement concerning the amnesty provision of the Lomé Agreement, the Secretary-General in the report on the establishment of the Special Court for Sierra Leone highlighted that the *„United Nations has consistently maintained the position that amnesty cannot be granted in respect of international crimes"*.[990] Consequently, Article 10 of the Statute of the SCSL determines that *„An amnesty granted to any person falling within the jurisdiction of the Special Court in respect of the crimes referred to in articles 2 to 4 of the present Statute shall not be a bar to prosecution."*[991] The crimes referred to in Articles 2 to 4 are crimes under international law.[992] The decisive question to be answered by the court was whether the amnesty provision of the Lomé Agreement precluded the judges from conducting criminal proceedings. This legal issue was raised in connection with four separate trials before the SCSL.[993] In 2004, the Appeals Chamber rendered a comprehensive decision on a challenge to jurisdiction in the case of **Prosecutor versus Kallon and Kamara.**[994] Kallon and Kamara, both former members of the RUF and accused of crimes against humanity and war crimes, argued that the amnesty provision prevents the court from exercising jurisdiction.[995] The judges assessed this matter quite differently and referred to the principle of universal jurisdiction.[996] They explained that even though a state is allowed to grant

988 Mallinder, 'Amnesties', 888; B. van Schaack and R. C. Slye, *International Criminal Law and Its Enforcement* (New York: Foundation Press, 2007), p. 875.

989 *Statute of the Special Court for Sierra Leone*. http://www.rscsl.org/Documents/scsl-statute.pdf (16 March 2017), Art. 1.

990 United Nations Security Council, *Report of the Secretary-General on the Establishment of a Special Court for Sierra Leone*, para. 22, *see* Chapter 3.2.2.

991 *Statute of the Special Court for Sierra Leone*.

992 Such as crimes against humanity, violations of Common Article 3 of the Geneva Conventions and other serious violations of international humanitarian law. *See* Statute of the Special Court for Sierra Leone, art. 2 to 4.

993 Williams, 'Amnesties in International Law', 272–3.

994 *Prosecutor v. Morris Kallon and Brima Bazzy Kamara, Decision on Challenge to Jurisdiction: Lomé Accord Amnesty* (Special Court for Sierra Leone, 13 March 2004).

995 Mallinder, *Amnesty, Human Rights and Political Transitions:*, pp. 258–60; Williams, 'Amnesties in International Law', 272–3.

996 Mallinder, *Amnesty, Human Rights and Political Transitions:*, pp. 258–60.

amnesties due to its sovereignty, this does not mean that other states are bound by these amnesties.[997] In the event that the amnesty encompasses grave international crimes which can be prosecuted according to universal jurisdiction, "*a State cannot deprive another State of its jurisdiction to prosecute the offender by the granting of an amnesty.*"[998] The judges concluded from this that the Sierra Leonean amnesty "*is also ineffective in depriving an international court such as the Special Court of jurisdiction.*"[999] This means that the SCSL is entitled to disregard the amnesty and, consequently, to prosecute crimes under international law. With regard to the general question of the legitimacy of amnesties under international law, the Appeals Chamber elaborated "*that there is a crystallising international norm that a government cannot grant amnesty for serious violations of crimes under international law.*"[1000] Thus, although the norm has not yet crystallised, "*it is accepted that such a norm is developing under international law.*"[1001] It is worth mentioning that the court did not carry out its own unbiased investigation and analysis of the state of international law and practice regarding amnesties, but drew upon the evaluation of the parties to the proceedings.[1002] In so doing the judges argued that there are several treaties requiring prosecution for serious crimes, such as the 1948 Convention on the Prevention and Punishment of the Crime of Genocide, the Convention against Torture and Other Cruel, Inhuman or Degrading Treatment or Punishment and the four Geneva Conventions.[1003] They referred to the statement that „*to the extent that the amnesty encompasses crimes against humanity, serious war crimes, torture and other gross violations of human rights its validity is highly doubtful.*"[1004] Finally, it was argued that „*Even if the opinion is held that Sierra Leone may not have breached customary law in granting an amnesty, this court is entitled in the exercise of its discretionary power, to attribute little or no weight to the grant of such amnesty which is*

997 *Prosecutor v. Morris Kallon and Brima Bazzy Kamara, Decision on Challenge to Jurisdiction: Lomé Accord Amnesty*, para. 67.

998 Ibid.

999 Ibid., para. 88.

1000 Ibid., para. 82.

1001 Ibid.

1002 Freeman, *Necessary Evils*, pp. 52–3; Freeman and Pensky, 'The Amnesty Controversy in International Law', 60–1; Williams, 'Amnesties in International Law', 307.

1003 *Prosecutor v. Morris Kallon and Brima Bazzy Kamara, Decision on Challenge to Jurisdiction: Lomé Accord Amnesty*, para.82.

1004 Ibid., para.83.

contrary to the direction in which customary international law is developing and which is contrary to the obligations in certain treaties and conventions the purpose of which is to protect humanity."[1005]

The amnesty question has also been raised in the subsequent cases **Prosecutor versus Kondewa**[1006], **Prosecutor versus Gbao**[1007] and **Prosecutor versus Fofana**[1008]. The Appeals Chamber reiterated its view on the scope of the amnesty and rejected all challenges to its jurisdiction.[1009] In the context of the decision in *Prosecutor vs. Kondewa*, Justice Robertson delivered a notable separate opinion. He made reference to the state practice of granting amnesties even for serious international crimes and concluded that "*the degree to which international criminal law forbids or nullifies amnesties must be open to some question.*"[1010] Justice Robertson, nevertheless, detected the development towards the prosecution of those most responsible for serious international crimes and hence the exclusion of amnesty in these cases.[1011] In his opinion, "*State practice is changing to conform with the consistent view that blanket amnesties are, at least 'in general', impermissible in international law for international crimes.*"[1012]

Just like the Inter-American Court of Human Rights, the Special Court for Sierra Leone did not consider the possibility that an amnesty might be necessary in order to prevent further serious human rights violations and re-establish peace.[1013] The judges of the SCSL furthermore neglected

1005 Ibid., para.84.

1006 *Prosecutor v. Allieu Kondewa, Decision on Lack of Jurisdiction/Abuse of Process: Amnesty Provided by the Lomé Accord* (Special Court for Sierra Leone, 25 May 2004).

1007 *Prosecutor v. Augustine Gbao, Decision on Preliminary Motion on the Invalidity of the Agreement between the United Nations and the Government of Sierra Leone on the Establishment of the Special Court* (Special Court for Sierra Leone, 25 May 2004).

1008 *Prosecutor v. Moinina Fofana, Decision on Preliminary Motion on Lack of Jurisdiction: Illegal Delegation of Jurisdiction by Sierra Leone* (Special Court for Sierra Leone, 25 May 2004).

1009 Williams, 'Amnesties in International Law', 272–3.

1010 *Prosecutor v. Allieu Kondewa, Decision on Lack of Jurisdiction/Abuse of Process: Amnesty Provided by the Lomé Accord,* paras. 30, 47–48; Freeman, *Necessary Evils*, pp. 52–3; Williams, 'Amnesties in International Law', 301.

1011 *Prosecutor v. Allieu Kondewa, Decision on Lack of Jurisdiction/Abuse of Process: Amnesty Provided by the Lomé Accord,* para. 48; Williams, 'Amnesties in International Law', 308.

1012 *Prosecutor v. Allieu Kondewa, Decision on Lack of Jurisdiction/Abuse of Process: Amnesty Provided by the Lomé Accord*, para. 48.

1013 *See* Chapter 3.1.2; Williams, 'Amnesties in International Law', 308.

the specific situation in Sierra Leone and the circumstances in which the amnesty was issued.[1014]

3.4.3 The European Court of Human Rights

The European Court of Human Rights (ECtHR) has not yet directly ruled on the compatibility of specific amnesty laws with the European Convention for the Protection of Human Rights and Fundamental Freedoms.[1015] This may be due to the different history and extent of amnesties compared to, for example, Latin-America. However, with regard to cases concerning serious human rights violations, the Court has referred to the duty to investigate and prosecute the perpetrators of these crimes and has thereby indirectly also taken a stand on amnesties.[1016] In 1996, the judges had to deal with the case **Aksoy versus Turkey**[1017] and decided that *"the fundamental importance of the prohibition of torture [...] and the especially vulnerable position of torture victims"* leads to an *"obligation on States to carry out a thorough and effective investigation of incidents of torture"* which is *"capable of leading to the identification and punishment of those responsible"*.[1018] An explicit obligation to prosecute and punish perpetrators of torture cannot be deduced from this statement.[1019] The obligation rather concerns the investigation itself which must be capable of leading to punishment.[1020] Several years later, however, in the cases **Yaman versus Turkey (2004)**[1021] and **Ould Dah versus France (2009)**[1022] the ECtHR pointed out, *obiter dic-*

1014 Ibid., p. 308.

1015 Bassiouni, *Introduction to International Criminal Law*, p. 977; UN Office of the High Commissioner for Human Rights, *Rule-of-Law Tools for Post-Conflict States*, p. 24; Transitional Justice Institute, *The Belfast Guidelines on Amnesty and Accountability*, p. 45.

1016 Transitional Justice Institute, *The Belfast Guidelines on Amnesty and Accountability*, p. 45.

1017 *Case of Aksoy v. Turkey* (European Court of Human Rights, 18 December 1996).

1018 Ibid., para. 98.

1019 Transitional Justice Institute, *The Belfast Guidelines on Amnesty and Accountability*, p. 44.

1020 Ibid., p. 44.

1021 *Case of Abdülsamet Yaman v. Turkey* (European Court of Human Rights, 02 November 2004), para. 55.

1022 *Case of Ely Ould Dah v. France* (European Court of Human Rights, 17 March 2009).

tum[1023], that the granting of amnesties for torture or ill-treatment should not be permissible, as this would undermine the obligation to prosecute and may be contrary to international law.[1024] In **Marguš versus Croatia (2012)** the judges went further and stated: *"Granting amnesty in respect of "international crimes" – which include crimes against humanity, war crimes and genocide – is increasingly considered to be prohibited by international law. This understanding is drawn from customary rules of international humanitarian law, human rights treaties, as well as the decisions of international and regional courts and developing State practice, as there has been a growing tendency for international, regional and national courts to overturn general amnesties enacted by Governments."*[1025] This view is in line with the jurisprudence of the Inter-American Court for Human Rights and the Special Court for Sierra Leone. But, unlike these courts, the European Court for Human Rights also considered the possibility that an amnesty might be necessary in order to prevent further serious human rights violations and re-establish peace.[1026] From this point of view, the ECtHR judges in their **2013 Tarbuk versus Croatia** decision found that *"even in such fundamental areas of the protection of human rights as the right to life, the State is justified in enacting [...] any amnesty laws it might consider necessary, with the proviso, however, that a balance is maintained between the legitimate interests of the State and the interests of individual members of the public"*.[1027] Thus the granting of amnesties even for international crimes might be acceptable provided that vital interests of the state such as peace and reconciliation are at stake.[1028]

1023 *Obiter dictum* – that is, an expression of opinion which is not essential to the decision and therefore not legally binding as a precedent, *see Oxford Dictionaries: Obiter Dictum*. https://en.oxforddictionaries.com/definition/obiter_dictum (21 March 2017).

1024 Kreß and Grover, 'International Criminal Law Restraints in Peace Talks to End Armed Conflicts of a Non-International Character', 51; Naqvi, *Impediments to Exercising Jurisdiction over International Crimes*, pp. 112–3; A. Buyse, *Amnesty and Torture*. http://echrblog.blogspot.de/2009/03/amnesty-and-torture.html (17 February 2017).

1025 *Case of Marguš v. Croatia* (European Court of Human Rights, 13 November 2012), para. 74.

1026 Transitional Justice Institute, *The Belfast Guidelines on Amnesty and Accountability*, p. 45.

1027 *Case of Tarbuk v. Croatia* (European Court of Human Rights, 29 April 2013), para. 50.

1028 Transitional Justice Institute, *The Belfast Guidelines on Amnesty and Accountability*, p. 45.

3.4.4 The International Criminal Tribunal for the former Yugoslavia

Contrary to the Statute of the Special Court for Sierra Leone, the statute of the *ad hoc* International Criminal Tribunal for the former Yugoslavia (ICTY), established in 1993, does not contain any specific provision on amnesties.[1029] Nor did the resolution of any case before the ICTY depend on the legal validity of an amnesty law.[1030] The court has nevertheless expressed its legal view on the legitimacy of amnesties — this was *obiter dictum*[1031].[1032] In 1998, in the case of **Prosecutor versus Furundzija**[1033] the trial chamber determined: „*The fact that torture is prohibited by a peremptory norm of international law has other effects at the inter-state and individual levels. At the inter-state level, it serves to internationally de-legitimise any legislative, administrative or judicial act authorising torture. It would be senseless to argue, on the one hand, that on account of the jus cogens value of the prohibition against torture, treaties or customary rules providing for torture would be null and void ab initio, and then be unmindful of a State say, taking national measures authorising or condoning torture or absolving its perpetrators through an amnesty law.*“[1034] This means that the judges of the ICTY concluded from the *jus cogens* character of the prohibition of torture an absolute obligation not to issue amnesties in those cases. In their view, the peremptory prohibition of torture and the resulting illegality of any treaty or agreement allowing such crime would be meaningless without the prohibition of granting impunity for perpetrators who have committed these atrocities classified as *jus cogens*.[1035] The trial chamber furthermore stated that perpetrators of torture who benefit from amnesties *"may nevertheless be held criminally responsible for torture, whether in a foreign State, or in their own State under a subsequent regime."*[1036] As for amnesty laws in general, the judges referred to General Comment No. 20 of the UN Human Rights

1029 Naqvi, *Impediments to Exercising Jurisdiction over International Crimes*, p. 85.

1030 Sadat, 'Individuel Progress in International Law', 348.

1031 *See* Footnote 938.

1032 Freeman and Pensky, 'The Amnesty Controversy in International Law', 59.

1033 *Prosecutor v. Anto Furundzija* (International Criminal Tribunal for the former Yugoslavia (ICTY), 10 December 1998).

1034 *Prosecutor v. Anto Furundzija*, para. 155.

1035 *See also*, Chapter 3.1.2 and the question ‚Is the International Obligation to Prosecute Absolute?‘.

1036 *Prosecutor v. Anto Furundzija*, para. 155.

Committee which came to the conclusion that *"amnesties are generally incompatible with the duty of States to investigate [acts of torture]."*[1037]

The frequently cited[1038] judgement in the *Furundzija* case is however open to criticism. Firstly, as already examined in Chapter 3.1.2, the peremptory character of the prohibition of torture does not necessarily lead to a peremptory duty to prosecute these crimes and thus has no reasonable impact on the legitimacy of respective amnesties.[1039] The court should therefore have elucidated its legal position in more depth.[1040] Furthermore, to substantiate its view on amnesties, it would have been essential for the trial chamber to conduct a thorough analysis of the state of international law and the practice of states with regard to the granting of amnesties.[1041] Finally, since the ICTY's stance on amnesties was *obiter dictum*, its significance for the assessment of amnesties should not be overestimated.[1042]

3.4.5 The Extraordinary Chambers in the Courts of Cambodia

Following peace negotiations between the Government of Cambodia and the oppressive Khmer Rouge communist group, an amnesty law, which

---

1037 Ibid., para. 155, n. 172 (*citing*, Compilation of General Comments and General Recommendations Adopted by Human Rights Treaty Bodies,U.N. Doc.HRI\GEN\1\Rev. 1 at 30 (1994)).

1038 *See* for example: United Nations Commission on Human Rights, *Independent Study on Best Practices, Including Recommendations, to Assist States in Strengthening Their Domestic Capacity to Combat all Aspects of Impunity, by Professor Diane Orentlicher*, E/CN.4/2004/88. http://www.unhchr.ch/Huridocda/Huridoca.nsf/0/94b45b7493a558cac1256e6e005a6d1d/$FILE/G0411355.pdf (20 March 2017), p. 11; UN Office of the High Commissioner for Human Rights, *Rule-of-Law Tools for Post-Conflict States*, pp. 29–30; Iliopoulos, *Afghan Amnesty Law a Setback for Peace*; International Federation for Human Rights (FIDH), *Afghanistan: Victims' Voice Must Be Heard*. http://www.fidh.org/Afghanistan-Victims-voice-must-be (13 March 2017).

1039 O'Keefe, *International Criminal law*, p. 476; *See also*, Chapter 3.1.2 and the question ‚Is the International Obligation to Prosecute Absolute?'.

1040 Freeman and Pensky, 'The Amnesty Controversy in International Law', 59–60.

1041 Ibid., 60; *see* Article 53 of the Vienna Convention on the Law of Treaties, which states that *"a peremptory norm of general international law is a norm accepted and recognized by the international community of States as a whole as a norm from which no derogation is permitted ....";* *see also* Chapter 3.1.2 and the question ‚Is the International Obligation to Prosecute Absolute?'.

1042 Ibid., 59.

explicitly excluded the leaders of the Khmer Rouge from its scope, was enacted in 1994.[1043] The amnesty law also provided that the King has the discretion to pardon.[1044] In 1996, the King exploited this legal opportunity and pardoned the former Deputy Prime Minister of the Khmer Rouge regime, Ieng Sary.[1045] A year later however the Cambodian Government and the United Nations started consultations on the establishment of an internationalised domestic tribunal to try those perpetrators who were most responsible.[1046]

After a further seven years, the "Law on the Establishment of the Extraordinary Chambers in the Courts of Cambodia [ECCC] for the Prosecution of Crimes Committed during the Period of Democratic Kampuchea"[1047] of 2004 was enacted. Article 40 of that law determines: *"[...] The scope of any amnesty or pardon that may have been granted prior to the enactment of this Law is a matter to be decided by the Extraordinary Chambers."* This meant that the scope of the 1996 pardon of Ieng Sary could be reviewed by the Extraordinary Chambers.[1048] The wording of Article 40 is somewhat surprising given that the legal question of the validity of the amnesty had not already been solved on that time.[1049]

Hence the legitimacy of the amnesty law and the pardon was examined by the ECCC in the decision on **Ieng Sary's Rule 89 Preliminary Objections**[1050] in 2011. Ieng Sary, accused of war crimes, crimes against

---

1043 Mallinder, 'Amnesties', 854.

1044 Ibid., 854–5.

1045 Ibid., 855; D. Scheffer, 'The Extraordinary Chambers in the Courts of Cambodia' in M. C. Bassiouni (ed.), *International Criminal Law, Volume III: International Enforcement*, 3rd edn. (Leiden: Martinus Nijhoff Publishers/Brill Academic, 2008), pp. 219–55, at p. 247.

1046 Mallinder, 'Amnesties', 855; Scheffer, 'The Extraordinary Chambers in the Courts of Cambodia', 247–8.

1047 *Law on the Establishment of the Extraordinary Chambers in the Courts of Cambodia for the Prosecution of Crimes Committed during the Period of Democratic Kampuchea*, S/RKM/1004/006. https://www.eccc.gov.kh/sites/default/files/legal-documents/KR_Law_as_amended_27_Oct_2004_Eng.pdf (21 March 2017).

1048 Scheffer, 'The Extraordinary Chambers in the Courts of Cambodia', 248.

1049 D. Jacobs, 'Puzzling over Amnesties: Defragmenting the Debate for International Criminal Tribunals' in L. van den Herik and C. Stahn (eds.), *The Diversification and Fragmentation of International Criminal Law*, Leiden studies on the frontiers of international law (Leiden, Boston: Martinus Nijhoff Publishers, 2012), pp. 305–45, at p. 323.

1050 *ECCC Trial Chamber – Decision on Ieng Sary's Rule 89 Preliminary Objections* (Extraordinary Chambers in the Courts of Cambodia, 03 November 2011).

humanity and genocide[1051], questioned the jurisdiction of the Court and argued that the royal amnesty and pardon was valid and would shield him from prosecution.[1052] The trial chamber disagreed and decided to attribute no weight to Ieng Sary's amnesty and pardon as it was contrary to the direction in which customary international law was developing and to Cambodia's international obligations.[1053] Consequently, the 1996 Royal Decree did not bar the trial chamber's exercise of jurisdiction over the accused.[1054] With regard to the legitimacy of amnesties in general, the judges of the ECCC noted that *"an emerging consensus prohibits amnesties in relation to serious international crimes, based on a duty to investigate and prosecute these crimes and to punish their perpetrators. As previously indicated, relevant treaty obligations impose an absolute prohibition in relation to genocide, torture and grave breaches of the 1949 Geneva Conventions (Section 4.5.1). Although state practice in relation to other serious international crimes is arguably insufficiently uniform to establish an absolute prohibition of amnesties in relation to them, this practice demonstrates at a minimum a retroactive right for third States, internationalised and domestic courts to evaluate amnesties and to set them aside or limit their scope should they be deemed incompatible with international norms."*[1055] This meant that the ECCC was convinced that an absolute prohibition of amnesties in relation to genocide, torture and grave breaches of the 1949 Geneva Conventions exists. With respect to other serious crimes, state practice is considered as insufficiently uniform to establish an absolute prohibition of amnesties. Unlike the SCSL and the ICTY, the ECCC trial chamber conducted an analysis of state practice concerning amnesties in order to substantiate its legal view.[1056] Furthermore, the judges mentioned the specific situation in Democratic Kampuchea and the circumstances in which the amnesty was issued.[1057] Just like the ECtHR, they were mindful of the possibility that an amnesty might be

1051 Radio Netherlands Worldwide, *Amnesty Not Applicable for KRouge Defendant.* http://www.rnw.nl/international-justice/article/amnesty-not-applicable-krouge-defendant (17 February 2014).

1052 *ECCC Trial Chamber – Decision on Ieng Sary's Rule 89 Preliminary Objections*, para. 1.

1053 Ibid., para. 54.

1054 Ibid., para. 55.

1055 Ibid., para. 53.

1056 Ibid., para. 40–52.

1057 *„It is uncontested that IENG Sary and a large number of combatants reintegrated with the Government as a result of the Royal Decree, and that this may have contributed to restoring peace in Cambodia. While the 1996 amnesty may have been a useful negotiation tool in ending the conflict,[…]"*, Ibid., para. 54.

necessary in order to end a violent conflict and re-establish peace. They did however criticise that the amnesty "*was unaccompanied by any truth or reconciliation process through which information regarding Accused IENG Sary's alleged crimes could be revealed or the internationally-enshrined rights of victims to an effective remedy otherwise acknowledge*".[1058]

3.4.6 Conclusion

The analysis of decisions rendered by various international, hybrid and regional human rights courts on amnesty regulations from around the world revealed that all of them reject domestic amnesties for serious human rights violations as they are in contradiction with several international treaties and in part with (emerging) customary international law.[1059] It has to be noted however that most amnesties assessed by the judges were wide-ranging self-amnesties.[1060] Whether the same applies to conditional and more nuanced amnesty laws has not yet been determined by any international court.

With regard to customary international law, the Special Court for Sierra Leone elaborated that there is a crystallising prohibition of amnesties for serious international crimes. The judges argued that there are several treaties requiring prosecution for serious crimes and mentioned that „*to the extent that the amnesty encompasses crimes against humanity, serious war crimes, torture and other gross violations of human rights its validity is highly doubtful.*"[1061] In his separate opinion, Justice Robertson, detected the development towards the prosecution of those most responsible for serious

1058 Ibid., para. 54.

1059 Freeman and Pensky, 'The Amnesty Controversy in International Law', 57; van Schaack and Slye, *International Criminal Law and Its Enforcement*, p. 875; Slye, 'The Legitimacy of Amnesties Under International Law and General Principles of Anglo-American Law', 179–80; UN Office of the High Commissioner for Human Rights, *Rule-of-Law Tools for Post-Conflict States: Prosecution Initiatives*, HR/PUB/06/4. http://www.ohchr.org/Documents/Publications/RuleoflawProsecutionsen.pdf (12 March 2017), p. 23; Sadat, 'Individuel Progress in International Law', 351.

1060 Seibert-Fohr, *Prosecuting Serious Human Rights Violations*, pp. 218–9.

1061 *Prosecutor v. Morris Kallon and Brima Bazzy Kamara, Decision on Challenge to Jurisdiction: Lomé Accord Amnesty*, para.83.

international crimes and hence the exclusion of amnesty in these cases.[1062] The jurisprudence of the Inter-American Court of Human Rights and the European Court for Human Rights are in line with this position. In almost all cases the judges of the Inter-American Court determined that the respective amnesty laws prevented the victims' next of kin and the surviving victims from being heard by a judge; that they violated the right to judicial protection; and that they prevented the investigation, capture, prosecution and conviction of those responsible. The Extraordinary Chambers in the Courts of Cambodia went further as the judges are convinced that an absolute prohibition of amnesties in relation to genocide, torture, and grave breaches of the 1949 Geneva Conventions already exists. With respect to other serious crimes, state practice is considered as insufficiently uniform to establish an absolute prohibition of amnesties. The International Criminal Tribunal for the former Yugoslavia extrapolated from the *jus cogens* character of the prohibition of torture to a peremptory duty to prosecute acts of torture and thus to an absolute prohibition of amnesties in these cases. Regrettably, apart from the IACtHR and the ECCC, no other court has conducted a thorough analysis of the state of international law and the practice of states concerning amnesties to substantiate its legal position.

It is also noteworthy that apart from the ECtHR and the ECCC and in one case the IACtHR, no other court has mentioned the possibility that an amnesty might be necessary in order to prevent further serious human rights violations, end a violent conflict and re-establish peace.[1063] The Inter-American Court of Human Rights examined Article 6 (5) of Protocol II Additional to the 1949 Geneva Conventions in the case of El Salvador and stated that amnesty laws are sometimes justified to pave the way to a return to peace. Nevertheless, the judges found that States also have an obligation to investigate and prosecute war crimes and crimes against humanity and therefore, the Salvadorian amnesty law can not be justified by the application of Article 6 (5) of Additional Protocol II.[1064]

To sum up, despite regional disparities and different circumstances, a common standard with respect to the assessment of amnesties can be defined. Although the reasoning as well as the comprehensiveness of the

1062 *Prosecutor v. Allieu Kondewa, Decision on Lack of Jurisdiction/Abuse of Process: Amnesty Provided by the Lomé Accord*, para. 48; Williams, 'Amnesties in International Law', 308.

1063 *See* Chapter 3.1.2; Seibert-Fohr, *Prosecuting Serious Human Rights Violations*, 107.

1064 *Case of the Massacres of el Mozote and Nearby Places v. El Salvador*, para.285, 286.

evidence varies depending on the respective court, it can be established that amnesties for serious human rights violations are either considered unlawful *per se* or the judges referred to a crystallising prohibition of such amnesties. Since the specific situations in the countries concerned and the circumstances in which the amnesty laws were issued have been neglected by almost all international courts, it may be assumed that these aspects were of minor importance for the assessment of the amnesty provisions.

As for the evaluation of the Afghan Amnesty Law, the international jurisprudence on different amnesties is applicable only to a limited extent since each case has its unique characteristics and hence is incomparable.[1065] It seems quite clear however that the blanket and unconditional Afghan amnesty — which neither led to peace nor did it prevent further serious human rights violations — would not have been accepted by one of the above-mentioned courts.

3.5 How Do Scholars Assess Amnesties?

In the course of this study, it has been established that neither explicit provisions nor solid customary international law or the general principles of law ban the Afghan Amnesty Law. The amnesty is nevertheless in contradiction to Afghanistan's international obligation to investigate and prosecute serious human rights violations. It is furthermore not in accordance with international jurisprudence concerning various amnesty laws from around the world and the current international trend towards the prohibition of blanket amnesties for serious crimes.

The interesting question to be answered in this chapter is how do scholars respond to this nebulous legal situation? Article 38 (1) (d) of the Statute of the International Court of Justice reads: "*[...] the teachings of the most highly qualified publicists of the various nations, as subsidiary means for the determination of rules of law.*" There exists no official list which determines who belongs to 'the most highly qualified publicists of the various nations'.[1066] This may be due to the fact that a scholar's expertise to a very large extent depends on the legal issue and thus, varies from case to case.[1067] Scholarly works comprise of, *inter alia*, publications by scholarly

1065 Freeman, *Necessary Evils*, p. 47; Seibert-Fohr, *Prosecuting Serious Human Rights Violations*, 109.

1066 Hoffman and Berring, *International Legal Research in a Nutshell*, p. 91.

1067 Ibid., p. 91.

associations, journal articles and articles in international law encyclopaedias.[1068] Just like 'judicial decisions' on amnesties, the 'teachings of the most highly qualified publicists of the various nations' do not have the status of a primary source of international law.[1069] They can nevertheless contribute to the determination of legal principles, particularly in terms of developing a general doctrine concerning certain topics.[1070]

With a view to the legitimacy of amnesties, the development of coherent criteria and principles, which may be applied when drafting or assessing amnesty law, would be very helpful.[1071] Even though of a non-binding character, such guidelines would provide legal certainty — not only for national authorities considering the enactment of an amnesty law, but also for courts and third states which have to evaluate the lawfulness of an amnesty.[1072] Furthermore, these criteria and principles could be designed in a way that national interests and international rules are reconciled as far as possible.[1073] This means in particular striking a balance between complete impunity and full accountability.[1074] Yet, in consideration of the complex legal issues surrounding the question of whether or not a certain amnesty is in accordance with international law, this is a challenging task.[1075] There is nevertheless "a new line of scholarship seeking to establish guidelines, tests, and parameters for "legitimate" amnesties", as one author describes it[1076] and this is shown in the next chapter.

1068 Ibid., p. 91.

1069 Eichhofer, 'Die Rechtsquellen des Völkerstrafrechts', 10–1; Werle, *Völkerstrafrecht*, p. 74.

1070 Eichhofer, 'Die Rechtsquellen des Völkerstrafrechts', 10–1.

1071 O'Shea, *Amnesty for Crime in International Law and Practice*, p. 320.

1072 Cassese, *The Oxford Companion to International Criminal Justice*, p. 158.

1073 O'Shea, *Amnesty for Crime in International Law and Practice*, p. 301; K. Henrard, 'The Viability of National Amnesties in View of the Increasing Recognition of Individual Criminal Responsibility at International Law', *Michigan State University-DCL Journal of International Law* 8 (1999), 595–649, at 634–6.

1074 M. Morris, 'International Guidelines Against Impunity: Facilitating Accountability', *Law and Contemporary Problems* 59 (1996), 29–40, at 29–34; Mallinder, *Amnesty, Human Rights and Political Transitions:*, pp. 24–5.

1075 Cassese, *The Oxford Companion to International Criminal Justice*, p. 158.

1076 L. J. Laplante, 'Outlawing Amnesty: The Return of Criminal Justice in Transitional Justice Schemes', *Virginia Journal of International Law* 49 (2009), 915–84, at 940.

3.5.1 Amnesty Guidelines

The majority of international scholars take the view that those most responsible for serious human rights violations must be prosecuted. However, they are willing to deviate from this principle in exceptional cases.[1077] The relevant guidelines developed by, *inter alia*, Lousie Mallinder, Mark Freeman and Ronald C. Slye as well as the Belfast Guidelines on Amnesty and Accountability are dealt with in the following:

To start with, the **"Belfast Guidelines on Amnesty and Accountability"**[1078] include not only a comprehensive analysis of the state of international law and practice regarding amnesties, but also well-founded principles which aim to assist all those seeking to make or evaluate decisions on amnesties and accountability.[1079] The drafters[1080] of the Belfast Guide-

1077 Seibert-Fohr, *Prosecuting Serious Human Rights Violations*, p. 214; Laplante, 'Outlawing Amnesty', 940–1.

1078 Transitional Justice Institute, *The Belfast Guidelines on Amnesty and Accountability*.

1079 Ibid., p. 1.

1080 The members of the Expert Group were:
- Barney Afako, Ugandan lawyer and a legal consultant in peace processes in Uganda and Darfur, Sudan
- Mahnoush H. Arsanjani, Commissioner, Bahrain Independent Commission of Inquiry and former Director of the Codification Division, UN Office of Legal Affairs
- Christine Bell, Professor of Public International Law, Edinburgh University
- Chaloka Beyani, Senior Lecturer in International Law, London School of Economics and UN Special Rapporteur on the Human Rights of Internally Displaced Persons
- Michael Broache, Fellow in the Doctorate Political Science program at Columbia University
- Colm Campbell, Professor of Law, Transitional Justice Institute, University of Ulster
- Mark Freeman, Executive Director, Institute for Integrated Transitions
- Tom Hadden, Emeritus Professor of Law, Queen's University Belfast and Professor of Law, Transitional Justice Institute, University of Ulster
- Brandon Hamber, Professor of Peace and Conflict and Director, International Conflict Research Institute, University of Ulster
- Hurst Hannum, Professor of International Law, Fletcher School of Law and Diplomacy, Tufts University
- David Kretzmer, Emeritus Professor of International Law, Hebrew University of Jerusalem
- Suzannah Linton, Professor of International Law, Bangor Law School
- Kieran McEvoy, Professor of Law and Transitional Justice, Institute of Criminology and Criminal Justice, Queen's University Belfast

lines are independent and internationally respected human rights and conflict resolution scholars and practitioners from around the world.[1081] Their findings are based on analyses of international treaties and customary international law; decisions by international criminal courts and human rights bodies; UN declarations, guidelines, resolutions and other standards; policy papers from the UN and other international organisations; national legislation; national case law; truth commission reports; peace agreements; scholarly writings; views expressed by the Expert Group as well as feedback received during the consultation process.[1082] The guidelines consist of four parts: general principles; scope of amnesty; amnesty conditions; and amnesty adoption, implementation and review.[1083] In the course of the guidelines, the obligations and objectives of states regarding the protection of human rights are described. Furthermore, the scholars dealt with the legal status and ideal design of amnesties as well as their role in transitional societies.[1084]

As a ***general principle***, Guideline 1 of the Belfast Guidelines establishes that in responding to mass violence, states have multiple obligations under international law to protect human rights and restore or establish peace and stability.[1085] This means, for example, that gross violations of human rights and international crimes must be investigated and prosecuted, but also that recurrence of the crimes and abuses must be prevented and

- Louise Mallinder, Reader in Human Rights and International Law, Transitional Justice Institute, University of Ulster
- William A. Schabas, Professor of International Law, Middlesex University; and Professor of Human Rights and Chairman, Irish Centre for Human Rights, National University of Ireland Galway
- Ronald C. Slye, Professor of Law, Seattle University School of Law; and a commissioner on the Truth, Justice and Reconciliation Commission, Kenya
- Yasmin Sooka, Executive Director, Foundation for Human Rights, South Africa
- Joe William, Founder Director and Senior Advisor, National Peace Council of Sri Lanka, Former Senior Development Advisor, Program Support Unit in Sri Lanka of the Canadian International Development Agency, and PhD student, School of Social and International Studies, University of Bradford, *see* ibid., pp. 2–4.

1081 Ibid., pp. 1–2; Kersten, *Rethinking Amnesty and Accountability*.

1082 Transitional Justice Institute, *The Belfast Guidelines on Amnesty and Accountability*, pp. 4–5.

1083 Ibid., p. 1.

1084 Ibid., p. 1.

1085 Ibid., Guideline 1 (a).

effective protection of human rights in the future must be ensured.[1086] In seeking to fulfil these obligations, states may be guided by broader policy objectives, such as ending conflict or repression; restoring public order and stability; establishing democratic structures and the rule of law; dealing with the underlying causes of conflict or repression; and promoting reconciliation, sustainable peace and other similar objectives.[1087] Like the first-mentioned obligations, these policy objectives often cannot be achieved simultaneously or rapidly and therefore may need to be balanced against each other and against the state's obligations.[1088] Guideline 1 (c) emphasises that amnesties can be designed to further a state's compliance with its legal obligations while also meeting its broader policy objectives.[1089] In their 'Explanatory Guidance on the Belfast Guidelines on Amnesty and Accountability' the drafters acknowledge that conflicted and transitional states may face enormous challenges in fulfilling their obligations.[1090] For example, the obligation to prosecute must be reconciled with other important and mandatory obligations of states, which could have the effect that an amnesty is necessary in order to prevent further serious human rights violations.[1091] However, as there is no binding law that could be applied to resolve any cases of conflict, the harmonisation of competing legal standards with the overall aim of protecting human rights and fulfilling the full range of states' obligations to the greatest extent possible is recommended.[1092] The guidelines which follow this are in line with the recommendation.

Guideline 2 states that in principle those responsible for gross violations of human rights or international crimes should be held accountable. Apart from legal mechanisms of accountability such as individual prosecutions, non-legal mechanisms may also come into question.[1093] According to Guideline 5, depending on their design and implementation, even amnesties can contribute to accountability. This means that amnesties can be designed to complement or operate sequentially with judicial and non-judicial accountability processes. The advantage of such combined approaches is for example that some form of truth and accountability for

---

1086 Ibid., Guideline 1 (a) (i) – (v).
1087 Ibid., Guideline 1 (b) (i) – (v).
1088 Ibid., Guideline 1 (b).
1089 Ibid., Guideline 1 (c).
1090 Ibid., p. 29.
1091 Ibid., p. 30.
1092 Ibid., p. 30.
1093 Ibid., Guideline 2.

cases which are not selected for prosecution can be delivered. In addition, limited prosecutorial resources can be focused on those cases which are deemed to be of a higher priority or where the perpetrator has failed to fulfil the conditions of the amnesty.[1094] Guideline 4 emphasises that *„In all contexts, where amnesties cover serious crimes, it is important to distinguish between illegitimate and legitimate amnesties. Illegitimate amnesties are generally unconditional and have the effect of preventing investigations and ensuring impunity for persons responsible for serious crimes. Amnesties are more likely to be viewed as legitimate where they are primarily designed to create institutional and security conditions for the sustainable protection of human rights, and require individual offenders to engage with measures to ensure truth, accountability and reparations.“*

In order to determine precisely whether or not a particular amnesty is legitimate under international law, the Belfast Guidelines contain several criteria concerning the ***scope of amnesties***. In Guideline 7 the **eligible offences**, that is, the acts which qualify for amnesty are defined. Since it is very difficult to find a balance between limiting the crimes covered by an amnesty and fulfilling the amnesty's objectives different options should be contemplated.[1095] Options that could be considered are: explicitly listing offences that are excluded from the scope of the amnesty; granting amnesty for a non-exhaustive list of conflict-related or political offences but with guidelines on how to distinguish political from ordinary offences; or granting amnesty for an exhaustive list of offences.[1096] According to Guideline 7 (c) (i) – (iii) *„the exclusion of the following acts from an amnesty may serve to increase its legitimacy and legality: serious international crimes; other serious acts of violence against persons that may not rise to the level of an international crime; acts or offences motivated by personal gain or malice.“* With regard to the **eligible beneficiaries**, that is, perpetrators who benefit from an amnesty, Guideline 8 (b) determines that distinctions can be made on the basis of allegiance or membership of a particular state institution or non-state body or on the basis of rank within the institution or body, or perceived level of responsibility therein. This means, for example, that amnesties that distinguish in terms of rank may exclude leaders while making amnesty feasible for lower-level offenders.[1097] Such an approach can however be suboptimal as high-ranking perpetrators are often key stake-

1094 Ibid., Guideline 5 (a) (b).
1095 Ibid., Guideline 7 (a).
1096 Ibid., Guideline 7 (b).
1097 Ibid., Guideline 8 (d).

holders in a political transition.[1098] The **temporal scope** of an amnesty should state the start and end dates within which eligible crimes must have been committed. The selection of these dates shall not be used strategically to exclude particular notorious events or crimes committed by only one faction because otherwise the amnesty could be regarded as illegitimate.[1099] Guideline 10 concerns the **geographic scope** of an amnesty, i.e. the amnesty may be restricted to offences committed within a certain region or applied in the whole country.

Apart from the precise scope of an amnesty, particular conditions must be fulfilled so that an amnesty can be considered legitimate under international law. Therefore, the Belfast Guidelines also include detailed explanations concerning ***amnesty conditions*** which should be imposed on individual offenders who wish to obtain amnesty. According to Guideline 11, specified conditions may enable an amnesty to contribute to preventing further violence and to facilitate accountability and the fulfilment of victims' rights to truth and reparations. Such conditions could be: submitting individual applications; surrendering and participating in disarmament, demobilisation and reintegration programmes; participating in traditional or restorative justice processes; fully disclosing personal involvement in offences, with penalties for false testimony; providing information on third party involvement with respect to offences; testifying (publicly or privately) in a truth commission, public inquiry or other truth-recovery process; testifying at the trial of those who were not granted or eligible for amnesty; surrendering assets illegitimately acquired; and contributing materially and/or symbolically to reparations.[1100] Where individuals fail to comply fully with applicable conditions, amnesty should be withheld.[1101] The beneficiaries of amnesties may also be subject to conditions that they must fulfil in order to avoid revocation of the benefits.[1102] Those conditions may include: not breaching the conditions on which the amnesty was originally granted; refraining from the commission of new conflict-related or political offences, or any other type of criminal activity; and time-limited bans on owning dangerous weapons, standing for election or public office, and/or serving in the police or armed forces.[1103] In the event

1098 Ibid.

1099 Transitional Justice Institute, *The Belfast Guidelines on Amnesty and Accountability*, Guideline 9 (a).

1100 Ibid., Guideline 11 (a) – (i).

1101 Ibid., Guideline 11.

1102 Ibid., Guideline 12.

1103 Ibid., Guideline 12 (a) (i) -(iii).

that beneficiaries abuse the amnesty process, they can be held accountable. It is intended that this will encourage amnesty beneficiaries to contribute to peace and reconciliation processes.[1104]

The fourth part of the Belfast Guidelines relates to ***amnesty adoption, implementation and review.*** In Guideline 14, the methods of enactment and public consultation are discussed. According to this guideline, amnesties may be enacted through a range of executive and legislative mechanisms.[1105] Public consultation may increase the legitimacy of an amnesty, especially when potentially marginalised groups such as victims, women, children, displaced persons, minorities and former combatants are involved.[1106] Apart from public consultations, national referenda in the form of holding votes on a peace agreement or new constitution that includes amnesty provisions can also serve to increase the legitimacy of an amnesty law.[1107] Self-amnesties, i.e. amnesties adopted unilaterally by regimes that are responsible for international crimes or gross violations of human rights, should be regarded as *prima facie* illegal and illegitimate.[1108]

As mentioned above, the Belfast Guidelines were drafted by renowned international scholars, including Louise Mallinder, William A. Schabas, Mark Freeman, Ronald C. Slye and Christine Bell. All of them have published books and/or articles on amnesties and accountability. Since the 'Belfast Guidelines on Amnesty and Accountability' to a large extent contain the views and recommendations of these scholars, the following section comprises only additions to or specifications of the issue.

Louise Mallinder developed 20 general guidelines on amnesties[1109], based on, *inter alia*, the cases in her Amnesty Law Database.[1110] Guideline 1 states that amnesty should be introduced in exceptional conditions and in good faith by all parties to meet clearly defined goals. According to Guideline 2, amnesty laws should be part of wider reform or post-conflict justice measures. Further guidelines determine that the extent of the threat of prosecutions should be considered before an amnesty is enacted (Guideline 3), that amnesty laws should be discrete and time-limited tools (Guideline 6) and that they must comply with a state's international legal obligations (Guideline 9). Furthermore, the territorial scope of an amnesty

1104 Ibid., Guideline 12 (a).
1105 Ibid., Guideline 14 (a).
1106 Ibid., Guideline 14 (b).
1107 Ibid., Guideline 14 (c).
1108 Ibid., Guideline 14 (e).
1109 Mallinder, 'Amnesties', 894–900.
1110 Ibid., 894.

cannot extend beyond the borders of the state in which it was introduced, because it is a recognized principle of international law that amnesties introduced in one state are not binding upon other states (Guideline 11). With regard to the temporal scope of the amnesty, Mallinder emphasises that this can be particularly problematic where the State has experienced human rights violations throughout changing political contexts, such as Afghanistan. The time limits that are chosen should reflect the objectives of the amnesty (Guideline 12). Finally, national amnesties could benefit from international assistance (Guideline 20).[1111]

In her book "Amnesty, Human Rights and Political Transitions: Bridging the Peace and Justice Divide" Mallinder describes several key issues which should be considered when introducing or assessing amnesty laws.[1112] They correspond to the Belfast Guidelines and include the following questions: How was the amnesty enacted? Did it have democratic approval? What crimes did the amnesty cover? Did the amnesty only immunise state agents from prosecution? Did the amnesty differentiate between different levels of culpability? Was the judicial system capable of prosecuting human rights violations and ensuring the accused the right to due process? Were appropriate alternative remedies made available to the victims? Were victims permitted to participate in the amnesty hearings? And if so, were resources made available to facilitate such participation and to support the victims after they had given testimony? Has the amnesty contributed to stability within the country? Is it likely that without the amnesty the violence would have continued? Did the state undertake measures to prevent a repetition of the human rights violations by investigating past violations and conducting institutional reforms? Did all the parties to the transition comply with the terms of the amnesty? Did the amnesty proposals/process receive international approval and support? Were efforts made to encourage targeted groups or individuals to participate in the amnesty process?[1113] Mallinder furthermore points out that the unique conditions within a state, such as the availability of resources and the duration of the conflict should duly be taken into account.[1114]

Mark Freeman also elaborated 'Guidelines for Effective Amnesty Design', noting that an amnesty's legitimacy depends on many elements.[1115]

1111 All guidelines are listed in, ibid., 894–900.

1112 Mallinder, *Amnesty, Human Rights and Political Transitions:*.

1113 Ibid., pp. 408–9.

1114 Ibid., p. 413.

1115 Freeman, *Necessary Evils*, p. 31.

In his view, an amnesty for human rights crimes should be enacted only as a last recourse, i.e. only in exceptional situations where fundamental interests are in danger.[1116] Furthermore, any other options[1117] that might be appropriate to end an exceptional situation must have been exhausted before enacting an amnesty for human rights crimes. In the event that the exceptional situation cannot be stopped with the aid of these measures, all leniency options, short of amnesty, should be exploited. Such leniency options could be, *inter alia*: the omission of criminal accountability, i.e. neither explicit prosecution nor explicit amnesty is declared; reduced sentencing schemes; alternative sentencing schemes and third-country asylum.[1118] If these measures do not lead to the desired objective and the introduction of an amnesty seems inevitable, the question of the amnesty's design must be answered. For this purpose, Freeman developed overarching criteria that should be applied to guide the specific amnesty design. These criteria comply with the above-mentioned 'Belfast Guidelines on Amnesty and Accountability' and include, for example, that: the amnesty should pursue a legitimate end, for example explicit public interest objectives; the amnesty should confer the minimum leniency possible on the beneficiaries, i.e. the crimes and persons it covers should be as narrow as possible; the amnesty should impose the maximum conditions possible on the beneficiaries; and that the amnesty should be accompanied by transitional justice mechanisms, such as victim reparation programs, institutional reforms and/or a truth commission.[1119] Finally, the author recommends an overall test of effective amnesty design: Is the amnesty crafted in good faith and in a manner that promises to fulfil a state's transitional obligations to the greatest extent possible in the particular context while impairing them as little as possible?[1120]

Another scholar, **Ronald C. Slye**, established six characteristics for a legitimate amnesty eligible for recognition and respect by foreign states and international tribunals.[1121] Such an "accountable amnesty" provides some accountability and more than minimal relief to victims.[1122] The

1116 Ibid., 110–111.
1117 Such options are, for example, political, economic, diplomatic, and legal measures, but also the use of armed force. *See* ibid., 110–111, 113–118.
1118 Ibid., 111, 118–122.
1119 Ibid., 111, 122–182.
1120 Ibid., p. 189.
1121 Slye, 'The Legitimacy of Amnesties Under International Law and General Principles of Anglo-American Law', 240, 245–247.
1122 Ibid., 245.

following criteria must be met: democratic creation of the amnesty; those most responsible for war crimes, crimes against humanity, and other serious violations of international criminal law must be excluded from the scope of the amnesty; some form of public procedure or accountability must be imposed on the amnesty recipients; an opportunity for victims to question and challenge an amnesty as well as concrete benefit, in the form of reparations must be provided; and finally, the amnesty must be designed to facilitate a transition to a more human-rights friendly regime.[1123] Slye concludes that by offering an alternative to traditional trials as a mechanism for justice, accountable amnesties are a possible institutional response to growing calls for restorative justice.[1124]

Although there are further tests, guidelines, and principles with regard to amnesties, these proposals by various authors[1125] will not be dealt with since it would amount to a duplication of information. The work of the scholars and practitioners from around the world leads to the conclusion that amnesties are not prohibited *per se* but rather must be limited in some way. Nevertheless, blanket self-amnesties for serious crimes under international law are increasingly deemed illegitimate. Conditional amnesties, on the other hand, which provide for some form of accountability may be legitimate under international law. In this sense, it is essential that an amnesty law has been crafted in good faith. It must be designed to further compliance with legal obligations to protect human rights while also meeting its broader policy objectives such as ending the conflict, establishing democratic structures, dealing with the underlying causes of the conflict

1123 Ibid., 245–246.

1124 Ibid., 246.

1125 *See* for example, scholars and their works: K. Ambos, 'The Legal Framework of Transitional Justice: A Systematic Study with a Special Focus on the Role of the ICC' in K. Ambos, J. Large and M. Wierda (eds.), *Building a Future on Peace and Justice: Studies on Transitional Justice, Conflict Resolution and Development.* The Nuremberg Declaration on Peace and Justice (Berlin: Springer, 2009), pp. 19–103, at pp. 49–52; C. P. Trumbull, 'Giving Amnesties a Second Chance', *Berkeley Journal of International Law* 25 (2007), 283–345, at 320–321, 324; 'International Guidelines on Post-Conflict Justice: The Chicago Principles' in M. C. Bassiouni (ed.), *The Pursuit of International Criminal Justice: A World Study on Conflicts, Victimization, and Post-Conflict Justice* (Antwerp, Oxford, Portland: Intersentia, 2010), pp. 41–65, at 43, 49–50; O'Shea, *Amnesty for Crime in International Law and Practice*, pp. 322–3; Seibert-Fohr, *Prosecuting Serious Human Rights Violations*, 215–217, 221; Bell, *The 'New Law' of Transitional Justice*, pp. 3–14; Cassel, 'Lessons from the Americas', 228–9.

and promoting reconciliation.[1126] Furthermore, where an amnesty covers serious crimes there must be a distinction between illegitimate amnesties, which are generally unconditional and have the effect of preventing investigations, and legitimate amnesties which create conditions for the sustainable protection of human rights, and require individual offenders to engage with measures to ensure truth, accountability and reparations.[1127] With regard to the temporal scope of an amnesty, the start and end dates within which eligible crimes must have been committed should be determined. Apart from the scope of an amnesty, particular conditions which should be imposed on individual offenders who wish to obtain amnesty must be fulfilled in order for an amnesty to be considered legitimate under international law. Such conditions might, for instance, include the participation in disarmament, demobilisation and reintegration programmes, participation in traditional or restorative justice processes, full disclosure of personal involvement in offences, testimony before a truth commission, and contribution materially and/or symbolically to reparations.[1128] Moreover, it is necessary to establish conditions that amnesty beneficiaries must fulfil in order to avoid revocation of the benefits.[1129] Finally, with respect to the legislative procedure for the adoption of an amnesty law, public consultation would increase the legitimacy of the law, especially if potentially marginalised groups such as victims, women, children, displaced persons, minorities and former combatants are involved.[1130]

3.5.2 Is the Afghan Amnesty Law Consistent with these Amnesty Guidelines?

Now that certain criteria concerning the legitimacy of amnesties have been presented in detail, the Afghan Amnesty Law will be reviewed on this basis. The decisive question in this context is whether the Afghan Amnesty Law has been crafted in good faith and in a manner that promises to fulfil

---

1126 Transitional Justice Institute, *The Belfast Guidelines on Amnesty and Accountability*, Guideline 1 (a) – (c).

1127 Transitional Justice Institute, *The Belfast Guidelines on Amnesty and Accountability*, Guideline 4.

1128 Ibid., Guideline 11 (a) – (i).

1129 Ibid., Guideline 12.

1130 Transitional Justice Institute, *The Belfast Guidelines on Amnesty and Accountability*, Guideline 14 (b).

Afghanistan's transitional obligations to the greatest extent possible in the particular context while impairing them as little as possible.[1131]

According to Mark Freeman, this also means that all leniency options, short of amnesty, must have been exploited. Such a leniency option could be the omission of criminal accountability, without explicitly declaring an amnesty.[1132] This was what happened during the 2001 Bonn negotiations dealing with the transition from the Taliban regime to peace and stability.[1133] Neither explicit efforts to prosecute nor an amnesty had been approved, thus leaving the issue of accountability entirely open.[1134] However, there is no doubt that this option did not lead to the desired objective given the fact that Afghanistan is still deeply rooted in conflict. Whether or not the subsequent introduction of the Afghan Amnesty Law, as a last recourse, was lawful depends largely on its design.

First of all, the Amnesty Law must be conceived to further Afghanistan's compliance with its legal obligations to protect human rights and establish peace and stability while also meeting its broader policy objectives such as ending the conflict, establishing democratic structures, dealing with the underlying causes of the conflict and promoting reconciliation.[1135] Since these obligations and objectives cannot be achieved simultaneously or rapidly, the overall aim is the protection of human rights and the fulfilment of the full range of Afghanistan's obligations to the greatest extent possible.[1136] The reasons given for the Afghan amnesty can be read in Article 1 of the corresponding law: *"This law is adopted for the purpose of strengthening the reconciliation and national stability, ensuring the supreme interests of the country, ending rivalries and building confidence among the belligerent parties …"*[1137] Relying only on the wording of this article, the motivations seem to be the promotion of peace and reconciliation as well as alleviating internal unrest. However, it may be that the real reasons for an amnesty are obscured. This is precisely what has occurred in the case

1131 Freeman, *Necessary Evils*, p. 189.

1132 Ibid., 110–111, 118–122.

1133 United Nations Security Council, *Agreement on Provisional Arrangements in Afghanistan Pending the Re-Establishment of Permanent Government Institutions*.

1134 Freeman, *Necessary Evils*, 118.

1135 Transitional Justice Institute, *The Belfast Guidelines on Amnesty and Accountability*, Guideline 1 (a) – (c).

1136 Ibid., p. 30.

1137 *See* „National Reconciliation, General Amnesty, and National Stability Law", Official Gazette, publishing date: 13 Qaus 1387 Serial No: (965) (unofficial English translation), in: Kouvo, *After Two Years in Legal Limbo*.

of Afghanistan. When members of parliament and government, who are at the same time alleged perpetrators of serious human rights violations,[1138] introduce a blanket amnesty, anyone might reasonable conclude that they primarily want to protect themselves from criminal investigation and punishment.[1139] Therefore the Afghan Amnesty Law can be qualified as a so-called self-amnesty.[1140]

Furthermore, where an amnesty covers serious crimes there must be a distinction between illegitimate amnesties, which are generally unconditional and have the effect of preventing investigations, and legitimate amnesties which create conditions for the sustainable protection of human rights, and require individual offenders to engage with measures to ensure truth, accountability and reparations.[1141] The blanket Afghan Amnesty Law, which makes no distinction between different types of perpetrators and covers all kinds of crimes, is unconditional and prevents the investigation of serious international crimes.[1142] Although the law contains an individual right of victims to bring charges against individual perpetrators[1143], this is unrealistic for many reasons. For example, many victims are intimidated by the superiority of warlords, or in relation to any potential trial. Apart from that, no investigative procedure exists to enforce the codified victim rights, making them meaningless.[1144]

1138 Among them were, for example, Muhammad Muhaqiq, Abdul Rasul Sayyaf and Burhanuddin Rabbani, See The Afghanistan Justice Project, *Amnesty Would Jeopardize National Reconciliation and Security*; Mühlmann, 'Afghanistan erteilt Massenmördern einen Freibrief'.

1139 Khan, 'Justice to the Extent Possible', 18–9; Wolkowa, 'Generalpardon für "heilige Krieger"'.

1140 Afghanistan Independent Human Rights Commission (AIHRC), *Discussion Paper on the Legality of Amnesties*, p. 9.

1141 Transitional Justice Institute, *The Belfast Guidelines on Amnesty and Accountability*, Guideline 4.

1142 Art. 3 (1) of the Amnesty Law provides: „All political factions and hostile parties who were involved in a way or another in hostilities before establishing of the Interim Administration shall be included in the reconciliation and general amnesty program for the purpose of reconciliation among different segments of society, strengthening of peace and stability and starting of new life in the contemporary political history of Afghanistan, and enjoy all their legal rights and shall not be legally and judicially prosecuted.".

1143 *See* Art. 3 (3) of the Amnesty Law: "The provisions set forth in clause (1) and (2) of this article shall not affect the claims of individuals against individuals based up on Haqullabd (rights of people) and criminal offences in respect of individual crimes.".

1144 Hartmann and Klonowiecka-Milart, *Impunity Prevails in Afghanistan*.

With regard to the temporal scope of an amnesty, the start and end dates within which eligible crimes must have been committed should be determined. In this respect, the Afghan Amnesty Law is formulated too broadly, as Article 3 (2) states that "*Those individuals and groups who are still in opposition to the Islamic Republic of Afghanistan and cease enmity after the enforcement of this resolution and join the process of national reconciliation, and respect the Constitution and other laws and abide them shall enjoy the benefits of this resolution.*" This means that not only perpetrators of past crimes are possible beneficiaries of the amnesty but also those who end violence only after the enforcement of the Amnesty Law. This is nothing other than an invitation to commit serious crimes, then join the reconciliation process and simply go unpunished.[1145] This approach surpasses many other amnesty regulations from around the world insofar as, in most cases, the crimes concerned must be perpetrated before the amnesty law is enacted.

Apart from the scope of an amnesty, particular conditions which should be imposed on individual offenders who wish to obtain amnesty must be fulfilled in order for an amnesty to be considered legitimate under international law. The only "condition" the Afghan Amnesty Law imposes on potential beneficiaries is participation in the process of national reconciliation and adherence to the Constitution and other enforced laws of the country.[1146] This is inadequate considering the intended purpose of conditional amnesties is to contribute not only to the prevention of further violence, but also to facilitate accountability and the fulfilment of victims' rights to truth and reparations.[1147] It should have been essential that the Afghan Amnesty Law incorporated conditions such as participation in disarmament, demobilisation and reintegration programmes, participation in traditional or restorative justice processes, full disclosure of personal involvement in offences, testimony before a truth commission, and contribution materially and/or symbolically to reparations.[1148]

Moreover, there is also a lack of conditions that amnesty beneficiaries must fulfil in order to avoid revocation of the benefits.[1149] These conditions could have been time-limited bans on owning dangerous weapons,

1145 Khan, 'Afghanistan: War Crimes, ICC and NGOs', 105.

1146 *See* Art. 1 and 3 (2) of the Afghan Amnesty Law.

1147 Transitional Justice Institute, *The Belfast Guidelines on Amnesty and Accountability*, Guideline 11.

1148 Ibid., Guideline 11 (a) – (i).

1149 Ibid., Guideline 12.

standing for election or public office, and/or serving in the police or armed forces.[1150]

Finally, the legislative procedure for the adoption of the Afghan Amnesty Law gives reason for serious concern. While at first glance the Amnesty Law seems to have been enacted by a democratically-elected parliament and government because it went through the lower and then upper house of parliament (Wolesi Jirga and Meshrano Jirga), was signed by former President Karzai and in the end, published and publicly announced[1151], it must nevertheless be borne in mind that the Afghan Amnesty Law was in legal limbo for almost three years[1152] and what's more, that it counts as a self-amnesty which renders it *prima facie* illegitimate.[1153] Apart from that, the Amnesty Law was not widely consulted about[1154], but rather introduced in secret. Public consultation would have increased the legitimacy of the Amnesty Law, especially if potentially marginalised groups such as victims, women, children, displaced persons, minorities and former combatants had been involved.[1155] In fact, however, the Afghan public would have rejected the Amnesty Law in this form.[1156] A survey conducted by the Afghan Civil Society Forum[1157] encompassing nine Afghan provinces and a total number of 3600 interviewees revealed that 39 % of respondents did not accept the Amnesty Law. In their view the law had not been approved by the nation but by the human rights violators themselves. This hinders the peace process and keeps the criminals in power.[1158] 38 % of interviewees conditionally accepted the Amnesty Law. This means that the law should be in the best interest of the people,

---

1150 Ibid., Guideline 12 (a) (i) -(iii).

1151 *See* Chapter 2.3.

1152 Ibid.

1153 Transitional Justice Institute, *The Belfast Guidelines on Amnesty and Accountability*, Guideline 14 (e); Afghanistan Independent Human Rights Commission (AIHRC), *Discussion Paper on the Legality of Amnesties*, p. 9; Khan, 'Justice to the Extent Possible', 18–9.

1154 Afghanistan Independent Human Rights Commission (AIHRC), *Discussion Paper on the Legality of Amnesties*, p. 9.

1155 Transitional Justice Institute, *The Belfast Guidelines on Amnesty and Accountability*, Guideline 14 (b).

1156 Afghanistan Independent Human Rights Commission (AIHRC), *Discussion Paper on the Legality of Amnesties*, p. 9.

1157 Afghan Civil Society Forum-organization (ACSFo), *A First Step on a Long Journey: How People Define Violence and Justice in Afghanistan (1958–2008)*. https://af.boell.org/sites/default/files/pdvj_final_20.4.2011.pdf (08 March 2017).

1158 Ibid., pp. 89–90.

but not a fraud. The opportunity for the return of human rights violators should be excluded.[1159] 23 % of respondents, mainly from the lower classes of society and the illiterate were unaware of the Amnesty Law.[1160]

In conclusion, the Afghan Amnesty Law has not been crafted in good faith and in a manner that promises to fulfil Afghanistan's transitional obligations to the greatest extent possible.-Thus, the blanket self-amnesty for serious crimes under international law would most probably be deemed illegitimate by 'the most highly qualified publicists of the various nations'.

3.6 Conclusion

Is the Afghan Amnesty Law legitimate under international law? In order to answer that question this chapter has dealt with international treaty law[1161], customary international law[1162], and general principles of law[1163] as well as judicial decisions[1164] and teachings of the most highly qualified publicists[1165].

With regard to the compatibility of the Afghan Amnesty Law with **international treaty law** it has been found that no international treaty explicitly prohibits or discourages the granting of amnesty for international crimes. As a consequence, the Afghan Amnesty Law cannot violate an international prohibition of certain amnesties, as no such prohibition so far exists.[1166] Even though international treaty law does not contain an explicit prohibition on amnesties, it does contain an explicit encouragement to enact them, namely Article 6 (5) of Additional Protocol II to the Geneva Conventions. Even if it is not clear from the wording of Article 6 (5) that amnesties for international crimes are exempted, the interpretation and application of the provision indicate this.[1167] This means that an

1159 Ibid., p. 91.
1160 Ibid., p. 91.
1161 *See* Chapter 3.1.
1162 *See* Chapter 3.2.
1163 *See* Chapter 3.3.
1164 *See* Chapter 3.4.
1165 *See* Chapter 3.5.
1166 *See The Case of the S.S. Lotus.*
1167 Henckaerts and Doswald-Beck (eds.), *Customary International Humanitarian Law*, p. 4043; Slye, 'The Legitimacy of Amnesties Under International Law and General Principles of Anglo-American Law', 178; UN Office of the High

unconditional amnesty for serious violations of human rights is certainly not permitted. Consequently, the blanket Afghan Amnesty Law, which grants impunity to all kinds of perpetrators and crimes, goes beyond the scope of Article 6 (5) and thus is not legitimised by this regulation. Since explicit provisions on amnesties are rare, the assessment of the legality of amnesty laws frequently focuses on obligations under international treaties to prosecute perpetrators of serious international crimes.[1168] These obligations could preclude the issuing of amnesties for the crimes in question. Afghanistan is obliged to investigate and prosecute international crimes according to the four Geneva Conventions and their Additional Protocols I and II, as well as the Convention against Torture, the Genocide Convention and the ICCPR. The blanket Afghan Amnesty Law is in violation of these obligations. However, since the duty to prosecute international crimes does not rise to the level of *jus cogens*, the Amnesty Law might be justified in light of further international obligations, in particular the effective protection of human rights and the prevention of their violation. Articles 23, 24 and 25 of the Draft Articles on Responsibility of States for Internationally Wrongful Acts enumerate certain exceptional circumstances which preclude "the wrongfulness of an act of a state not in conformity with an international obligation of that state." Yet the Afghan Amnesty Law cannot be justified on these grounds.

Since Afghanistan is a State Party to the Rome Statute of the International Criminal Court the duty to investigate and prosecute international crimes as well as the duty to implement the Rome Statute into Afghan law[1169] and the duty to cooperate fully with the Court[1170] do arise. For

Commissioner for Human Rights, *Rule-of-Law Tools for Post-Conflict States*, p. 16; United Nations Commission on Human Rights, *Report of the Special Rapporteur on the Independence of Judges and Lawyers, Leandro Despouy*, p. 16; Henckaerts and Doswald-Beck (eds.), *Customary International Humanitarian Law*, p. 4043.

1168 Mallinder, 'Amnesties', 420.

1169 *See* Preamble of the Rome Statute of the International Criminal Court: "Affirming that the most serious crimes of concern to the international community as a whole must not go unpunished and that their effective prosecution must be ensured by taking measures at the national level and by enhancing international cooperation" [...] "Recalling that it is the duty of every State to exercise its criminal jurisdiction over those responsible for international crimes".

1170 *See* Article 86 of the Rome Statute of the International Criminal Court.

a long time no significant progress was made in this regard.[1171] More recently, in May 2017, the Afghan parliament however adopted a new Penal Code which now explicitly incorporates Rome Statute crimes.[1172] Notwithstanding this, the Afghan authorities completely ignored the principles contained in the Rome Statute of the ICC in enacting the Amnesty Law in 2010. Yet neither the Rome Statute nor its Rules of Procedure and Evidence explicitly prohibit or discourage the granting of amnesty for international crimes. However, the Rome Statute contains some provisions which can be interpreted as allowing the court to acknowledge national amnesties under certain circumstances and in consequence to stop ongoing investigations. In this light, the Afghan Amnesty Law could play a role in the framework of preliminary examinations into alleged international crimes committed in Afghanistan.[1173] The legal analysis of Article 53 in conjunction with Article 17 of the Rome Statute however revealed that the preliminary investigation consisting of considerations by the prosecutor with respect to jurisdiction, admissibility (complementary and gravity) and the interests of justice led to the decision that the unconditional and comprehensive Afghan Amnesty Law does not justify a closure of the proceedings. In conclusion it may be stated that although no international treaty explicitly prohibits or discourages the granting of amnesty for international crimes, the Afghan Amnesty Law is nevertheless inconsistent with international treaty law requiring the investigation and prosecution of serious international crimes.

The objective of the chapter on **customary international law** was to explore whether a prohibition of amnesties in cases of serious international crimes exists. The result of the analysis of the practice of several states, as well as of the United Nations, can be summarised as follows: With regard to the state practice it has been determined that although Latin American countries have made significant progress, as many of them abolished or restricted their comprehensive amnesty laws, this regional trend[1174] can not be transferred to other parts of the world since each case has its unique

1171 Moen and Mohammadi, *International Criminal Court (ICC) in Afghanistan*, p. 4; Khan, 'Afghanistan: War Crimes, ICC and NGOs', 103.

1172 International Criminal Court (ICC) – The Office of the Prosecutor, *Situation in the Islamic Republic of Afghanistan*, para. 273.

1173 Barbour and Weed, *The International Criminal Court (ICC)*, p. 14.

1174 That is, the development with regard to amnesties in South America as described by Louise Mallinder, *see* Mallinder, 'The End of Amnesty or Regional Overreach?', 671.

characteristics and hence is incomparable.[1175] Nor does this trend mean that amnesties are completely rejected.[1176] In other words, states continue to enact amnesties for international crimes. Even where the term amnesty is not explicitly used or in cases in which an amnesty law excludes severe human rights violations from its scope, the situation is nevertheless characterised by impunity, that is, by *de facto* amnesty. This result can be further substantiated by the fact that those states, which commented on amnesties of other states, also tend to support rather than criticise them.[1177] Even in the case of the most serious crimes, amnesties have been encouraged by the international community. The analysis of the practice of the United Nations has demonstrated that on the one hand there is a trend towards outlawing blanket amnesties for serious international crimes as the policy of various UN organisations, in particular of the UN human rights bodies, shows. But on the other hand, this approach has so far not been applied consistently. Above all, the Security Council as well as the Secretary-General do not always oppose and even support peace agreements which include amnesties for perpetrators of heinous crimes. Apart from that, a general declaration on amnesties or their rejection in cases of the most serious crimes has not been able to be enforced within the Security Council. The result of the study indicates that the practice of states and the United Nations regarding a prohibition of amnesties for international crimes is not sufficiently uniform and widespread enough to establish a new rule of customary international law. That is, even though the international community has identified a common issue, it has not acted in concert to cope with the issue. The consequence is that a customary rule has not (yet) emerged and thus amnesties for the most serious crimes are not (yet) prohibited by customary international law.[1178] It follows that the

1175 Freeman, *Necessary Evils*, p. 47; Seibert-Fohr, *Prosecuting Serious Human Rights Violations*, 109.

1176 Mallinder, 'The End of Amnesty or Regional Overreach?', 671, 677–678; Freeman, *Necessary Evils*, p. 30.

1177 Ludwin King, 'Amnesties in a Time of Transition', 605; Osiel, *Making Sense of Mass Atrocity*, p. 234; Mallinder, 'Power, Pragmatism, and Prisoner Abuse', 333; Mallinder, *Amnesty, Human Rights and Political Transitions:*, p. 329.

1178 Mallinder, 'The End of Amnesty or Regional Overreach?', 671, 677–678; O'Keefe, *International Criminal law*, pp. 468–70; Cassese and Gaeta, *Cassese's International Criminal Law*, pp. 310–2; Ludwin King, 'Amnesties in a Time of Transition', 604–6; Freeman, *Necessary Evils*, p. 33; Seibert-Fohr, *Prosecuting Serious Human Rights Violations*, pp. 285–6; Mallinder, *Amnesty, Human Rights and Political Transitions:*, 9, 122, 135; Scharf, 'Trading Justice for Peace', 258; Freeman and Pensky, 'The Amnesty Controversy in International Law', 57.

Afghan Amnesty Law is not illegitimate according to current customary international law.

Nonetheless, provided that the trend towards outlawing blanket amnesties for serious international crimes continues and expands further[1179], the legitimacy of the Afghan Amnesty Law would have to be judged differently. Due to its extensive scope and unconditional application, the Afghan Amnesty Law would most probably become unlawful. In this context it has been elaborated that Afghanistan does not hold the status of a persistent objector and thus would be bound by a possible future prohibition of amnesties for serious international crimes in customary international law. However, if customary international law develops only subsequent to the Afghan Amnesty Law, it can have an effect at the earliest from the moment of its formation. This means that a new rule of customary international law would have no influence on any acts adopted on the basis of the Amnesty Law between 2010 and the emergence of this new customary rule.[1180] The legal situation would be quite different if rules of *jus cogens* were affected. In the event that a peremptory norm of general international law needs to be safeguarded and the newly established customary international law would serve this purpose, the Afghan Amnesty Law would become null and void *ab initio*.[1181] Yet since it is

1179 Ludwin King, 'Amnesties in a Time of Transition', 606; Afghanistan Independent Human Rights Commission (AIHRC), *Discussion Paper on the Legality of Amnesties*, pp. 4–5; Naqvi, *Impediments to Exercising Jurisdiction over International Crimes*, p. 119; Iliopoulos, *Afghan Amnesty Law a Setback for Peace*.

1180 For comparison: In international treaty law the principle of non-retroactivity is firmly anchored: see Art. 28 Vienna Convention on the Law of Treaties: *"Non-retroactivity of treaties: Unless a different intention appears from the treaty or is otherwise established, its provisions do not bind a party in relation to any act or fact which took place or any situation which ceased to exist before the date of the entry into force of the treaty with respect to that party."*.

1181 For comparison: In international treaty law the Joint Declaration of Judges Shi and Koroma with reference to the 'Case Concerning Application of the Convention on the Prevention and Punishment of the Crime of Genocide' (Bosnia and Herzegovina v. Serbia and Montenegro) (Judgment of 26 February 2007) is worth mentioning: *"Nevertheless, in some respects the interpretation of a treaty's provisions cannot be divorced from developments in the law subsequent to its adoption. Thus, even though a treaty when concluded did not conflict with any rule of jus cogens, it will become void if there subsequently emerges a new rule of jus cogens with which it is in conflict. [...]"* (para. 2), *see International Court of Justice, Joint Declaration of Judges Shi and Koroma with reference to the 'Case Concerning Application of the Convention on the Prevention and Punishment of the Crime of Genocide'*; Kotzur, 'Intertemporal Law', 4.

lex ferenda, i.e. desirable future law, it cannot be assessed at this stage whether an absolute prohibition on amnesties for international crimes[1182] safeguarded by customary international law will ever take shape.[1183]

Since both international treaty law and customary international law do not provide for a prohibition of amnesties in cases of serious human rights violations[1184], the **general principles of law**, that is, those legal principles which can be derived from national laws of a large number of states[1185], can be used to fill the gap.[1186] However, the comparison of constitutions from around the world led to the conclusion that a common legal principle concerning the prohibition of amnesties for international crimes does not exist. This is not surprising in view of the results obtained so far. Therefore, the general principles of law cannot be used to fill the gap[1187] and the Afghan Amnesty Law cannot be declared unlawful on that basis.

Following the primary sources of international law, **judicial decisions** on amnesties as subsidiary means for the determination of rules of law have been analysed. The examination of judgements rendered by various international, hybrid and regional human rights courts on amnesty regulations from around the world revealed that all of them reject domestic amnesties for serious human rights violations as they are in contradiction with several international treaties and in part with (emerging) customary international law.[1188] Thus, despite regional disparities and different circumstances, a common standard with respect to the assessment of amnesties can be defined. Although the reasoning as well as the com-

---

1182 An absolute prohibition to issue amnesties for international crimes cannot be derived from the jus cogens prohibition of these crimes, *See* Chapter 3.1.2.

1183 Mallinder, *Amnesty, Human Rights and Political Transitions:*, p. 9; Freeman and Pensky, 'The Amnesty Controversy in International Law', 57.

1184 The general principles of law are a subsidiary source and will only be used when neither international treaty law nor international customary law provide for relevant provisions. *See* Werle, *Völkerstrafrecht*, p. 69.

1185 *See* Art. 21 (1) (c) Rome Statute of the International Criminal Court; Thirlway, 'The Sources of International Law', 109.

1186 Apple, *What are General Principles of International Law?*; Werle, *Völkerstrafrecht*, p. 69.

1187 Seibert-Fohr, *Prosecuting Serious Human Rights Violations*, p. 277.

1188 Freeman and Pensky, 'The Amnesty Controversy in International Law', 57; van Schaack and Slye, *International Criminal Law and Its Enforcement*, p. 875; Slye, 'The Legitimacy of Amnesties Under International Law and General Principles of Anglo-American Law', 179–80; UN Office of the High Commissioner for Human Rights, *Rule-of-Law Tools for Post-Conflict States*, p. 23; Sadat, 'Individuel Progress in International Law', 351.

prehensiveness of the evidence varies depending on the court, it can be established that amnesties for serious human rights violations are either considered unlawful *per se* or the judges referred to a crystallising prohibition of such amnesties. Since the specific situations in the countries concerned and the circumstances in which the amnesty laws were issued have been neglected by almost all international courts, it may be assumed that these aspects were of minor importance for the assessment of the amnesty provisions. As for the evaluation of the Afghan Amnesty Law, international jurisprudence on different amnesties is applicable only to a limited extent since each case has its unique characteristics and hence is incomparable.[1189] It seems quite clear however that the blanket and unconditional Afghan amnesty — which neither led to peace nor prevented further serious human rights violations — would not have been accepted by one of the above-mentioned courts.

Finally, another subsidiary source of international law, namely **the teachings of the most highly qualified publicists of the various nations**, has been assessed. The relevant guidelines developed by, *inter alia*, Lousie Mallinder, Mark Freeman and Ronald C. Slye as well as the Belfast Guidelines on Amnesty and Accountability establish the general principle that amnesties are not prohibited *per se* but rather must be limited in some way. Nevertheless, blanket self-amnesties for serious crimes under international law are increasingly deemed illegitimate. Conditional amnesties which provide for some form of accountability may be legitimate under international law. Afghanistan's blanket self-amnesty for serious crimes under international law has not been crafted in good faith and in a manner which promises to fulfil Afghanistan's transitional obligations to the greatest extent possible and would therefore most probably be considered illegitimate by the fore-mentioned scholars.

The initial question of whether or not the Afghan Amnesty Law is legitimate under international law can therefore be answered as follows: While neither international treaty law nor current customary international law nor the general principles of law prohibit the Afghan Amnesty Law, there is nevertheless a trend towards outlawing blanket amnesties for serious international crimes as the practice of Latin American states and several UN organisations indicates.[1190] Apart from that, the blanket amnesty is

1189 Freeman, *Necessary Evils*, p. 47; Seibert-Fohr, *Prosecuting Serious Human Rights Violations*, 109.

1190 Mallinder, 'The End of Amnesty or Regional Overreach?', 671; Schabas, *Unimaginable Atrocities*, p. 182; Seibert-Fohr, *Prosecuting Serious Human Rights*

in violation of Afghanistan's duty to prosecute international crimes and cannot be justified by further international obligations. Taking into account the subsidiary sources of international law, i.e. judicial decisions on amnesties and the teachings of the most highly qualified publicists of the various nations, a condemnation of blanket self-amnesties for serious crimes under international law can be ascertained. The Afghan Amnesty Law is consequently not in line with these secondary sources, developing customary international law or the obligation to prosecute international crimes.[1191]

According to Article 29 of the Draft Articles on Responsibility of States for Internationally Wrongful Acts, *"the legal consequences of an internationally wrongful act [...] do not affect the continued duty of the responsible State to perform the obligation breached."* This means that — regardless of the Amnesty Law — Afghanistan is still obliged to perform its duty to prosecute international crimes. Article 30 of the Draft Articles further determines *"that the State responsible for the internationally wrongful act is under an obligation to cease that act, if it is continuing"*. Thus, in order to perform the obligation to prosecute, Afghanistan must abrogate or amend its Amnesty Law to remove the blanket amnesty provision. There are various ways in which the Afghan Amnesty Law could theoretically be abolished or at least limited. One option would be to bring a case before the national courts of Afghanistan.[1192] The prospects for success would largely depend on the (personal) view of the judges concerned with the amnesty challenge. In order to succeed it would therefore be necessary for conservative judges who advocate the Amnesty Law to be replaced by human-rights oriented judges.[1193] Further options are the use of a referendum and the nullification or amendment of the law by the legislature.[1194]

It is however unlikely that the Afghan authorities will take action in this regard.[1195] This is clear not just from the recently signed peace deal between Ashraf Ghani, current President of Afghanistan and Gulbuddin Hekmatyar, leader of the insurgent group Hezb-e Islami, which grants

---

Violations, pp. 286–7; Bassiouni, 'Accountability for Violations of International Humanitarian Law and Other Serious Violations of Human Rights', 17–8.

1191 Khan, 'Justice to the Extent Possible', 20–1; Afghanistan Independent Human Rights Commission (AIHRC), *Discussion Paper on the Legality of Amnesties*, p. 9.

1192 Freeman, *Necessary Evils*, pp. 185–6.

1193 Ibid., pp. 185–6; Gossman and Kouvo, *Tell Us How This Ends*, p. 50.

1194 Freeman, *Necessary Evils*, pp. 186–7.

1195 Khan, 'Justice to the Extent Possible', 21.

amnesty for international crimes[1196], but also from the fact that the Afghan parliament would need a two-thirds majority to abolish the Amnesty Law, which seems difficult, if not impossible, to achieve[1197].

Given this situation, it is essential that the international community adopts measures which help to remove or amend the Amnesty Law.[1198] Such measures could be support for the Afghan nongovernmental organisations[1199] and lawyers who might challenge the blanket amnesty as well as the initiation of public debates about the Amnesty Law and alternative solutions.[1200] Furthermore, the international community must remind the Afghan Government of its obligations under international law.[1201] Regrettably, no serious efforts have been made so far. The international community is very reluctant to criticise the Afghan Amnesty Law, let alone demand its repeal or amendment.[1202]

1196 Article 9 of the agreement says that the government "provides guarantee for the judicial immunity of the leader and members of Hezb-e Islami concerning the party's past political and military actions.", *see* Osman, *Peace With Hekmatyar*, p. 4; Bengali and Faizy, 'Afghanistan Takes a Step Toward Peace With Notorious Ex-Warlord'; Osman, *Peace With Hekmatyar*, p. 1.

1197 L. Manley, *Physicians for Human Rights – Afghan Panel on Human Rights and Transitional Justice*. http://physiciansforhumanrights.org/blog/guftegu-afghan-panel-on-human-rights-and-transitional-justice.html (08 March 2017).

1198 International Center for Transitional Justice (ICTJ), *Sustainable Peace After Mass Atrocities: The Case for Transitional Justice: Recommendations of the Working Group on Transitional Justice and SDG16+*. https://www.ictj.org/news/recommendations-working-group-transitional-justice-and-sdg16 (08 February 2019).

1199 Transitional Justice Coordination Group – Afghanistan, *TJCG Statement on the Amnesty Law: Accountability, Not Impunity: Only Victims Have the Right to Forgive*. http://tjcgafghanistan.wordpress.com/2010/03/01/tjcg-statement-on-the-amnesty-law/ (20 March 2017).

1200 Freeman, *Necessary Evils*, p. 188.

1201 International Center for Transitional Justice (ICTJ), *ICTJ Statement on Afghanistan: Amnesty Law*. http://www.saajs.org/eng/index.php?option=com_content&view=article&id=47:-ictj-statement-on-afghanistan-amnesty-law&catid=42&Itemid=2 (16 October 2012).

1202 Neither the Communiqué of the 2014 London Conference on Afghanistan nor that of the 2016 Brussels Conference on Afghanistan included a statement on the Amnesty Law or the issue of accountability, see *The London Conference on Afghanistan: Afghanistan and International Community: Commitments to Reforms and Renewed Partnership*, Communique. https://www.gov.uk/government/uploads/system/uploads/attachment_data/file/383205/The-London-Conference-on-Afghanistan-Communique.pdf (10 January 2015); *Brussels Conference on Afghanistan, Partnership for Prosperity and Peace: Communiqué of the Participants*. http://www.consilium.europa.eu/en/press/press-releases/2016/10/05-afghanistan-conference-joint-communique/ (11 October 2016); *See also*, chapter 3.2.

Despite, or precisely because of, these poor prospects it is necessary to make proposals with respect to a transitional justice process in Afghanistan. This process may also include an amnesty which must however be legitimate under international law, i.e. an amnesty that is conditional and individualised. In the following part of the study this issue will be dealt with in more depth.

4 Determination of the Conditions under which an Afghan Amnesty Law would be Legitimate under International Law

Having established that the Afghan Amnesty Law in its current form is incompatible with various sources of international law[1203], it will be explored how an Afghan amnesty law could be designed in order to fulfil the requirements of international law. Since the 'Belfast Guidelines on Amnesty and Accountability' include well-founded and comprehensive principles which aim to assist all those seeking to make decisions on amnesties and accountability[1204], these guidelines serve as a basis for the following explanations. The national laws of Afghanistan, tribal and Sharia law as well as the legal order of the Taliban are not considered in this chapter. This means that the potential national legal basis for a legitimate amnesty law is not considered, as it only deals with the legitimacy of an Afghan amnesty under international law. However, in addition to aspects of international law the political, social, and cultural circumstances in Afghanistan also play a significant role for the design and successful implementation of an amnesty law.[1205] Therefore these specific circumstances are adequately integrated in the analysis.

First of all, the classification of an amnesty within the wider process of transitional justice requires an evaluation of the specifics in the case of Afghanistan.[1206] It has been acknowledged that Afghanistan is one of the world's most complex peace- and state-building operations[1207] and that it presents one of the most confronting case studies of transitional

---

1203 Namely with the international jurispridence on amnesties, the teachings of the most highly qualified legal experts of the various nations as well as developing customary international law and the obligation to prosecute international crimes.

1204 Transitional Justice Institute, *The Belfast Guidelines on Amnesty and Accountability*, p. 1; *see* chapter 3.5.1.

1205 United Nations Security Council, *The Rule of Law and Transitional Justice in Conflict and Post-Conflict Societies, Report of the Secretary-General*, p. 1; Thier, 'Introduction:', 1–2; Dickinson, 'Transitional Justice in Afghanistan', 33; Mallinder, *Amnesty, Human Rights and Political Transitions:*, p. 10.

1206 Winterbotham, *The State of Transitional Justice in Afghanistan*, p. 30; The Afghanistan Justice Project, *Casting Shadows:*, p. 7.

1207 International Center for Transitional Justice (ICTJ), *Challenges to Peace and Justice in Afghanistan*, p. 1.

justice[1208]. The country has been through a long period of war with various perpetrators, leaders, factions and international actors. Moreover, it is still deeply rooted in conflict and the perpetrators of serious crimes remain influential which makes it all the more difficult to implement any transitional justice mechanisms.[1209] Hence strategies which have been employed in other countries may not be suitable for the unique nature of the Afghan transition.[1210]

The approach that has been taken so far in the case of Afghanistan was based on the expectation that postponing justice and accountability will lead to peace and stability.[1211] For example, unlike other UN-supported peace agreements, the 2001 Bonn Agreement[1212] made no references to the issues of transitional justice or accountability for human rights violations.[1213] Furthermore, the negotiations did not involve representatives

1208 Danchin, 'Transitional Justice in Afghanistan', 3.

1209 Afghanistan Research and Evaluation Unit (AREU), *When Will Transitional Justice in Afghanistan Become a Part of the Transitional Decade?: A Roundtable Discussion*. http://www.areu.org.af/Uploads/EditionPdfs/1612E%20When%20Will%20Transitional%20Justice%20in%20Afghanistan1.pdf (28 November 2016), pp. 7–8; B. D. Hollinder, *How to Build a Better Truth Commission: Applying Lessons from Past Truth Commissions to the Selection of Commissioners for an Afghanistan Truth Commission* (2006), pp. 20–1.

1210 Nadery, 'Afghans Struggle to Restore Justice in their Country', brief 28, 53; Danchin, 'Transitional Justice in Afghanistan', 41.

1211 P. Anderson, *Calls Grow to Tackle Afghan War Crimes* (2005). http://news.bbc.co.uk/2/hi/programmes/from_our_own_correspondent/4258343.stm (10 March 2017); P. Gossman, *The Past as Present: War Crimes, Impunity and the Rule of Law*, State Reconstruction and International Engagement in Afghanistan (2003), p. 1; Hartmann and Klonowiecka-Milart, *Impunity Prevails in Afghanistan*; D. Friedman, L. Pactat and A. Weisell, *Accountability and Impunity: Afghanistan, Kosovo and Argentina*. http://www.gpia.info/files/practicum/28/2008%20Spring%20-%20Human%20Rights%20Watch%20-%20Accountability%20and%20Impunity.pdf (12 June 2012), p. 25; Human Rights Watch, *Seductions of "Sequencing"*, pp. 4–5.

1212 United Nations Security Council, *Agreement on Provisional Arrangements in Afghanistan Pending the Re-Establishment of Permanent Government Institutions*.

1213 A. J. Benish, *Between Impunity And Accountability: A Comparative Overview of Transitional Justice Processes in Two Post-Conflict South Asian Countries: Nepal and Afghanistan*. http://www.watchafghanistan.org/files/Between_Impunity_and_Accountability_english.pdf (06 March 2012), p. 10; Wardak, Saba and Kazem, *Afghanistan Human Development Report 2007*, p. 77; Winterbotham, *Healing the Legacies of Conflict in Afghanistan*, p. 17; Niland, 'Impunity and Insurgency: a Deadly Combination in Afghanistan', 933, 936; B. R. Rubin, 'Transitional Justice and Human Rights in Afghanistan', *International Affairs* 79 (2003), 567–81, at 570.

of victims, women's groups or human rights organisations, but instead well-known warlords had been welcomed.[1214] This meant that political objectives for peace and stability took priority over justice and accountability.[1215] The approach taken at Bonn was however wrong as "peace without justice is an illusion"[1216].[1217] This is demonstrated by the fact that the ongoing conflict in Afghanistan results not least from the failure to address the atrocities of former times, i.e. blanket impunity has encouraged more violence and hindered the political process of peacebuilding.[1218] Despite this reality, neither the Afghan authorities nor the international community has learned from past mistakes.[1219] None of the subsequent international conferences on Afghanistan addressed the massive human rights violations and the continuing impunity.[1220]

The question which arises is therefore: What needs to be done differently to pave the way for a successful transitional justice process? Since the blanket Amnesty Law is the main reason for the continuing violence and the failed peacebuilding process in Afghanistan, the approach based on impunity must be replaced with an approach based on accountability for

---

1214 Niland, 'Impunity and Insurgency: a Deadly Combination in Afghanistan', 933.

1215 Wisner, 'Is Time Ripe for Transitional Justice in Afghanistan?', 1–2.

1216 Richard Goldstone, cited in: Khan, 'Justice to the Extent Possible', 12.

1217 Wardak, Saba and Kazem, *Afghanistan Human Development Report 2007*, p. 76; Khan, 'Afghanistan: War Crimes, ICC and NGOs', 117.

1218 Khan, 'Justice to the Extent Possible', 12; Gossman, 'Kabul's Stealth Attack on Human Rights'; Human Rights Watch, *World Report 2011:*, pp. 4–5; The Afghanistan Justice Project, *Casting Shadows:*, p. 155; R. Mani, *Ending Impunity and Building Justice in Afghanistan*. http://unpan1.un.org/intradoc/groups/public/documents/apcity/unpan016655.pdf (19 March 2017), 1, 38; Human Rights Watch, *Seductions of "Sequencing"*, pp. 5–6; Winterbotham, *Healing the Legacies of Conflict in Afghanistan*, pp. 23–4; Wisner, 'Is Time Ripe for Transitional Justice in Afghanistan?', 1–2.

1219 Amnesty International, *Afghanistan: Addressing the Past to Secure the Future*. https://www.amnesty.org/en/documents/asa11/003/2005/en/ (28 March 2017), p. 1.

1220 *See* Bonn Conference 2011, Auswärtiges Amt, *Afghanistan nach der Bonner Konferenz*. http://www.auswaertiges-amt.de/DE/Aussenpolitik/RegionaleSchwerpunkte/AfghanistanZentralasien/Bonn_Konferenz_2011/111227-AFG-nach-Bonnkonferenz-node.html (14 May 2012); London Conference 2014, *The London Conference on Afghanistan: Afghanistan and International Community: Commitments to Reforms and Renewed Partnership*, Communique; Brussels Conference 2016, *Brussels Conference on Afghanistan, Partnership for Prosperity and Peace: Communiqué of the Participants.*

human rights violations.[1221] This means that without justice, truth and reparations, there will be no lasting peace, reconciliation[1222] and stability in the country.[1223] Although it is always a delicate decision to hold (still) powerful perpetrators to account, especially in such a fragile situation, a genuine process of accountability and emerging respect for human rights will help to bring peace and long-term stability to Afghanistan.[1224] The alternative would be that these perpetrators of serious international crimes continue to destabilise the political process and transition in the country.[1225] However, given that accountability must play a crucial role in the framework of a possible future transitional justice process, it seems questionable whether an amnesty, i.e. impunity, can be justified in this context.

1221 Mani, *Ending Impunity and Building Justice in Afghanistan*, 1, 7, 30–31; Joint report by the Advisory Council on International Affairs (AIV) and the Advisory Committee on Issues of Public International Law (CAVV), *Transitional Justice*, p. 32; Sharifzada, *Eide Concerned at Amnesty Law*; CTV News, *No Peace without Justice, Says Envoy to Afghanistan*. http://www.ctvnews.ca/no-peace-without-justice-says-envoy-to-afghanistan-1.503738 (27 March 2017); International Center for Transitional Justice (ICTJ), *Afghanistan Mapping Report Opportunity to Break Cycles of Abuse*; Thier, 'Introduction:', 9–10; Khan, 'Justice to the Extent Possible', 27.

1222 P. Clark, 'Reconciliation, Peace, Justice: A Conceptual Framework for Transitional Justice and Rebuilding Society', *IP Journal* (2010), 19–25, at 20; E. Mobekk, 'Transitional Justice in Post-Conflict Societies – Approaches to Reconciliation' in A. Ebnother and P. Fluri (eds.), *After Intervention: Public Security Management in Post-Conflict Societies – From Intervention to Sustainable Local Ownership* (Geneva, 2005), pp. 261–92, at 263, 268–269.

1223 Bassiouni, *Introduction to International Criminal Law*, p. 997; Amnesty International, *Afghanistan: Addressing the Past to Secure the Future*, p. 1; International Crisis Group, *Afghanistan*, p. 2; UN Office of the High Commissioner for Human Rights, *Rule-of-Law Tools for Post-Conflict States*, p. 45; Human Rights Watch, *Seductions of "Sequencing"*, p. 19; Friedman, Pactat and Weisell, *Accountability and Impunity:*, p. 4; Friedman, Pactat and Weisell, *Accountability and Impunity:*, p. 80.

1224 Human Rights Watch, *Blood-Stained Hands: Past Atrocities in Kabul and Afghanistan's Legacy of Impunity*. http://www.hrw.org/sites/default/files/reports/afghanistan0605.pdf (21 March 2017), p. 126; Kaleck, *Mit zweierlei Maß*, pp. 100–1.

1225 Human Rights Watch, *Blood-Stained Hands*, p. 126; M. P. Scharf and N. Rodley, 'International Law Principles on Accountability' in M. C. Bassiouni (ed.), *Post-Conflict Justice* (Ardsley, New York: Transnational Publishers, 2002), pp. 89–96, at pp. 90–1.

As indicated in Chapter 2 ("Amnesties in the Age of Accountability") of this study, apart from amnesties and prosecutions, truth commissions[1226], reparation programs[1227], lustration policies and institutional reforms[1228] as well as traditional justice initiatives[1229] are also important transitional justice mechanisms.[1230] In this regard, it has been emphasised that a holistic approach is essential for success of the transitional justice process.[1231] This means that the application of single mechanisms is not advisable as they will not lead to peace and reconciliation by themselves.[1232] Instead, the mechanisms must be balanced in order to be most expedient.[1233] This is also true for prosecutions and amnesties. As decisive as criminal proceedings may be, it should not be overlooked that Afghanistan is incapable of holding each and every perpetrator to account.[1234] Decades of war resulted

---

1226 Truth Commissions are temporary bodies officially sanctioned by the state or an international governmental organization to investigate a pattern of past abuses and issue a report, *see* Olsen, Payne and Reiter, *Transitional Justice in Balance*, p. 34; United Nations, *What is Transitional Justice? A Backgrounder*, pp. 3–4; International Center for Transitional Justice (ICTJ), *What is Transitional Justice?*.

1227 Reparation programs are state-sponsored initiatives that aim to contribute to repairing the material and moral consequences of past abuses experienced by victims, *see* United Nations, *What is Transitional Justice? A Backgrounder*, pp. 3–4; International Center for Transitional Justice (ICTJ), *What is Transitional Justice?*; International Center for Transitional Justice (ICTJ), *What is Transitional Justice?*.

1228 E.g., vetting, the creation of new constitutions, judicial and security sector reforms.

1229 International Center for Transitional Justice (ICTJ), *What is Transitional Justice?*; Greiff, *Transitional Justice, Security, and Development*, p. 2; Buckley-Zistel, 'Einleitung', 9–10.

1230 Werle and Jessberger, *Principles of International Criminal Law*, pp. 84–7; Olsen, Payne and Reiter, *Transitional Justice in Balance*, p. 1; Boraine, 'Transitional Justice', 319; United Nations Security Council, *The Rule of Law and Transitional Justice in Conflict and Post-Conflict Societies, Report of the Secretary-General*, p. 4.

1231 Olsen, Payne and Reiter, 'The Justice Balance', 1004–5; Joint report by the Advisory Council on International Affairs (AIV) and the Advisory Committee on Issues of Public International Law (CAVV), *Transitional Justice*, p. 9.

1232 Olsen, Payne and Reiter, 'The Justice Balance', 1004–5; Rubin, 'Transitional Justice and Human Rights in Afghanistan', 576.

1233 Olsen, Payne and Reiter, 'The Justice Balance', 1004–5; Human Security Network, *Annual Ministerial Meeting*, p. 5; Kaleck, *Mit zweierlei Maß*, pp. 113–4.

1234 Olsen, Payne and Reiter, *Transitional Justice in Balance*, pp. 154–5; Mallinder, *Amnesty, Human Rights and Political Transitions:*, pp. 24–5; Winterbotham, *Healing the Legacies of Conflict in Afghanistan*, pp. 56–7.

in an extensive number of crimes committed by numerous offenders.[1235] Conditional and individualised amnesties combined with other transitional justice mechanisms can be applied to limit the number of criminal proceedings.[1236] This is in accordance with the findings of Chapter 3.5.1 ("Amnesty Guidelines") which led to the conclusion that amnesties are not prohibited *per se* but rather must be limited in some way. With this is mind, the UN Rule-of-Law Tools on Amnesties determined that *„It has been recognized that amnesties can play a valuable role in ending armed conflicts, reconciling divided communities and restoring human rights [...].*"[1237] Nevertheless, blanket self-amnesties for serious crimes under international law are deemed to be illegitimate. Conditional amnesties, on the other hand, which provide for some form of accountability may be legitimate under international law. It should also be mentioned that Islamic notions of forgiveness and amnesty are firmly anchored in Afghan culture.[1238] Even in cases of severe crimes, such as murder, Islam encourages victims and/or their relatives to forgive. A corresponding tenet of the Prophet Mohammad became part of Sharia law.[1239] Another example is an old Afghan saying: *"Even a knife cannot cut a soft throat if bowed before you."*[1240] Hence, although many Afghans favour the prosecution of those most responsible for the worst crimes, they would support forgiveness for minor human rights violations.[1241] Thus, criminal proceedings may be conducted in parallel with the application of amnesties.[1242]

The next question raised is, how can a blanket amnesty be avoided? Or to put it more precisely, what conditions must be met to ensure that

---

1235 Rubin, 'Transitional Justice and Human Rights in Afghanistan', 567; Mani, *Ending Impunity and Building Justice in Afghanistan*, p. 27; Winterbotham, *Healing the Legacies of Conflict in Afghanistan*, pp. 56–7.

1236 Olsen, Payne and Reiter, *Transitional Justice in Balance*, pp. 154–5; Mallinder, *Amnesty, Human Rights and Political Transitions:*, 14, 24–25.

1237 UN Office of the High Commissioner for Human Rights, *Rule-of-Law Tools for Post-Conflict States*, p. 44.

1238 Nadery, 'Afghans Struggle to Restore Justice in their Country', brief 28, 52; Afghanistan Independent Human Rights Commission (AIHRC), *A Call for Justice*, p. 21.

1239 *See* Nadery, 'Afghans Struggle to Restore Justice in their Country', brief 28, 52

1240 *See* Nadery, 'Afghans Struggle to Restore Justice in their Country', brief 28, 52.

1241 Wardak, Saba and Kazem, *Afghanistan Human Development Report 2007*, p. 76; Echavez, Chona R., Pilongo, Leah Wilfreda RE, Jayakody, Noorzai, Ahmad Saboor Hamza, Markova and Narasimhaiah, *Transitional Justice*, 2, 16–7.

1242 The exact material and personal scope of an amnesty and cases in which prosecutions are required are determined further below.

an Afghan amnesty can cope with the demands of international law? In this respect, the overall test of effective amnesty design, developed by Mark Freeman[1243], should be employed. According to this guideline, the amnesty must be crafted in good faith and in a manner that promises to fulfil Afghanistan's transitional obligations to the greatest extent possible in the particular context, while impairing them as little as possible.[1244] Louise Mallinder adds that the amnesty should be accompanied by other transitional justice mechanisms and institutional reforms.[1245] In order to further specify this maxim, the well-founded and comprehensive principles contained in the 'Belfast Guidelines on Amnesty and Accountability'[1246] are applied. Consequently, these guidelines serve as a basis for the determination of the conditions under which an Afghan amnesty law would be legitimate under international law.

First of all, the amnesty law would need to be **democratically legitimated**. Even though amnesties may be enacted through a range of executive and legislative mechanisms, it is imperative that potentially marginalised groups such as victims, women, displaced persons, minorities and former combatants are involved. Thus, a unilaterally adopted self-amnesty is out of the question.

Furthermore, the **scope of the amnesty** must be defined. This comprises the eligible offences, i.e. the acts which qualify for amnesty, and the eligible beneficiaries, i.e. perpetrators who benefit from an amnesty. Besides that, the temporal and the geographic scope are to be specified.

Apart from the precise scope, particular conditions which should be imposed on individual offenders who wish to obtain amnesty must be fulfilled so that the amnesty can be considered legitimate under international law. These **amnesty conditions** may contribute to preventing further violence and to facilitating accountability and the fulfilment of victims' rights to truth and reparations. Such conditions are: submitting individual applications; participating in traditional or restorative justice processes; surrendering and participating in disarmament, demobilisation and reintegration programmes; testifying (publicly or privately) in a truth commission, public inquiry or other truth-recovery; and contributing materially

1243 *See* Chapter 3.5.1.

1244 Freeman, *Necessary Evils*, p. 189.

1245 Mallinder, *Amnesty, Human Rights and Political Transitions:*, p. 18.

1246 Transitional Justice Institute, *The Belfast Guidelines on Amnesty and Accountability*, p. 1; *see* Chapter 3.5.1.

and/or symbolically to reparations. Where individuals fail to comply fully with applicable conditions, amnesty should be withheld.

The beneficiaries of amnesties should also be subject to conditions that they must fulfil in order to avoid revocation of the benefits. This means that amnesty recipients must not breach the conditions on which the amnesty was originally granted and furthermore, that they must refrain from the commission of new conflict-related or political offences, or any other type of criminal activity. Another contribution to peace and the rule of law is the imposition of time-limited bans on owning dangerous weapons, standing for election or public office, and/or serving in the police or armed forces. In the event that beneficiaries abuse the amnesty process, they can be held accountable. It is furthermore essential that reliable state institutions are built. For this purpose, reforms of, *inter alia*, the judiciary and the government institutions must be pursued.[1247]

All the listed conditions would help to find a balance between an amnesty and Afghanistan's international obligations.[1248] Moreover, the Afghan people would most likely be supportive of such a balanced approach. Various surveys[1249] which provided a forum where Afghans were allowed to describe their perceptions of justice, reconciliation and peace, have further clarified how transitional mechanisms in the specific context of Afghanistan may be applied.[1250] The interviews have indicated that processes of justice, peace and reconciliation were interdependent and overlapping, whereby achieving peace is the key priority.[1251] Criminal

1247 D. Tolbert and W. J.M. van Genugten, *International Justice in a Time of Transition*, International Peace Institute (IPI) Policy Forum (The Hague, 2012); International Center for Transitional Justice (ICTJ), *Stabilizing Afghanistan: Legitimacy and Accountability in Governance*. http://www.ictj.org/sites/default/files/ICTJ-Afghanistan-Stabilizing-Accountability-2010-English.pdf (19 March 2017), p. 3.

1248 The Afghanistan Justice Project, *Casting Shadows:*, p. 7.

1249 Such as, Winterbotham, *Healing the Legacies of Conflict in Afghanistan*; Afghanistan Independent Human Rights Commission (AIHRC), *Afghan People's Dialogue on Peace: Laying the Foundations for an Inclusive Peace Process*. http://www.aihrc.org.af/media/files/People%27s%20Dialogue%20FINAL%20report.pdf (08 March 2017); Afghanistan Independent Human Rights Commission (AIHRC), *A Call for Justice*; Afghan Civil Society Forum-organization (ACSFo), *A First Step on a Long Journey*; The Afghanistan Justice Project, *Casting Shadows:*

1250 Winterbotham, *Healing the Legacies of Conflict in Afghanistan*, p. 7.

1251 Ibid., pp. 88–9.

accountability is likewise important for most Afghans.[1252] With regard to forgiveness and amnesty it has already been mentioned that although many Afghans favour the prosecution of those most responsible for the worst crimes[1253], they would support forgiveness for minor human rights violations.[1254] Blanket amnesties were rejected by most of the interviewees.[1255] Instead, they supported a combination of mechanisms aimed at dealing with the past and contributing to peace and reconciliation. From this point of view, processes of truth-seeking and documentation[1256], reparations[1257] and restitution of victims' rights[1258] as well as the fulfilment of certain conditions, such as the renunciation of violence and public apology[1259] are desired. In order to build credible state institutions, Afghans demand punitive measures in the form of vetting or lustration, i.e. those responsible for serious crimes must be dismissed from Government and nongovernmental posts.[1260]

Having elaborated the conditions for a legitimate Afghan amnesty law, it is noteworthy that Afghanistan itself established a holistic approach regarding transitional justice in its Action Plan on Peace, Justice and

1252 Ibid., pp. 88–9; Afghanistan Independent Human Rights Commission (AIHRC), *A Call for Justice*, p. 17; Wisner, 'Is Time Ripe for Transitional Justice in Afghanistan?', 2–3.

1253 Afghanistan Independent Human Rights Commission (AIHRC), *Afghan People's Dialogue on Peace*, p. 11; Afghan Civil Society Forum-organization (ACSFo), *A First Step on a Long Journey*, 74, 84–86.

1254 Wardak, Saba and Kazem, *Afghanistan Human Development Report 2007*, p. 76; Winterbotham, *Healing the Legacies of Conflict in Afghanistan*, pp. 74–5; Wisner, 'Is Time Ripe for Transitional Justice in Afghanistan?', 2–3.

1255 Winterbotham, *Healing the Legacies of Conflict in Afghanistan*, pp. 74–5.

1256 Ibid., pp. 76–8; Wisner, 'Is Time Ripe for Transitional Justice in Afghanistan?', 2–3; Afghan Civil Society Forum-organization (ACSFo), *A First Step on a Long Journey*, pp. 84–6; The Afghanistan Justice Project, *Casting Shadows:*, p. 4.

1257 Wisner, 'Is Time Ripe for Transitional Justice in Afghanistan?', 2–3.

1258 Afghan Civil Society Forum-organization (ACSFo), *A First Step on a Long Journey*, pp. 84–6.

1259 Winterbotham, *Healing the Legacies of Conflict in Afghanistan*, pp. 82–4; Afghan Civil Society Forum-organization (ACSFo), *A First Step on a Long Journey*, p. 74.

1260 Winterbotham, *Healing the Legacies of Conflict in Afghanistan*, pp. 88–9; Wisner, 'Is Time Ripe for Transitional Justice in Afghanistan?', 2–3; Afghan Civil Society Forum-organization (ACSFo), *A First Step on a Long Journey*, p. 74; The Afghanistan Justice Project, *Casting Shadows:*, p. 4.

Reconciliation (APPRJ)[1261] in 2005.[1262] As already mentioned in Chapter 2.2 ("The Case of Afghanistan — History of Conflicts") the Action Plan contains five key areas: acknowledgement of the suffering of the Afghan people, ensuring credible and accountable state institutions, truth-seeking and documentation, reconciliation and national unity as well as the establishment of effective and reasonable accountability mechanisms.[1263] The Afghan Government reiterated that the many cases of human rights violations need to be seriously dealt with. However, it became apparent that the promise to end impunity was nothing more than lip service. The Government disregarded the Action Plan[1264] and radically undermined its provisions and objectives by introducing the blanket Amnesty Law in 2007. It is therefore not surprising that then President Karzai denied the extension of the Action Plan which expired in March 2009.[1265] Apart from that, none of the objectives of the APPRJ has been fully implemented.[1266]

In conclusion, according to both international guidelines on legitimate amnesty design and the Afghan people, a blanket self-amnesty must and can be avoided by the introduction of an amnesty that is democratically legitimised, limited in scope and conditional. Appropriate conditions are: submitting individual applications, participating in traditional or restorative justice processes, surrendering and participating in disarmament, demobilisation and reintegration programmes, testifying (publicly or privately) in a truth commission, public inquiry or other truth-recovery, contributing materially and/or symbolically to reparations, and institutional reforms. Furthermore, the beneficiaries of amnesties must not breach the conditions on which the amnesty was granted and refrain from the commission of new conflict-related or political offences, or any other type of criminal activity. It should, however, be remembered that in cases of serious international crimes accountability in the form of criminal proceedings must play a decisive role within the framework of the proposed tran-

1261 Government of the Islamic Republic of Afghanistan, *Action Plan on Peace, Reconciliation and Justice in Afghanistan*.

1262 Afghanistan Independent Human Rights Commission (AIHRC), *Discussion Paper on the Legality of Amnesties*, p. 7.

1263 Government of the Islamic Republic of Afghanistan, *Action Plan on Peace, Reconciliation and Justice in Afghanistan*.

1264 Hartmann and Klonowiecka-Milart, *Impunity Prevails in Afghanistan*.

1265 Winterbotham, *The State of Transitional Justice in Afghanistan*, p. 7.

1266 International Center for Transitional Justice (ICTJ), *Challenges to Peace and Justice in Afghanistan*, pp. 1–2; Winterbotham, *The State of Transitional Justice in Afghanistan*, p. 2.

sitional justice process. Particular aspects of a legitimate Afghan amnesty law are described in detail in the following chapters.

4.1 Democratic Legitimacy of the Amnesty Law

With regard to the first aspect of the proposed Afghan amnesty law it has to be emphasised that apart from the content of an amnesty, the procedure of its adoption is equally important.[1267] In other words, the way in which an amnesty is enacted has consequences not only for the legitimacy of the amnesty process, but also for the impact the amnesty may have on peace and reconciliation.[1268] The legitimacy of the adoption procedure is enhanced when it is as consultative and democratic as possible.[1269] This means that an amnesty law which is approved by the Afghan people or their elected representatives will be regarded as democratically legitimised.[1270] Nevertheless, a range of executive and legislative mechanisms exist through which an amnesty may be enacted.[1271]

One option could be an **executive decree**, i.e. a presidential decree or proclamation. This approach, however, provides only limited legitimacy since the amnesty law would not have been directly approved by the Afghan people.

Another option is holding **public consultations**. The involvement of victims, women[1272], children, displaced persons, minorities and former combatants helps local realities to be understood, as well as the experi-

1267 Basic literature on „procedural justice", e.g.: Tyler T. R. (ed.), *Procedural Justice*, The international library of essays in law and society (Aldershot: Ashgate, 2005); Röhl K. F. (ed.), *Procedural Justice*, Oñati international series in law and society (Aldershot, Hants: Dartmouth, 1997).

1268 Mallinder, *Amnesty, Human Rights and Political Transitions:*, p. 29; Joint report by the Advisory Council on International Affairs (AIV) and the Advisory Committee on Issues of Public International Law (CAVV), *Transitional Justice*, p. 32.

1269 Freeman, *Necessary Evils*, p. 111.

1270 Mallinder, *Amnesty, Human Rights and Political Transitions:*, pp. 33–4.

1271 Transitional Justice Institute, *The Belfast Guidelines on Amnesty and Accountability*, Guideline 14 (a).

1272 Winterbotham, *Healing the Legacies of Conflict in Afghanistan*, p. 98; E. Winterbotham, *Legacies of Conflict: Healing Complexes and Moving Forwards in Ghazni Province*. http://www.refworld.org/docid/4e92ba3a2.html (10 March 2017), p. 48; Tolbert and van Genugten, *International Justice in a Time of Transition*.

ences, needs and expectations of all actors.[1273] According to the UNOHCHR 'Rule-of-Law Tools on National Consultations on Transitional Justice'[1274] such consultations are required under international human rights law.[1275] From this point of view, Article 25 of the ICCPR determines that *"Every citizen shall have the right and the opportunity, [...] (a) To take part in the conduct of public affairs, directly or through freely chosen representatives"*. Consequently the Human Rights Committee stated that citizens are entitled to be consulted on the design and implementation of transitional justice programmes.[1276] Interestingly, the now-expired APPRJ acknowledged *"that any mechanism for building peace and justice must be carried out with the active and meaningful participation of all national stakeholders, including justice authorities, civil society, professional associations, mujahedeen, traditional and religious groups, victims, ex-combatants and (non-criminal) elements of former regimes. Special attention must be given to ensuring the active participation of women in the process."*[1277] Public consultations can be performed either quantitatively or qualitatively.[1278] The primary quantitative consultation technique is the public opinion survey to assess, for example, expectations of how to deal with the past.[1279] Qualitative consultations may include workshops, seminars, community meetings and other forms of debate.[1280] In any case the public must be informed of the realistic options available.[1281] For example, television and radio programs focused on providing

1273 Freeman, *Necessary Evils*, p. 123; UN Office of the High Commissioner for Human Rights, *Rule-of-Law Tools for Post-Conflict States: National Consultations on Transitional Justice*, HR/PUB/09/2. http://www.ohchr.org/Documents/Publications/NationalConsultationsTJ_EN.pdf (23 March 2017), V, 2; United Nations, *Guidance Note of the Secretary-General: United Nations Approach to Transitional Justice*. https://www.un.org/ruleoflaw/files/TJ_Guidance_Note_March_2010FINAL.pdf (17 March 2017), p. 9; Transitional Justice Coordination Group – Afghanistan, *TJCG Statement on the Amnesty Law*.

1274 UN Office of the High Commissioner for Human Rights, *Rule-of-Law Tools for Post-Conflict States*.

1275 Ibid., p. 4.

1276 Ibid., p. 4.

1277 Government of the Islamic Republic of Afghanistan, *Action Plan on Peace, Reconciliation and Justice in Afghanistan*, p. 3.

1278 UN Office of the High Commissioner for Human Rights, *Rule-of-Law Tools for Post-Conflict States*, 7, 9–10.

1279 Ibid., p. 7.

1280 Ibid., p. 9.

1281 International Crisis Group, *Afghanistan*, p. 18; G. Kippen, 'The Long Democratic Transition' in A. J. Thier (ed.), *The Future of Aghanistan* (Washington D.C., 2009), pp. 35–44, at pp. 37–8.

information and on seeking comments on the transitional process could be initiated.[1282] Furthermore, Afghan citizens should be educated about their (human) rights in this matter.[1283] As shown in the previous chapter, various surveys[1284] which provided a forum where Afghans were allowed to describe their perceptions of justice, reconciliation and peace have been successfully conducted and thus should be further supported and expanded.[1285]

In addition to public consultations, a **national referendum** in the form of holding votes on the proposed amnesty law can serve to increase its legitimacy.[1286] This option is included in Article 65 of the Afghan Constitution, which reads as follows: *"On important national, political, social as well as economic issues the President can call for a referendum of the people of Afghanistan. The referendum shall not be contrary to the provisions of this Constitution or require its amendment.*"[1287]

Another possibility of coming to an understanding on a conditional amnesty law is a **negotiated peace agreement**. Such a national agreement could involve representatives of the government, the parties in conflict[1288] and the international community.[1289] The conclusions of the International Afghanistan Conference in Bonn in 2011 stress *"the need for a political solu-*

1282 International Crisis Group, *Talking About Talks*, pp. I–III.

1283 Nadery, 'A Human Rights Awakening?', 61–2; United States Agency for International Development (USAID), *Afghanistan Rule of Law Project: Field Study of Informal and Customary Justice in Afghanistan and Recommendations on Improving Access to Justice and Relations Between Formal Courts and Informal Bodies.* http://www.usip.org/files/file/usaid_afghanistan.pdf (15 March 2017), p. 14.

1284 Such as Winterbotham, *Healing the Legacies of Conflict in Afghanistan*; Afghanistan Independent Human Rights Commission (AIHRC), *Afghan People's Dialogue on Peace*; Afghanistan Independent Human Rights Commission (AIHRC), *A Call for Justice*; Afghan Civil Society Forum-organization (ACSFo), *A First Step on a Long Journey*; The Afghanistan Justice Project, *Casting Shadows.*

1285 UN Office of the High Commissioner for Human Rights, *Rule-of-Law Tools for Post-Conflict States*, pp. 1–2; Afghanistan Independent Human Rights Commission (AIHRC), *A Call for Justice*, p. 54; Winterbotham, *Healing the Legacies of Conflict in Afghanistan*, 67–70, 91; International Crisis Group, *Afghanistan*, pp. 20–1.

1286 R. Synovitz, *Afghanistan: Amnesty Law Draws Criticism*. http://www.rferl.org/content/article/1075272.html (18 March 2017); Mallinder, *Amnesty, Human Rights and Political Transitions:*, pp. 34–5.

1287 *The Constitution of the Islamic Republic of Afghanistan*. http://www.afghanembassy.com.pl/afg/images/pliki/TheConstitution.pdf (31 August 2017).

1288 International Crisis Group, *Talking About Talks*, pp. I–II.

1289 Mallinder, *Amnesty, Human Rights and Political Transitions:*, pp. 32–3.

tion in order to achieve peace and security in Afghanistan. [...] a political process is necessary, of which negotiation and reconciliation are essential elements. [...] Mindful of the relevant UN resolutions, the International Community concurs with Afghanistan that the peace and reconciliation process and its outcome must be based on the following principles: (a) The process leading to reconciliation must be truly Afghan-led and Afghan-owned; as well as inclusive, representing the legitimate interests of all the people of Afghanistan, regardless of gender or social status."[1290] This is in accordance with the view of many Afghans, who furthermore emphasise that international actors, in particular those with military forces in Afghanistan, should not participate in peace negotiations.[1291] These people refuse to accept solutions from outside and instead demand national proposals.[1292] However, some Afghans considered the participation of the United Nations in possible peace talks.[1293] The most challenging question concerning peace negotiations is whether or not the Taliban should be involved and, if so, whether they would be willing to attend.[1294] According to a survey, the majority of Afghans recognises the need for negotiations with the Taliban, as this would be the only way to restore peace.[1295] They nevertheless insist on the fulfilment of certain conditions, for example that those responsible for serious human rights violations should be excluded from the negotiations and should instead be prosecuted.[1296] From today's perspective it must be noted that the Taliban participated in peace talks with prominent Afghan politicians, many of them former enemies.[1297] However, the Afghan Government did not attend the talks.[1298] Apart from these negotiations, military action is still

1290 *International Afghanistan Conference in Bonn, 5 December 2011 – Conference Conclusions*. http://afghanistan-un.org/wp-content/uploads/2011/12/Konferenzschlussfolgerung_engl.pdf (14 March 2017), pp. 3–4.

1291 Winterbotham, *Healing the Legacies of Conflict in Afghanistan*, pp. 79–80.

1292 Ibid., p. 80.

1293 Ibid., p. 81.

1294 Human Rights Watch, *World Report 2012: Afghanistan*. http://www.hrw.org/sites/default/files/related_material/afghanistan_2012.pdf.pdf (08 March 2017), p. 1; Irving, *Talking With Taliban*.

1295 Winterbotham, *Healing the Legacies of Conflict in Afghanistan*, pp. 82–4.

1296 Ibid., pp. 82–4.

1297 A. Higgins and M. Mashal, 'Taliban Peace Talks in Moscow End With Hope the U.S. Exits, if Not Too Quickly', The New York Times, 06 February 2019.

1298 E. Graham-Harrison and A. Roth, *Taliban and Afghan Groups Find Common Ground in Landmark Talks: Insurgents attend Moscow peace summit, but Afghan president is excluded*. https://www.theguardian.com/world/2019/feb/06/taliban-say-they-have-no-plans-to-seize-afghanistan-by-force (07 February 2019).

the Talibans' method of choice and nothing indicates that this will change in the near future.[1299]

Finally, the proposed amnesty law could be ratified by a **democratically elected legislature.**[1300] Compared to an executive decree, a ratified law has greater legitimacy since it is debated and negotiated.[1301] This would nonetheless presuppose that Afghanistan is a peaceful and democratic society and that the legislature is free from warlords and other criminals.[1302]

To sum up, a possible approach to democratically legitimise the proposed amnesty would be to conduct public consultations in order to inform the Afghan people and to learn about their stance towards the proposed amnesty and its conditions. In addition to these consultations, the outcome of a national referendum[1303] on the proposed amnesty law could then be adequately integrated into peace negotiations between the government and the parties in conflict with participation of the UN.[1304] The final version of the agreement could subsequently be ratified by a democratically elected legislature. Although such an approach would greatly enhance the legitimacy of the adoption procedure, it is questionable whether this is achievable given the realities in Afghanistan. The democratic process of adoption is only one aspect in assessing the legitimacy of an Afghan amnesty law, the exact content has to be determined as well.

4.2 The Scope of the Amnesty Law

The personal and material scope of an amnesty is the determinant factor for assessing the legitimacy of an amnesty law under international law. This means that the crimes which must be excluded from the scope of the amnesty (material scope) because of their severity, extent or international condemnation have to be specified. Furthermore, the perpetrators which are eligible for an amnesty must be determined and which are not (personal scope). Moreover, the temporal and geographic scope of the amnesty must be defined.

1299 Osman, *Peace With Hekmatyar*, 10.

1300 For details of the legislative process in Afghanistan, *see* Wardak, Saba and Kazem, *Afghanistan Human Development Report 2007*, pp. 105–8.

1301 Mallinder, *Amnesty, Human Rights and Political Transitions:*, p. 33.

1302 Ibid., p. 34.

1303 *See* Article 65 of the Afghan Constitution.

1304 UN Office of the High Commissioner for Human Rights, *Rule-of-Law Tools for Post-Conflict States*, p. 27.

The crimes that occurred during the decades of war in Afghanistan include large scale war crimes, crimes against humanity, and other serious human rights violations — in principle everything that is prohibited.[1305] With respect to the perpetrators, it has been found that up to one million individuals have committed crimes during the conflicts.[1306] A survey in 2010 estimated that there were 32 000 to 40 000 combatants in Afghanistan with 8 000 to 10 000 full-time fighters, whereby illegal networks and criminal gangs were not recorded.[1307] Thus, the determination of the material and personal scope requires extensive balancing and careful consideration.

The material scope of the amnesty can be specified in various ways. For example, the offences that are not covered by the scope of the amnesty could be explicitly listed. In this regard, the Belfast Guidelines on Amnesty and Accountability emphasise that the exclusion of serious international crimes, such as war crimes, crimes against humanity, enforced disappearance and torture as well as other serious acts of violence against persons that may not rise to the level of an international crime from an amnesty may serve to increase its legitimacy and legality.[1308] This is in line with the view of many Afghans, who would be supportive of amnesties for non-serious crimes, such as looting, informing or burning houses, and furthermore stated that trials could be restricted to those responsible for serious human rights violations.[1309] In this respect, the now-expired APPRJ had underlined that there can be no excuse for *„genocide, war crimes, crimes against humanity and other gross violations of human rights. On the contrary, bold action against these crimes is itself a universally accepted moral principle. […] The commission of such crimes does not fall into the scope of amnesty on the basis of the principles of the sacred religion of Islam and internationally accepted*

1305 Rubin, 'Transitional Justice and Human Rights in Afghanistan', 567; Wardak, Saba and Kazem, *Afghanistan Human Development Report 2007*, p. 75.

1306 Nadery, 'Afghans Struggle to Restore Justice in their Country', brief 28, 50.

1307 T. Sajjad, *Peace at all Costs: Reintegration and Reconciliation in Afghanistan*. http://www.refworld.org/docid/4cb411692.html (12 April 2017), pp. 12–3.

1308 Transitional Justice Institute, *The Belfast Guidelines on Amnesty and Accountability*, Guideline 7 (c) (i) – (iii).

1309 Winterbotham, *Healing the Legacies of Conflict in Afghanistan*, pp. 44–50; Afghanistan Independent Human Rights Commission (AIHRC), *Afghan People's Dialogue on Peace*, p. 11; Afghanistan Independent Human Rights Commission (AIHRC), *A Call for Justice*, pp. 21–2.

standards."[1310] However, the Action Plan has not been implemented as has been explained above.

With regard to the eligible beneficiaries, that is, perpetrators who benefit from an amnesty, a distinction can be made on the basis of rank or level of responsibility. This means, for example, that amnesties that distinguish in terms of rank may exclude leaders while making amnesty feasible for lower-level offenders.[1311] Since the most serious crimes can be attributed to forces with command structures and identifiable political leaders, decision makers or senior officers, it is quite possible to determine who will not be covered by the personal scope of the amnesty.[1312] Lower-ranking perpetrators or subordinates, i.e. those individuals who followed the legally binding orders of a superior, could be eligible for amnesty provided that certain conditions were fulfilled, such as the investigation of the crimes concerned, reparations for victims and the application of alternative justice mechanisms.[1313] According to a survey, most of the Afghan people interviewed agree with this distinction. They stated that leaders of the conflicts must be prosecuted, whereas followers, collaborators, bystanders or other ordinary militants should be absolved of guilt because these people merely followed orders.[1314] The interviewees furthermore identified particular leaders who would not be eligible for amnesty, namely the communist government, the leaders of the mujahedeen factions and Taliban forces as well as the Karzai government which included well-known warlords.[1315] Apart from Afghan leaders, foreign forces and external powers, such as Pakistan, Iran and the United States have also been accused of serious international crimes.[1316]

1310 Government of the Islamic Republic of Afghanistan, *Action Plan on Peace, Reconciliation and Justice in Afghanistan*, pp. 2–3.

1311 Transitional Justice Institute, *The Belfast Guidelines on Amnesty and Accountability*, Guideline 8 (d).

1312 International Crisis Group, *Afghanistan*, 17, 19; Bassiouni, 'Accountability for Violations of International Humanitarian Law and Other Serious Violations of Human Rights', 26–8.

1313 Mallinder, *Amnesty, Human Rights and Political Transitions:*, pp. 100–2.

1314 Winterbotham, *Healing the Legacies of Conflict in Afghanistan*, pp. 49–50.

1315 Ibid., pp. 37–40; Danchin, 'Transitional Justice in Afghanistan', 18; Mani, *Ending Impunity and Building Justice in Afghanistan*, p. 29; Khan, 'Afghanistan: War Crimes, ICC and NGOs', 95.

1316 Winterbotham, *Healing the Legacies of Conflict in Afghanistan*, pp. 37–40; Danchin, 'Transitional Justice in Afghanistan', 18, 39; Niland, 'Impunity and Insurgency: a Deadly Combination in Afghanistan', 948–9.

As indicated above, the temporal and geographic scope of the amnesty has to be defined as well. The temporal scope should state the start and end dates within which eligible crimes must have been committed. In order to safeguard a holistic approach towards transitional justice and to avoid unjustified unequal treatment the period should be very long. This means that all eligible crimes which have been perpetrated in the recent history of conflict in Afghanistan, starting with the Communist Revolution and People's Democratic Party of Afghanistan (PDPA) government in 1978, would be covered by the amnesty. Notwithstanding this, offences that are committed only after the enforcement of the amnesty can in no case be included. Thus, the crimes concerned must be perpetrated before the amnesty law is enacted. The geographic scope of the amnesty should not be restricted to crimes committed within a certain region, but enclose the whole country as to a varying degree all parts of Afghanistan have been affected by the various violent conflicts.[1317]

Having established that serious international crimes and other serious acts of violence against persons that may not rise to the level of an international crime are excluded from the scope of the proposed amnesty, the next step is to examine how the political leaders, decision makers or senior officers who are most responsible for these crimes can be held accountable.

4.3 Prosecution of Serious International Crimes and Other Serious Acts of Violence against Persons

The prosecution of serious international crimes, such as war crimes, crimes against humanity, enforced disappearance and torture, as well as other serious acts of violence against persons that may not rise to the level of an international crime, is not only required by international law, but also the Afghan people[1318] and the now-expired APPRJ[1319] have demanded

1317 Winterbotham, *Wartime Suffering*, p. 39.

1318 Winterbotham, *Healing the Legacies of Conflict in Afghanistan*, pp. 44–9; *Demonstrators in Kabul Call for Bringing War Criminals to Justice* (Xinhua | English.news.cn, 2011); Afghan Civil Society Forum-organization (ACSFo), *A First Step on a Long Journey*, p. 84; Wisner, 'Is Time Ripe for Transitional Justice in Afghanistan?', 2–3.

1319 Key Action 5 of the APPRJ concerning the Establishment of effective and reasonable accountability mechanisms provides that *"In order to end impunity in Afghanistan and ensure that there will be no amnesty for war crimes, crimes against humanity and other gross human rights violations, the conditions for fair*

that those most responsible for these crimes will be prosecuted. However, as already mentioned earlier, the exclusion of those most responsible for these crimes, namely political leaders, decision makers or senior officers, from the amnesty can be precarious as high-ranking perpetrators are often key stakeholders in a political transition.[1320] On the other hand, it must be admitted that such an approach could lead to a clean break from the past and, moreover, to wider political and judicial reforms as well as increased awareness of and respect for human rights.[1321] Furthermore, if high-ranking perpetrators were indeed prosecuted, this would prevent them from regaining power and deter others from committing similar crimes.[1322]

A key issue to be debated is the relevant time period in which the crimes must have been perpetrated in order to be investigated and prosecuted.[1323] With a view to the temporal scope of the amnesty, it seems reasonable to focus on the recent history of conflict in Afghanistan, starting with the Communist Revolution and People's Democratic Party of Afghanistan (PDPA) government in 1978. It is further necessary not on-

---

and effective justice procedures are established in accordance with the principles of the sacred religion of Islam, international law and transitional justice. a) A Taskforce will be established on the presidential decree. The Taskforce has the duty to provide recommendations to the President for a legal, procedural and institutional framework necessary for Afghanistan's implementation of its international legal obligations, and gives priority to removing continued threats to peace and stability in Afghanistan. Lead: President's Office – The President to appoint a five-member Task Force, including one member nominated by UNAMA and one member nominated by AIHRC. Timeframe: Task force to be established by December 2005, Task Force recommendations to be presented to the President no later than end 2007", see Government of the Islamic Republic of Afghanistan, *Action Plan on Peace, Reconciliation and Justice in Afghanistan*, pp. 10–1.

1320 Afghanistan Independent Human Rights Commission (AIHRC), *A Call for Justice*, p. 50; Winterbotham, *Healing the Legacies of Conflict in Afghanistan*, p. 56; Danchin, 'Transitional Justice in Afghanistan', 51.

1321 Mallinder, *Amnesty, Human Rights and Political Transitions:*, p. 103; Winterbotham, *Healing the Legacies of Conflict in Afghanistan*, pp. 8–9; United Nations Security Council, *The Rule of Law and Transitional Justice in Conflict and Post-Conflict Societies, Report of the Secretary-General*, pp. 13–4; Kaleck, *Mit zweierlei Maß*, pp. 100–1; Danchin, 'Transitional Justice in Afghanistan', 51.

1322 Mallinder, *Amnesty, Human Rights and Political Transitions:*, p. 103; United Nations Security Council, *The Rule of Law and Transitional Justice in Conflict and Post-Conflict Societies, Report of the Secretary-General*, pp. 13–4; Human Rights Watch, *Selling Justice Short*, pp. 123–4; Danchin, 'Transitional Justice in Afghanistan', 51.

1323 Danchin, 'Transitional Justice in Afghanistan', 46.

ly to address the past, but also the present state of impunity.[1324] In the following, a short overview lists the different phases of the conflict including the worst crimes and main perpetrators. The Communist Revolution and PDPA government was characterised by arrests, disappearances and summary executions.[1325] The Afghanistan intelligence agency, i.e. the Department for Safeguarding the Interests of Afghanistan (AGSA) and later the Workers' Intelligence Department (KAM) were most responsible for these crimes.[1326] Furthermore, the Kerala massacre and the bombardment of Herat in 1979 occurred during this phase of the war.[1327] This period was followed by the Soviet occupation and rule of Afghanistan from 1979 till 1989.[1328] During this time systematic violations of human rights, such as arbitrary detentions, forced disappearance, torture, indiscriminate bombardments against civilians, the destruction of cultivated fields, forced displacement and mass executions took place.[1329] The subsequent phase was the fall of the Najibullah government, which had been responsible for bombardments and severe abuses of human rights,[1330] and the following civil war period from 1989 till 1996.[1331] Armed mujahidin forces as well as all other major factions to the conflict[1332] committed incredible atrocities such as massacres, mass rapes, bombardments, torture, and mass executions.[1333] From 1996 onwards, the hard-line Taliban regime brutally ruled the country by perpetrating massacres, torture, burnings, and deliberate destruction.[1334] Basic rights and freedoms of Afghans, especially of

---

1324 Mani, *Ending Impunity and Building Justice in Afghanistan*, p. 7.

1325 Gossman, *Afghanistan: The Past as a Prologue*, p. 3.

1326 Ibid., p. 3.

1327 Ibid., p. 3.

1328 Winterbotham, *Wartime Suffering*, p. 1.

1329 The Afghanistan Justice Project, *Casting Shadows:*, p. 2; Nadery, 'Afghans Struggle to Restore Justice in their Country', brief 28, 52–3.

1330 Gossman, *Afghanistan: The Past as a Prologue*, p. 3.

1331 Winterbotham, *Wartime Suffering*, p. 1.

1332 Including Hezb-e Islami, the Islamic party (led by Gulbuddin Hekmatyar); Jamiat-i Islami/Shura-i Nazar (led by Burhanudin Rabbani and Ahmad Shah Massoud); Junbish-i Milli (led by Abdul Rashid Dostum); Hizb-e Wahdat (led by Abdul Ali Mazari); and Ittihad-i Islami (led by Abd al-Rabb al-Rasul Sayyaf), *see* United Nations, *UN Mapping Report Afghanistan – unpublished*. http://www.flagrancy.net/salvage/UNMappingReportAfghanistan.pdf (20 April 2017).

1333 Gossman, *Afghanistan: The Past as a Prologue*, p. 3; Human Rights Watch, *Blood-Stained Hands*.

1334 Nadery, 'Afghans Struggle to Restore Justice in their Country', brief 28, 52–3; Khan, 'Afghanistan: War Crimes, ICC and NGOs', 90–1.

Afghan women, were severely limited or even abolished.[1335] This phase lasted until 2001, when the United States and its allies invaded and defeated the Taliban regime. The following post-Taliban transitional period is still ongoing. Despite great hope and proclamations that the violence will be over, serious human rights violations and a bloody conflict between the Afghan government and its international supporters on the one hand and various non-state armed groups[1336] on the other are still reality.[1337] In several parts of the country aerial bombardments, suicide attacks, torture and enforced disappearances still occur.[1338] International military forces, especially the US Army and NATO forces have been accused of arbitrary detentions and indiscriminate civilian casualties by air strikes.[1339] The ICC Report on Preliminary Examination Activities in 2016 furthermore states that *"in the course of interrogating [...] detainees, and in conduct supporting those interrogations, members of the US armed forces and the US Central Intelligence Agency ("CIA") resorted to techniques amounting to the commission of the war crimes of torture, cruel treatment, outrages upon personal dignity, and rape.* "[1340] It is also noted that these crimes were committed *„pursuant to plans or policies approved at senior levels of the US Government, following careful and extensive deliberations.* "[1341]

Detailed analyses of the most heinous crimes and perpetrators who were responsible for these atrocities were prepared by the United Nations in 2006[1342] and by the Afghan Independent Human Rights Commission (AIHRC) in 2011. The 800-page report by the AIHRC, titled „Conflict

1335 Nadery, 'Afghans Struggle to Restore Justice in their Country', brief 28, 52–3.

1336 Such as the Taliban, the Haqqani network and Hezb-e Islami, *see* United Nations Assistance Mission in Afghanistan (UNAMA), *Afghanistan Midyear Report 2011*, ii.

1337 Jackson, *The Cost of War*, pp. 3–4.

1338 Winterbotham, *Healing the Legacies of Conflict in Afghanistan*, p. 36; The Afghanistan Justice Project, *Casting Shadows:*, pp. 155–6; Human Rights Watch, *Blood-Stained Hands*, p. 3.

1339 Khan, 'Afghanistan: War Crimes, ICC and NGOs', 92–3; Wisner, 'Is Time Ripe for Transitional Justice in Afghanistan?', 6; Amnesty International, *Getting away with Murder?: The Impunity of International Forces in Afghanistan*. https://doc.es.amnesty.org/cgi-bin/ai/BRSCGI/GETTING%20AWAY%20WITH%20MURDER?CMD=VEROBJ&MLKOB=29040884646 (07 April 2017), p. 5; Danchin, 'Transitional Justice in Afghanistan', 39.

1340 International Criminal Court (ICC) – The Office of the Prosecutor, *Report on Preliminary Examination Activities 2016*, 47.

1341 Ibid., 50.

1342 United Nations, *UN Mapping Report Afghanistan – unpublished.*

Mapping in Afghanistan Since 1978"[1343], encompasses the period from 1978 to 2001.[1344] The report lists the names of more than 500 former and current warlords or officials, some still in positions of power and some of whom have already died as well as the locations and details of 180 mass graves.[1345] Among the main perpetrators are the former First Vice-President Mohammed Fahim and the former Second Vice-President Karim Khalili as well as General Atta Mohammed Noor, now Governor of the Northern Province of Balkh and General Abdul Rashid Dostum, former Uzbek warlord and currently First Vice-President.[1346] Further named perpetrators are, *inter alia*, Gulbuddin Hekmatyar[1347], Mullah Fazul Akhund and Mullah Khairullah Khirkawa.[1348] Another report on crimes and perpetrators of the civil war period drafted by Human Rights Watch also listed former Energy Minister Ismail Khan and lawmaker Abdul Rasul Sayyaf as among those most responsible for serious human rights violations.[1349] Apart from Afghan war lords and officials, external perpetrators of serious human rights violations have also been mentioned by several civil society groups.[1350] Among them are General Gromove of the Soviet Union, Lieutenant General Yosfue, General Aslam Big, General Naseerullah Babar, General Hamid Gul, General Akhtar Mohammad, Carnal Amam of Pakistan, Najafi, the Iranian ambassador during 1991, and William Kasi of the United States.[1351]

Having established that those most responsible for serious international crimes as well as other serious acts of violence against persons which occurred from 1978 onwards must be held accountable, the question arises whether perpetrators of other nationalities should be prosecuted in

---

1343 Nordland, 'Top Afghans Tied to '90s Carnage, Researchers Say'; Kazim, 'Kriegsverbrecher-Studie: Massaker-Berichte belasten afghanische Politiker'.

1344 The release of the report has been prevented by the Afghan Government and by the US., *see* Nordland, 'Top Afghans Tied to '90s Carnage, Researchers Say'; Human Rights Watch, *World Report 2015: Afghanistan*.

1345 Nordland, 'Top Afghans Tied to '90s Carnage, Researchers Say'; Kazim, 'Kriegsverbrecher-Studie: Massaker-Berichte belasten afghanische Politiker'.

1346 Nordland, 'Top Afghans Tied to '90s Carnage, Researchers Say'; Kazim, 'Kriegsverbrecher-Studie: Massaker-Berichte belasten afghanische Politiker'.

1347 Mühlmann, 'Afghanistan erteilt Massenmördern einen Freibrief'.

1348 Nordland, 'Top Afghans Tied to '90s Carnage, Researchers Say'; Kazim, 'Kriegsverbrecher-Studie: Massaker-Berichte belasten afghanische Politiker'.

1349 Human Rights Watch, *Blood-Stained Hands*; Synovitz, *Afghanistan: Amnesty Law Draws Criticism*.

1350 Nadery, 'Afghans Struggle to Restore Justice in their Country', brief 28, 50.

1351 Ibid., 50.

addition to Afghans.[1352] Leaving aside the practical challenges and imponderables of criminal proceedings against foreigners, any process striving for justice should not be selective and no-one should be treated differently.[1353] This means that anyone, whether Afghan or any other nationality, allegedly most responsible for serious human rights violations must be investigated and if necessary be prosecuted.[1354]

Another issue that has to be addressed is which norms of international law are applicable in the course of any potential trial. In this context, a differentiation with respect to the nature of the armed conflicts (international or internal) as well as the nationality and the legal status (state or non-state actor) of the perpetrators has to be made. The nature of the longstanding armed conflict in Afghanistan has already been described in Chapter 3.1. It has been shown that the armed conflict in Afghanistan was in part of an international, a non-international or an internationalised character.[1355] However, the classification is not always easy. Hence, it is also not always easy to determine which rules of international humanitarian law are applicable to the different phases. An international armed conflict is governed by the four Geneva Conventions and the Protocol Additional to the Geneva Conventions of 1949, and Relating to the Protection of Victims of International Armed Conflicts (Additional Protocol I). In domestic armed hostilities, however, Article 3 common to the four Geneva Conventions (Common Article 3) as well as the Protocol Additional to the Geneva Conventions of 12 August 1949, and Relating to the Protection of Victims of Non-International Armed Conflicts (Additional

1352 Danchin, 'Transitional Justice in Afghanistan', 46.

1353 International Crisis Group, *Afghanistan*, p. 19.

1354 Amnesty International, *Afghanistan: Addressing the Past to Secure the Future*, p. 8; Khan, 'Justice to the Extent Possible', 34; R. Nordland, 'Old Atrocities, Now Official, Galvanize Afghanistan', The New York Times, 30 September 2013.

1355 The first period from 1978 till 1989, comprising the Communist Revolution and PDPA government as well as the Soviet occupation, was an international armed conflict. The subsequent civil war from 1989 until 1996 can be designated as an internal armed conflict. The third phase, the Taliban regime from 1996 onwards was of an internal nature, but due to foreign involvement, the conflict may have become internationalised. When the United States and its allies invaded and defeated the Taliban regime in 2001 the hostilities turned again into a pure international conflict. Since June 2002 when the transitional government was set up it has been an internal conflict. *See* Chapter 3.1 Is the Afghan Amnesty Law Consistent with Relevant International Treaties?.

Protocol II) contain the relevant standards.[1356] In addition, the regulations of customary international humanitarian law are applicable to all types of armed conflict.[1357] This means that almost all of the regulations governing international armed conflicts are equally applicable to non-international armed conflicts.[1358] Thus in cases like Afghanistan, the difficulties in distinguishing between internal and international armed hostilities as well as the challenge of determining the respective provisions of international humanitarian law can be overcome by the application of customary international humanitarian law.

The relevant international treaties to which Afghanistan is a party and which are thus applicable in the case of Afghan perpetrators have been identified in Chapter 3.1.[1359] With regard to perpetrators of foreign states it is noteworthy that all states contributing to the international forces present in Afghanistan are bound by the four Geneva Conventions of 1949 as well as by the rules of customary international law.[1360] Non-state actors, such as the Taliban, cannot formally become parties to international humanitarian and human rights treaties. However, according to the practice of states, international case law, and scholarship it is an indisputable fact that non-state actors are nevertheless bound by Common Article 3.[1361]

In order to conduct any future criminal proceedings it is essential to obtain the necessary evidence, testimony and documentation.[1362] Although

1356 Bellal, Giacca and Casey-Maslen, 'International Law and Armed Non-State Actors in Afghanistan', 52–3.

1357 Pejic, 'The Protective Scope of Common Article 3', 196.

1358 State Library of New South Wales, *Non-International Armed Conflict*.

1359 International humanitarian treaties by which Afghanistan is bound are the Geneva Conventions of 1949 and the 1977 Additional Protocols thereto. With regard to international human rights treaties, Afghanistan acceded or signed and ratified the Convention against Torture and Other Cruel, Inhuman or Degrading Treatment or Punishment (CAT) and the International Covenant on Civil and Political Rights (ICCPR). Relevant international criminal law treaties applicable in the case of Afghanistan are the Convention on the Prevention and Punishment of the Crime of Genocide, the Convention on the Non-Applicability of Statutory Limitations to War Crimes and Crimes against Humanity and the Rome Statute of the International Criminal Court. *See* Chapter 3.1 Is the Afghan Amnesty Law Consistent with Relevant International Treaties?.

1360 United Nations Assistance Mission in Afghanistan (UNAMA), *Afghanistan Midyear Report 2011*, pp. ii–iii.

1361 Bellal, Giacca and Casey-Maslen, 'International Law and Armed Non-State Actors in Afghanistan', 55–6.

1362 International Crisis Group, *Afghanistan*, p. 16.

the above-mentioned reports by the United Nations[1363] and the Afghan Independent Human Rights Commission (AIHRC)[1364] entail important information and documentation at least until 2001, they had not been published to date.[1365] Also the analyses conducted by Human Rights Watch[1366], the Afghanistan Justice Project[1367] and the Physicians for Human Rights[1368] include evidence of serious human rights abuses and information on mass graves. However, they encompass only limited timeframes or are unofficial documents. Thus it is absolutely necessary to initiate an official investigation that covers the relevant period from 1978 until today and which is independent and impartial.[1369] The international community should support such an approach through financial contributions and technical assistance.[1370] The collection and protection of evidence, such as that contained in mass graves should be pursued and existing documentation should be recorded in a common database.[1371]

Having discussed several prior issues, the decisive question with regard to possible future criminal proceedings is which jurisdiction is competent and capable of dealing with the relevant cases. In this respect, different options come into consideration – trials before the national courts of Afghanistan, the establishment of an *ad hoc* international tribunal or a hybrid court as well as proceedings before the International Criminal

1363 United Nations, *UN Mapping Report Afghanistan – unpublished.*

1364 Nordland, 'Top Afghans Tied to '90s Carnage, Researchers Say'; Kazim, 'Kriegsverbrecher-Studie: Massaker-Berichte belasten afghanische Politiker'.

1365 Winterbotham, *Healing the Legacies of Conflict in Afghanistan*, p. 58; Human Rights Watch, *Blood-Stained Hands*, p. 2; International Center for Transitional Justice (ICTJ), *Afghanistan: Addressing the Past*, pp. 4–6; Gossman, *Afghanistan: The Past as a Prologue*, pp. 2–3.

1366 Human Rights Watch, *Blood-Stained Hands*; Human Rights Watch, *Afghanistan: Bring War Criminals to Justice: Special Court Needed for Past Atrocities*. http://www.hrw.org/news/2005/07/07/afghanistan-bring-war-criminals-justice (26 April 2017).

1367 The Afghanistan Justice Project, *Casting Shadows.*

1368 Winterbotham, *Healing the Legacies of Conflict in Afghanistan*, p. 25.

1369 Ibid., p. 59; International Crisis Group, *Afghanistan*, pp. 18–9.

1370 International Crisis Group, *Afghanistan*, pp. 18–9; Wisner, 'Is Time Ripe for Transitional Justice in Afghanistan?', 8.

1371 S. Worden and R. Steele, *Telling the Story: Documentation Lessons for Afghanistan from the Cambodian Experience*. http://dspace.cigilibrary.org/jspui/bitstream/123456789/25297/1/Telling%20the%20Story%20-%20Documentation%20Lessons%20for%20Afghanistan%20from%20the%20Cambodian%20Experience.pdf?1 (10 April 2017), pp. 15–6.

Court or under the principle of universal jurisdiction.[1372] This means that, where the crimes concerned rise to the level of international crimes, not only national courts but also international or hybrid tribunals as well as the jurisdiction of third states (universal jurisdiction) is in principle possible.[1373] The advantages and disadvantages of each particular option as well as their feasibility and usefulness are presented in the following chapters.

4.3.1 National Courts

The first option is to conduct trials before the national courts of Afghanistan. According to Principle 20 of the United Nations' Updated Set of Principles for the Protection and Promotion of Human Rights through Action to Combat Impunity, *"It remains the rule that States have primary responsibility to exercise jurisdiction over serious crimes under international law. In accordance with the terms of their statutes, international and internationalized criminal tribunals may exercise concurrent jurisdiction when national courts cannot offer satisfactory guarantees of independence and impartiality or are materially unable or unwilling to conduct effective investigations or prosecutions."*[1374] Thus although national prosecutions should be the usual case, states which are emerging from conflict or states as Afghanistan where the conflict is still ongoing may be unable or unwilling to do so.[1375] In that case, international and internationalised criminal tribunals can exercise concurrent jurisdiction.

1372 Human Security Network, *Annual Ministerial Meeting*, p. 9; United Nations Commission on Human Rights, *Report of the Independent Expert to Update the Set of Principles to Combat Impunity, Diane Orentlicher, Addendum*, Principle 20 and 21.

1373 Joint report by the Advisory Council on International Affairs (AIV) and the Advisory Committee on Issues of Public International Law (CAVV), *Transitional Justice*, pp. 9–10; Khan, 'Justice to the Extent Possible', 27–8; M. A. Drumble, 'Rights, Culture, and Crime: The Role of Rule of Law for the Women of Afghanistan', *Columbia Journal of Transnational Law* 42 (2004), 349–90, at 388–9; Winterbotham, *The State of Transitional Justice in Afghanistan*, p. 22; Bassiouni, 'Accountability for Violations of International Humanitarian Law and Other Serious Violations of Human Rights', 27–8.

1374 United Nations Commission on Human Rights, *Report of the Independent Expert to Update the Set of Principles to Combat Impunity, Diane Orentlicher, Addendum*, Principle 20.

1375 United Nations Human Rights Council, *Analytical Study on Human Rights and Transitional Justice*, p. 9.

The advantages of proceedings in the country where the crime has occurred are manifold. Not only are the victims of the offence or their relatives present, but also it is the rules and values of a community in that country that have been violated.[1376] Furthermore, it is there that most evidence can be collected.[1377] Another advantage of national trials is that the citizens would most likely support such an approach[1378] and that it would demonstrate the greatest legitimacy.[1379] However, a domestic response to past atrocities, namely to war crimes, crimes against humanity, genocide and other serious violations of human rights has been the absolute exception.[1380] This may be due to the fact that any national trial must comply with international standards. This means that the development of national investigative and prosecutorial capacities, an independent and effective judiciary, adequate legal defense, witness and victims' protection as well as the conduct of fair, impartial and independent processes is necessary.[1381] The creation of such an environment after years of destruction requires huge financial and logistical resources as well as qualified personnel.[1382] None of these requirements for criminal proceedings before national courts is met in the case of Afghanistan.[1383] The justice system is in bad condition, the physical infrastructure of the courts has been devastated by years of war and judges are appointed without a university degree in law or proper educational and training background.[1384] Afghan

---

1376 Cassese, *The Oxford Companion to International Criminal Justice*, p. 123.

1377 Ibid., p. 123.

1378 Winterbotham, *Healing the Legacies of Conflict in Afghanistan*, p. 89.

1379 O. Miazad, 'Transitional Justice in Post-War Afghanistan', *Human Rights Brief* 9 (2002), 1–5, at 5.

1380 J. D. van der Vyver, 'The United Nations and International Criminal Law', *The University of Queensland Law Journal* 24 (2005), 317–36, at 335.

1381 United Nations, *Guidance Note of the Secretary-General*, p. 7; Amnesty International, *Afghanistan: Addressing the Past to Secure the Future*, p. 8; Khan, 'Afghanistan: War Crimes, ICC and NGOs', 96–7.

1382 Mallinder, *Amnesty, Human Rights and Political Transitions:*, p. 14; Cassese, *The Oxford Companion to International Criminal Justice*, p. 125.

1383 Khan, 'Justice to the Extent Possible', 21–3.

1384 Wardak, Saba and Kazem, *Afghanistan Human Development Report 2007*, p. 28; Khan, 'Afghanistan: War Crimes, ICC and NGOs', 102–3; N. Choudhury, 'Reconceptualising Legal Pluralism in Afghanistan', Selected Proceedings of the Annual Canadian Law Student Conference, *Windsor Review of Legal and Social Issues* Inaugural Volume (2010), 21–52, at 34; Winterbotham, *Healing the Legacies of Conflict in Afghanistan*, pp. 19–20; Human Rights Watch, *World Report 2011:*, p. 4; Afghanistan National Development Strategy Secretariat/Islamic Republic of Afghanistan, *Afghanistan National Development Strategy (ANDS)*.

judges suffer from a lack of economic and physical security as well as from poor working conditions.[1385] They receive low salaries and cannot access the resources necessary to hold trials, such as legal text books.[1386] Further shortcomings exist in the area of witness protection and the provision of appropriate defence counsel.[1387] Other problems stem from the fact that the criminal justice system in Afghanistan is marked by severe human rights violations, including the use of torture and the application of the death penalty.[1388]

It is because of this sad reality that the Afghan criminal justice system has to struggle with even ordinary crimes.[1389] Dealing with international crimes would thus be an almost impossible task for Afghan courts.[1390] It is noteworthy in this context that war crimes, genocide and crimes against humanity are not defined in Afghanistan's national legislation, that is, they are not criminal offences according to the Afghan penal code or any other Afghan law.[1391] Consequently, perpetrators of these crimes cannot be prosecuted before Afghan courts since the necessary jurisdiction is lacking.[1392]

---

http://www.undp.org.af/publications/KeyDocuments/ANDS_Full_Eng.pdf (16 March 2017), p. 65.

1385 Wardak, Saba and Kazem, *Afghanistan Human Development Report 2007*, p. 28; Afghanistan National Development Strategy Secretariat/Islamic Republic of Afghanistan, *Afghanistan National Development Strategy (ANDS)*, p. 65.

1386 Wardak, Saba and Kazem, *Afghanistan Human Development Report 2007*, 28, 91–93; Afghanistan National Development Strategy Secretariat/Islamic Republic of Afghanistan, *Afghanistan National Development Strategy (ANDS)*, p. 65; Khan, 'Afghanistan: War Crimes, ICC and NGOs', 102.

1387 Afghanistan Independent Human Rights Commission (AIHRC), *A Call for Justice*, p. 50.

1388 Amnesty International, *Afghanistan: Addressing the Past to Secure the Future*, p. 10.

1389 Winterbotham, *Healing the Legacies of Conflict in Afghanistan*, 20, 52–53, 89; United Nations Assistance Mission in Afghanistan (UNAMA), *Afghanistan Mid Year Report on Protection of Civilians in Armed Conflict 2010*, p. 11.

1390 Winterbotham, *Healing the Legacies of Conflict in Afghanistan*, p. 20; Khan, 'Justice to the Extent Possible', 26–7; Human Rights Watch, *Blood-Stained Hands*, p. 129; Wisner, 'Is Time Ripe for Transitional Justice in Afghanistan?', 6.

1391 Hartmann, 'Casualties of Myopia', 183; Joint report by the Advisory Council on International Affairs (AIV) and the Advisory Committee on Issues of Public International Law (CAVV), *Transitional Justice*, p. 36.

1392 Joint report by the Advisory Council on International Affairs (AIV) and the Advisory Committee on Issues of Public International Law (CAVV), *Transitional Justice*, p. 36; Hazdra, 'Verurteilen – Vergessen – Versöhnen. Die wichtigsten Ansätze zur Konfliktaufarbeitung im Überblick', 157.

The bad condition of the Afghan justice system was clearly evident in the trials of Abdullah Shah in 2002 and Asadullah Sarwary in 2005/6, which did not meet the basic standards of fair process.[1393] In the case of Abdullah Shah, a mujahedeen commander who had been accused of killings and tried according to ordinary criminal law[1394], several standards of due process were violated: he had no defence counsel, was tortured in detention and his case was heard in camera. Finally, he was sentenced to death and then executed.[1395] The trial of Asadullah Sarwary, head of the communist intelligence agency, namely the Department for Safeguarding the Interests of Afghanistan (AGSA) and charged with torture and multiple murders, was likewise unfair.[1396] He was arrested in 1992 and kept in pre-trial detention until 2004.[1397] During the proceedings, Sarwary was not given the opportunity to question witnesses or challenge the evidence against him.[1398] His death sentence was later reduced to twenty years imprisonment.[1399]

On the basis of the above, it can be concluded that Afghanistan is currently unable to investigate and prosecute those responsible for serious international crimes. In this event and with reference to Principle 20 of the United Nations' Updated Set of Principles[1400], international and internationalised criminal tribunals may exercise concurrent jurisdiction.

1393 Winterbotham, *Healing the Legacies of Conflict in Afghanistan*, p. 20; International Center for Transitional Justice (ICTJ), *Challenges to Peace and Justice in Afghanistan*, p. 2.

1394 Rubin, 'Transitional Justice and Human Rights in Afghanistan', 570; C. Gall, 'With Killer's Execution, Karzai Signals Move on Warlords', The New York Times, 03 May 2004.

1395 Amnesty International, *Afghanistan: "First Execution since Fall of Taliban"*. http://reliefweb.int/report/afghanistan/afghanistan-first-execution-fall-taliban (27 April 2017).

1396 Hartmann and Klonowiecka-Milart, *Impunity Prevails in Afghanistan*; TRIAL, *TRIAL WATCH: Assadullah Sarwari*. http://www.trial-ch.org/en/resources/trial-watch/trial-watch/profiles/profile/452/action/show/controller/Profile.html (01 June 2012).

1397 Hartmann and Klonowiecka-Milart, *Impunity Prevails in Afghanistan*; TRIAL, *TRIAL WATCH: Assadullah Sarwari*.

1398 Gossman and Kouvo, *Tell Us How This Ends*, p. 40.

1399 Hartmann and Klonowiecka-Milart, *Impunity Prevails in Afghanistan*; TRIAL, *TRIAL WATCH: Assadullah Sarwari*; Gossman and Kouvo, *Tell Us How This Ends*, p. 41.

1400 United Nations Commission on Human Rights, *Report of the Independent Expert to Update the Set of Principles to Combat Impunity, Diane Orentlicher, Addendum*, Principle 20.

According to revised Principle 21 (2) states may satisfy their obligations aimed at ensuring prosecution of certain offences not only by instituting prosecutions, but also by surrendering suspects for prosecution before an international or internationalised criminal tribunal.[1401]

4.3.2 *Ad hoc* International Tribunal

An advantage of international tribunals is, for example, that they may be more impartial than national courts since international judges have no connection to the state where the crimes have occurred.[1402] International judges are moreover selected due to their competence in the area of international criminal law and they benefit from proper equipment.[1403] In the context of international crimes as well as the fact that universal rights have been violated, it seems furthermore adequate to conduct proceedings before an international tribunal which applies international principles and rules.[1404]

The establishment of an *ad hoc* international tribunal is one way of dealing with serious human rights violations at the international level. *Ad hoc* international tribunals have been established by the UN Security Council in the case of the former Yugoslavia[1405] in 1993 and in the case of Rwanda[1406] in 1994.[1407] These tribunals are subsidiary organisations of the United Nations and located in The Hague (Netherlands)[1408] and Arusha (United Republic of Tanzania)[1409], thus outside the territories where the crimes had occurred.[1410]

1401 United Nations Commission on Human Rights, *Report of the Independent Expert to Update the Set of Principles to Combat Impunity, Diane Orentlicher*, p. 13.

1402 Cassese, *The Oxford Companion to International Criminal Justice*, p. 127.

1403 Ibid., p. 127.

1404 Ibid., p. 127.

1405 International Criminal Tribunal for the Former Yugoslavia.

1406 International Criminal Tribunal for Rwanda.

1407 United Nations Security Council, *The Rule of Law and Transitional Justice in Conflict and Post-Conflict Societies, Report of the Secretary-General*, p. 13; UN Office of the High Commissioner for Human Rights, *Rule-of-Law Tools for Post-Conflict States*, p. 29.

1408 International Criminal Tribunal for the Former Yugoslavia.

1409 International Criminal Tribunal for Rwanda.

1410 United Nations Security Council, *The Rule of Law and Transitional Justice in Conflict and Post-Conflict Societies, Report of the Secretary-General*, p. 13; UN

In 2001, various experts considered the possibility of establishing an international sponsored regime in the form of an *ad hoc* international criminal tribunal at the investigation and prosecution of those most responsible for serious international crimes in Afghanistan.[1411] However, due to the fact that peace took priority over justice, there was no support for such a regime.[1412] Furthermore, as in the above-mentioned cases of Yugoslavia and Rwanda, the UN Security Council would be the competent authority in this regard.[1413] But there has been no indication that the Security Council plans to set up an *ad hoc* tribunal for Afghanistan.[1414] Given that the Council is a political body, it can be assumed that, for example, the US and/or Russia would put a veto on the establishment of an *ad hoc* tribunal which could possibly prosecute their nationals.[1415] Even in the unlikely event that the Security Council would support the creation of an *ad hoc* tribunal, it must be taken into account that there is a risk that the mandate of the tribunal is too narrow with respect to perpetrators, crimes or the period of time.[1416]

Apart from the unlikelihood of an *ad hoc* international criminal tribunal for Afghanistan, it should no longer be necessary since the International Criminal Court has been established in order to deal with serious international crimes.[1417] In addition, in the cases of the *ad hoc* tribunals for Yugoslavia and Rwanda the expenditure of time and money, problems of translation as well as the limited success rate in prosecuting those most

---

Office of the High Commissioner for Human Rights, *Rule-of-Law Tools for Post-Conflict States*, p. 29.

1411 Khan, 'Justice to the Extent Possible', 28.

1412 Ibid., p. 28.

1413 Amnesty International, *Afghanistan: Addressing the Past to Secure the Future*, p. 14.

1414 Danchin, 'Transitional Justice in Afghanistan', 47; N. J. Kritz, 'Promoting a Formal System of Justice in Post-Taliban Afghanistan', *Conn. J. Int'l L.* 17 (2001–2002), 451–9, at 454.

1415 Danchin, 'Transitional Justice in Afghanistan', 47; M. Gerding, 'Völkerstrafrecht vor Internationalen Strafgerichten' in H.-H. Kühne, R. Esser and M. Gerding (eds.), *Völkerstrafrecht*, 1st edn. (Osnabrück: Julius Jonscher Verlag, 2007), pp. 251–91, at p. 291.

1416 Amnesty International, *Afghanistan: Addressing the Past to Secure the Future*, p. 14.

1417 Kritz, 'Progress and Humility', 75; Tolbert and van Genugten, *International Justice in a Time of Transition*.

responsible for international crimes has been criticised.[1418] Besides this, the interaction with local people, especially with victims and witnesses as well as the collecting of evidence has been made more difficult.[1419] Another argument against the establishment of *ad hoc* international tribunals is that it could be considered as victor's justice or as imposed on the state and the people concerned.[1420] Moreover, there would possibly be a disparity between western cultural norms and the local traditions of Afghanistan.[1421]

The option of an *ad hoc* international criminal tribunal in the case of Afghanistan has thus to be rejected. As an alternative, the creation of a hybrid court, i.e. a mixed court combining international and national elements, should be considered.

4.3.3 Hybrid Court

A hybrid court, also referred to as internationalised court, special court or mixed tribunal is a temporary criminal tribunal that would bring Afghan and international judges, prosecutors and defence lawyers together in order to conduct proceedings in cases of serious human rights violations.[1422] Unlike *ad hoc* international tribunals, hybrid courts are located in the country concerned. There are various ways in which such a court could possibly be set up, for example by the UN Security Council, through national legislation or on the basis of a treaty.[1423] In the cases of the Special Court for Sierra Leone and the Extraordinary Chambers in the Courts of Cambodia, a treaty between each respective government and the UN was the basis for their creation.[1424] In view of the high costs of the International Criminal Tribunal for the Former Yugoslavia and

---

1418 Van der Vyver, 'The United Nations and International Criminal Law', 329; N. Eisikovits, *Transitional Justice*. http://plato.stanford.edu/entries/justice-transitional/ (05 May 2017), p. 5.

1419 United Nations Security Council, *The Rule of Law and Transitional Justice in Conflict and Post-Conflict Societies, Report of the Secretary-General*, pp. 14–5.

1420 Eisikovits, *Transitional Justice*, p. 5.

1421 Ibid., p. 6.

1422 Amnesty International, *Afghanistan: Addressing the Past to Secure the Future*, p. 14.

1423 Ibid., p. 14; Hazdra, 'Verurteilen – Vergessen – Versöhnen. Die wichtigsten Ansätze zur Konfliktaufarbeitung im Überblick', 161.

1424 Amnesty International, *Afghanistan: Addressing the Past to Secure the Future*, pp. 14–5; UN Office of the High Commissioner for Human Rights, *Rule-of-Law Tools for Post-Conflict States*, p. 30.

for Rwanda, the financing of the mixed tribunals for Sierra Leone and for Cambodia relied on voluntary contributions.[1425] This however led to uncertainty since an assured and continuous source of funding was missing.[1426] Nevertheless, a hybrid court would have several advantages over an *ad hoc* tribunal, such as Afghan ownership of the process as well as greater impact on and easier interaction with the Afghan population.[1427] Another benefit of such a tribunal is its contribution to national capacity building within the domestic legal system.[1428] This means not only that the skills of national justice personnel would be enhanced, but also that the physical infrastructure including buildings, equipment and furniture would be left to Afghanistan.[1429] Furthermore, a court located inside Afghanistan is in close vicinity to evidence, victims and witnesses.[1430] In accordance with this assessment, the UNOHCHR Rule-of-Law Tool with regard to prosecution initiatives emphasises that *"If at all possible, a tribunal should be developed in the country where the crimes occurred, as it will have more impact and may assist to develop domestic capacity."*[1431] The creation of a hybrid court for Afghanistan would hence be a reasonable option.[1432] This is also in line with the view of the Afghan people themselves. According to a survey 79.5 % of the respondents are in favour of trials being held inside rather than outside Afghanistan and 49.6 % support a court with a mixture

1425 United Nations Security Council, *The Rule of Law and Transitional Justice in Conflict and Post-Conflict Societies, Report of the Secretary-General*, pp. 14–5.

1426 Ibid., pp. 14–5.

1427 Amnesty International, *Afghanistan: Addressing the Past to Secure the Future*, p. 15; UN Office of the High Commissioner for Human Rights, *Rule-of-Law Tools for Post-Conflict States*, p. 31; Kritz, 'Progress and Humility', 74.

1428 Amnesty International, *Afghanistan: Addressing the Past to Secure the Future*, p. 15; UN Office of the High Commissioner for Human Rights, *Rule-of-Law Tools for Post-Conflict States*, p. 31; United Nations Security Council, *The Rule of Law and Transitional Justice in Conflict and Post-Conflict Societies, Report of the Secretary-General*, p. 15; Kritz, 'Progress and Humility', 74; Dickinson, 'Transitional Justice in Afghanistan', 37–9.

1429 United Nations Security Council, *The Rule of Law and Transitional Justice in Conflict and Post-Conflict Societies, Report of the Secretary-General*, p. 15.

1430 Ibid., p. 15.

1431 UN Office of the High Commissioner for Human Rights, *Rule-of-Law Tools for Post-Conflict States*, p. 30.

1432 Mani, *Ending Impunity and Building Justice in Afghanistan*, 5,33; Dickinson, 'Transitional Justice in Afghanistan', 39–42; Khan, 'Justice to the Extent Possible', 28–9.

of international and Afghan judges as the most trusted option for fair trials of war criminals.[1433]

Before establishing a hybrid court in Afghanistan several prior issues would have to be considered. In this regard, the above-mentioned UNOHCHR Rule-of-Law Tool on Prosecution Initiatives lists various important topics[1434], such as the initial question of whether the international assistance should take the form of assistance to the domestic legal system or whether criminal trials should be conducted before a "special" court sitting outside the ordinary court structure, but of course inside the country.[1435] The establishment of a special (hybrid) court is more convincing as it is a well-defined project which may receive sufficient support and resources.[1436] In order to be internationally legitimised a hybrid court for Afghanistan should be set up under the auspices of the United Nations.[1437]

With respect to the capacity and impartiality of the court on the one hand and the local legitimacy on the other, a careful balancing is essential.[1438] Thus, a large number of international personnel may be unnecessary and could lead to local reluctance. International know-how is nonetheless required in technical fields such as forensics or in relation to administrative tasks.[1439] However investigations, including interrogations and witness support as well as outreach and public information, will be best achieved through Afghan personnel.[1440]

Furthermore, capacity-building and the legacy of the hybrid court should form parts of its core mandate. This means that not only initiatives such as mentoring, training and capacity-building of civil society should be integrated, but also that international personnel need to learn about Afghanistan's history, culture and legal tradition.[1441] Other relevant issues are, for example, the creation of adequate defence capacity; preventing ten-

1433 21.5 % prefer a court with Afghan judges and 27.6 % favour a fully international court, *see* Afghanistan Independent Human Rights Commission (AIHRC), *A Call for Justice*, pp. 24–6.

1434 *See* UN Office of the High Commissioner for Human Rights, *Rule-of-Law Tools for Post-Conflict States*, pp. 32–8.

1435 Ibid., p. 32.

1436 Ibid., p. 32.

1437 Ibid., pp. 32–3.

1438 Ibid., p. 33.

1439 Ibid., p. 33.

1440 Ibid., pp. 33–4.

1441 Ibid., pp. 34–5.

sions between international and national staff; security challenges; prison conditions and witness protection.[1442]

In light of the uncertainty and unreliability of voluntary contributions, the funding for a future hybrid court should be arranged by other means[1443], for example, by continuous and specified payments from the United Nations or supportive states. This, however, would require a clearly defined mandate, a fixed timeframe and efficient functioning of the court.

Another very important issue concerns the enforcement powers of hybrid courts. Without a Security Council resolution[1444] placing binding legal obligations on states to cooperate with tribunals, it is extremely difficult for hybrid courts to obtain custody of the accused sheltering outside the country.[1445] Also problematic are Bilateral Immunity/Security Agreements, such as the *"Security and Defence Cooperation Agreement Between the United States of America and the Islamic Republic of Afghanistan"* of 2015[1446] which states in its Article 13 (1) that *„Afghanistan [...] agrees that the United States shall have the exclusive right to exercise jurisdiction over such persons in respect of any criminal or civil offenses committed in the territory of Afghanistan.“*[1447] Furthermore, Article 13 (5) determines that *„Afghanistan and the United States agree that members of the force and of the civilian component may not be surrendered to, or otherwise transferred to, the custody of an international tribunal or any other entity or state without the express consent of the United States."*[1448] In order to increase the overall efficacy of hybrid courts and to ensure adequate cooperation from other states, these courts need a capacity to develop state relations that enable them to operate

1442 Ibid., pp. 35–6.

1443 Ibid., pp. 37–8.

1444 Under Chapter VII of the Charter of the United Nations a Security Council resolution may place binding legal obligations on states to cooperate with tribunals. *See* ibid., p. 36.

1445 Ibid., pp. 36–7.

1446 Ministry of Foreign Affairs (Government of Afghanistan), *Security and Defense Cooperation Agreement Between the United States of America and the Islamic Republic of Afghanistan*, Pre-decisional Document as of November 2013. http://mfa.gov.af/Content/files/2013-11-18%20BSA%20TEXT.pdf (01 April 2017); C. Recknagel, *Explainer: Key Points in U.S.-Afghan Bilateral Security Agreement*. http://www.rferl.org/content/explainer-bsa-afghan-us-security-agreement-bsa/26613884.html (09 January 2015).

1447 Ministry of Foreign Affairs (Government of Afghanistan), *Security and Defense Cooperation Agreement Between the United States of America and the Islamic Republic of Afghanistan*, p. 14.

1448 Ibid., p. 14.

without obstacles.[1449] Such a strategy may involve staff with experience in diplomatic relations and negotiating agreements as well as groups of supportive states.[1450] Given the participation of various international actors in the Afghan conflicts, it is all the more important to take an approach based on the aforementioned considerations.

Taking into account some of these prior issues, the Afghan Independent Human Rights Commission (AIHRC) as well as Human Rights Watch has made proposals with respect to the establishment of a special court or special chamber for Afghanistan. The AIHRC has recommended a permanent specialised investigative capacity within the criminal justice system called a "Special Prosecutor's Office", which should receive technical assistance and support from other governments, the United Nations, and the ICC.[1451] The Special Prosecutor's Office would investigate and prosecute those most responsible for current or past serious violations of human rights.[1452] Furthermore, a specialised chamber should be established through an agreement between the Afghan Government and the UN with the mandate to hear cases of war crimes and crimes against humanity committed during the conflict.[1453] The specialised chamber should be comprised of both Afghan and international judges. Apart from that, a capacity for defence lawyers as well as outreach and public information programmes has to be developed.[1454]

Human Rights Watch suggested the creation of an independent and impartial Special Court in order to investigate and prosecute war crimes, crimes against humanity, and other serious human rights crimes committed during the armed conflicts in Afghanistan since 1978.[1455] The court should be a mixed court and involve Afghan and international judges, with an international majority.[1456] The prosecutor's office should also be led by an international prosecutor.[1457] In the event that it is not feasible to locate the Special Court inside Afghanistan because of security risks and

---

1449 UN Office of the High Commissioner for Human Rights, *Rule-of-Law Tools for Post-Conflict States*, p. 37.

1450 Ibid., p. 37.

1451 Afghanistan Independent Human Rights Commission (AIHRC), *A Call for Justice*, pp. 50–2.

1452 Ibid., pp. 50–2.

1453 Ibid., pp. 50–2.

1454 Ibid., pp. 50–2.

1455 Human Rights Watch, *Blood-Stained Hands*, pp. 129–30.

1456 Ibid., p. 9.

1457 Ibid., p. 9.

the ongoing armed conflict, Human Rights Watch has recommended the establishment of the court outside of the country.[1458] In any case, the court must meet international fair trial standards and should include an effective protection programme for victims and witnesses.[1459]

Notwithstanding these proposals and the previous considerations, there are currently various obstacles which may hinder the establishment of a hybrid court for Afghanistan. The main reason is a lack of interest and political will to support such an approach. Neither the international community, including the United Nations, nor the Afghan Government has made serious efforts in this regard.[1460] A fundamental change in thinking is therefore absolutely essential.

4.3.4 The International Criminal Court

As an alternative to a hybrid court for Afghanistan, the International Criminal Court (ICC) could be an appropriate forum for the investigation and prosecution of serious international crimes. The decisive question in this context is whether and under what conditions is this possible? And apart from that, how realistic and advisable are proceedings before the ICC?

As already mentioned in Chapter 3.1.3[1461], the most comprehensive legal framework with regard to the fight against impunity is the Rome Statute of the International Criminal Court. In February 2003, Afghanistan became a States Party to the statute and since 2007 the then prosecutor of the ICC Moreno-Ocampo undertook preliminary investigations into alleged international crimes committed by anti-government groups, i.e. the Taliban and other armed groups, as well as by Afghan National Security Forces, US armed forces and the CIA in Afghanistan.[1462] His successor, Fatou Bensouda, has recently completed the preliminary in-

1458 Ibid., pp. 126–7.

1459 Ibid., pp. 129–30.

1460 Kersten, *The ICC in Afghanistan*; S. Harris Rimmer, *Building Democracy and Justice After Conflict: The Afghanistan Independent Human Rights Commission.* http://regnet.anu.edu.au/sites/default/files/BD-WorkingPaper5.pdf (11 June 2012), p. 10.

1461 Chapter 3.1.3 The Afghan Amnesty Law and the Rome Statute of the International Criminal Court.

1462 Barbour and Weed, *The International Criminal Court (ICC)*, p. 14.

vestigations and requested authorisation from the Court's Judges to open formal investigations.[1463]

According to Article 53 (1) (a) – (c) of the Rome Statute, the preliminary examination consists of considerations by the prosecutor with respect to jurisdiction, admissibility (complementary and gravity) and the interests of justice.[1464] The examination in the context of Chapter 3.1.3 has shown that, *inter alia*, due to the blanket Amnesty Law currently in force, Afghanistan does not pass the complementarity test.[1465] In the final phase of the preliminary examination with a focus on the question of whether there are *"substantial reasons to believe that an investigation would not serve the interests of justice"*[1466], Chapter 3.1.3 explored that the prosecutor has not accepted the current Afghan Amnesty Law, since an unconditional and comprehensive amnesty applying to those most responsible for serious human rights violations is absolutely contrary to the object and purpose of the Rome Statute.[1467] Thus, the current Afghan Amnesty Law is in any case not an appropriate way of stopping the investigations by the Office of the Prosecutor.

In the event that Afghanistan adopts the proposed amnesty law, i.e. an amnesty law which is designed to fulfil the requirements of international law, it is open to question how the ICC will deal with such an amnesty. For the purpose of this chapter, it is hence important to establish whether and how the proposed legitimate amnesty law and possible ICC proceedings go together. The legal analysis starts with Article 53 in conjunction with Article 17 of the Rome Statute, because these provisions are directly applicable. Since the examination has focused on the admissibility of

1463 International Criminal Court (ICC) – The Office of the Prosecutor, *Situation in Afghanistan*.

1464 International Criminal Court (ICC) – The Office of the Prosecutor, *Report on Preliminary Examination Activities 2016*, p. 2.

1465 International Criminal Court (ICC) – The Office of the Prosecutor, *Situation in the Islamic Republic of Afghanistan*; Robinson, 'Serving the Interests of Justice', 501; Kreß and Grover, 'International Criminal Law Restraints in Peace Talks to End Armed Conflicts of a Non-International Character', 70; Mallinder, *Amnesty, Human Rights and Political Transitions:*, p. 283; Seibert-Fohr, 'The Relevance of the Rome Statute of the International Criminal Court for Amnesties and Truth Commissions', 588; Joint report by the Advisory Council on International Affairs (AIV) and the Advisory Committee on Issues of Public International Law (CAVV), *Transitional Justice*, pp. 20–1.

1466 *See* Article 53 (1) (c) Rome Statute of the International Criminal Court.

1467 Robinson, 'Serving the Interests of Justice', 484; *See* Chapter 3.1.3.

potential cases[1468], that is, the Office of the Prosecutor has analysed *inter alia* whether the requirements for complementarity of Article 17 of the Rome Statute are met[1469], the following remarks focus on this issue. As mentioned above, the principle of complementary entails the assessment of national proceedings and other efforts to ensure justice and accountability.[1470] In this respect, Article 17 (1) (a) of the Rome Statute determines that *"[...] the Court shall determine that a case is inadmissible where: (a) The case is being investigated or prosecuted by a State which has jurisdiction over it, unless the State is unwilling or unable genuinely to carry out the investigation or prosecution."* In a policy paper the Office of the Prosecutor emphasised the importance of different approaches to combat impunity. This means that not only prosecutions provide a response to international crimes, but also truth seeking, reparations, institutional reform and traditional justice mechanisms can be decisive factors as regards the principle of complementarity.[1471] Ultimately, a comprehensive strategy in which all efforts are as complementary to each other as possible is necessary.[1472] In practice, this means, for example, that the government of a society in transition may prosecute only those perpetrators most responsible for serious human rights violations and additionally, a truth commission and amnesties for lower-level criminals could be employed in order to satisfy the responsibilities under international law and to comply with the principle of complementarity.[1473] The proposed amnesty law can consequently be recognised

---

1468 *See International Criminal Court: Preliminary Examinations*, Afghanistan. https://www.icc-cpi.int/pages/preliminary-examinations.aspx?ln=en (02 August 2016); International Criminal Court (ICC) – The Office of the Prosecutor, *Situation in the Islamic Republic of Afghanistan*, paras. 261–363.

1469 *See* Article 53 (1) (b) Rome Statute of the International Criminal Court.

1470 Kersten, *The ICC in Afghanistan*; International Criminal Court (ICC) – The Office of the Prosecutor, *Report on Preliminary Examination Activities 2015*, p. 31.

1471 International Criminal Court (ICC) – The Office of the Prosecutor, *Policy Paper on the Interests of Justice*, pp. 7–8; M. Valinas, 'Interpreting Complementarity and Interest of Justice in the Presence of Restorative-Based Alternative Forms of Justice' in C. Stahn and L. van den Herik (eds.), *Future Perspectives on International Criminal Justice* (The Hague: T.M.C. Asser Press, 2010), pp. 267–88, at p. 287.

1472 International Criminal Court (ICC) – The Office of the Prosecutor, *Policy Paper on the Interests of Justice*, p. 8.

1473 Robinson, 'Serving the Interests of Justice', 500–1; Mallinder, *Amnesty, Human Rights and Political Transitions:*, p. 285; Seibert-Fohr, 'The Relevance of the Rome Statute of the International Criminal Court for Amnesties and Truth Commissions', 588.

by the ICC as it only applies to lower-level offenders and provides for accountability in the form of criminal proceedings with regard to those perpetrators who are most responsible for serious international crimes. The amnesty law would furthermore be subject to the condition that perpetrators participate in traditional or restorative justice processes, and that they testify (publicly or privately) in a truth commission, public inquiry or other truth-recovery. Further relevant conditions are, for example, surrendering and participating in disarmament, demobilisation and reintegration programmes; contributing materially and/or symbolically to reparations; and institutional reforms. Although this comprehensive strategy would presumably satisfy the ICC, it has been shown in Chapter 4.3.1 that Afghanistan is currently *"[...] unable genuinely to carry out the investigation or prosecution* "(Article 17 (1) (a) of the Rome Statute). From this it follows that the prosecutor will not consider a case inadmissible and thus that the ICC would be the competent authority. In such a case, the legal analyses would focus on the final phase of the preliminary examination, namely whether there are *"substantial reasons to believe that an investigation would not serve the interests of justice"*.[1474] The situation is quite different when a hybrid court[1475] would be established in order to investigate and prosecute those most responsible for serious international crimes. In this event, the prosecutor of the ICC could rely on Article 53 (1) (b) in conjunction with Article 17 of the Rome Statute and consider a case inadmissible.

Leaving aside the option of establishing a hybrid court for Afghanistan and assuming that due to its inability to investigate and prosecute serious human rights violations, Afghanistan will not pass the complementarity test, the following analysis deals with the final phase of the preliminary examination — the interests of justice. This means that where an investigation would not serve the interests of justice, the Office of the Prosecutor will not continue with its endeavours.[1476] As has been elaborated in Chapter 3.1.3, the prosecutor follows the approach that "only in exceptional circumstances [...] an investigation or a prosecution may not serve the interests of justice"[1477], i.e. "there is a presumption in favour of investigation

1474 *See* Article 53 (1) (c) Rome Statute of the International Criminal Court.

1475 *See* Chapter 4.3.3.

1476 International Criminal Court (ICC) – The Office of the Prosecutor, *Policy Paper on the Interests of Justice*, p. 1.

1477 Ibid., p. 3.

or prosecution"[1478].[1479] Furthermore, it has been demonstrated that there are no concrete indications as to whether the prosecutor would approve amnesty under certain conditions and stop an investigation.[1480] However, Article 53 (2) (c) of the Rome Statute determines that "*A prosecution is not in the interests of justice, taking into account all the circumstances, including the gravity of the crime, the interests of victims and the age or infirmity of the alleged perpetrator, and his or her role in the alleged crime [...]*". For minor crimes or in cases where the role of the perpetrator is less important, the prosecutor might accept an amnesty and conclude that there is not a sufficient basis for a prosecution.[1481] This means that, contrary to unconditional and comprehensive amnesties, amnesties which are restricted to lower-level criminals and accompanied by other transitional justice mechanisms, such as a truth commission, are not against the object and purpose of the Rome Statute of the International Criminal Court.[1482] This is all the more true when it is stipulated that perpetrators most responsible for international crimes must be prosecuted. In this respect, it has been explained in the introduction to Chapter 4[1483] why accountability for these crimes must play a crucial role in the framework of a possible future transitional justice process in Afghanistan. Investigations and prosecutions in these cases will consequently serve the interests of justice.

To sum up, it emerges from the legal analysis of Article 53 in conjunction with Article 17 of the Rome Statute that the preliminary examination consisting of considerations by the prosecutor regarding jurisdiction, admissibility (complementary and gravity) and the interests of justice would presumably lead to the acceptance of the proposed amnesty law and hence to the decision not to open formal investigations. In cases of serious international crimes committed by high-ranking perpetrators, such as political

---

1478 Ibid., p. 1.

1479 International Criminal Court (ICC) – The Office of the Prosecutor, *International Seminar on the Imperatives of the Observance of Human Rights and International Humanitarian Law Norms in International Security Operations*, p. 6.

1480 The examples of Uganda and Libya are illustrating the unclear situation with regard to national peace negotiations including amnesties and their consideration by the ICC., see Chapter 3.1.3 The Afghan Amnesty Law and the Rome Statute of the International Criminal Court.

1481 F. Razesberger, *The International Criminal Court: The Principle of Complementarity*, Völkerrecht, Europarecht und internationales Wirtschaftsrecht (Frankfurt am Main: Peter Lang, 2006), vol. 1, p. 183.

1482 Ibid., p. 184.

1483 Chapter 4 Determination of the Conditions under which an Afghan Amnesty Law would be Legitimate under International Law.

leaders, decision makers or senior officers, investigations and prosecutions are, however, indispensable. However, it has been shown that the Afghan justice system is unable to conduct criminal proceedings of such a magnitude. Thus, investigations and prosecutions are the responsibility of either a hybrid court for Afghanistan or the International Criminal Court itself.

Article 14 of the Rome Statute, which deals with the referral of a situation by a State Party, provides a further possibility for initiating investigations and prosecutions by the ICC. The article states that "*A State Party may refer to the Prosecutor a situation in which one or more crimes within the jurisdiction of the Court appear to have been committed requesting the Prosecutor to investigate the situation for the purpose of determining whether one or more specific persons should be charged with the commission of such crimes.*" This means that the Afghan authorities themselves could request assistance from the ICC and refer a situation to the court.[1484]

As mentioned at the beginning of this chapter, the Office of the Prosecutor has undertaken preliminary investigations into alleged international crimes committed by members of the US armed forces and members of the CIA. Similar to criminal proceedings against international actors before a hybrid court, the question arises of whether there are any obstacles to the institution of such proceedings. First of all, it is necessary to establish whether the ICC has jurisdiction over crimes committed by nationals of states that are not parties to the Rome Statute.[1485] The answer to this problem can be derived from Article 13 (c) in connection with Article 12 (2) (a) of the Rome Statute, which states that "*[...] the Court may exercise its jurisdiction if one or more of the following States are Parties to this Statute or have accepted the jurisdiction of the Court in accordance with paragraph 3: (a) The State on the territory of which the conduct in question occurred [...]*". Since Afghanistan, the state where the crimes occurred, acceded to the Rome Statute in February 2003, the ICC may exercise its jurisdiction over foreign perpetrators as well.[1486] According to Article 12 (3) of the

1484 Afghanistan Independent Human Rights Commission (AIHRC), *A Call for Justice*, p. 50; L. Charbonneau, *ICC Prosecutor Eyes Possible Afghanistan War Crimes* (Reuters, 2009); Amnesty International, *Taleban Should Be Prosecuted for War Crimes in Afghanistan*. https://www.amnestyusa.org/press-releases/afghanistan-taliban-should-be-prosecuted-for-war-crimes-2/ (13 May 2017).

1485 For example, Russia and the US have not ratified the Rome Statute of the ICC.

1486 International Criminal Court (ICC) – The Office of the Prosecutor, *Situation in the Islamic Republic of Afghanistan*, para. 44; Barbour and Weed, *The International Criminal Court (ICC)*, p. 15.

Rome Statute[1487], Afghanistan could even accept the ICC's jurisdiction over a time period prior to February 2003. Consequently, the prosecutor could be empowered to investigate international crimes which occurred in Afghanistan after July 1, 2002, when the Rome Statute entered into force.

In addition to the determination of jurisdiction, the prosecutor must consider whether the further requirements described in Article 53 and in Article 17 are met in order to open formal investigations against international actors. With regard to the principle of complementarity, US officials affirmed that any alleged wrongdoing would be properly investigated and prosecuted, if necessary, under the US military justice system.[1488] They therefore emphasised that the ICC must not arrest or prosecute members of the US armed forces.[1489] The ICC prosecutor, however, deemed the endeavours by the United States to be insufficient[1490] and stated that the information available indicates that no national investigations or prosecutions have been conducted or are ongoing against those who appear most responsible for the crimes allegedly committed by members of the US armed forces or the CIA.[1491] Hence it might be the case that the Pre-Trial Chamber decides to open formal investigations into crimes committed by US nationals. In that event, another problem may arise, namely whether US suspects can be extradited to the ICC. According to Article 89 (1) of the Rome Statute[1492], states parties, such as Afghanistan, are obliged to comply with an extradition request from the ICC. However, due to the already mentioned Bilateral Immunity Agreements (BIAs) between the US

1487 Art. 12 (3) of the Rome Statute determines: „*If the acceptance of a State which is not a Party to this Statute is required under paragraph 2, that State may, by declaration lodged with the Registrar, accept the exercise of jurisdiction by the Court with respect to the crime in question. The accepting State shall cooperate with the Court without any delay or exception in accordance with Part 9.*".

1488 Barbour and Weed, *The International Criminal Court (ICC)*, p. 15.

1489 Ibid., p. 15.

1490 *See* International Criminal Court (ICC) – The Office of the Prosecutor, *Report on Preliminary Examination Activities 2016*, 47, 49–50; International Criminal Court (ICC) – The Office of the Prosecutor, *Report on Preliminary Examination Activities 2015*, pp. 28–31.

1491 International Criminal Court (ICC) – The Office of the Prosecutor, *Situation in Afghanistan*, paras. 39–42.

1492 Article 89 (1) of the Rome Statute of the ICC states that „*The Court may transmit a request for the arrest and surrender of a person,[...], to any State on the territory of which that person may be found and shall request the cooperation of that State in the arrest and surrender of such a person. States Parties shall, in accordance with the provisions of this Part and the procedure under their national law, comply with requests for arrest and surrender.*"

and Afghanistan as well as many other states, it seems highly questionable whether these states will extradite US suspects to the ICC.[1493] The BIAs are aimed at preventing other countries from surrendering US nationals to the ICC without US consent.[1494] According to Article 98 (2) of the Rome Statute, *"The Court may not proceed with a request for surrender which would require the requested State to act inconsistently with its obligations under international agreements pursuant to which the consent of a sending State is required to surrender a person of that State to the Court, unless the Court can first obtain the cooperation of the sending State for the giving of consent for the surrender.*" So far, the Office of the prosecutor has not delivered an opinion on the question whether or not the BIAs pre-empt an extradition request from the ICC.[1495]

Ultimately, it should be considered whether proceedings before the ICC are realistic and generally advisable. As has been noticed in the previous chapter, the establishment of a hybrid court faces many challenges, such as a lack of interest and political will on the part of the international community, including the United Nations and the Afghan Government.[1496] The same applies to possible proceedings before the ICC.[1497] This is illustrated, *inter alia*, by the fact that, to this day, the Afghan authorities have not taken any practical steps to draft and adopt an ICC cooperation law[1498], although they are obliged to do so.[1499]

1493 Moen and Mohammadi, *International Criminal Court (ICC) in Afghanistan*, p. 12; Barbour and Weed, *The International Criminal Court (ICC)*, pp. 7–8.

1494 Barbour and Weed, *The International Criminal Court (ICC)*, p. 2.

1495 Ibid., 2, 8–10, 16–17.

1496 Kersten, *The ICC in Afghanistan*; Harris Rimmer, *Building Democracy and Justice After Conflict:*, p. 10.

1497 Winterbotham, *Healing the Legacies of Conflict in Afghanistan*, p. 21; Asian Centre for Human Rights, *Afghan Charter of Impunity: President Karzai as the Lame Duck*; Moen and Mohammadi, *International Criminal Court (ICC) in Afghanistan*, p. 12.

1498 Moen and Mohammadi, *International Criminal Court (ICC) in Afghanistan*, p. 4; Khan, 'Afghanistan: War Crimes, ICC and NGOs', 103; Winterbotham, *The State of Transitional Justice in Afghanistan*, p. 20.

1499 Since February 2003, when Afghanistan became a party to the Rome Statute, several duties, such as the duty to investigate and prosecute international crimes as well as the duty to implement the Rome Statute into Afghan law and to cooperate fully with the court, have been imposed upon it. *See* Preamble of the Rome Statute of the International Criminal Court: „*Affirming that the most serious crimes of concern to the international community as a whole must not go unpunished and that their effective prosecution must be ensured by taking measures at the national level and by enhancing international cooperation*" *[...]*

In accordance with these concerns – and shortly before this thesis was finalised – Pre-Trial Chamber II of the ICC rejected the request of the Prosecutor to proceed with an investigation into the situation in Afghanistan.[1500] The judges stated *"that the request establishes a reasonable basis to consider that crimes within the ICC jurisdiction have been committed in Afghanistan and that potential cases would be admissible before the Court."*[1501] However, they also noted *"the lack of cooperation that the Prosecutor has received and which is likely to go scarcer should an investigation be authorized hampering the chances of successful investigation and prosecution"* and *"the need for the Court to use its resources prioritizing activities that would have better chances to succeed."*[1502] The Chamber furthermore found that *"it is unlikely that pursuing an investigation would result in meeting the objectives listed by the victims favouring the investigation."*[1503] An investigation into the situation in Afghanistan would thus not serve the interests of justice.[1504] The arguments put forward by the judges are not convincing since a lack of resources should never be used as a reason for refraining from criminal investigations.[1505] What is essential is that criminal proceedings against those responsible for severe human rights violations principally serves the interests of the victims and the interests of justice. In duly substantiated exceptional cases only, the Court may derogate from this principle.[1506] However, it seems as though the Chamber had made a political decision.[1507]

Apart from that, it must be highlighted that the ICC does not have retroactive jurisdiction. This means that the court is responsible only from the date on which the Rome Statute comes into effect in a particular

---

„*Recalling that it is the duty of every State to exercise its criminal jurisdiction over those responsible for international crimes*“ and Article 86 of the Rome Statute of the International Criminal Court.

1500 International Criminal Court (ICC), *ICC Judges Reject Opening of an Investigation Regarding Afghanistan Situation*, ICC-CPI-20190412-PR1448. https://www.icc-cpi.int//Pages/item.aspx?name=pr1448 (23 April 2019).

1501 Ibid.

1502 Ibid.

1503 Ibid.

1504 Ibid.

1505 P. Thielbörger and Ö. Özdemir, *"Afghanistan" als Risikofall: Machtspiele am IStGH in Den Haag*. https://www.lto.de/recht/justiz/j/istgh-icc021733-afghanistan-usa-kriegsverbrechen-keine-untersuchung/ (23 April 2019).

1506 Ibid.

1507 According to some critics, the Court had capitulated to intensive pressure from the United States administration. *See* e.g. M. Simons, R. Gladstone and C. Rosenberg, 'Hague Court Abandons Afghanistan War Crimes Inquiry', 12 April 2019; Thielbörger and Özdemir, *"Afghanistan" als Risikofall*.

state.[1508] Thus in the case of Afghanistan, where the Statute became effective in February 2003, crimes committed before that date are, in principle, not covered by the jurisdiction of the ICC.[1509] According to Article 12 (3) of the Rome Statute[1510], Afghanistan could additionally accept the ICC's jurisdiction from July 1, 2002 onwards, when the Rome Statute entered into force.[1511] However, since it is necessary to focus on the whole (recent) history of conflict in Afghanistan, starting with the Communist Revolution and People's Democratic Party of Afghanistan (PDPA) government in 1978, the impact of restricted proceedings before the ICC would be doubtful.[1512] Not only would some of those perpetrators who are most responsible for serious human rights violations be ignored, but also the holistic process of transitional justice as well as victims' rights would be at stake.[1513]

Hence although the proposed amnesty law for Afghanistan is in accordance with the Rome Statute of the International Criminal Court and investigations and prosecutions of those most responsible for international crimes would theoretically be possible, there are nevertheless serious concerns about such an approach. Apart from challenges with regard to criminal proceedings against international actors, in particular against US personnel, as well as the lack of interest and will, the main problem concerns the temporal limitation of any proceedings before the ICC. It is this limitation which is a strong argument against the ICC, but in favour of the establishment of a hybrid court that could operate without temporal limits.

1508 Winterbotham, *The State of Transitional Justice in Afghanistan*, pp. 19–20.

1509 Kersten, *The ICC in Afghanistan*.

1510 Art. 12 (3) of the Rome Statute determines: *„If the acceptance of a State which is not a Party to this Statute is required under paragraph 2, that State may, by declaration lodged with the Registrar, accept the exercise of jurisdiction by the Court with respect to the crime in question. The accepting State shall cooperate with the Court without any delay or exception in accordance with Part 9.*".

1511 Danchin, 'Transitional Justice in Afghanistan', 47.

1512 Winterbotham, *The State of Transitional Justice in Afghanistan*, pp. 19–20; Khan, 'Afghanistan: War Crimes, ICC and NGOs', 109–10.

1513 Winterbotham, *The State of Transitional Justice in Afghanistan*, pp. 19–20.

4.3.5 Universal Jurisdiction

Another possibility of investigating and prosecuting severe human rights violations is provided by the principle of universal jurisdiction[1514]. Apart from the national courts of the country where the crimes occurred, and international or hybrid tribunals, perpetrators most responsible for atrocious crimes can also be held accountable before the national courts of any other state.[1515] The nationality of the perpetrator, victim or the location of the crimes does not matter.[1516] This is legally possible due to the universality principle, which is based on the approach that certain crimes are so grave that all countries have an interest in prosecuting them.[1517] Since universal jurisdiction is an exceptional form of jurisdiction, criminal proceedings in third states are restricted to only the most serious crimes and can only be conducted when the country where the crimes took place is either unwilling or unable to do so.[1518] In theory, there are several ways in which universal jurisdiction could be employed: when the suspect is present in the state which is willing to exercise universal jurisdiction; when the suspect is not present, by investigating crimes and requesting the suspect's extradition for trial; or when states agree to share responsibility for exercising universal jurisdiction.[1519]

1514 Basic literature on „universal jurisdiction", e.g.: Macedo S. (ed.), *Universal Jurisdiction: National Courts and the Prosecution of Serious Crimes under International Law*, Pennsylvania studies in human rights (Philadelphia, Pa.: Univ. of Pennsylvania Press, 2004); L. Reydams, *Universal Jurisdiction: International and Municipal Legal Perspectives*, Oxford monographs in international law (Oxford: Oxford Univ. Press, 2003); D. Hovell, 'The Authority of Universal Jurisdiction', *European Journal of International Law* 29 (2018), 427–56; M. Inazumi, *Universal Jurisdiction in Modern International Law: Expansion of National Jurisdiction for Prosecuting Serious Crimes under International Law*, Teilw. zugl.: Utrecht, Univ., Diss., 2004, School of Human Rights research series (Antwerpen: Intersentia, 2005), vol. 19.

1515 United Nations Security Council, *The Rule of Law and Transitional Justice in Conflict and Post-Conflict Societies, Report of the Secretary-General*, p. 16.

1516 Amnesty International, *Afghanistan: Addressing the Past to Secure the Future*, p. 7; Khan, 'Justice to the Extent Possible', 29–30.

1517 United Nations Security Council, *The Rule of Law and Transitional Justice in Conflict and Post-Conflict Societies, Report of the Secretary-General*, p. 16.

1518 Ibid., p. 16; Amnesty International, *Afghanistan: Addressing the Past to Secure the Future*, p. 4; Khan, 'Justice to the Extent Possible', 29–30.

1519 Amnesty International, *Afghanistan: Addressing the Past to Secure the Future*, pp. 13–4.

In connection with the Afghan conflict, the exercise of universal jurisdiction in four cases has been the sole source of accountability so far.[1520] These cases concern the investigation and prosecution of Afghans for their role in the commission of international crimes.[1521] From 2005 until 2007, the United Kingdom (UK) and the Netherlands (NL) exercised universal jurisdiction against Afghans present in their countries.[1522]

The first proceeding in the UK in July 2005 was initiated against Faryadi Sarwar Zardad, a former commander of Hezb-e Islami who had come to the UK in 1998.[1523] He was prosecuted for the crimes of torture and hostage-taking in Afghanistan between 1992 and 1996, and finally sentenced to 20 years in prison.[1524] His appeal was dismissed in 2007.[1525]

In October 2005, the Netherlands conducted trials against Hesamuddin Hesam and Habibullah Jalalzoy[1526], who were high-ranking members of Afghanistan's communist-era intelligence service (KhAD) and had come to the Netherlands in the early 1990s.[1527] They were prosecuted for their involvement in war crimes, crimes against humanity and acts of torture

---

1520 Khan, 'Justice to the Extent Possible', 29–33.

1521 Ibid., pp. 29–33.

1522 Khan, 'Afghanistan: War Crimes, ICC and NGOs', 111.

1523 Ibid., p. 111; Khan, 'Justice to the Extent Possible', 29–33; TRIAL, *TRIAL WATCH: Faryadi Sarwar Zardad*. https://trialinternational.org/latest-post/faryadi-sarwar-zardad/ (01 May 2017); S. Laville, *UK Court Convicts Afghan Warlord: Zardad Found Guilty of Torture after Landmark Old Bailey Retrial*. http://www.guardian.co.uk/uk/2005/jul/19/afghanistan.world (02 May 2017).

1524 Khan, 'Afghanistan: War Crimes, ICC and NGOs', 111; TRIAL, *TRIAL WATCH: Faryadi Sarwar Zardad*; Laville, *UK Court Convicts Afghan Warlord*.

1525 Khan, 'Justice to the Extent Possible', 29–33; TRIAL, *TRIAL WATCH: Faryadi Sarwar Zardad*.

1526 LJN: AV1489 and LJN: AV1163, District Court, 09/751005–04, cases against Hesamuddin Hesam and Habibullah Jalalzoy, 14 October 2005.

1527 Khan, 'Justice to the Extent Possible', 29–33; Khan, 'Afghanistan: War Crimes, ICC and NGOs', 111; L. Zegveld, 'Dutch Cases on Torture Committed in Afghanistan: The Relevance of the Distinction between Internal and International Armed Conflict', *Journal of International Criminal Justice* (2006), 878–80, at 878; C. Ryngaert, *Another Afghan Case in the Hague District Court: Universal Jurisdiction over Violations of Common Article 3*. http://www.haguejusticeportal.net/Docs/Miscellaneous/Portal%20Ryngaert%20Commentary%20Abdullah%20F%2012-9-2007.pdf (03 May 2017), p. 1; TRIAL, *TRIAL WATCH: Heshamuddin Hesam*. https://trialinternational.org/latest-post/heshamuddin-hesam/ (30 April 2017); TRIAL, *TRIAL WATCH: Habibullah Jalalzoy*. https://trialinternational.org/latest-post/habibullah-jalalzoy/ (01 May 2017).

and sentenced to 12 years and nine years imprisonment, respectively.[1528] Their appeals[1529] were unsuccessful as well.[1530]

In the fourth criminal proceeding, which was held in the Netherlands in June 2007, the accused Abdullah F., an Afghan military official in the 1980s, was acquitted.[1531] The judges of the Hague District Court emphasised the difficulties and challenges that arise in cases where the crimes were committed in a foreign country many years ago.[1532] They mentioned problems with the hearing of witnesses, as well as cultural and political differences.[1533] For these reasons, i.e. for lack of proof, Abdullah F. could not be convicted for the commission of physical violence, cruel and inhuman treatment and torture.[1534]

Although the exercise of universal jurisdiction in the other three cases has of course contributed to accountability and might have had a general deterrent effect on perpetrators seeking protection in other states, it must nevertheless be considered that the prosecution of Afghan nationals in western states could be seen as an imposition of western conceptions of justice.[1535] This is even more true in view of the fact that only Afghans have so far had to take responsibility for their acts. Thus it is also necessary to apply the principle of universal jurisdiction in cases where international actors are alleged to have committed serious crimes against the Afghan people.[1536] Further shortcomings of proceedings in third states are such as mentioned by the Hague District Court in the case of Abdullah F. and include, for example, that the interaction with the local people, especially

---

1528 Khan, 'Afghanistan: War Crimes, ICC and NGOs', 111; TRIAL, *TRIAL WATCH: Heshamuddin Hesam*; TRIAL, *TRIAL WATCH: Habibullah Jalalzoy*.

1529 LJN: AZ9366, Court of Appeal The Hague, 09–751005–04, case against Habibullah Jalalzoy, 29 January 2007; LJN: AZ9365, Court of Appeal The Hague, 09–751004–04 and 09–750006–05, case against Hesamuddin Hesam, 29 January 2007.

1530 Khan, 'Afghanistan: War Crimes, ICC and NGOs', 111; Khan, 'Justice to the Extent Possible', 29–33; TRIAL, *TRIAL WATCH: Heshamuddin Hesam*; TRIAL, *TRIAL WATCH: Habibullah Jalalzoy*.

1531 LJN: BA9575, District Court The Hague, 09/750001–06, case against Abdullah F., 25 June 2007; Khan, 'Justice to the Extent Possible', 29–33.

1532 Ibid., pp. 29–33.

1533 Ibid., pp. 29–33.

1534 Ibid., pp. 29–33; Ryngaert, *Another Afghan Case in the Hague District Court*, p. 1.

1535 Khan, 'Justice to the Extent Possible', 33.

1536 Ibid., p. 33.

with victims and witnesses as well as the collecting of evidence is extremely difficult.[1537]

4.3.6 Conclusion

Having elaborated the various ways of prosecuting serious international crimes and other serious acts of violence against persons, it can be concluded that trials before the national courts of Afghanistan are highly unlikely as the Afghan justice system is in a bad condition and struggles with even ordinary crimes.[1538] Dealing with international crimes would thus be an almost impossible task for Afghan courts.[1539] Furthermore, the establishment of an *ad hoc* international tribunal has been rejected, as there is no indication that the Security Council plans to set up an *ad hoc* tribunal for Afghanistan.[1540] Apart from that, the location of such a tribunal outside Afghanistan would make the interaction with the local people, especially with victims and witnesses as well as the collecting of evidence more difficult.[1541] Another argument against the establishment of an *ad hoc* international tribunal is that it could be considered as being imposed on Afghanistan and its people.[1542] Moreover, there would possibly be a disparity between the western cultural norms and local traditions of Afghanistan.[1543] These problems also arise with regard to criminal proceedings under the principle of universal jurisdiction. They are conducted be-

1537 UN Office of the High Commissioner for Human Rights, *Rule-of-Law Tools for Post-Conflict States*, p. 29.

1538 Winterbotham, *Healing the Legacies of Conflict in Afghanistan*, 20, 52–53, 89; United Nations Assistance Mission in Afghanistan (UNAMA), *Afghanistan Mid Year Report on Protection of Civilians in Armed Conflict 2010*, p. 11.

1539 Winterbotham, *Healing the Legacies of Conflict in Afghanistan*, p. 20; Khan, 'Justice to the Extent Possible', 26–7; Human Rights Watch, *Blood-Stained Hands*, p. 129; Wisner, 'Is Time Ripe for Transitional Justice in Afghanistan?', 6.

1540 Danchin, 'Transitional Justice in Afghanistan', 47; Kritz, 'Promoting a Formal System of Justice in Post-Taliban Afghanistan', 454.

1541 United Nations Security Council, *The Rule of Law and Transitional Justice in Conflict and Post-Conflict Societies, Report of the Secretary-General*, pp. 14–5.

1542 Eisikovits, *Transitional Justice*, p. 5.

1543 Ibid., p. 6.

fore the national courts of a third state[1544], that is, outside Afghanistan and without any link to the perpetrator, the victims or the crime concerned[1545].

The exercise of universal jurisdiction nevertheless contributes to accountability and might have a general deterrent effect on perpetrators seeking protection in other states. It is however also necessary to apply the principle of universal jurisdiction in cases where international actors are alleged to have committed serious crimes against the Afghan people.[1546]

In addition to proceedings under the universality principle, either the International Criminal Court or a hybrid tribunal comes into consideration. A hybrid court would be located inside Afghanistan and bring Afghan and international judges, prosecutors and defence lawyers together.[1547] It would have several advantages over an *ad hoc* tribunal, such as Afghan ownership of the process as well as greater impact on and easier interaction with the Afghan population.[1548] Another benefit of a hybrid court is its contribution to national capacity building within the domestic legal system.[1549] Furthermore, a court located inside Afghanistan is in close vicinity to evidence, victims and witnesses.[1550]

With regard to proceedings before the International Criminal Court, it has been shown that the proposed amnesty law for Afghanistan is in accordance with the Rome Statute and investigations and prosecutions of those most responsible for international crimes would theoretically be possible. There are nevertheless various challenges concerning both the establishment of a hybrid court and proceedings before the ICC, such as a lack of interest and political will on the part of the international communi-

1544 United Nations Security Council, *The Rule of Law and Transitional Justice in Conflict and Post-Conflict Societies, Report of the Secretary-General*, p. 16.

1545 Amnesty International, *Afghanistan: Addressing the Past to Secure the Future*, p. 7; Khan, 'Justice to the Extent Possible', 29–30.

1546 Khan, 'Justice to the Extent Possible', 33.

1547 Amnesty International, *Afghanistan: Addressing the Past to Secure the Future*, p. 14.

1548 Ibid., p. 15; UN Office of the High Commissioner for Human Rights, *Rule-of-Law Tools for Post-Conflict States*, p. 31; Kritz, 'Progress and Humility', 74.

1549 Amnesty International, *Afghanistan: Addressing the Past to Secure the Future*, p. 15; UN Office of the High Commissioner for Human Rights, *Rule-of-Law Tools for Post-Conflict States*, p. 31; United Nations Security Council, *The Rule of Law and Transitional Justice in Conflict and Post-Conflict Societies, Report of the Secretary-General*, p. 15; Kritz, 'Progress and Humility', 74; Dickinson, 'Transitional Justice in Afghanistan', 37–9.

1550 United Nations Security Council, *The Rule of Law and Transitional Justice in Conflict and Post-Conflict Societies, Report of the Secretary-General*, p. 15.

ty and the Afghan Government[1551] as well as obstacles in respect of trials against international actors, in particular against US personnel. However, the main problem concerns the temporal limitation of any proceedings before the ICC. It is this limitation which is a strong argument against the ICC, but in favour of the establishment of a hybrid court that could operate without temporal limits.

4.4 The Role of Traditional Justice Processes

Apart from prosecuting those most responsible for serious international crimes, such as war crimes, crimes against humanity, enforced disappearance and torture as well as other serious acts of violence against persons that may not rise to the level of an international crime, an amnesty for lower-level offenders and minor crimes[1552] is possible. As has been highlighted in the introductory chapter, a legitimate amnesty must, however, be conditional in order to prevent further violence and to facilitate accountability and the fulfilment of victims' rights. The participation of amnesty beneficiaries in traditional justice processes[1553] within customary legal systems may serve this purpose.[1554]

Afghanistan is charactarised by a highly complex legal pluralism. Customary legal systems exist beyond the state justice system, but both coexist in the same social setting.[1555] In Afghanistan, the formal legal system consists of the Afghan Constitution, statutory laws, Islamic Sharia law and the associated state institutions, such as courts.[1556] In most rural parts of

1551 Kersten, *The ICC in Afghanistan*; Harris Rimmer, *Building Democracy and Justice After Conflict:*, p. 10.

1552 Such as looting, informing or burning houses.

1553 Instead of the term ‚traditional justice processes', other similar terms are used by scholars and practitioners, such as, for example, ‚customary legal mechanisms', ‚tradition-based justice', ‚community-based justice', ‚restorative justice processes'.

1554 United Nations Security Council, *The Rule of Law and Transitional Justice in Conflict and Post-Conflict Societies, Report of the Secretary-General*, p. 4.

1555 Choudhury, 'Reconceptualising Legal Pluralism in Afghanistan', 22.

1556 Afghanistan National Development Strategy Secretariat/Islamic Republic of Afghanistan, *Afghanistan National Development Strategy (ANDS)*, p. 64; C. Jones-Pauly and N. Nojumi, 'Balancing Relations between Society and State: Legal Steps Toward National Reconciliation and Reconstruction of Afghanistan', *The American Journal of Comparative Law* 52 (2004), 825–55, at 825–6; Wardak, Saba and Kazem, *Afghanistan Human Development Report 2007*,

the country informal legal mechanisms are in effect, that is, customary rules are applied by traditional tribunals.[1557] Having established that the national courts of Afghanistan are currently unable to conduct any criminal proceedings with regard to the decades-long conflict, the question of whether and to what extent traditional processes can contribute to transitional justice in Afghanistan is now dealt with.

Tradition-based justice mechanisms[1558] are restorative approaches to justice.[1559] In contrast to retributive approaches which include prosecutions and criminal penalties, traditional justice processes focus on apology, social forgiveness, reconciliation and the reintegration of former combatants.[1560] They aim at restoring peace and community harmony as well as redressing the harm done to the victims and holding perpetrators accountable for their actions.[1561] The basis for the restorative justice processes in Afghanistan is formed by non-state institutions of dispute resolution, i.e. traditional tribunals as *jirgas*, *shuras* or *mookee khans*.[1562] *Jirgas*[1563], mainly exist within Pashtun communities, are permanent and quasi-permanent

---

p. 5; F. Ahmed, 'Shari'a, Custom, and Statutory Law: Comparing State Approaches to Islamic Jurisprudence, Tribal Autonomy, and Legal Development in Afghanistan and Pakistan', *Global Jurist* 7 (2007), at 4–6.

1557 Afghanistan National Development Strategy Secretariat/Islamic Republic of Afghanistan, *Afghanistan National Development Strategy (ANDS)*, p. 64; Jones-Pauly and Nojumi, 'Balancing Relations between Society and State', 825–6; Wardak, Saba and Kazem, *Afghanistan Human Development Report 2007*, p. 5; Ahmed, 'Shari'a, Custom, and Statutory Law: Comparing State Approaches to Islamic Jurisprudence, Tribal Autonomy, and Legal Development in Afghanistan and Pakistan', 4–6.

1558 Freeman, *Necessary Evils*, p. 168.

1559 Mallinder, *Amnesty, Human Rights and Political Transitions:*, 184.

1560 Ibid., 184; Ludwin King, 'Amnesties in a Time of Transition', 611–2; Afghanistan National Development Strategy Secretariat/Islamic Republic of Afghanistan, *Afghanistan National Development Strategy (ANDS)*, p. 64; Wardak, Saba and Kazem, *Afghanistan Human Development Report 2007*, p. 5.

1561 Wardak, Saba and Kazem, *Afghanistan Human Development Report 2007*, pp. 40–1; N. Coburn and J. Dempsey, *Informal Dispute Resolution in Afghanistan*. http://www.usip.org/files/resources/sr247_0.pdf (25 May 2017), pp. 2–3.

1562 Afghanistan National Development Strategy Secretariat/Islamic Republic of Afghanistan, *Afghanistan National Development Strategy (ANDS)*, p. 64; Wardak, Saba and Kazem, *Afghanistan Human Development Report 2007*, p. 5; A. Senier, 'Rebuilding the Judicial Sector in Afghanistan: The Role of Customary Law', *The Fletcher School Online Journal for issues related to Southwest Asia and Islamic Civilization* (2006), 1–10, at 2.

1563 *Jirga* is a Pashtu word, meaning ‚circle', *see* T. Barfield, N. Nojumi and A. J. Thier, *The Clash of Two Goods: State and Non-State Dispute Resolution in*

local councils and have persistent membership.[1564] *Shuras*[1565], on the other hand, exist within non-Pashtun communities[1566] for more *ad hoc* meetings in order to solve a particular dispute.[1567] All kinds of traditional tribunals at the village, district or provincial levels consist of community elders and leaders, usually men, who interact with the respective community.[1568]

These tribunals use the Afghan customary law or *orf* as a guideline for local dispute settlement concerning political, economic and social conflicts as well as criminal cases.[1569] Afghan customary law has been described "*as those law-like unwritten social/moral codes of behavior that are deeply present in the collective conscience of members of a community (tribe, ethnic group, village), which have binding effects (socially and morally) on members.*"[1570]

Afghanistan. http://www.usip.org/files/file/clash_two_goods.pdf (04 May 2017), p. 7.

1564 T. J. Röder, 'Kollisionen zwischen shari'a, Gesetz und Stammestradition in Afghanistan' in M. Kötter and G. F. Schuppert (eds.), *Normative Pluralität ordnen: Rechtsbegriffe, Normenkollisionen und Rule of Law in Kontexten dies- und jenseits des Staates*, 1st edn. (Baden-Baden: Nomos, 2009), pp. 257–301, at pp. 284–8; The Country of Origin Information Centre (Landinfo), *Afghanistan: Blood Feuds, Traditional Law (Pashtunwali) and Traditional Conflict Resolution*. http://www.landinfo.no/asset/1940/1/1940_1.pdf (17 May 2017), pp. 12–3; Choudhury, 'Reconceptualising Legal Pluralism in Afghanistan', 35; United States Agency for International Development (USAID), *Afghanistan Rule of Law Project*, p. 52.

1565 *Shura* is a Dari word, meaning ‚to consult', *see* Barfield, Nojumi and Thier, *The Clash of Two Goods*, p. 7.

1566 For example, within Tajik-, Hazara- or Uzbek-communities, *see* Röder, 'Kollisionen zwischen shari'a, Gesetz und Stammestradition in Afghanistan', 284–8.

1567 Ibid., 284–8; Choudhury, 'Reconceptualising Legal Pluralism in Afghanistan', 35; United States Agency for International Development (USAID), *Afghanistan Rule of Law Project*, p. 52.

1568 Coburn and Dempsey, *Informal Dispute Resolution in Afghanistan*, pp. 2–3; United States Agency for International Development (USAID), *Afghanistan Rule of Law Project*, 9, 56–57; Barfield, Nojumi and Thier, *The Clash of Two Goods*, p. 7.

1569 Wardak, Saba and Kazem, *Afghanistan Human Development Report 2007*, p. 44; Coburn and Dempsey, *Informal Dispute Resolution in Afghanistan*, pp. 2–3; United States Agency for International Development (USAID), *Afghanistan Rule of Law Project*, pp. 7–8.

1570 Wardak, Saba and Kazem, *Afghanistan Human Development Report 2007*, p. 44; *see also*, Barfield, Nojumi and Thier, *The Clash of Two Goods*, p. 5; The Liaison Office, *Linkages between State and Non-State Justice Systems in Eastern Afghanistan: Evidence from Jalalabad, Nangarhar and Ahmad Aba, Paktia*. http://www.tlo-afghanistan.org/sites/default/files/Working-Paper-Series/TLO-Linka

There are approximately 55 distinct ethnic groups and as many customary legal systems in Afghanistan.[1571]

It is worth pointing out that due to the various traditional conflict resolution mechanisms which settle more than 80 % of disputes in the country[1572], Afghan communities have been able to maintain local stability and social order.[1573] These mechanisms not only comply with people's demands for justice, but also prevent major conflicts and escalating violence.[1574] Moreover, traditional tribunals have helped resolve particular wartime disputes[1575], revealed the truth and thus contributed to transitional justice in Afghanistan[1576].[1577] Hence the majority of Afghans refuses to accept the fragmented, ineffective and corrupt formal justice system and instead relies on traditional tribunals as trustworthy, efficient and less corrupt informal bodies.[1578]

There are however certain shortcomings with respect to the composition and the procedure of traditional tribunals, as well as the possible outcome of restorative justice processes.[1579] Procedural problems concern,

---

ges-between-state-and-non-state-justice-systems-in-eastern-Afghanistan.pdf (30 April 2017), p. 6.

1571 Senier, 'Rebuilding the Judicial Sector in Afghanistan', 2; International Legal Foundation, *The Customary Laws of Afghanistan*. http://www.usip.org/files/file/ilf_customary_law_afghanistan.pdf (06 May 2017).

1572 A. Wardak, 'State and Non-State Justice Systems in Afghanistan: the Need for Synergy', *U. Pa. J. Int'l L.* 32 (2011), 1305–24, at 1314; Wardak, Saba and Kazem, *Afghanistan Human Development Report* 2007, p. 91.

1573 R. Gang, *Community-Based Dispute Resolution Processes in Kabul City*. https://areu.org.af/wp-content/uploads/2016/02/1107E-CBDR-Processes-in-Kabul-City-CS-2011-web.pdf (19 May 2017), p. 1.

1574 Coburn and Dempsey, *Informal Dispute Resolution in Afghanistan*, p. 3.

1575 Winterbotham, *Healing the Legacies of Conflict in Afghanistan*, p. 77.

1576 Khan, 'Afghanistan: War Crimes, ICC and NGOs', 102.

1577 R. Shaw and L. Waldorf, 'Introduction: Localizing Transitional Justice' in R. Shaw, L. Waldorf and P. Hazan (eds.), *Localizing Transitional Justice: Interventions and Priorities After Mass Violence* (Stanford, Calif: Stanford University Press, 2010), pp. 3–26, at 15, 16, 17; United States Agency for International Development (USAID), *Afghanistan Rule of Law Project*, pp. 7–8.

1578 Wardak, Saba and Kazem, *Afghanistan Human Development Report 2007*, p. 91; J. Dempsey and N. Coburn, *Traditional Dispute Resolution and Stability in Afghanistan*. http://www.usip.org/files/resources/PB%2010%20Traditional%20Dispute%20Resolution%20and%20Stability%20in%20Afghanistan.pdf (27 May 2017), pp. 2–3.

1579 Dempsey and Coburn, *Traditional Dispute Resolution and Stability in Afghanistan*, pp. 2–3; Joint report by the Advisory Council on International Affairs (AIV) and the Advisory Committee on Issues of Public International

for example, the presumption of innocence, the collection of evidence and witness protection.[1580] Apart from that, *jirgas* and *shuras* usually consist of male elders and leaders, whereas women are generally excluded from the decision making procedure.[1581] Further disregard for the human rights of women results from *baad*, that is, the practice of offering a woman from the offender's family into marriage with a close relative of the victim as a possible outcome in a dispute resolution.[1582] Another highly problematic outcome is the burning down of the offender's house.[1583] It must however be noted that both *baad* and the burning of houses are applied only very rarely by traditional tribunals.[1584] Instead, reconciliation of the parties in conflict and compensation of the victim are paramount for a successful dispute resolution.[1585]

The abovementioned shortcomings, nevertheless, raise the question of whether the traditional processes fulfil the requirements of international law. First of all, although customary legal mechanisms are contrary to Western concepts of justice, the international community must recognise the great significance and impact of tradition-based justice in

---

Law (CAVV), *Transitional Justice*, pp. 38–9; L. McGregor, 'International Law as a 'Tiered Process': Transitional Justice at the Local, National and International Level' in K. McEvoy and L. McGregor (eds.), *Transitional Justice from Below: Grassroots Activism and the Struggle for Change* (Oxford and Portland, Oregon: Hart Pub., 2008), pp. 47–73, at p. 61; Barfield, Nojumi and Thier, *The Clash of Two Goods*, p. 3; Nadery, 'A Human Rights Awakening?', 59–60.

1580 N. Zupan and S. Servaes, *Transitional Justice & Dealing with the Past*, Guidance Paper Transitional Justice (Bonn, Germany, 2007), pp. 5–6.

1581 Wardak, 'State and Non-State Justice Systems in Afghanistan: the Need for Synergy', 1317; Barfield, Nojumi and Thier, *The Clash of Two Goods*, p. 17.

1582 Wardak, 'State and Non-State Justice Systems in Afghanistan: the Need for Synergy', 1318; Wardak, Saba and Kazem, *Afghanistan Human Development Report 2007*, p. 93; Barfield, Nojumi and Thier, *The Clash of Two Goods*, p. 17; A.-C. Claude, *Afghanistan – Justice and Reconciliation: The Informal Justice System in Afghanistan*. http://reliefweb.int/sites/reliefweb.int/files/resources/6AC2F49A58EF764B492577EF00071C46-Full_Report.pdf (19 May 2017), p. 5.

1583 Wardak, Saba and Kazem, *Afghanistan Human Development Report 2007*, p. 93.

1584 Ibid., p. 93; The Country of Origin Information Centre (Landinfo), *Afghanistan: Blood Feuds, Traditional Law (Pashtunwali) and Traditional Conflict Resolution*, pp. 13–4.

1585 Wardak, Saba and Kazem, *Afghanistan Human Development Report 2007*, p. 94; The Country of Origin Information Centre (Landinfo), *Afghanistan: Blood Feuds, Traditional Law (Pashtunwali) and Traditional Conflict Resolution*, pp. 13–4.

Afghanistan.[1586] At the same time, it must be ensured that international human rights standards are not ignored.[1587] Hence a good balance must be achieved between maintaining the informal legal mechanisms and respecting human rights.[1588] This means that, without modifying the traditional proceedings from the ground up[1589], practices such as *baad* or the burning of houses should disappear since they will never be tolerable.[1590] With regard to procedural standards it has to be carefully considered whether the demand for defence rights and other due process guarantees may undermine the customary legal system and its operating principles.[1591]

In conclusion, apart from certain issues that need be addressed, traditional justice approaches are a meaningful component of a possible future amnesty process in Afghanistan. Informal dispute resolution mechanisms can contribute to local stability and social order and thus, to transitional justice in Afghanistan.

1586 A. L. Hinton, 'Introduction: Toward an Anthropology of Transitional Justice' in A. L. Hinton (ed.), *Transitional Justice: Global Mechanisms and Local Realities after Genocide and Mass Violence* (New Brunswick: Rutgers University Press, 2011), pp. 1–22, at p. 5; Coburn and Dempsey, *Informal Dispute Resolution in Afghanistan*, p. 5.

1587 Mobekk, 'Transitional Justice in Post-Conflict Societies – Approaches to Reconciliation', 287.

1588 Kritz, 'Progress and Humility', 80.

1589 This happened in the case of the customary *gacaca*-tribunals in Rwanda, which were transformed into formalised, politicised and coercive state structures in order to deal with lower-level perpetrators of the mass violence between the rival Tutsis and Hutus groups and the genocide of 1994. However, this approach was not effective and led to unintended consequences which undermined peace and reconciliation. *See* Mallinder, *Amnesty, Human Rights and Political Transitions:*, pp. 107–9; Shaw and Waldorf, 'Introduction', 17–8; J. E. Burnet, '(In)Justice: Truth, Reconciliation, and Revenge in Rwanda's Gacaca' in A. L. Hinton (ed.), *Transitional Justice: Global Mechanisms and Local Realities after Genocide and Mass Violence* (New Brunswick: Rutgers University Press, 2011), pp. 95–118, at 97–98, 112–115; R. Duthie, 'Afterword: The Consequences of Transitional Justice in Particular Context' in A. L. Hinton (ed.), *Transitional Justice: Global Mechanisms and Local Realities after Genocide and Mass Violence* (New Brunswick: Rutgers University Press, 2011), pp. 249–56, at pp. 253–4; Hinton, 'Introduction', 12; Buckley-Zistel, 'Einleitung', 19; B. Ingelaere, 'The Gacaca Courts in Rwanda' in L. Huyse and M. Salter (eds.), *Traditional Justice and Reconciliation after Violent Conflict: Learning from African Experiences* (Stockholm, Sweden, 2008), pp. 25–59, at 49–51, 57.

1590 Wardak, Saba and Kazem, *Afghanistan Human Development Report 2007*, pp. 107–9.

1591 Kritz, 'Progress and Humility', 80.

4.5 *Encouraging Participation in Disarmament, Demobilisation and Reintegration Programmes*

To ensure that the Afghan amnesty process will be successful and the proposed concept of transitional justice will bear fruit, the participation of target groups in disarmament, demobilisation and reintegration programmes (DDR programmes) is essential.[1592] The following explanations illustrate 'who' should be involved in these programmes and 'how' this can best be achieved.

As has been elaborated in Chapter 4.2[1593], there are up to one million individuals who committed crimes during the Afghan conflicts.[1594] Furthermore, a survey in 2010 estimated that there are 32 000 to 40 000 combatants in Afghanistan with 8 000 to 10 000 full-time fighters, whereby illegal networks and criminal gangs were not recorded.[1595] Lower-ranking perpetrators responsible for non-serious crimes[1596] are possible amnesty beneficiaries provided that they fulfil certain conditions which contribute, *inter alia*, to preventing further violence. It has been established above that surrendering and participating in disarmament, demobilisation and reintegration programmes may constitute such a condition.[1597] The combination of amnesty and DDR programmes could encourage combatants to participate in the process of transitional justice since they will not be prosecuted and will receive assistance to change their lives.[1598]

According to the United Nations, *disarmament* includes the collection of small arms and light and heavy weapons.[1599] *Demobilisation* means that the conflict parties disband their military structures and combatants begin

---

1592 Mallinder, *Amnesty, Human Rights and Political Transitions:*, p. 379; Thier, 'Introduction:', 7; Rubin, 'Transitional Justice and Human Rights in Afghanistan', 576, 577; International Center for Transitional Justice (ICTJ), *Stabilizing Afghanistan*, p. 3.

1593 Chapter 4.2 The Scope of the Amnesty Law.

1594 Nadery, 'Afghans Struggle to Restore Justice in their Country', brief 28, 50.

1595 Sajjad, *Peace at all Costs*, pp. 12–3.

1596 Such as looting, informing or burning houses.

1597 *See* Chapter 4 Determination of the Conditions under which an Afghan Amnesty Law would be Legitimate under International Law.

1598 Mallinder, *Amnesty, Human Rights and Political Transitions:*, p. 382.

1599 United Nations Security Council, *Report of the Secretary-General on the Role of United Nations Peacekeeping in Disarmament, Demobilization and Reintegration*, S/2000/101. http://www.un.org/en/ga/search/view_doc.asp?symbol=S/2000/101 (31 May 2017), para. 6 (a).

the transformation into civilian life.[1600] It generally entails registration of former combatants, some kind of assistance to enable them to meet their immediate basic needs, and discharge and transportation to their home communities.[1601] *Reintegration* refers to the process which allows ex-combatants and their families to adapt, economically and socially, to a productive civilian life.[1602] It generally entails the provision of a package of cash or in-kind compensation, training, and job- and income-generating projects.[1603]

It has to be mentioned that various DDR-programmes have already been implemented in Afghanistan since 2001.[1604] Key Action 4 of the now-expired Action Plan for Peace, Reconciliation and Justice, which concerns the promotion of reconciliation and national unity, stated, *inter alia*, that the return and re-integration into society of all Afghans shall be encouraged through *"a range of programmes such as the Disarmament, Demobilisation and Reintegration programme (DDR), Disarmament of Illegal Armed Groups (DIAG) and the Strengthening Peace Programme [...]"*.[1605] The following remarks refer to the most significant programmes and highlight their achievements as well as their fundamental flaws. The *Disarmament, Demobilisation and Reintegration programme (DDR)* lasted from 2003 until 2005 and aimed at the collection of heavy weapons, the destruction of anti-personnel mines and ammunition stockpiles, and the disbandment of illegally armed groups.[1606] Although the programme was successful inasmuch as 70 000 weapons were collected from approximately 63 000 ex-combatants and 259 military units were decommissioned, it was hampered by a narrow time frame as well as by manipulation by local strongmen and militia commanders.[1607]

1600 Ibid., para. 6 (b).
1601 Ibid., para. 6 (b).
1602 Ibid., para. 6 (c).
1603 Ibid., para. 6 (c).
1604 D. Derksen, *The Politics of Disarmament and Rearmament in Afghanistan*. http://www.usip.org/sites/default/files/PW110-The-Politics-of-Disarmament-and-Rearmament-in-Afghanistan.pdf (16 December 2015), p. 5.
1605 Government of the Islamic Republic of Afghanistan, *Action Plan on Peace, Reconciliation and Justice in Afghanistan*, 4–11, Key Action 4 (e).
1606 Sajjad, *Peace at all Costs*, p. 5.
1607 Ibid., p. 5; P. Gossman, *Transitional Justice and DDR: The Case of Afghanistan*. http://ictj.org/sites/default/files/ICTJ-DDR-Afghanistan-ResearchBrief-2009-English.pdf (12 May 2017), pp. 1–3; United Nations Development Programme Afghanistan, *Afghanistan's New Beginnings Programme (ANBP)*. http://www.un

The *Disbandment of Illegal Armed Groups Programme (DIAG)* lasted from 2005 until 2011 and focused on the disarmament and disbandment of illegally armed groups as well as on development projects.[1608] *DIAG* has collected approximately 54 000 weapons and 760 illegally armed groups announced that they had disbanded their units.[1609] Notwithstanding this, the programme suffered from a lack of national and international support.[1610]

The *Strengthening Peace Programme (PTS)* was established in 2005 with the objective of encouraging combatants, in particular the Taliban and Hezb-e-Islami, to recognise the government, to accept the constitution, and to change their lives.[1611] This programme was characterised by weak management, corruption, insufficient resources and a lack of political will as well as a lack of participation.[1612]

Finally, the *Afghanistan Peace and Reintegration Programme (APRP)* was launched in 2010 in order to promote disarmament, reintegration and reconciliation.[1613] As has been mentioned in Chapter 2.3[1614], the proclamation of the *APRP* at the London Conference in January 2010[1615] can be associated with the worsening security situation in the country and Karzai's efforts to talk to the Taliban.[1616] Hence the main components of the programme were social outreach, confidence-building and negotia-

dp.org.af/whoweare/undpinafghanistan/Projects/psl/prj_anbp.htm (07 May 2012).

1608 Sajjad, *Peace at all Costs*, p. 6; United Nations Development Programme Afghanistan, *Afghanistan's New Beginnings Programme (ANBP)*.

1609 United Nations Development Programme Afghanistan, *Afghanistan's New Beginnings Programme (ANBP)*; United Nations Development Programme Afghanistan, *Disbandment of Illegal Armed Groups (DIAG): Annual Project Report 2010*. http://www.undp.org.af/Projects/Report2011/diag/2011-03-21-%20Annual%20Progress%20Report%20of%20DIAG.pdf (07 May 2012), pp. 3–4.

1610 F. Vendrell, 'The International Community's Failures in Afghanistan' in W. Mason (ed.), *The Rule of Law in Afghanistan* (Cambridge: Cambridge University Press, 2011), pp. 53–60, at p. 55.

1611 Sajjad, *Peace at all Costs*, pp. 7–8.

1612 Ibid., p. 8.

1613 Ibid., 1, 22–23; United Nations Development Programme Afghanistan, *Afghanistan Peace and Reintegration Programme (APRP) – UNDP Support: Third Quarter Report 2011*. http://www.undp.org.af/Projects/Report2011/APRP/3rdQ/APRP_00076674_QPR_Q3_2011.pdf (17 April 2012).

1614 Chapter 2.3 The Afghan Amnesty Law 2010.

1615 UNDP in Afghanistan, *Afghanistan Peace and Reintegration Programme (APRP)*.

1616 Human Rights Watch, *Afghanistan: Repeal Amnesty Law*.

tions; demobilisation; and consolidation of peace.[1617] The *APRP*, furthermore, included various initiatives for Taliban insurgents, such as offering work, education, land and pensions on condition that they renounced violence.[1618] The Project Progress Report from 2015 stated that 10 578 ex-combatants had renounced arms and joined the peace programme since 2010.[1619] The total number of weapons collected or registered by *APRP* was 8 101.[1620] However, according to experts these numbers are low and it should also be noted that the Taliban did not attend any peace negotiations.[1621] Furthermore, there were problems with abuse and manipulation by local commanders[1622] as well as a lack of security for ex-combatants[1623].

Thus although altogether these four programmes have demobilised tens of thousands of armed combatants and contributed to temporary improvements in security[1624], it must be assumed that the programmes have not reached their objectives.[1625] This is clearly illustrated by the ongoing conflict, the vast numbers of armed men and the instability prevailing in the country.[1626] This may be due to the uncoordinated and inconsistent approach of the DDR programmes as well as the manipulation and corruption in some cases.[1627] In addition, a comprehensive concept applying throughout Afghanistan was missing.[1628]

1617 Winterbotham, *Healing the Legacies of Conflict in Afghanistan*, p. 22; ISAF – International Security Assistance Force, *Afghanistan Peace and Reintegration Program*. http://www.isaf.nato.int/article/focus/afghanistan-peace-and-reconcili ation-program.html (18 April 2012).

1618 Winterbotham, *The State of Transitional Justice in Afghanistan*, pp. 9–10; UNDP in Afghanistan, *Afghanistan Peace and Reintegration Programme (APRP)*.

1619 UNDP in Afghanistan, *Afghanistan Peace and Reintegration Programme: 2015 Third Quarter Project Progress Report*. http://www.af.undp.org/content/dam/afgh anistan/docs/crisisprev/APRP/APRP-3QPR-2015.pdf (02 June 2017), p. 6.

1620 Ibid., p. 6.

1621 Al Jazeera, *Afghan Official: No Plans to Revive Taliban Peace Talks* Derksen, *The Politics of Disarmament and Rearmament in Afghanistan*, p. 19.

1622 Sajjad, *Peace at all Costs*, pp. 14–5.

1623 D. Derksen, *Impact or Illusion? Reintegration under the Afghanistan Peace and Reintegration Program*. http://www.usip.org/files/resources/PB%20106.pdf (18 April 2017), p. 2.

1624 Derksen, *The Politics of Disarmament and Rearmament in Afghanistan*, p. 5.

1625 Ibid., p. 5; International Crisis Group, *Talking About Talks*, pp. 17–8; Kippen, 'The Long Democratic Transition', 37.

1626 Derksen, *The Politics of Disarmament and Rearmament in Afghanistan*, p. 5; International Crisis Group, *Talking About Talks*, pp. 17–8; Kippen, 'The Long Democratic Transition', 37.

1627 Sajjad, *Peace at all Costs*, p. 1.

1628 Ibid., p. 1.

To ensure that a future disarmament, demobilisation and reintegration programme in Afghanistan will be effective and successful, certain conditions are indispensable. First of all, any DDR programme is embedded in the wider political context and as long as the armed conflict continues and powerful warlords do not support, but undermine, these programmes, they will fail.[1629] This means that political will is essential — the international community, the Afghan Government, the civilian population as well as the armed combatants of the various groups must strive for peace and reconciliation.[1630] Furthermore, to improve DDR programmes a coordinated, cooperative and transparent approach is crucial.[1631] With a view to the previous chapter and the role of tradition-based justice mechanisms concerning reconciliation and the reintegration of former combatants[1632], recognition of local realities and expectations is also necessary.[1633]

4.6 Testifying before a Truth Commission

In cases where the transitional justice process entails a regulation on amnesty it is important not to neglect the 'right to know the truth'.[1634] Hence the UNOHCHR has emphasised that amnesties must never be used

---

1629 Derksen, *The Politics of Disarmament and Rearmament in Afghanistan*, pp. 45–8; International Peace Academy (IPA), *A Framework for Lasting Disarmament, Demobilization, and Reintegration of Former Combatants in Crisis Situations.* https://www.ipinst.org/wp-content/uploads/publications/framework_for_ddr.pdf (02 May 2017), pp. 3–4.

1630 International Peace Academy (IPA), *A Framework for Lasting Disarmament, Demobilization, and Reintegration of Former Combatants in Crisis Situations*, p. 2.

1631 Sajjad, *Peace at all Costs*, 26, 36–41.

1632 Mallinder, *Amnesty, Human Rights and Political Transitions:*, 184; Ludwin King, 'Amnesties in a Time of Transition', 611–2; Afghanistan National Development Strategy Secretariat/Islamic Republic of Afghanistan, *Afghanistan National Development Strategy (ANDS)*, p. 64; Wardak, Saba and Kazem, *Afghanistan Human Development Report 2007*, p. 5.

1633 Sajjad, *Peace at all Costs*, pp. 36–41.

1634 *See* United Nations Commission on Human Rights, *Report of the Independent Expert to Update the Set of Principles to Combat Impunity, Diane Orentlicher, Addendum*, Principle 24 (b), which determines that: „ *[…] amnesty and other measures of clemency shall be kept within the following bounds: […] (b) Amnesties and other measures of clemency shall be without effect with respect to the victims' right to reparation, to which principles 31 through 34 refer, and shall not prejudice the right to know;"*.

to limit, deny or impair the right to the truth.[1635] Instead, amnesties and truth commissions can co-exist and complement.[1636] It has been affirmed that individual victims have a right to know the truth about their suffering and that society has a right to know the truth about past events.[1637] Thus the right to truth has an individual as well as a collective dimension.[1638] From this point of view, the United Nations' Updated Set of Principles to Combat Impunity states that: *"Every people has the inalienable right to know the truth about past events concerning the perpetration of heinous crimes and about the circumstances and reasons that led, through massive or systemic violations, to the perpetration of those crimes."*[1639] Furthermore *"victims and their families have the imprescriptible right to know the truth about the circumstances in which violations took place and, in the event of death or disappearance, the victims' fate."*[1640]

In Afghanistan several proposals concerning the establishment of a truth commission have already been made.[1641] In 2002, for example, then President Karzai recommended such a commission in order to reveal the truth and to heal the wounds of the Afghan people.[1642] The expired Action Plan for Peace, Reconciliation and Justice of 2005 included a provision on 'Truth-seeking and Documentation' emphasising that *"Through truth-seeking and documentation, evaluate the facts of the conflicts and injustices*

1635 *See* UN Office of the High Commissioner for Human Rights, *Rule-of-Law Tools for Post-Conflict States*, p. 31.

1636 Mallinder, *Amnesty, Human Rights and Political Transitions:*, 165; M. Schoiswohl, '"Transitional Justice" in Afghanistan: Vergangenheitsbewältigung der nächsten Generation', *juridikum – zeitschrift im rechtsstaat* (2005), 94–8, at 95–7.

1637 UN Office of the High Commissioner for Human Rights, *Rule-of-Law Tools for Post-Conflict States*, p. 31.

1638 Ibid., p. 31.

1639 *See* United Nations Commission on Human Rights, *Report of the Independent Expert to Update the Set of Principles to Combat Impunity, Diane Orentlicher, Addendum*, Principle 2.

1640 *See* ibid., Principle 4.

1641 For example, *see* A. Shuja, *Key Afghan Opposition Leader Calls for a Truth Commission, Says Negotiation with Insurgents Possible*. http://www.undispatch.com/key-afghan-opposition-leader-calls-for-truth-commissions-says-negotiation-with-insurgents-possible (16 May 2017); L. Bai, *Truth and Reconciliation Commission on Afghanistan*. http://www.bharat-rakshak.com/SRR/Volume13/laxmibai.html (16 July 2012), p. 1.

1642 Hamid Karzai, Opening remarks at the first National Human Rights workshop on 9th March, Kabul, Afghanistan, *see* Wardak, Saba and Kazem, *Afghanistan Human Development Report* 2007, p. 76; International Crisis Group, *Afghanistan*, pp. 15–6.

happened in the past, [...] through acknowledging the oppression and expressing the belief in justice, while supporting reconciliation and recognising that there are 'multiple truths'."[1643] The Action Plan went even further and demanded *"a consultative process seeking views on truth-seeking mechanisms from civil society, academia, community leaders, religious leaders etc. to formulate recommendations for a truthseeking mechanism in Afghanistan, giving special consideration to the participation of women in the consultation and how to deal with gender-based violence and other crimes against women."*[1644] However, as has been mentioned earlier, the government disregarded the Action Plan[1645] and radically undermined its provisions and objectives by introducing the unconditional Amnesty Law in 2007. Apart from that, no official enquiry into human rights violations and the Afghan conflict has been published to date.[1646] Given this sad reality, there is all the more reason to establish a truth-seeking process in Afghanistan. Although the concept of a truth commission is almost unknown in the country, the vast majority of the Afghan people are in favour of establishing the truth of the decades-long war and the crimes occurred.[1647]

A truth commission can best be defined as an official, temporary, non-judicial or quasi-judicial investigative body, which maps patterns of past violence, and unearths the causes and consequences of these destructive events, which usually occurred over a number of years.[1648]

1643 Government of the Islamic Republic of Afghanistan, *Action Plan on Peace, Reconciliation and Justice in Afghanistan*, Key Action 3.

1644 Ibid., Key Action 3.

1645 Hartmann and Klonowiecka-Milart, *Impunity Prevails in Afghanistan*.

1646 Winterbotham, *Healing the Legacies of Conflict in Afghanistan*, p. 58; Human Rights Watch, *Blood-Stained Hands*, p. 2; International Center for Transitional Justice (ICTJ), *Afghanistan: Addressing the Past*, pp. 4–6; Gossman, *Afghanistan: The Past as a Prologue*, pp. 2–3.

1647 Afghanistan Independent Human Rights Commission (AIHRC), *A Call for Justice*, pp. 29–32.

1648 UN Office of the High Commissioner for Human Rights, *Rule-of-Law Tools for Post-Conflict States: Truth Commissions*, HR/PUB/06/1. http://www.ohchr.org/Documents/Publications/RuleoflawTruthCommissionsen.pdf (30 January 2017), p. 1; United Nations Commission on Human Rights, *Report of the Independent Expert to Update the Set of Principles to Combat Impunity, Diane Orentlicher, Addendum*, p. 6; United Nations, *Guidance Note of the Secretary-General*, p. 8; P. B. Hayner, *Unspeakable Truths: Facing the Challenge of Truth Commissions* (New York: Routledge Chapman & Hall, 2002), p. 24.

In comparison to criminal proceedings, truth-seeking processes investigate human rights violations in a wider political context.[1649] The UNOHCHR Rule-of-Law Tool on Truth Commissions emphasises that the work of the commission may help to understand and acknowledge a contested or denied history.[1650] Although each truth commission is unique, there are nonetheless certain components which can be found in almost every case. These include, *inter alia*, collecting statements from victims and witnesses; the participation of both victims and perpetrators; conducting thematic research, such as gender and children analysis of violations; organizing public hearings and other awareness programs; and publishing a final report outlining findings and recommendations for institutional and policy reforms.[1651] In this way truth commissions can contribute to the acknowledgement of past abuses, accountability, the needs of victims and reconciliation.[1652] In the absence of effective and fair criminal proceedings, a truth commission may be a viable and more appropriate alternative.[1653] Their benefits may, however, be hampered by unfavourable conditions, such as political instability, victim and witness fears about testifying, a weak civil society or inadequate funding and support.[1654]

With regard to a truth-seeking process in Afghanistan several issues need to be addressed. The mandate of a possible future Truth Commission (TC) for Afghanistan has to be defined precisely, including the composition of the Commission, their funding and period of operation. Further aspects concern the functioning of the TC as well as guarantees for victims, witnesses and perpetrators.

First of all, it has to be determined what is meant by **'truth'** in the case of Afghanistan. In contrast to the truth commissions that were established in Latin America and Eastern Europe, a possible Afghan TC would have a different focus. In Latin America, truth commissions were needed to un-

1649 Mallinder, *Amnesty, Human Rights and Political Transitions:*, p. 167; Hayner, *Unspeakable Truths*, p. 24.

1650 UN Office of the High Commissioner for Human Rights, *Rule-of-Law Tools for Post-Conflict States*, pp. 1–2.

1651 Ibid., p. 1; United Nations, *Guidance Note of the Secretary-General*, p. 8; Mallinder, *Amnesty, Human Rights and Political Transitions:*, p. 167; Hayner, *Unspeakable Truths*, p. 24.

1652 UN Office of the High Commissioner for Human Rights, *Rule-of-Law Tools for Post-Conflict States*, p. 1; Hayner, *Unspeakable Truths*, p. 24.

1653 Mallinder, *Amnesty, Human Rights and Political Transitions:*, p. 168.

1654 United Nations Security Council, *The Rule of Law and Transitional Justice in Conflict and Post-Conflict Societies, Report of the Secretary-General*, p. 17.

cover the truth about disappearances, torture and other serious violations of human rights which were committed in secret as well as to make the invisible victims visible and to explain the system behind these atrocities.[1655] In Eastern Europe, the opening up of state archives and historical commissions helped to break the silence and to acknowledge the past as well as to reveal the extent, origin and nature of the crimes.[1656] In Afghanistan, on the other hand, the nature and extent of the crimes are widely known and also their underlying reasons.[1657] Hence an Afghan TC should combine truth-seeking with further-reaching and forward-looking questions of transitional justice.[1658] This means that the commission could document past abuses, give the victims the opportunity to tell their stories and organise public hearings, but also that the commission could initiate discussions on institutional and policy reforms as well as other aspects of transitional justice.[1659] This is in line with the demands of many Afghans. According to a survey, they desire the recognition of their suffering, the documentation and investigation of war-time events and the impact of conflict on their communities as well as reconciliation and social reconstruction.[1660] Given the fact that during the Afghan conflict all sides, including foreign actors, committed severe human rights violations, it is furthermore important to avoid only partial truth-seeking, since such an approach would lead to accusations of bias and thus obstruct any peacebuilding process.[1661] Instead, an Afghan Truth Commission should establish a 'national history' which is acceptable to all Afghans.[1662]

The **temporal mandate**, i.e. the period of time under investigation, should encompass the recent history of conflict in Afghanistan, start-

---

1655 Danchin, 'Transitional Justice in Afghanistan', 48–9; Roht-Arriaza, *Transitional Justice and Peace Agreements*, p. 2.

1656 Roht-Arriaza, *Transitional Justice and Peace Agreements*, p. 2.

1657 Danchin, 'Transitional Justice in Afghanistan', 48–9.

1658 Ibid., pp. 48–9; Bai, *Truth and Reconciliation Commission on Afghanistan*, p. 4; Kritz, 'Promoting a Formal System of Justice in Post-Taliban Afghanistan', 457–8.

1659 Danchin, 'Transitional Justice in Afghanistan', 48–9; Maass, 'National Reconciliation in Afghanistan.', 25; Kritz, 'Promoting a Formal System of Justice in Post-Taliban Afghanistan', 457–8.

1660 Winterbotham, *Healing the Legacies of Conflict in Afghanistan*, pp. 57–61.

1661 Y. Sooka, 'Dealing With the Past and Transitional Justice: Building Peace Through Accountability', *International Review of the Red Cross* 88 (2006), 311–25, at 315–6; Winterbotham, *Healing the Legacies of Conflict in Afghanistan*, pp. 61–3; Bai, *Truth and Reconciliation Commission on Afghanistan*, p. 4.

1662 Maass, 'National Reconciliation in Afghanistan.', 35–6.

ing with the Communist Revolution and People's Democratic Party of Afghanistan (PDPA) government in 1978. The mandate should not be limited to select periods in Afghanistan's history in order to avoid the appearance of bias.[1663] Apart from that, the Commission should not be tasked with investigating events which take place only after their establishment.[1664] These events are better dealt with by the national human rights commission or the public prosecutor.[1665]

The UNOHCHR emphasises that the **establishment** of a truth commission requires political will and active support on the part of the Government as well as interest and preparedness to cooperate with the commission on the part of perpetrators, victims and witnesses.[1666] Given the fragmented Afghan society and culture, with its different ethnicities and religions, it seems to be very difficult to develop truth-seeking policies that ensure widespread acceptance.[1667]

The Updated Set of Principles to Combat Impunity identifies certain further aspects which have to be considered when setting up a truth commission. According to Principle 6 *"To the greatest extent possible, decisions to establish a truth commission, define its terms of reference and determine its composition should be based upon broad public consultations in which the views of victims and survivors especially are sought. Special efforts should be made to ensure that men and women participate in these deliberations on a basis of equality."*[1668] Furthermore, the commission's independence, impartiality and competence must be ensured.[1669]

With regard to the **composition** of an Afghan TC it is important to take the above-mentioned diversity of the Afghan society and culture into account, and to appoint commissioners who represent as many groups as possible.[1670] In addition, consideration should be given to the appoint-

---

1663 UN Office of the High Commissioner for Human Rights, *Rule-of-Law Tools for Post-Conflict States*, pp. 8–13.

1664 Ibid., pp. 8–13.

1665 Ibid., pp. 8–13.

1666 Ibid., pp. 2–3; B. D. Hollinder, *How to Build a Better Truth Commission: Applying Lessons from Past Truth Commissions to the Selection of Commissioners for an Afghanistan Truth Commission* (2006), 14, 19.

1667 Hollinder, *How to Build a Better Truth Commission*, pp. 18–9.

1668 United Nations Commission on Human Rights, *Report of the Independent Expert to Update the Set of Principles to Combat Impunity, Diane Orentlicher, Addendum*, Principle 6.

1669 Ibid., Principle 7.

1670 At least the four major ethnic groups – the Pashtoons, Tajiks, Hazaras and Uzbeks should be included. *See* Hollinder, *How to Build a Better Truth Com-*

ment of some international commissioners, provided that they understand Afghan and Islamic culture and are respected by the Afghan people.[1671] The local ownership of the Truth Commission must nevertheless be guaranteed and international actors should assist, but not control, the process.[1672] Furthermore, the participation of women is essential since they often lack power and a say in their own affairs.[1673] This is in accordance with Principle 7 (c) of the Updated Set of Principles to Combat Impunity which states that *"In determining membership, concerted efforts should be made to ensure adequate representation of women as well as of other appropriate groups whose members have been especially vulnerable to human rights violations."*[1674] In order to work successfully and reach out to as many Afghans as possible, the Truth Commission should consist of **"local Truth Committees"**[1675] which incorporate local norms and methods, such as the procedure of a *loya jirga*.[1676]

It is moreover necessary to differentiate between the **competence** of a possible future Truth Commission and the jurisdiction of courts, which means that the TC is not intended to act as a substitute for the civil, administrative or criminal courts.[1677] In particular, criminal courts alone have jurisdiction in establishing individual criminal responsibility, with a view as appropriate to passing judgement and imposing a sentence.[1678] Notwithstanding this, by collecting evidence and testimony as well as documenting human rights violations the Truth Commission could con-

---

mission, 41–42, 50–54; Hazdra, 'Verurteilen – Vergessen – Versöhnen. Die wichtigsten Ansätze zur Konfliktaufarbeitung im Überblick', 166.

1671 Hollinder, *How to Build a Better Truth Commission*, pp. 50–4.

1672 Ibid., pp. 47–9.

1673 Ibid., 12–13, 50–54.

1674 United Nations Commission on Human Rights, *Report of the Independent Expert to Update the Set of Principles to Combat Impunity, Diane Orentlicher, Addendum*, pp. 8–11.

1675 J.* Mohr, 'Negotiation, Reconciliation and Outreach: What Are the Options on the Table?' in W. Danspeckgruber (ed.), *Petersberg Papers on Afghanistan and the Region*, Liechtenstein Colloquium Report (2009), pp. 103–15, at p. 115.

1676 Hollinder, *How to Build a Better Truth Commission*, pp. 50–4; Mohr, 'Negotiation, Reconciliation and Outreach: What Are the Options on the Table?', 115.

1677 United Nations Commission on Human Rights, *Report of the Independent Expert to Update the Set of Principles to Combat Impunity, Diane Orentlicher, Addendum*, Principle 8.

1678 Ibid., Principle 8.

tribute to solving criminal cases which are dealt with by courts.[1679] The disclosure of information is however precluded in cases where testimony is collected with a confidentiality agreement, which needs to be respected.[1680] Here, Principle 8 (f) of the Updated Set of Principles determines that the Commission's terms of reference *"should clarify the conditions that will govern access to their documents, including conditions aimed at preventing disclosure of confidential information while facilitating public access to their archives."*[1681]

Another aspect that has to be considered is how **investigation and documentation** will be performed by the Truth Commission. In view of the lengthy conflict involving many factions and different phases, documentation is urgently needed, but at the same time difficult to obtain.[1682] It has been already mentioned that detailed analyses of the most heinous crimes and perpetrators who are responsible for these atrocities as well as locations and details of mass graves have been prepared by the United Nations in 2006[1683] and by the Afghan Independent Human Rights Commission (AIHRC) in 2011[1684]. Although these reports contain important information and documentation up to at least 2001, they have not been published to date.[1685] Also the analyses conducted by Human Rights Watch[1686], the Afghanistan Justice Project[1687] and the Physicians for Human Rights[1688] include evidence of serious human rights abuses and information on mass graves. However, they encompass only limited

1679 Miazad, 'Transitional Justice in Post-War Afghanistan', 4–5; UN Office of the High Commissioner for Human Rights, *Rule-of-Law Tools for Post-Conflict States*, p. 27; Roht-Arriaza, *Transitional Justice and Peace Agreements*, p. 5.

1680 UN Office of the High Commissioner for Human Rights, *Rule-of-Law Tools for Post-Conflict States*, p. 27.

1681 United Nations Commission on Human Rights, *Report of the Independent Expert to Update the Set of Principles to Combat Impunity, Diane Orentlicher, Addendum*, pp. 8–11.

1682 Worden and Steele, *Telling the Story*, pp. 1–2.

1683 United Nations, *UN Mapping Report Afghanistan – unpublished.*

1684 Nordland, 'Top Afghans Tied to '90s Carnage, Researchers Say'; Kazim, 'Kriegsverbrecher-Studie: Massaker-Berichte belasten afghanische Politiker'.

1685 Winterbotham, *Healing the Legacies of Conflict in Afghanistan*, p. 58; Human Rights Watch, *Blood-Stained Hands*, p. 2; International Center for Transitional Justice (ICTJ), *Afghanistan: Addressing the Past*, pp. 4–6; Gossman, *Afghanistan: The Past as a Prologue*, pp. 2–3.

1686 Human Rights Watch, *Blood-Stained Hands*; Human Rights Watch, *Afghanistan: Bring War Criminals to Justice*.

1687 The Afghanistan Justice Project, *Casting Shadows:*

1688 Winterbotham, *Healing the Legacies of Conflict in Afghanistan*, p. 25.

timeframes or are unofficial documents. Thus it is absolutely necessary to initiate an official investigation that covers the relevant period from 1978 until today and which is independent and impartial.[1689] For this purpose, the great amount of evidences and information which can be found in paper files, audio and video recordings, mementos, photo albums and mass graves must be preserved.[1690] There are various techniques to gather and organise each type of information which include, *inter alia*, conducting interviews and performing forensic analysis as well as establishing databases, cataloguing and protecting accurate information.[1691] In addition, classified documents, for example those relating to the Soviet occupation, should be declassified and made accessible.[1692] Apart from the foregoing, it must be noted that several difficulties and challenges, such as fear of retribution from still powerful warlords and the instability in the country may obstruct any documentation process in Afghanistan.[1693]

A possible future Afghan Truth Commission, furthermore, would have to give **guarantees** to alleged perpetrators as well as victims and witnesses. Alleged perpetrators must be allowed to *"provide a statement setting forth their version of the facts either at a hearing convened by the commission while conducting its investigation or through submission of a document equivalent to a right of reply for inclusion in the commission's file."*[1694] With regard to victims and witnesses testifying on their behalf, Principle 10 of the Updated Set of Principles specifies that *"Effective measures shall be taken to ensure the security, physical and psychological well-being, and, where requested, the privacy of victims and witnesses who provide information to the commission."*[1695]

For the Commission to be able to work independently and in a credible manner, their transparent **funding** and the provision of sufficient material and human resources must be ensured.[1696] As mentioned above, it is also necessary to determine the **period of operation** of the Truth Commission. This means that start and end dates (including the possibility of one or

1689 Ibid., p. 59; International Crisis Group, *Afghanistan*, pp. 18–9.

1690 Worden and Steele, *Telling the Story*, 1–2, 5.

1691 Ibid., 5, 10–13, 15–16.

1692 The Afghanistan Justice Project, *Casting Shadows:*, p. 6.

1693 Ibid., p. 7.

1694 United Nations Commission on Human Rights, *Report of the Independent Expert to Update the Set of Principles to Combat Impunity, Diane Orentlicher, Addendum*, Principle 9.

1695 Ibid., pp. 8–11.

1696 Ibid., Principle 11; Hazdra, 'Verurteilen – Vergessen – Versöhnen. Die wichtigsten Ansätze zur Konfliktaufarbeitung im Überblick', 166.

more short-term extensions) for the operation of the commission should be established.[1697]

Lastly, the **final report** of the Truth Commission should include recommendations concerning, for example, possible reform processes or reparation programmes.[1698] It is advisable to require serious consideration of the recommendations by executive, legislative and judicial authorities as well as regular public reporting on their implementation.[1699] The report shall be made public in full and as widely available to the general public as possible.[1700]

4.7 *Reparations for Victims*

Apart from the 'right to know the truth', transitional justice processes must incorporate the 'right to reparations'. This means that it is essential to secure the legal rights of victims, of course also in cases where an amnesty for perpetrators has been granted. If amnesties refuse these rights, the suffering of victims will be exacerbated.[1701] Mechanisms of providing reparations could well be combined with truth commissions, since appropriate reparations require fact-finding on the situation of victims and documentation.[1702] Moreover, as has been mentioned above, the final report of

1697 UN Office of the High Commissioner for Human Rights, *Rule-of-Law Tools for Post-Conflict States*, p. 8.

1698 United Nations Commission on Human Rights, *Report of the Independent Expert to Update the Set of Principles to Combat Impunity, Diane Orentlicher, Addendum*, Principle 12; Zupan and Servaes, *Transitional Justice & Dealing with the Past*
, pp. 18–9.

1699 UN Office of the High Commissioner for Human Rights, *Rule-of-Law Tools for Post-Conflict States*, p. 13; United Nations Commission on Human Rights, *Independent Study on Best Practices, Including Recommendations, to Assist States in Strengthening Their Domestic Capacity to Combat all Aspects of Impunity, by Professor Diane Orentlicher*, p. 9.

1700 United Nations Commission on Human Rights, *Report of the Independent Expert to Update the Set of Principles to Combat Impunity, Diane Orentlicher, Addendum*, Principle 13; United Nations Commission on Human Rights, *Independent Study on Best Practices, Including Recommendations, to Assist States in Strengthening Their Domestic Capacity to Combat all Aspects of Impunity, by Professor Diane Orentlicher*, p. 10.

1701 Mallinder, *Amnesty, Human Rights and Political Transitions:*, pp. 11–2.

1702 Afghanistan Independent Human Rights Commission (AIHRC), *A Call for Justice*, p. 54; United Nations Security Council, *The Rule of Law and Transitional*

the Truth Commission should include recommendations concerning, for example, reparation programmes.[1703]

Various human rights conventions and United Nations resolutions entail provisions on the 'right to an effective remedy'.[1704] According to the "UN General Assembly's Basic Principles and Guidelines on the Right to a Remedy and Reparation for Victims of Gross Violations of International Human Rights Law and Serious Violations of International Humanitarian Law", the right to a remedy is a composite right, i.e. it consists of the right to equal and effective access to justice; access to relevant information concerning violations and reparation mechanisms; and also of adequate, effective and prompt reparation for harm suffered.[1705] The Basic Principles and Guidelines further determine that states are generally required to provide effective remedies to victims, including reparation[1706] as well as that reparation should redress *"gross violations of international human rights law or serious violations of international humanitarian law."*[1707] Reparation must be *"proportional to the gravity of the violations and the harm suffered."*[1708] There are various forms of reparation, which are enumerated in Principles 19 to 23 of the Basic Principles and Guidelines and encompass *"restitution, compensation, rehabilitation, satisfaction and guarantees of non-repetition."* Restitution may include the *"restoration of liberty, enjoyment of human rights, identity, family life and citizenship, return to one's place of residence, restoration of employment and return of property."*[1709] Compensation *"should be provided for any economically assessable damage, [...] such as: physical or mental harm;[...]; material damages and loss of earnings, including loss of earn-*

Justice in Conflict and Post-Conflict Societies, Report of the Secretary-General, pp. 18–9.

1703 United Nations Commission on Human Rights, *Report of the Independent Expert to Update the Set of Principles to Combat Impunity, Diane Orentlicher, Addendum*, Principle 12; Zupan and Servaes, *Transitional Justice & Dealing with the Past*
, pp. 18–9.

1704 For example, Article 8 of the Universal Declaration of Human Rights and Article 2 of the ICCPR.

1705 United Nations General Assembly, *Basic Principles and Guidelines on the Right to a Remedy and Reparation for Victims of Gross Violations of International Human Rights Law and Serious Violations of International Humanitarian Law*, annex, Principle 11.

1706 Ibid., annex, Principle. 3 (d).

1707 Ibid., annex, Principle 15.

1708 Ibid., annex, Principle 15.

1709 Ibid., annex, Principle 19.

ing potential; [...]; costs required for legal or expert assistance, medicine and medical services, and psychological and social services."[1710] Principle 21 states that *"rehabilitation should include medical and psychological care as well as legal and social services"* and Principle 22 defines that satisfaction should involve, *inter alia*, *"effective measures aimed at the cessation of continuing violations; [...]; the search for the whereabouts of the disappeared, for the identities of the children abducted, and for the bodies of those killed, and assistance in the recovery, identification and reburial of the bodies in accordance with the expressed or presumed wish of the victims, or the cultural practices of the families and communities; [...]; public apology, including acknowledgement of the facts and acceptance of responsibility; [...]; commemorations and tributes to the victims;[...]."*And finally, guarantees of non-repetition encompass, for example, *"ensuring effective civilian control of military and security forces; [...]; providing, on a priority and continued basis, human rights and international humanitarian law education to all sectors of society and training for law enforcement officials as well as military and security forces; [...]; promoting mechanisms for preventing and monitoring social conflicts and their resolution; reviewing and reforming laws contributing to or allowing gross violations of international human rights law and serious violations of international humanitarian law."*[1711] This list emphasises that non-monetary reparations, such as rehabilitation programmes or symbolic measures as well as material forms of reparations, such as compensation come into question.[1712] Although, in particular, in post-conflict situations it is virtually impossible to implement reparations programmes which include all of the categories, it is nevertheless necessary that states use the Basic Principles and Guidelines as a source of inspiration and a tool for victim-oriented policies.[1713]

In Afghanistan, according to a survey, the people have deemed it necessary that financial or material compensation will be paid[1714] as well as that

---

1710 Ibid., annex, Principle 20.

1711 Ibid., annex, Principle 23.

1712 United Nations Security Council, *The Rule of Law and Transitional Justice in Conflict and Post-Conflict Societies, Report of the Secretary-General*, pp. 18–9; United Nations Human Rights Council, *Analytical Study on Human Rights and Transitional Justice*, p. 11.

1713 UN Office of the High Commissioner for Human Rights, *Rule-of-Law Tools for Post-Conflict States: Reparations Programmes*, HR/PUB/08/1. http://www.ohchr.org/Documents/Publications/ReparationsProgrammes.pdf (31 January 2013), pp. 7–9; Kritz, 'Promoting a Formal System of Justice in Post-Taliban Afghanistan', 458.

1714 Afghanistan Independent Human Rights Commission (AIHRC), *A Call for Justice*, 33–34.

symbolic reparation in the form of memorialisation will be provided.[1715] The respondents proposed monetary payouts; assistance with rebuilding houses, schools and hospitals; assistance for disabled people as well as the renaming of squares and streets with the names of ordinary victims and the building of sculptures near sites of previous war atrocities.[1716]

The expired Action Plan for Peace, Reconciliation and Justice in its Key Action 1 set out the objective that, by acknowledging the suffering of the Afghan people, the healing of the nation and the building of a peaceful Afghanistan has to be facilitated.[1717] Several activities were defined in order to achieve this objective. For example, *"the assignment of a National Remembrance Day, the day of victims of human rights violations and war crimes in Afghanistan, for instance 4th Jan (14 Jadi) – the day that Afghanistan's new Constitution was approved – as a national day to commemorate the victims of war crimes and human rights violations in Afghanistan. The day would be announced during a brief ceremony for recognition and respect of the victims of the conflicts at the Loya Jirga tent, in the presence of war disabled, families of martyrs and victims, civil society groups, community elders, religious leaders, academics and women's groups"* as well as *"the establishment of national memorial sites. Proposed location for the main memorial: near the National Assembly building in Kabul. Architects and artists from around the world will be requested to submit designs for such memorials. Roads and squares in Kabul, Herat and other cities can be named 24 Hut, 3 Hut or other similar days."*[1718] Furthermore, the *"Establishment of a national museum commemorating the victims and designed to educate younger generations by presenting the history and symbols of three decades of war, including pictures and names of victims, photographs and films of the war, destructions, executions and etc."* had been envisaged.[1719]

Regrettably, the intentions of the APPRJ have scarcely been achieved. The proposed National Remembrance Day, the day of victims of human rights violations and war crimes, was only held in 2006 and 2007 and has since been disregarded by the Afghan Government.[1720] The commemoration of the *mujahidin* on the other hand, has not been overlooked. There are public holidays, such as the Celebration of the Islamic Revolu-

1715 Winterbotham, *Healing the Legacies of Conflict in Afghanistan*, pp. 63–7.
1716 Ibid., pp. 63–7.
1717 Government of the Islamic Republic of Afghanistan, *Action Plan on Peace, Reconciliation and Justice in Afghanistan*.
1718 Ibid.
1719 Ibid.
1720 Winterbotham, *Healing the Legacies of Conflict in Afghanistan*, p. 19.

tion in Afghanistan and The Great Ahmad Shah Massoud Day as well as memorials, such as the Massoud Circle and the Mazari memorial in Kabul in honour of the *mujahidin*.[1721] Until 2009, just 1 % of victims and /or their relatives had received any compensation or apology for the harm suffered.[1722]

However, it should also be mentioned that some progress regarding commemorative activities has been made. For example, in Kabul an annual ceremony to remember the events of February 1993[1723] takes place.[1724] In Bamiyan, the entrance to a graveyard is marked by a board listing the names of individuals who were killed by the Taliban.[1725] In addition, although Afghanistan does not have a comprehensive reparation and compensation programme, it pays compensation for disability or death as result of war.[1726] It is above all the Afghan civil society and the Afghanistan Independent Human Rights Commission who commit themselves to the commemoration of victims.[1727] Victims' support networks established a travelling theatre and personal stories have been interchanged.[1728] Furthermore, the AIHRC established a war museum which shows, *inter alia* a great many photos and names of victims.[1729] In addition international actors, for example the US, Canada, Australia and Germany, contribute to reparation and compensation for civilians suffering from collateral damages.[1730] However, even though several *ad hoc* mechanisms exist to pay compensation where a civilian has been harmed, these mechanisms are uncoordinated, arbitrary and inconsistent.[1731]

In order to implement a promising and comprehensive reparation policy in Afghanistan it is crucial that the Afghan Government takes action

1721 Ibid., p. 19.

1722 Jackson, *The Cost of War*, p. 4.

1723 In February 1993, bombardments took place as Shura-i Nazara and Hezb-i Islami shelled each other's positions.

1724 Winterbotham, *Healing the Legacies of Conflict in Afghanistan*, p. 64.

1725 Ibid., p. 64.

1726 Ibid., p. 67.

1727 Ibid., pp. 24–5.

1728 Ibid., pp. 24–5; International Center for Transitional Justice (ICTJ), *A Year of Change – A Decade of Hope: Annual Report 2011*. http://ictj.org/sites/default/files/ICTJ-Global-Annual-Report-2011-English_0.pdf (24 June 2017), p. 13.

1729 Winterbotham, *Healing the Legacies of Conflict in Afghanistan*, pp. 24–5.

1730 Amnesty International, *Getting away with Murder?*, p. 16.

1731 Ibid., p. 16.

and supports such a policy.[1732] On the basis of the final report of the proposed Afghan Truth Commission[1733] further national museums and memorials focusing on wartime suffering should be created.[1734] Furthermore Victims' Day[1735] should be publically marked every year and the government should symbolically and publically apologise on behalf of previous regimes.[1736] Financial compensation, reparation and rehabilitation measures must be adequate and consistent.[1737] According to the Report of the Independent Expert to Update the Set of Principles to Combat Impunity, the effective design of reparation programmes encompasses various key aspects.[1738] This means, *inter alia* that the programme should take all victims, including women and minority groups, as well as a broad set of relevant crimes into account. However, this does not mean that all victims have to receive the same amount.[1739] The programme must furthermore provide for a variety of material and symbolic benefits, which are mutually supportive.[1740] Finally, it is essential that victims are involved in the process of designing and implementing the programme.[1741]

4.8 Institutional Reforms

Another important issue and core task of transitional justice is the prevention of further human rights violations by conducting institutional reforms.[1742] It is essential that institutions which have abused human rights

---

1732 Transitional Justice Coordination Group – Afghanistan, *TJCG Statement on the Amnesty Law*.

1733 *See* Chapter 4.6 Testifying in a Truth Commission.

1734 Winterbotham, *Healing the Legacies of Conflict in Afghanistan*, pp. 94–5.

1735 *See* e.g. Public holidays as „kulturelle Identitätselemente", in: P. Häberle, *Der Sonntag als Verfassungsprinzip*, Schriften zum Öffentlichen Recht, 2. Aufl. (Berlin: Duncker & Humblot, 2006), vol. 551, 81–83, 108–111.

1736 Winterbotham, *Healing the Legacies of Conflict in Afghanistan*, pp. 94–5.

1737 Ibid., pp. 94–5.

1738 United Nations Commission on Human Rights, *Report of the Independent Expert to Update the Set of Principles to Combat Impunity, Diane Orentlicher*, p. 17.

1739 Ibid., p. 17.

1740 Ibid., p. 17.

1741 Ibid., p. 17; N. Zupan and S. Servaes.

1742 UN Office of the High Commissioner for Human Rights, *Rule-of-Law Tools for Post-Conflict States: Vetting: an Operational Framework*, HR/PUB/06/5. http://www.ohchr.org/Documents/Publications/RuleoflawVettingen.pdf (31 January 2017), p. 3.

and served criminal regimes are transformed into institutions which protect human rights, enjoy civic trust and serve the rule of law.[1743] Besides this, without functioning institutions a legitimate and effective amnesty process cannot be achieved. Due to the fact that employees make up an institution, a main aspect of institutional reform should be personnel reform through vetting and lustration.[1744] By the process of vetting the suitability of individuals for particular posts is assessed.[1745] Lustration means that the integrity of persons currently holding positions is evaluated in order to decide whether or not they are suitable for continued service. In this way it is possible to refrain from employing or to remove from office those who are responsible for serious human rights violations. Personnel reform can thus contribute to non-criminal accountability and the fulfilment of victims' rights.[1746] Various surveys carried out in Afghanistan have indicated that the vast majority of respondents demand the removal of perpetrators who are responsible for serious international crimes from their (governmental) posts and the institutionalisation of vetting procedures.[1747]

The questions considered in the following concern, on the one hand, which initiatives have been taken to reform institutions in Afghanistan, including the question of their effectiveness and, on the other hand, which additional or necessary steps can achieve the objective of institutional reform. Since these questions are not easy to answer, and are moreover very complex, the following explanations only provide an overview and focus on key points. Particular attention is paid to the Afghan Government and Parliament as well as to the justice system, because these institutions play a crucial role in the amnesty process and in contributing to peace and justice in Afghanistan.

The first initiation of a reform of Afghan institutions was in 2001 when the *"Agreement on Provisional Arrangements in Afghanistan Pending*

1743 Ibid., p. 3.

1744 Ibid., p. 4.

1745 Ibid., p. 4; Afghanistan Independent Human Rights Commission (AIHRC), *A Call for Justice*, pp. 46–50; United Nations Security Council, *The Rule of Law and Transitional Justice in Conflict and Post-Conflict Societies, Report of the Secretary-General*, pp. 17–8.

1746 UN Office of the High Commissioner for Human Rights, *Rule-of-Law Tools for Post-Conflict States*, p. 5.

1747 Afghanistan Independent Human Rights Commission (AIHRC), *A Call for Justice*, p. 28; Afghan Civil Society Forum-organization (ACSFo), *A First Step on a Long Journey*, p. 74; Winterbotham, *Healing the Legacies of Conflict in Afghanistan*, pp. 50–1; The Afghanistan Justice Project, *Casting Shadows:*, p. 4.

the Re-establishment of Permanent Government Institutions" — the so-called "Bonn Agreement"[1748] — was adopted. However, this opportunity was lost and Afghanistan still suffers from insecurity, corruption and poverty, and many perpetrators of appalling atrocities still hold political power.[1749] The approach taken at the Bonn Conference was to approve a model of state-building where warlords and perpetrators of international crimes became part of the government.[1750]

In subsequent years, some efforts regarding institutional reform have been made in Afghanistan. In this respect Articles 85 and 86 of the new Afghan Constitution, which was passed in January 2004, are noteworthy. Article 85 determines that *"The individual who becomes a candidate or appointed to the membership of the National Assembly, […], shall have the following qualifications: […]; 2. Shall not have been convicted of crimes against humanity, as well as a crime or deprivation from civil rights by a court; […]"*.[1751] According to Article 86, *„Elections credentials of members of the National Assembly shall be reviewed by the Independent Elections Commission in accordance with the provisions of the law.“*[1752] These provisions provide that those who have been found guilty of having committed crimes against humanity are not allowed to become members of the Afghan National Assembly.[1753] However, given that the justice system in Afghanistan is

---

1748 United Nations Security Council, *Agreement on Provisional Arrangements in Afghanistan Pending the Re-Establishment of Permanent Government Institutions*.

1749 Friedman, Pactat and Weisell, *Accountability and Impunity:*, 25–6, 74–5; Kippen, 'The Long Democratic Transition', 35–6; International Center for Transitional Justice (ICTJ), *ICTJ Statement on Afghanistan*; Rubin, 'The Transformation of the Afghan State', 18; Khan, 'Afghanistan: War Crimes, ICC and NGOs', 106–9; Wisner, 'Is Time Ripe for Transitional Justice in Afghanistan?', 4–6; Thier, 'Introduction:', 7; NDR, *Auswärtiges Amt zeichnet in vertraulichem Bericht düsteres Afghanistan-Lagebild*. https://www.ndr.de/der_ndr/presse/mitteilungen/Auswaertiges-Amt-zeichnet-in-vertraulichem-Bericht-duesteres-Afghanistan-Lagebild-,pressemeldungndr16542.html (15 December 2015); Afghanistan Research and Evaluation Unit (AREU), *When Will Transitional Justice in Afghanistan Become a Part of the Transitional Decade?: A Roundtable Discussion*. http://www.areu.org.af/Uploads/EditionPdfs/1612E%20When%20Will%20Transitional%20Justice%20in%20Afghanistan1.pdf (28 November 2016), pp. 7–8; Benish, *Between Impunity And Accountability*, pp. 16–7.

1750 Afghan Civil Society Forum-organization (ACSFo), *A First Step on a Long Journey*, p. 83; Friedman, Pactat and Weisell, *Accountability and Impunity:*, p. 20.

1751 *The Constitution of the Islamic Republic of Afghanistan*.

1752 Ibid.

1753 Amnesty International, *Afghanistan: Addressing the Past to Secure the Future*, p. 4.

unable to prosecute and convict those responsible for serious international crimes, Article 85 of the Constitution cannot be put into effect.[1754] Another criticism is that the provision does not refer to all other crimes under international law, such as war crimes and enforced disappearances.[1755]

It is also worth mentioning that an objective of the expired Action Plan for Peace, Reconciliation and Justice was to ensure credible and accountable state institutions and purge human rights violators and criminals from these in order to restore the trust of people and victims in the state.[1756] To achieve this, several activities were planned, such as the use of transparent and fair appointment and vetting procedures, and the development of an inclusive strategy for the general reform of the justice sector, so as to ensure the establishment of a fair and effective justice system and to prevent patterns of human rights abuses of the past from being repeated.[1757]

Although the Independent Afghanistan Reform and Civil Service Commission, the Electoral Complaints Commission and the Advisory Panel on Senior Appointments have been brought into being[1758], they all have had limited success in achieving institutional and personnel reform.[1759] Vetting initiatives for candidates for parliamentary elections and senior political appointments did not include vetting on the basis of the candidate's human rights record, since it was deemed unconstitutional.[1760] The complaints procedure did not lead to the removal of candidates.[1761] In summary, the exclusion of those who committed serious human rights violations from official posts did not take place, because of the absence of an effective vetting system.[1762]

1754 Ibid., p. 4.
1755 Ibid., p. 4.
1756 Government of the Islamic Republic of Afghanistan, *Action Plan on Peace, Reconciliation and Justice in Afghanistan*.
1757 Ibid., Key Action 2.
1758 United Nations Human Rights Council, *Analytical Study on Human Rights and Transitional Justice*, p. 13; Winterbotham, *The State of Transitional Justice in Afghanistan*, pp. 13–4.
1759 International Center for Transitional Justice (ICTJ), *Afghanistan: Addressing the Past*, pp. 5–6; Nadery, 'A Human Rights Awakening?', 57–8; M. Mashal, 'Afghanistan's Electoral Reform Plan Is Met With Skepticism', The New York Times, 31 August 2015.
1760 International Center for Transitional Justice (ICTJ), *Afghanistan: Addressing the Past*, pp. 5–6.
1761 Ibid., pp. 5–6.
1762 Vendrell, 'The International Community's Failures in Afghanistan', 57.

With respect to the judiciary, various national and international initiatives and strategies have been carried out to rebuild and improve the system. These started with the formation of the Afghan Judicial Commission in 2001[1763] and was followed by several similar approaches, such as the 2005 Justice for All strategy, the 2008 Afghanistan National Development Strategy, the National Justice Sector Strategy, the National Justice Program, the 2010 Afghanistan National Development Strategy Prioritization and Implementation Plan as well as the Justice Sector Reform strategy agreed on at the London Conference in 2014.[1764] Although wide-ranging reforms and improvements have not occurred, Afghanistan's state justice system has nevertheless developed.[1765] For example, judges and prosecutors have been trained, some justice institutions have been renovated or newly built and an Independent National Legal Training Centre has been established.[1766] However, the different strategies failed to achieve the desired objectives and there are still severe shortcomings such as corruption, professional incompetence and an inadequate infrastructure.[1767] Furthermore, despite the intention to explore possible links and develop a relationship between the formal and the informal/traditional justice system[1768], the efforts remain insufficient.[1769] The government's "Draft Law on Dispute

1763 *See* United Nations Security Council, *Agreement on Provisional Arrangements in Afghanistan Pending the Re-Establishment of Permanent Government Institutions*, p. 4, which states that the Afghan Judicial Commission is tasked with rebuilding the domestic justice system in accordance with Islamic principles, international standards, the rule of law and Afghan legal traditions; Wardak, 'State and Non-State Justice Systems in Afghanistan: the Need for Synergy', 1305–6.

1764 Wardak, 'State and Non-State Justice Systems in Afghanistan: the Need for Synergy', 1305–6; Wardak, Saba and Kazem, *Afghanistan Human Development Report 2007*, pp. 100–2; M. Tondini, *Statebuilding and Justice Reform: Post-Conflict Reconstruction in Afghanistan* (London and New York: Routledge, 2010), pp. 31–105; Islamic Republic of Afghanistan, *Realizing Self-Reliance: Commitments to Reforms and Renewed Partnership*, London Conference on Afghanistan. http://www.afghanistan-un.org/wp-content/uploads/2014/12/REALIZING-FINAL-SELF-RELIANCE-25-November-2014.pdf (12 January 2015), p. 11.

1765 Wardak, 'State and Non-State Justice Systems in Afghanistan: the Need for Synergy', 1307–13.

1766 Ibid., pp. 1307–13.

1767 Ibid., pp. 1307–13; *see also*, Chapter 4.3.1 National Courts.

1768 *See* Chapter 4.4 The Role of Traditional Justice Processes.

1769 ; S. Schmeidl, 'Engaging Traditional Justice Mechanisms in Afghanistan: State-Building Opportunity or Dangerous Liaison?' in W. Mason (ed.), *The Rule of Law in Afghanistan* (Cambridge: Cambridge University Press, 2011), pp. 149–71, at p. 150; Coburn and Dempsey, *Informal Dispute Resolution in Afghanistan*, pp. 3–5; Claude, *Afghanistan – Justice and Reconciliation*, pp. 5–6.

Resolution, Shuras and Jirgas" of 2010 ceased to exist – perhaps because it would have proven infeasible.[1770]

There is an apparent discrepancy between the objectives and requirements codified in official documents and the actions and results that can be listed so far. A more comprehensive approach should therefore be made in order to succeed in reforming Afghanistan's institutions.

As a first step, the Afghan Government should no longer disregard the competence of the Afghan Independent Human Rights Commission (AIHRC)[1771] by preventing the release of the report „Conflict Mapping in Afghanistan Since 1978".[1772] Since the report contains a record of serious violations of international law from 1978 to 2001 in Afghanistan and lists the names of more than 500 former and current warlords or officials, some still in positions of power[1773], it would serve as a firm foundation for any vetting and lustration process.[1774] Those most responsible for serious crimes should be removed from positions of power.[1775] It is also necessary to improve and strengthen the Independent Afghanistan Reform and Civil Service Commission, the Electoral Complaints Commission and the Advisory Panel on Senior Appointments in order to further develop existing vetting procedures and to ensure that perpetrators are excluded from public offices.[1776] In addition, there should be internal oversight mechanisms within institutions[1777], which must however be fair and in accordance with international human rights standards.[1778] Hence legitimate

---

1770 The Liaison Office, *Building Dispute Resolution Institutions in Southern Afghanistan: Lessons from The Liaison Office Justice Shuras in Helmand, Uruzgan, and Nimruz*. http://www.usip.org/sites/default/files/ROL/TLO%20-%20Building%20Dispute%20Resolution%20Institutions%20in%20Southern%20Afghanistan%20%282%29.pdf (16 March 2014), VII, 37; Claude, *Afghanistan – Justice and Reconciliation*, pp. 5–6.

1771 Harris Rimmer, *Building Democracy and Justice After Conflict:*, 1–2, 4–7, 11.

1772 Nordland, 'Top Afghans Tied to '90s Carnage, Researchers Say'; Kazim, 'Kriegsverbrecher-Studie: Massaker-Berichte belasten afghanische Politiker'; Human Rights Watch, *World Report 2015: Afghanistan*.

1773 Nordland, 'Top Afghans Tied to '90s Carnage, Researchers Say'; Kazim, 'Kriegsverbrecher-Studie: Massaker-Berichte belasten afghanische Politiker'; Human Rights Watch, *World Report 2015: Afghanistan*.

1774 Winterbotham, *Healing the Legacies of Conflict in Afghanistan*, p. 91.

1775 Ibid., p. 91; The Afghanistan Justice Project, *Casting Shadows:*, p. 8.

1776 Winterbotham, *Healing the Legacies of Conflict in Afghanistan*, 3, 91; International Center for Transitional Justice (ICTJ), *Stabilizing Afghanistan*, p. 3.

1777 Winterbotham, *Healing the Legacies of Conflict in Afghanistan*, p. 3.

1778 United Nations Security Council, *The Rule of Law and Transitional Justice in Conflict and Post-Conflict Societies, Report of the Secretary-General*, pp. 17–8.

vetting processes require, *inter alia*, that the human rights of those who are alleged to have committed serious international crimes are respected.[1779] This means, for example, that due process safeguards and the principle of non-discrimination are to be applied.[1780]

Apart from removing perpetrators through vetting mechanisms, further efforts are necessary in order to transform public institutions into institutions which protect human rights, enjoy civic trust and serve the rule of law.[1781] These efforts should include measures such as the establishment of adequate institutional frameworks, procedures and resources, the creation of civil complaint procedures, the development of ethical guidelines and codes of conduct, the introduction of good governance practices and transparency provisions, the prevention of corruption as well as the provision of adequate salaries, equipment and infrastructure.[1782] With regard to the justice system it is important to ensure the independent, impartial and effective operation of courts according to international standards of due process.[1783] It is furthermore necessary that a critical evaluation of the various initiatives takes place and that an effective coordination between donor countries and Afghan state institutions is assured.[1784] As for the relationship between the formal and the informal justice system, a more pragmatic approach is needed. This means that restoring and improving

---

1779 Ibid., pp. 17–8.

1780 Ibid., pp. 17–8; United Nations Commission on Human Rights, *Report of the Independent Expert to Update the Set of Principles to Combat Impunity, Diane Orentlicher, Addendum*, Principle 36.

1781 Afghanistan Independent Human Rights Commission (AIHRC), *A Call for Justice*, pp. 46–50.

1782 UN Office of the High Commissioner for Human Rights, *Rule-of-Law Tools for Post-Conflict States*, p. 4; United Nations Commission on Human Rights, *Report of the Independent Expert to Update the Set of Principles to Combat Impunity, Diane Orentlicher, Addendum*, Principle 36; Afghanistan Independent Human Rights Commission (AIHRC), *A Call for Justice*, pp. 46–50; Kippen, 'The Long Democratic Transition', 40–1; Nadery, 'A Human Rights Awakening?', 56–7; International Center for Transitional Justice (ICTJ), *Stabilizing Afghanistan*, p. 3; Winterbotham, *Healing the Legacies of Conflict in Afghanistan*, p. 85; Rubin, 'The Transformation of the Afghan State', 19.

1783 United Nations Commission on Human Rights, *Report of the Independent Expert to Update the Set of Principles to Combat Impunity, Diane Orentlicher, Addendum*, Principle 36.

1784 F. Ahmed, 'Judicial Reform in Afghanistan: A Case Study in the New Criminal Procedure Code', *Hastings Int'l & Comp. L. Rev.* 29 (2005–2006), 93–134, at 96–7; Wardak, 'State and Non-State Justice Systems in Afghanistan: the Need for Synergy', 1307–13.

the laws, processes and institutions of the formal justice sector has to be accompanied by recognising the value of the less formal sector, namely traditional mechanisms[1785].[1786] Thus the crucial question is how the formal and the informal justice system can be reconciled.[1787] Several authors[1788] have considered this issue and some of them propose a hybrid model for Afghanistan. The aim is to deliver accessible, effective, transparent and restorative justice to the Afghan people[1789] and to establish a sustainable justice system which links informal to formal mechanisms.[1790] The hybrid model encompasses the creation of Alternative Dispute Resolution (ADR) Units (including *Jirgas* and *Shuras*) and Human Rights Units alongside the state justice system.[1791] ADR Units would deal with minor crimes and civil cases, whereas the state justice system would be concerned with serious criminal cases.[1792] The Human Rights Units which consists, *inter alia*, of members of the Afghanistan Independent Human Rights Commission (AIHRC) would be responsible for monitoring decisions made by ADR Units.[1793] Very important components of the hybrid model are mutual recognition as well as constructive and complementary interactions

---

1785 *See* Chapter 4.4 The Role of Traditional Justice Processes.

1786 United Nations Security Council, *The Rule of Law and Transitional Justice in Conflict and Post-Conflict Societies, Report of the Secretary-General*, pp. 12–3; Senier, 'Rebuilding the Judicial Sector in Afghanistan', 7.

1787 Wardak, Saba and Kazem, *Afghanistan Human Development Report 2007*, p. 25; Choudhury, 'Reconceptualising Legal Pluralism in Afghanistan', 31, 32; Thier, 'Introduction:', 4–5.

1788 Wardak, 'State and Non-State Justice Systems in Afghanistan: the Need for Synergy', 1319–23; Schmeidl, 'Engaging Traditional Justice Mechanisms in Afghanistan', 169; Coburn and Dempsey, *Informal Dispute Resolution in Afghanistan*, p. 11; Röder, 'Kollisionen zwischen shari'a, Gesetz und Stammestradition in Afghanistan', 288–93; Friedman, Pactat and Weisell, *Accountability and Impunity:*, p. 28; Wardak, Saba and Kazem, *Afghanistan Human Development Report 2007*; Barfield, Nojumi and Thier, *The Clash of Two Goods*, 2–5, 24–28; Jones-Pauly and Nojumi, 'Balancing Relations between Society and State', 842–5.

1789 Wardak, 'State and Non-State Justice Systems in Afghanistan: the Need for Synergy', 1307, 1324.

1790 Ibid., pp. 1319–23.

1791 Ibid., pp. 1319–23; Wardak, Saba and Kazem, *Afghanistan Human Development Report 2007*, 31–33, 146–52.

1792 Wardak, 'State and Non-State Justice Systems in Afghanistan: the Need for Synergy', 1319–23.

1793 Ibid., pp. 1319–23; Wardak, Saba and Kazem, *Afghanistan Human Development Report 2007*, 31–33, 146–52.

between the formal courts, ADR mechanisms and the Human Rights Units.[1794]

4.9 Conclusion

The purpose of Part 4 was to draft an amnesty programme for Afghanistan which is in accordance with the requirements of international law and which adequately integrates the specific political, social and cultural circumstances of the country. It is essential that justice and accountability are included as a central component in any amnesty process. Apart from this, several other mechanisms have been explored in order to design an amnesty which will meet the needs of victims and the Afghan society. The following crucial elements should be incorporated in a possible future transitional justice process:

First of all, it has to be emphasised that apart from the content of an amnesty, the procedure of its adoption is equally important.[1795] In other words, the way in which an amnesty is enacted has consequences not only for the legitimacy of the amnesty process, but also for the impact the amnesty may have on peace and reconciliation.[1796] To enhance the legitimacy of the adoption of the amnesty law, the procedure should be as consultative and democratic as possible.[1797] This means that an amnesty law which is approved by the Afghan people or their elected representatives will be regarded as democratically legitimised.[1798]

Serious international crimes such as war crimes, crimes against humanity, enforced disappearance and torture as well as other serious acts of violence against persons that may not rise to the level of an international crime must be excluded from the scope of the proposed amnesty. Those

1794 Wardak, Saba and Kazem, *Afghanistan Human Development Report 2007*, p. 151; Barfield, Nojumi and Thier, *The Clash of Two Goods*, p. 22; United States Agency for International Development (USAID), *Afghanistan Rule of Law Project*, p. 14.

1795 Basic literature on „procedural justice“, e.g.: Tyler (ed.), *Procedural Justice*; Röhl (ed.), *Procedural Justice*.

1796 Mallinder, *Amnesty, Human Rights and Political Transitions:*, p. 29; Joint report by the Advisory Council on International Affairs (AIV) and the Advisory Committee on Issues of Public International Law (CAVV), *Transitional Justice*, p. 32.

1797 Freeman, *Necessary Evils*, p. 111.

1798 Mallinder, *Amnesty, Human Rights and Political Transitions:*, pp. 33–4.

most responsible for these crimes, namely the political leaders, decision makers or senior officers shall be held accountable, preferably before a hybrid court.

In cases of non-serious crimes, such as looting, informing or burning houses and lower-ranking criminals or subordinates, i.e. those individuals who followed the legally binding orders of a superior, an amnesty comes into consideration provided that certain conditions are fulfilled.[1799]

In order to prevent further violence and to facilitate accountability and the fulfilment of victims' rights, the participation of amnesty beneficiaries in traditional justice processes[1800] within customary legal systems is expedient.[1801] In this way informal dispute resolution mechanisms can contribute to local stability and social order.

To ensure that the Afghan amnesty process will be successful and the proposed concept of transitional justice will bear fruit, the participation of target groups in disarmament, demobilisation and reintegration programmes (DDR programmes) is essential.[1802]

It is furthermore important not to neglect the 'right to know the truth'.[1803] It has been emphasised that amnesties must never be used to limit, deny or impair the right to the truth.[1804] Instead, amnesties and truth commissions can co-exist.[1805] With regard to a truth-seeking process

1799 Ibid., pp. 100–2.

1800 Instead of the term ‚traditional justice processes', other similar terms are used by scholars and practitioners, such as, for example, ‚customary legal mechanisms', ‚tradition-based justice', ‚community-based justice', ‚restorative justice processes'.

1801 United Nations Security Council, *The Rule of Law and Transitional Justice in Conflict and Post-Conflict Societies, Report of the Secretary-General*, p. 4.

1802 Mallinder, *Amnesty, Human Rights and Political Transitions:*, p. 379; Thier, 'Introduction:', 7; Rubin, 'Transitional Justice and Human Rights in Afghanistan', 576, 577; International Center for Transitional Justice (ICTJ), *Stabilizing Afghanistan*, p. 3.

1803 *See* United Nations Commission on Human Rights, *Report of the Independent Expert to Update the Set of Principles to Combat Impunity, Diane Orentlicher, Addendum*, Principle 24 (b), which determines that: „ *[…] amnesty and other measures of clemency shall be kept within the following bounds: […] (b) Amnesties and other measures of clemency shall be without effect with respect to the victims' right to reparation, to which principles 31 through 34 refer, and shall not prejudice the right to know;"*.

1804 *See* UN Office of the High Commissioner for Human Rights, *Rule-of-Law Tools for Post-Conflict States*, p. 31.

1805 Mallinder, *Amnesty, Human Rights and Political Transitions:*, 165; Schoiswohl, '"Transitional Justice" in Afghanistan', 95–7.

in Afghanistan several issues need to be addressed. The mandate of a possible future Truth Commission for Afghanistan has to be defined precisely, including the composition of the commission, their funding and period of operation. Further aspects concern the functioning of the TC as well as guarantees for victims, witnesses and perpetrators.

Apart from the 'right to know the truth', transitional justice processes must incorporate the 'right to reparations' in order to secure the legal rights of victims. Mechanisms of providing reparations could well be combined with truth commissions since appropriate reparations require fact-finding on the situation of victims and documentation.[1806] Moreover, the final report of the Truth Commission should include recommendations concerning, for example, reparation programmes.[1807]

Another important issue and core task in the context of transitional justice is the prevention of further human rights violations by conducting institutional reforms.[1808] Institutions which have abused human rights and served criminal regimes must be transformed into institutions which protect human rights, enjoy civic trust and serve the rule of law.[1809] Besides this, without functioning institutions a legitimate and effective amnesty process cannot be achieved. Due to the fact that employees make up institutions, a main aspect of institutional reform should be personnel reform through vetting and lustration.[1810] Since there is an apparent discrepancy between the objectives and requirements codified in official documents and the actions and results that can be listed so far, a more comprehensive approach to achieve success in reforming Afghanistan's institutions is necessary.

The proposed future amnesty process for Afghanistan with its various mechanisms and components is largely theoretical and it remains to be

---

1806 Afghanistan Independent Human Rights Commission (AIHRC), *A Call for Justice*, p. 54; United Nations Security Council, *The Rule of Law and Transitional Justice in Conflict and Post-Conflict Societies, Report of the Secretary-General*, pp. 18–9.

1807 United Nations Commission on Human Rights, *Report of the Independent Expert to Update the Set of Principles to Combat Impunity, Diane Orentlicher, Addendum*, Principle 12; Zupan and Servaes, *Transitional Justice & Dealing with the Past*
, pp. 18–9.

1808 UN Office of the High Commissioner for Human Rights, *Rule-of-Law Tools for Post-Conflict States*, p. 3.

1809 Ibid., p. 3.

1810 Ibid., p. 4.

seen if the situation in Afghanistan moves in this direction.[1811] Apart from the specific circumstances in Afghanistan, Louise Mallinder has pointed out that amnesty processes do not usually contain all of the described mechanisms, but rather only some of them.[1812] Other factors which must be taken into account are that tensions may arise between different components of the proposed transitional justice strategy or that possible amnesty beneficiaries are discouraged by the various conditions that must be fulfilled in order to obtain amnesty.[1813] Besides these uncertainties, and although the proper implementation of each mechanism is extremely challenging, a holistic approach — in which different mechanisms that complement and reinforce each other are combined — is crucial for the success of a transitional justice process in Afghanistan.[1814]

1811 Rather critical: A. S. Amin, 'Transitional Justice and the Culture of Impunity in Afghanistan', Dissertation, University of Erfurt (2013), pp. 86–7.

1812 L. Mallinder, 'Amnesties in the Pursuit of Reconciliation, Peacebuilding, and Restorative Justice' in J. J. Llewellyn and D. Philpott (eds.), *Restorative Justice, Reconciliation, and Peacebuilding* (Oxford: Oxford University Press, 2014), pp. 138–73, at p. 164; Mallinder, *Amnesty, Human Rights and Political Transitions:*, 199.

1813 Mallinder, 'Amnesties in the Pursuit of Reconciliation, Peacebuilding, and Restorative Justice', 164.

1814 United Nations, *What is Transitional Justice? A Backgrounder*, pp. 3–4; Duthie, 'Afterword', 254–6; *See also*, Chapter 2. Amnesties in the Age of Accountability.

5 Final Remarks and Future Prospects

The above analysis of the Afghan Amnesty Law has shown that amnesties during transitions continue to play a vital role. **Part 2** (**Amnesties in the Age of Accountability**) has dealt with the development of amnesties, a form of providing impunity and especially with their relationship to criminal proceedings. The meaning of "amnesty" depends on the legal, cultural and political background of the society affected. This means that, not only blanket or unconditional, but also conditional amnesties, self-amnesties and *de facto* amnesties are possible. In the case of Afghanistan, the government introduced a controversial blanket amnesty law which entered into force in 2010.

Part 3 (**The Legitimacy of the Afghan Amnesty Law under International Law**) concerned the crucial question of whether the regulations of the Afghan Amnesty Law are compatible with Afghanistan's obligations under international law. In this regard, a full examination of relevant international law was necessary, while taking into account the specific situation in Afghanistan and the exact details of the Afghan Amnesty Law in order to determine its legitimacy under international law. Hence this part of the study encompassed different stages of legal examination. Following the sources of international law, as contained in Article 38 (1) of the Statute of the International Court of Justice, the compatibility of the Afghan Amnesty Law with international conventions, international custom, the general principles of law as well as judicial decisions and the teachings of the most highly qualified publicists has been looked at.[1815] The analy-

1815 *See* Statute of the International Court of Justice, Article 38:
"*(1) The Court, whose function is to decide in accordance with international law such disputes as are submitted to it, shall apply:*
a. international conventions, whether general or particular, establishing rules expressly recognized by the contesting states;
b. international custom, as evidence of a general practice accepted as law;
c. the general principles of law recognized by civilized nations;
d. subject to the provisions of Article 59, judicial decisions and the teachings of the most highly qualified publicists of the various nations, as subsidiary means for the determination of rules of law.",
United Nations, *Statute of the International Court of Justice*, 18 April 1946, http://www.refworld.org/docid/3deb4b9c0.html (08 February 2016).

sis revealed that neither international treaty law nor current customary international law nor the general principles of law prohibit the Afghan Amnesty Law (Chapter 3.1, 3.2 and 3.3). However, there is nevertheless a trend towards outlawing blanket amnesties for serious international crimes as the practice of Latin American states and several UN organisations indicates (Chapter 3.2).[1816] Apart from that, the blanket amnesty is in violation of Afghanistan's duty to prosecute international crimes and cannot be justified by further international obligations. Taking into account the subsidiary sources of international law, i.e. judicial decisions on amnesties and the teachings of the most highly qualified publicists of various nations, a condemnation of blanket self-amnesties for serious crimes under international law can be ascertained (Chapter 3.4 and 3.5). The Afghan Amnesty Law is consequently not in line with these secondary sources, developing customary international law and the obligation to prosecute international crimes.[1817] In order to perform the obligation to prosecute, Afghanistan must abrogate or amend its Amnesty Law to remove the blanket amnesty provision.

On these grounds, **Part 4 (Determination of the Conditions under which an Afghan Amnesty Law would be Legitimate under International Law)** explored how an Afghan amnesty law could be designed to fulfil the requirements of international law. The national laws of Afghanistan, tribal and Sharia law as well as the legal order of the Taliban have not been considered in this chapter. However, in addition to aspects of international law the political, social and cultural circumstances in Afghanistan also play a significant role for the design and successful implementation of an amnesty law.[1818] Therefore, these specific circumstances have been adequately integrated in the analysis. As a central component in any amnesty process justice and accountability must be included. Apart from that, several other mechanisms have been explored in order to design an amnesty which will meet the needs of victims and the Afghan

---

1816 Mallinder, 'The End of Amnesty or Regional Overreach?', 671; Schabas, *Unimaginable Atrocities*, p. 182; Seibert-Fohr, *Prosecuting Serious Human Rights Violations*, pp. 286–7; Bassiouni, 'Accountability for Violations of International Humanitarian Law and Other Serious Violations of Human Rights', 17–8.

1817 Khan, 'Justice to the Extent Possible', 20–1; Afghanistan Independent Human Rights Commission (AIHRC), *Discussion Paper on the Legality of Amnesties*, p. 9.

1818 United Nations Security Council, *The Rule of Law and Transitional Justice in Conflict and Post-Conflict Societies, Report of the Secretary-General*, p. 1; Thier, 'Introduction:', 1–2; Dickinson, 'Transitional Justice in Afghanistan', 33; Mallinder, *Amnesty, Human Rights and Political Transitions:*, p. 10.

society. To enhance the legitimacy of the adoption of the amnesty law the procedure should be as consultative and democratic as possible.[1819] This means that an amnesty law which is approved by the Afghan people or their elected representatives will be regarded as democratically legitimised (Chapter 4.1).[1820] Serious international crimes as well as other serious acts of violence against persons that may not rise to the level of an international crime must be excluded from the scope of the proposed amnesty (Chapter 4.2). Those most responsible for these crimes, namely the political leaders, decision makers or senior officers shall be held accountable, preferably before a hybrid court (Chapter 4.3). In cases of non-serious crimes and lower-ranking criminals or subordinates an amnesty comes into question provided that certain conditions are fulfilled.[1821] In order to prevent further violence and to facilitate accountability and the fulfilment of victims' rights, the participation of amnesty beneficiaries in traditional justice processes within customary legal systems[1822] (Chapter 4.4) as well as in disarmament, demobilisation and reintegration programmes (DDR programmes) (Chapter 4.5) is essential.[1823] It is furthermore important to not neglect the 'right to know the truth'.[1824] It has been emphasised that amnesties must never be used to limit, deny or impair the right to the truth.[1825] Instead, amnesties and truth commissions can co-exist and complement (Chapter 4.6).[1826] Apart from the 'right to know the truth', transitional justice processes must incorporate the 'right to reparations' in

---

1819 Freeman, *Necessary Evils*, p. 111.

1820 Mallinder, *Amnesty, Human Rights and Political Transitions:*, pp. 33–4.

1821 Ibid., pp. 100–2.

1822 United Nations Security Council, *The Rule of Law and Transitional Justice in Conflict and Post-Conflict Societies, Report of the Secretary-General*, p. 4.

1823 Mallinder, *Amnesty, Human Rights and Political Transitions:*, p. 379; Thier, 'Introduction:', 7; Rubin, 'Transitional Justice and Human Rights in Afghanistan', 576, 577; International Center for Transitional Justice (ICTJ), *Stabilizing Afghanistan*, p. 3.

1824 *See* United Nations Commission on Human Rights, *Report of the Independent Expert to Update the Set of Principles to Combat Impunity, Diane Orentlicher, Addendum*, Principle 24 (b), which determines that: „ *[…] amnesty and other measures of clemency shall be kept within the following bounds: [...] (b) Amnesties and other measures of clemency shall be without effect with respect to the victims' right to reparation, to which principles 31 through 34 refer, and shall not prejudice the right to know;*".

1825 *See* UN Office of the High Commissioner for Human Rights, *Rule-of-Law Tools for Post-Conflict States*, p. 31.

1826 Mallinder, *Amnesty, Human Rights and Political Transitions:*, 165; Schoiswohl, '"Transitional Justice" in Afghanistan', 95–7.

order to secure the legal rights of victims. Mechanisms of providing reparations could well be combined with truth commissions since appropriate reparations require fact-finding on the situation of victims and documentation.[1827] Moreover, the final report of the Truth Commission should include recommendations concerning, for example, reparation programmes (Chapter 4.7).[1828] Another important issue and core task in the context of transitional justice is the prevention of further human rights violations by conducting institutional reforms.[1829] It is essential that institutions which have abused human rights and served criminal regimes are transformed into institutions which protect human rights, enjoy civic trust and serve the rule of law (Chapter 4.8).[1830] Although such a holistic amnesty process would be crucial for Afghanistan's peaceful future[1831], it remains to be seen whether or not the situation in Afghanistan moves in this direction.[1832] Apart from that, amnesty processes do not usually contain all of the mentioned mechanisms, but rather only some of them.[1833]

The case of Afghanistan has clearly demonstrated the current status of amnesties with regard to their legitimacy under international law. Even though the teachings of the most highly qualified publicists, international jurisprudence as well as the United Nations condemn blanket amnesties for serious international crimes and accept conditional amnesties under certain circumstances, no binding law exists at present that can be applied

---

1827 Afghanistan Independent Human Rights Commission (AIHRC), *A Call for Justice*, p. 54; United Nations Security Council, *The Rule of Law and Transitional Justice in Conflict and Post-Conflict Societies, Report of the Secretary-General*, pp. 18–9.

1828 United Nations Commission on Human Rights, *Report of the Independent Expert to Update the Set of Principles to Combat Impunity, Diane Orentlicher, Addendum*, Principle 12; Zupan and Servaes, *Transitional Justice & Dealing with the Past*, pp. 18–9.

1829 UN Office of the High Commissioner for Human Rights, *Rule-of-Law Tools for Post-Conflict States*, p. 3.

1830 Ibid., p. 3.

1831 United Nations, *What is Transitional Justice? A Backgrounder*, pp. 3–4; Duthie, 'Afterword', 254–6; *See also*, Chapter 2. Amnesties in the Age of Accountability.

1832 Rather critical: Amin, 'Transitional Justice and the Culture of Impunity in Afghanistan', pp. 86–7.

1833 Mallinder, 'Amnesties in the Pursuit of Reconciliation, Peacebuilding, and Restorative Justice', 164; Mallinder, *Amnesty, Human Rights and Political Transitions:*, 199.

to determine the legitimacy of an existing amnesty law or to draft an amnesty which is in accordance with international law.[1834]

The question thus arises of whether, and if so how, rules determining the legitimacy of (proposed) amnesty provisions should be codified (*lex ferenda*) as binding law within the international legal order. The status as well as the acceptance of amnesties within the framework of international law is decisive for their future application and assessment. The following considerations focus on central issues in the context of further establishing amnesty guidelines, without exploring this matter in depth.

As already mentioned, one option to establish amnesty criteria would be their codification, in other words the creation of binding law, which would require an international treaty. Proponents of binding law on amnesties argue that it is the most effective way for the progressive development of international law. Binding international law would have further advantages, for instance providing legal certainty with respect to the formulation of amnesty provisions[1835] or the mandatory and non-negotiable character of codified amnesty criteria.[1836] The often prevailing "might is right" approach to peace negotiations could be considerably diminished by a legally binding framework with regard to amnesties.

There are various proposals by international experts concerning the codification of rules on amnesties. One suggestion is to adopt a multilateral treaty, for example in the form of an Additional Protocol to the Convention on the Non-Applicability of Statutory Limitations to War Crimes and Crimes against Humanity, which would contain an explicit prohibition of amnesties for perpetrators of war crimes, genocide and crimes against humanity.[1837] Another possibility of codifying amnesty guidelines would be to develop a special international agreement that includes a set of guidelines determining the conditions under which the international community would recognise an amnesty.[1838] According to O'Shea these guidelines

---

1834 O'Shea, *Amnesty for Crime in International Law and Practice*, p. 320.

1835 K. Oellers-Frahm, 'The Evolving Role of Treaties in International Law' in R. A. Miller and R. M. Bratspies (eds.), *Progress in International Law* (Leiden, Boston: Martinus Nijhoff Publishers, 2008), pp. 173–96, at p. 175.

1836 Ibid., 175; A. E. Boyle and C. M. Chinkin, *The Making of International Law*, Foundations of public international law (Oxford, New York: Oxford University Press, 2007), p. 215.

1837 Ntoubandi, *Amnesty for Crimes against Humanity under International Law*, pp. 231–2.

1838 O'Shea, *Amnesty for Crime in International Law and Practice*, 319, 328–29.

could be incorporated in a Protocol to the ICC Rome Statute.[1839] In his view, this approach would also underline how national amnesties can be reconciled with international criminal law.[1840]

However, an argument against the adoption of an international treaty is the fact that the amnesty question has been regularly posed during multilateral treaty negotiations, but the parties were unable to come to agreement.[1841] It can be deduced from this that an agreement on the incorporation of amnesty guidelines, for example in a Protocol to the Rome Statute, is quite unlikely.[1842]

The crucial question therefore is how binding rules on amnesties can be brought into being. The most notable institution concerned with the development and codification of international law is the International Law Commission (ILC)[1843], established by the United Nations General Assembly in 1948.[1844] Its thirty-four members represent "the main forms of civilization and of the principal legal systems of the world" (Article 8 ILC Statute[1845]).[1846] Due to the multinational and multicultural nature of the ILC it might be ideally equipped for finding a way to reach a consensus on the implementation of internationally accepted amnesty provisions. According to Articles 1 and 15 of the ILC Statute, the commission's main functions are *"the progressive development of international law and its codification"*. That is, the preparation of draft conventions on subjects which have not yet been regulated by international law or in regard to which the law has not yet been sufficiently developed in states' practice. And also, the more precise formulation and systematization of rules of international law in fields where there already has been extensive state practice, precedent and doctrine. Of particular interest with regard to the formation of a law on amnesties are existing state practice, international case-law and the relevant academic debate. Article 20 of the ILC Statute determines that *„The Commission shall prepare its drafts in the form of articles and shall*

1839 Ibid., 319, 328–29.

1840 Ibid., 319, 328–29.

1841 Freeman, *Necessary Evils*, pp. 32–3.

1842 Seibert-Fohr, 'The Relevance of the Rome Statute of the International Criminal Court for Amnesties and Truth Commissions', 589–90.

1843 *International Law Commission*. http://legal.un.org/ilc/ (02 December 2017).

1844 K. Ipsen, *Völkerrecht: Ein Studienbuch*, 6th edn. (München: C.H. Beck, 2014), p. 487.

1845 *Statute of the International Law Commission*. http://legal.un.org/docs/?path=./ilc/texts/instruments/english/statute/statute.pdf&lang=EF (02 December 2017).

1846 Villiger, *Customary International Law and Treaties*, vol. 28, pp. 75–6.

submit them to the General Assembly together with a commentary [...]." The subsequent procedure contains, *inter alia*, the opportunity for governments to submit comments within a reasonable time (Article 21 (2) ILC Statute) as well as the preparation of a final draft and an explanatory report by the ILC, which it shall submit with its recommendations through the Secretary-General to the General Assembly (Article 22 ILC Statute). According to Article 23 (1) (c) of the statute „*The Commission may recommend to the General Assembly: [...] To recommend the draft to Members with a view to the conclusion of a convention; [...]*".[1847] Having described the codification process, the likelihood that the ILC will deal with the issue of amnesties has to be assessed. The selection of topics is described in Articles 16 to 18 of the statute and „*should reflect the needs of States in respect of the progressive development and codification of international law. The topic furthermore should be at a sufficiently advanced stage in terms of State practice to permit progressive development and codification and the Commission should not restrict itself to traditional topics, but should also consider those that reflect new developments in international law and pressing concerns of the international community as a whole.*"[1848] Notwithstanding these guiding principles, the ILC has not yet taken up the amnesty issue and thus, has yet to elucidate the status of amnesties in international law. The reason may be that the topic is too politically sensitive to deal with it within the procedural framework of the ILC.[1849]

But beyond that, in some cases the codification of international law could also be counterproductive since binding law also has disadvantages. An argument against the codification of amnesty guidelines is the inflexibility of codified law. This means that a set of codified and legally binding rules on the design of amnesties does not allow for individual solutions in unique transitional situations.[1850] One also has to bear in mind the great complexity and the immense amount of time required for the entire treaty-making process.[1851] This is all the more true in the heavily disputed

1847 Ibid., p. 80.

1848 United Nations, *The Work of the International Law Commission*, 6th edn. (New York: United Nations, 2004), pp. 29–30.

1849 Boyle and Chinkin, *The Making of International Law*, pp. 175–6.

1850 Seibert-Fohr, *Prosecuting Serious Human Rights Violations*, pp. 216–7; Mallinder, *Amnesty, Human Rights and Political Transitions:*, p. 408; Bell, *The 'New Law' of Transitional Justice*, p. 16.

1851 Oellers-Frahm, 'The Evolving Role of Treaties in International Law', 176–7; Seibert-Fohr, 'The Relevance of the Rome Statute of the International Criminal Court for Amnesties and Truth Commissions', 589.

area of amnesties, as the controversies surrounding the negotiations of the ICC Rome Statute, the Convention on the Non-Applicability of Statutory Limitations to War Crimes and Crimes against Humanity or the International Convention for the Protection of All Persons from Enforced Disappearance have illustrated.[1852] Moreover, the uniformity of the substance of an international treaty may be undermined by reservations made by different parties to that treaty.[1853]

Another option for establishing amnesty criteria would be its application in the form of non-binding guidelines, so-called "soft law".[1854] The theoretical background to this approach stems from the "New Haven School", a policy-oriented perspective on international law.[1855] The advantage of non-binding soft law would be its flexibility.[1856] Moreover, it would leave more room for discussion and for achieving a consensus on sensitive issues, such as the prohibition of some forms of amnesties. Furthermore, since states are usually reluctant to bind themselves to treaties which may restrict their sovereignty, it might be easier to reach agreement if the law in question is non-binding.[1857] Another advantage of using soft law guidelines concerning amnesties in the context of peace-negotiations is that they may provide more immediate evidence of international support and consensus than "hard law" does.[1858]

Having presented the advantages and disadvantages of hard (binding) law on the one hand and soft law on the other, the best approach for establishing criteria on amnesties needs to be explored. In this context, it is noteworthy that most of the multilateral conventions on human rights have been preceded by non-binding declarations.[1859] The benefit of establishing such non-binding standards is that it is the most pragmatic solution to avoid a complex and time-consuming treaty-making process. In the event that states are increasingly willing to comply with these

---

1852 Seibert-Fohr, *Prosecuting Serious Human Rights Violations*, 171–172, 181–183, 217;Freeman, *Necessary Evils*, pp. 32–3.

1853 Oellers-Frahm, 'The Evolving Role of Treaties in International Law', 179–80.

1854 A. E. Boyle, 'Soft Law in International Law-Making' in M. D. Evans (ed.), *International Law*, 3rd edn. (Oxford, New York: Oxford University Press, 2010), pp. 122–40, at p. 122.

1855 Cassel, 'Lessons from the Americas', 229–30.

1856 Boyle and Chinkin, *The Making of International Law*, p. 214.

1857 Ibid., p. 214.

1858 D. Shelton, 'International Law and 'Relative Normativity'' in M. D. Evans (ed.), *International Law*, 3rd edn. (Oxford, New York: Oxford University Press, 2010), pp. 141–71, at p. 168.

1859 Ibid., 166–7.

standards, they nonetheless have the potential to develop into hard law. The best approach therefore is using soft law guidelines which may serve as a starting point for the gradual formation of binding law concerning amnesties.[1860]

In this respect, the Rule-of-Law Tool for Post-Conflict States on Amnesties issued by the UNOHCHR in 2009[1861] is worth emphasising once again, since it is probably the most significant international set of rules governing amnesties. The principles contained should guide United Nations personnel when dealing with amnesties that may contradict international law.[1862] Apart from that, transitional administrations and civil society receive assistance to better deal with (post-) conflict situations.[1863] Even though of a non-binding character, the legal principles of the Rule-of-Law Tool nevertheless restrict the discretion of States and the United Nations.[1864]

Another set of non-binding guidelines are the "Belfast Guidelines on Amnesty and Accountability"[1865] which have been presented in detail above. They include not only a comprehensive analysis of the state of international law and practice regarding amnesties, but also well-founded principles which aim to assist all those seeking to make or evaluate decisions on amnesties and accountability.[1866]

The approach of using the just mentioned soft law guidelines should be applied in Afghanistan in the way described above (Part 4). This would contribute towards the establishment of a holistic process of transitional justice. However, no matter how important its contribution may be, a transitional justice process on its own cannot lead to fundamental transformation and lasting peace in the country. Rather, further efforts must be made and changes must take place in the political, economic and social

1860 Oellers-Frahm, 'The Evolving Role of Treaties in International Law', 192–3; Shelton, 'International Law and 'Relative Normativity'', 166–7; Boyle, 'Soft Law in International Law-Making', 125.

1861 UN Office of the High Commissioner for Human Rights, *Rule-of-Law Tools for Post-Conflict States*.

1862 Ibid., p. 1.

1863 Ibid., V.

1864 Ibid., p. 2.

1865 Transitional Justice Institute, *The Belfast Guidelines on Amnesty and Accountability*.

1866 Ibid., p. 1.

area as well.[1867] Emily Winterbotham[1868] concludes that *"a peaceful and united country may be difficult to achieve, but [that] it is not too much to ask."*[1869]

1867 Duthie, 'Afterword', 254–6; J. Lamey and E. Winterbotham, *Painful Steps: Justice, Forgiveness and Compromise in Afghanistan's Peace Process*. https://areu.org.af/archives/publication/1129 (12 October 2017), p. 4; Thier, 'Introduction:', 7, 11; Rubin, 'The Transformation of the Afghan State', 20–1; Benish, *Between Impunity And Accountability*, pp. 19–20.

1868 Emily Winterbotham's expertise lies in transitional justice, peacebuilding and reconciliation, particularly in Afghanistan and Pakistan. *See* http://www.emilywinterbotham.com/bio/ (26 October 2017).

1869 Winterbotham, *Healing the Legacies of Conflict in Afghanistan*, p. 99.

6 References

A Declaration of Commitment to End Sexual Violence in Conflict. https://www.gov.uk/government/uploads/system/uploads/attachment_data/file/244849/A_DECLARATION_OF_COMMITMENT_TO_END_SEXUAL_VIOLENCE_IN_CONFLICT__TO_PRINT...pdf (24 January 2017).

Abrão, P. and Torelly, M. D., 'Resistance to Change: Brazil's Persistent Amnesty and its Alternatives for Truth and Justice' in F. Lessa and L. A. Payne (eds.), *Amnesty in the Age of Human Rights Accountability: Comparative and International Perspectives* (Cambridge, New York: Cambridge University Press, 2012), pp. 152–81.

Adams, M., Husa, J. and Oderkerk, M. (eds.), *Comparative Law Methodology*, The international library of comparative law (Cheltenham, UK, Northampton, MA, USA: Edward Elgar Publishing, 2017), vol. 3.

Adhikari G., *Nepal Inches Towards Truth About War*. http://www.thehindu.com/news/international/south-asia/nepal-inches-towards-truth-about-war/article4526543.ece (18 January 2017).

adveniat – Blickpunkt Lateinamerika, *Chile: Schleppende Aufarbeitung von Militärdiktatur*. http://www.blickpunkt-lateinamerika.de/news-details/article/schleppende-aufarbeitung-von-militaerdiktatur.html?no_cache=1&cHash=de4bd055606f8b214b963d9df7809aff (08 January 2015).

Afghan Civil Society Forum-organization (ACSFo), *A First Step on a Long Journey: How People Define Violence and Justice in Afghanistan (1958-2008)*. https://af.boell.org/sites/default/files/pdvj_final_20.4.2011.pdf (08 March 2017).

Afghanistan Independent Human Rights Commission. http://www.aihrc.org.af/ (22.01.16).

Afghanistan Independent Human Rights Commission (AIHRC), *A Call for Justice: A National Consultation on past Human Rights Violations in Afghanistan*. http://www.refworld.org/pdfid/47fdfad50.pdf (11 January 2017).

Afghanistan Independent Human Rights Commission (AIHRC), *Discussion Paper on the Legality of Amnesties*. http://www.aihrc.org.af/media/files/Reports/Thematic%20reports/Amnesties_paper_23_Feb_2010.pdf (25 January 2016).

Afghanistan Independent Human Rights Commission (AIHRC), *Afghan People's Dialogue on Peace: Laying the Foundations for an Inclusive Peace Process*. http://www.aihrc.org.af/media/files/People%27s%20Dialogue%20FINAL%20report.pdf (08 March 2017).

Afghanistan National Development Strategy Secretariat/Islamic Republic of Afghanistan, *Afghanistan National Development Strategy (ANDS)*. http://www.undp.org.af/publications/KeyDocuments/ANDS_Full_Eng.pdf (16 March 2017).

Afghanistan Research and Evaluation Unit (AREU), *Afghanistan Research Newsletter Number 24, January/February 2010*. http://www.areu.org.af/Uploads/EditionPdfs/1006E-Afghanistan%20Research%20Newsletter%2024%20Jan-Feb%202010.pdf (26 January 2016).

Afghanistan Research and Evaluation Unit (AREU), *When Will Transitional Justice in Afghanistan Become a Part of the Transitional Decade?: A Roundtable Discussion*. http://www.areu.org.af/Uploads/EditionPdfs/1612E%20When%20Will%20Transitional%20Justice%20in%20Afghanistan1.pdf (28 November 2016).

Afghanistan: Immunity to Perpetrators of Mass Atrocities Greenlights Impunity (IRIN, 2010).

Afghanistan: Justice Action Plan Heading for Oblivion (IRIN Asia, 2010).

Aguilar, P., 'The Spanish Amnesty Law of 1977 in Comparative Perspective: From a Law for Democracy to a Law for Impunity' in F. Lessa and L. A. Payne (eds.), *Amnesty in the Age of Human Rights Accountability: Comparative and International Perspectives* (Cambridge, New York: Cambridge University Press, 2012), pp. 315–35.

Ahmed, F., 'Judicial Reform in Afghanistan: A Case Study in the New Criminal Procedure Code', *Hastings Int'l & Comp. L. Rev.* 29 (2005-2006), 93–134.

Ahmed, F., 'Shari'a, Custom, and Statutory Law: Comparing State Approaches to Islamic Jurisprudence, Tribal Autonomy, and Legal Development in Afghanistan and Pakistan', *Global Jurist* 7 (2007).

Al Jazeera, *Afghan Official: No Plans to Revive Taliban Peace Talks*. http://www.aljazeera.com/news/2016/07/afghan-official-plans-revive-taliban-peace-talks-160714083916947.html (11 October 2016).

Al Jazeera America, *Nepal Parliament Passes Amnesty Bill*. http://www.aljazeera.com/news/asia/2014/04/nepal-parliament-passes-amnesty-bill-20144271502645838.html (18 January 2017).

Al Jazeera America, *UN Rights Chief: War Crimes Not to Be Part of Any Syria Amnesty Deal*. http://america.aljazeera.com/articles/2016/2/1/un-rights-chief-war-crimes-not-to-be-part-of-any-syria-amnesty-deal.html (08 February 2016).

al Sharjabi A. M., *Yemen's Revolutionary Ideals Stumble*. http://www.al-monitor.com/pulse/security/2015/01/yemen-revolution-saleh-hadi-garden-public-space-mohsen.html (16 January 2017).

Alford-Jones K., *Guatemala's New 'Right-wing' Attorney General Raises Questions and Fears*. http://upsidedownworld.org/main/guatemala-archives-33/4851-guatemalas-new-right-wing-attorney-general-raises-questions-and-fears- (15 December 2016).

Al-Samei M., *Derailment of Transitional Justice Law Provokes Exchange of Wild Accusations*. http://www.yementimes.com/en/1592/report/1189/Derailment-of-Transitional-Justice-Law-provokes-exchange-of-wild-accusations.html (15 January 2017).

Ambos, K., 'The Legal Framework of Transitional Justice: A Systematic Study with a Special Focus on the Role of the ICC' in K. Ambos, J. Large and M. Wierda (eds.), *Building a Future on Peace and Justice: Studies on Transitional Justice, Conflict Resolution and Development*. The Nuremberg Declaration on Peace and Justice (Berlin: Springer, 2009), pp. 19–103.

Ambos, K., *Internationales Strafrecht: Strafanwendungsrecht, Völkerstrafrecht, Europäisches Strafrecht, Rechtshilfe*, 4th edn. (München: C.H. Beck, 2014).

American Non-Governmental Organizations Coalition for the International Criminal Court (AMICC), *Countries Concluding Bilateral Immunity Agreements.* http://www.amicc.org/usicc/bialist (26 January 2017).

Amin, A. S., 'Transitional Justice and the Culture of Impunity in Afghanistan', Dissertation, University of Erfurt (2013).

Amnesty International, *Annul Report: Algeria 2015/2016.* https://www.amnesty.org/en/countries/middle-east-and-north-africa/algeria/report-algeria/ (23 January 2017).

Amnesty International, *Chile – Transition at the Crossroads: Human Rights Violations under Pinochet Rule Remain the Crux.* https://www.amnesty.org/download/Documents/172000/amr220011996en.pdf (04 January 2019).

Amnesty International, *International Criminal Court: US Efforts to Obtain Impunity for Genocide, Crimes Against Humanity and War Crime*, IOR 40/025/2002. http://www.amicc.org/docs/aiusimpunity.pdf (27 January 2017).

Amnesty International, *Afghanistan: "First Execution since Fall of Taliban".* http://reliefweb.int/report/afghanistan/afghanistan-first-execution-fall-taliban (27 April 2017).

Amnesty International, *Afghanistan: Addressing the Past to Secure the Future.* https://www.amnesty.org/en/documents/asa11/003/2005/en/ (28 March 2017).

Amnesty International, *Getting away with Murder?: The Impunity of International Forces in Afghanistan.* https://doc.es.amnesty.org/cgi-bin/ai/BRSCGI/GETTING%20AWAY%20WITH%20MURDER?CMD=VEROBJ&MLKOB=29040884646 (07 April 2017).

Amnesty International, *Afghanistan: 10-Point Human Rights Agenda for President Karzai.* https://www.amnesty.nl/sites/default/files/public/afghanistan_10point_human_rights_agenda_for_president_karzai.pdf (12 January 2017).

Amnesty International, *Taleban Should Be Prosecuted for War Crimes in Afghanistan.* https://www.amnestyusa.org/press-releases/afghanistan-taliban-should-be-prosecuted-for-war-crimes-2/ (13 May 2017).

Amnesty International, *The Time for Justice Is Now: New Strategy Needed in The Democratic Republic of the Congo*, AFR 62/006/2011. https://www.amnesty.org/en/documents/AFR62/006/2011/en/ (09 January 2017).

Amnesty International, *Yemen's Immunity Law: Breach of International Obligations.* https://doc.es.amnesty.org/cgi-bin/ai/BRSCGI/mde310072012en?CMD=VEROBJ&MLKOB=30564653838 (15 January 2017).

Amnesty International, *Democratic Republic Of The Congo: Annual Report 2013.* http://www.amnestyusa.org/research/reports/annual-report-democratic-republic-of-congo-2013?page=show (09 January 2017).

Amnesty International, *Annual Report: Suriname 2013.* http://www.amnestyusa.org/research/reports/annual-report-suriname-2013 (20 December 2016).

Amnesty International, *Ukraine: Abuses and War Crimes by the Aidar Volunteer Battalion in the North Luhansk Region*, AI Index: EUR 50/040/2014. https://www.amnesty.org/en/documents/EUR50/040/2014/en/ (24 January 2017).

Amnesty International, *Annual Report – Democratic Republic of the Congo 2015/2016*. https://www.amnesty.org/en/countries/africa/democratic-republic-of-the-congo/report-democratic-republic-of-the-congo/ (11 January 2017).

Amnesty International, *Amnesty International Report 2017/18 – Yemen*. https://www.refworld.org/publisher,AMNESTY,ANNUALREPORT,YEM,5a99382fa,0.html (05 February 2019).

Anderson P., *Calls Grow to Tackle Afghan War Crimes* (2005). http://news.bbc.co.uk/2/hi/programmes/from_our_own_correspondent/4258343.stm (10 March 2017).

Apple J. G., *What are General Principles of International Law?* http://www.judicialmonitor.org/archive_0707/generalprinciples.html (06 March 2017).

Asian Centre for Human Rights, *Afghan Charter of Impunity: President Karzai as the Lame Duck*. http://www.achrweb.org/Review/2007/155-07.htm (25 January 2016).

Auswärtiges Amt, *Afghanistan nach der Bonner Konferenz*. http://www.auswaertiges-amt.de/DE/Aussenpolitik/RegionaleSchwerpunkte/AfghanistanZentralasien/Bonn_Konferenz_2011/111227-AFG-nach-Bonnkonferenz-node.html (14 May 2012).

Azanian Peoples Organisation (AZAPO) and Others v President of the Republic of South Africa and others: Case CCT 17/96, Explanatory Note. http://www.saflii.org/za/cases/ZACC/1996/16media.pdf (05 February 2019).

Bai L., *Truth and Reconciliation Commission on Afghanistan*. http://www.bharat-rakshak.com/SRR/Volume13/laxmibai.html (16 July 2012).

Baker, R. B., 'Customary International Law in the 21st Century: Old Challenges and New Debates', *European Journal of International Law* 21 (2010), 173–204.

Barbour E. C. and Weed M. C., *The International Criminal Court (ICC): Jurisdiction, Extradition, and U.S. Policy*. http://www.amicc.org/docs/R41116_20100316.pdf (01 August 2016).

Barfield T., Nojumi N. and Thier A. J., *The Clash of Two Goods: State and Non-State Dispute Resolution in Afghanistan*. http://www.usip.org/files/file/clash_two_goods.pdf (04 May 2017).

Bassiouni, M. C., 'Accountability for Violations of International Humanitarian Law and Other Serious Violations of Human Rights' in M. C. Bassiouni (ed.), *Post-Conflict Justice* (Ardsley, New York: Transnational Publishers, 2002), pp. 3–54.

Bassiouni, M. C., 'Proposed Guiding Principles for Combating Impunity for International Crimes' in M. C. Bassiouni (ed.), *Post-Conflict Justice* (Ardsley, New York: Transnational Publishers, 2002), pp. 255–82.

Bassiouni, M. C., 'Reflections on Contemporary Developments in International Criminal Justice' in B. S. Brown (ed.), *Research Handbook on International Criminal Law*, Research handbooks in international law (Cheltenham, UK, Northampton, MA: Edward Elgar, 2011), pp. 409–17.

Bassiouni, M. C., *Introduction to International Criminal Law*, Second revised edition (Leiden, Boston: Martinus Nijhoff Publishers, 2013).

BBC, *Ex-Paramilitaries Jailed for Guatemala Massacre*. http://www.bbc.co.uk/news/world-latin-america-17454434 (14 December 2016).

BBC, *David Cameron: Safe Passage for Syria's Assad Acceptable*. http://www.bbc.co.uk/news/world-middle-east-20223759 (16 January 2017).

BBC, *Nepal to Investigate Civil War Crimes*. http://www.bbc.com/news/world-asia-37118106 (19 January 2017).

Beaudoin S., *Appeals Court's Decision Suspends Genocide Trial*. http://www.ijmonitor.org/2015/10/appeals-courts-decision-suspends-genocide-trial/ (17 December 2015).

Beaudoin S., *Guatemala Opens a New Court to Hear Cases Related to Grave Crimes*. http://www.ijmonitor.org/2015/11/guatemala-opens-a-new-court-to-hear-cases-related-to-grave-crimes/ (17 December 2015).

Bell, C., *The 'New Law' of Transitional Justice*, Building a Future on Peace and Justice, "Workshop 1 – From Mediation to Sustainable Peace" (Nuremberg, 2007).

Bellal, A., Giacca, G. and Casey-Maslen, S., 'International Law and Armed Non-State Actors in Afghanistan', *International Review of the Red Cross* 93 (2011), 47–79.

Bengali, S. and Faizy, S., 'Afghanistan Takes a Step Toward Peace With Notorious Ex-Warlord', Los Angeles Times, 22 September 2016.

Benish A. J., *Between Impunity And Accountability: A Comparative Overview of Transitional Justice Processes in Two Post-Conflict South Asian Countries: Nepal and Afghanistan*. http://www.watchafghanistan.org/files/Between_Impunity_and_Accountability_english.pdf (06 March 2012).

Binder, C., 'The Prohibition of Amnesties by the Inter-American Court of Human Rights', *German Law Journal* 12 (2011), 1203–30.

Blum C. P., Magarrell L. and Wierda M., *Prosecuting Abuses of Detainees in U.S. Counter- terrorism Operations: Criminal Justice for Criminal Policy*. https://www.ictj.org/sites/default/files/ICTJ-USA-Criminal-Justice-2009-English.pdf (25 January 2017).

Boone J., *Afghanistan Quietly Brings into Force Taliban Amnesty Law*. http://www.guardian.co.uk/world/2010/feb/11/taliban-amnesty-law-enacted (27 January 2016).

Boraine, A., 'Transitional Justice' in S. Chesterman, M. Ignatieff and R. C. Thakur (eds.), *Making States Work: State Failure and the Crisis of Governance* (Tokyo, New York, Paris: United Nations University Press, 2005), pp. 318–38.

Borger J., *Smuggled Syrian Documents Enough to Indict Bashar al-Assad, Say Investigators*. http://www.theguardian.com/world/2015/may/12/smuggled-syrian-documents-indict-assad-investigators (01 June 2015).

Bos, A., 'From the International Law Commission to the Rome Conference (1994-1998)' in A. Cassese, P. Gaeta and J. R. W. D. Jones (eds.), *The Rome Statute of the International Criminal Court: A Commentary*, 3 vols. (Oxford, New York: Oxford University Press, 2002), vol. 1, pp. 35–66.

Boyle, A. E., 'Soft Law in International Law-Making' in M. D. Evans (ed.), *International Law*, 3rd edn. (Oxford, New York: Oxford University Press, 2010), pp. 122–40.

Boyle, A. E. and Chinkin, C. M., *The Making of International Law*, Foundations of public international law (Oxford, New York: Oxford University Press, 2007).

Braid, E. and Roht-Arriaza, N., 'De Facto and De Jure Amnesty Laws: The Central American Case' in F. Lessa and L. A. Payne (eds.), *Amnesty in the Age of Human Rights Accountability: Comparative and International Perspectives* (Cambridge, New York: Cambridge University Press, 2012), pp. 182–209.

'Brazil to Focus on Past Abuses', The New York Times, 01 April 2014.

Brodzinsky S. and Watts J., *Former Guatemalan Dictator Convicted of Genocide and Jailed for 80 Years*. http://www.theguardian.com/world/2013/may/11/guatemalan-dictator-rios-montt-jailed-genocide (14 December 2016).

Brussels Conference on Afghanistan, Partnership for Prosperity and Peace: Communiqué of the Participants. http://www.consilium.europa.eu/en/press/press-releases/2016/10/05-afghanistan-conference-joint-communique/ (11 October 2016).

Buckley-Zistel, S., 'Einleitung: Nach Krieg, Gewalt und Repression' in S. Buckley-Zistel and T. Kater (eds.), *Nach Krieg, Gewalt und Repression: Vom schwierigen Umgang mit der Vergangenheit*, 1st edn. (Baden-Baden: Nomos, 2011), pp. 7–20.

Burke-White, W. W., 'Reframing Impunity: Applying Liberal International Law Theory to an Analysis of Amnesty Legislation', *Harvard International Law.Journal* 42 (2001), 467–533.

Burnet, J. E., '(In)Justice: Truth, Reconciliation, and Revenge in Rwanda's Gacaca' in A. L. Hinton (ed.), *Transitional Justice: Global Mechanisms and Local Realities after Genocide and Mass Violence* (New Brunswick: Rutgers University Press, 2011), pp. 95–118.

Buyse A., *Amnesty and Torture*. http://echrblog.blogspot.de/2009/03/amnesty-and-torture.html (17 February 2017).

Carasik L., *Rios Montt Edges Closer to Escaping Accountability for Genocide*. http://america.aljazeera.com/opinions/2013/11/rios-montt-guatemalagenocidetrial.html (17 February 2017).

Casey, N., 'Colombia's Congress Approves Peace Accord With FARC', The New York Times, 30 November 2016.

Cassel, D., 'Lessons from the Americas: Guidelines for International Response to Amnesties for Atrocities', *Law and Contemporary Problems* 59 (1996), 197–230.

Cassese, A., *The Oxford Companion to International Criminal Justice* (Oxford, New York: Oxford University Press, 2009).

Cassese, A. and Gaeta, P., *Cassese's International Criminal Law*, 3rd edn. (Oxford: Oxford University Press, 2013).

Castillo M. and Vasquez P., *Guatemala Genocide Trial Hits Hurdles: Rios Montt Accused in Massacres of 1,700 Ixil Mayans in '80s*. http://www.wptz.com/guatemala-genocide-trial-hits-hurdles/30559846 (07 January 2015).

Center for Constitutional Rights, *Military Commissions Act of 2006: A Summary of the Law*. http://ccrjustice.org/sites/default/files/assets/files/report_MCA.pdf (26 January 2017).

Centro de Estudios Legales y Sociales (CELS), *Estadísticas*. http://www.cels.org.ar/blogs/estadisticas/ (02 December 2016).

Cespedes T. and Wade T., *Peru's Fujimori Gets 25 Years Prison for Massacres*. http://www.reuters.com/article/us-peru-fujimori-idUSTRE5363RH20090407 (09 December 2016).

Charbonneau, L., *ICC Prosecutor Eyes Possible Afghanistan War Crimes* (Reuters, 2009).

Charbonneau L., *Hague Prosecutor Urges Libya Not to Grant Amnesty for War Crimes*. http://www.reuters.com/article/2012/11/07/us-libya-icc-idUSBRE8A629N20121107 (16 January 2017).

Choudhury, N., 'Reconceptualising Legal Pluralism in Afghanistan', Selected Proceedings of the Annual Canadian Law Student Conference, *Windsor Review of Legal and Social Issues* Inaugural Volume (2010), 21–52.

Clark, P., 'Reconciliation, Peace, Justice: A Conceptual Framework for Transitional Justice and Rebuilding Society', *IP Journal* (2010), 19–25.

Claude A.-C., *Afghanistan – Justice and Reconciliation: The Informal Justice System in Afghanistan*. http://reliefweb.int/sites/reliefweb.int/files/resources/6AC2F49A58EF764B492577EF00071C46-Full_Report.pdf (19 May 2017).

Close J., *Amnesty Provisions in the Constitutions of the World: A Comparative Analysis*. https://aninternationallawblog.wordpress.com/2015/01/05/amnesty-provisions-in-the-constitutions-of-the-world-a-comparative-analysis/ (08 March 2017).

Coburn N. and Dempsey J., *Informal Dispute Resolution in Afghanistan*. http://www.usip.org/files/resources/sr247_0.pdf (25 May 2017).

Cockburn K., *How to Prove a Role of Customary International Criminal Law: Re-imaging a Definition of CIL*. http://www.publiclaw.uct.ac.za/usr/public_law/LLMPapers/cockburn.pdf (03 November 2016).

Cryer, R., *Prosecuting International Crimes: Selectivity and the International Criminal Law Regime*, Cambridge studies in international and comparative law (Cambridge, New York: Cambridge University Press, 2005).

Cryer, R., 'International Criminal Law' in M. D. Evans (ed.), *International Law*, 3rd edn. (Oxford, New York: Oxford University Press, 2010), pp. 752–83.

Cryer, R., Friman, H., Robinson, D. and Wilmshurst, E., *An Introduction to International Criminal Law and Procedure*, 2nd edn. (Cambridge, New York: Cambridge University Press, 2010).

CTV News, *No Peace without Justice, Says Envoy to Afghanistan*. http://www.ctvnews.ca/no-peace-without-justice-says-envoy-to-afghanistan-1.503738 (27 March 2017).

DailyMail – MailOnline, *Court: Murder Trial Against Suriname President Must Continue*. http://www.dailymail.co.uk/wires/ap/article-3634186/Court-Murder-trial-against-Suriname-leader-continue.html (20 December 2016).

Danchin, P. G., 'Transitional Justice in Afghanistan: Confronting Violations of International Humanitarian and Human Rights Law', *Yearbook of International Humanitarian Law* 4 (2001), 3–51.

Dayal A., *The Institutional Returns of Amnesty?: Evaluating Security Sector Reform in Post-Conflict Cases*. http://citation.allacademic.com/meta/p413445_index.html (07 January 2016).

Decree of the Presidency of the Interim Administration of Afghanistan on the Establishment of an Afghan Independent Human Rights Commission (2002).

Del Vecchio, G., *General Principles of Law* (Littleton, Colo.: F.B. Rothman, 1986, 1956).

Democratic Republic of Congo: Peace Agreement Between the Government and the Congrès National pour la Défense du Peuple (CNDP), Goma, March 23, 2009. http://friendsofthecongo.org/images/pdf/cndp_accord.pdf (09 January 2017).

Demonstrators in Kabul Call for Bringing War Criminals to Justice (Xinhua | English.news.cn, 2011).

Dempsey J. and Coburn N., *Traditional Dispute Resolution and Stability in Afghanistan*. http://www.usip.org/files/resources/PB%2010%20Traditional%20Dispute%20Resolution%20and%20Stability%20in%20Afghanistan.pdf (27 May 2017).

Derksen D., *Impact or Illusion? Reintegration under the Afghanistan Peace and Reintegration Program*. http://www.usip.org/files/resources/PB%20106.pdf (18 April 2017).

Derksen D., *The Politics of Disarmament and Rearmament in Afghanistan*. http://www.usip.org/sites/default/files/PW110-The-Politics-of-Disarmament-and-Rearmament-in-Afghanistan.pdf (16 December 2015).

Detainee Treatment Act of 2005, Public Law 109-148 of December 30, 2007, Title X; 119 STAT. 2739. https://www.dni.gov/index.php/about/organization/ic-legal-reference-book/ref-book-detainee-treatment-act-of-2005 (24 January 2017).

Deutsche Welle (DW), *UN to Set Up War Crimes Panel for Syria Investigations*. http://www.dw.com/en/un-to-set-up-war-crimes-panel-for-syria-investigations/a-36869596?maca=en-Twitter-sharing (04 February 2017).

Deutschlandfunk, *Bundesregierung Lobt Friedensabkommen Zwischen Kabul und Hisb-e Islami* (2016).

Dickinson, L. A., 'Transitional Justice in Afghanistan: The Promise of Mixed Tribunals', *Denver Journal of International Law and Policy* 31 (2002-2003), 23–42.

Dinstein, Y., *The Interaction between Customary International Law and Treaties*, Recueil des cours (Leiden: Martinus Nijhoff Publishers, 2007), vol. 322.

Drumble, M. A., 'Rights, Culture, and Crime: The Role of Rule of Law for the Women of Afghanistan', *Columbia Journal of Transnational Law* 42 (2004), 349–90.

Duthie, R., 'Afterword: The Consequences of Transitional Justice in Particular Context' in A. L. Hinton (ed.), *Transitional Justice: Global Mechanisms and Local Realities after Genocide and Mass Violence* (New Brunswick: Rutgers University Press, 2011), pp. 249–56.

Easterday J., *No Justice Cascade in Spain*. http://www.intlawgrrls.com/2012/03/no-justice-cascade-in-spain.html (14 January 2017).

Echavez, Chona R., Pilongo, Leah Wilfreda RE, Jayakody A., Noorzai, Ahmad Saboor Hamza, Markova M. and Narasimhaiah S., *Transitional Justice: Views from the Ground on How Afghanistan Fares*. https://areu.org.af/wp-content/uploads/2016/12/1622E-Transitional-Justice-Views-from-the-Ground-on-How-Afghanistan-Fares.pdf (30 November 2017).

Eichhofer, A., 'Die Rechtsquellen des Völkerstrafrechts' in H.-H. Kühne, R. Esser and M. Gerding (eds.), *Völkerstrafrecht*, 1st edn. (Osnabrück: Julius Jonscher Verlag, 2007), pp. 1–22.

Eisikovits N., *Transitional Justice*. http://plato.stanford.edu/entries/justice-transitional/ (05 May 2017).

Ending Recruitment and Use of Children by Armed Forces and Groups: Contributing to Peace, Justice and Development, N'DJAMENA DECLARATION – N'Djamena, 7–9 June 2010. https://www.unicef.org/protection/files/DDR_Conference_Declarations_de_NDjamena.pdf (23 January 2017).

Engstrom, P. and Pereira, G., 'From Amnesty to Accountability: The Ebbs and Flows in the Search for Justice in Argentina' in F. Lessa and L. A. Payne (eds.), *Amnesty in the Age of Human Rights Accountability: Comparative and International Perspectives* (Cambridge, New York: Cambridge University Press, 2012), pp. 97–122.

Escudero, R., 'Road to Impunity: The Absence of Transitional Justice Programs in Spain', *Human Rights Quarterly* 36 (2014), 123–46.

FARC-EP International, *Agreement Victims*. http://farc-epeace.org/peace-process/agreements/agreements/item/939-agreement-victims (22 December 2016).

Federal Political Department, *Official Records of the Diplomatic Conference on the Reaffirmation and Development of International Humanitarian Law Applicable in Armed Conflicts: Volume IX*. http://www.loc.gov/rr/frd/Military_Law/pdf/RC-records_Vol-9.pdf (23 February 2016).

Ferdinandusse, W. N., *Direct Application of International Criminal Law in National Courts* (The Hague, West Nyack, NY: TMC Asser Press; Cambridge University Press, 2006).

Ferreira-Hidaka L. J., *Accountability for Gross Human Rights Violations in Brazil: The Araguaia Case and Its Repercussions*. http://lostintranslationbrazil.wordpress.com/2013/12/10/accountability-for-gross-human-rights-violations-in-brazil-the-araguaia-case-and-its-repercussions/ (19 December 2016).

Ferrié, J.-N., 'The Uncertainties of Democratic Promotion in Afghanistan' in Z. Laidi (ed.), *EU Foreign Policy in a Globalized World: Normative Power and Social Preferences*, 1st edn. (Oxon: Routledge, 2008), pp. 134–42.

Figgins S., *After Libya's Elections, Transitional Justice in the Balance*. http://www.egyptindependent.com/news/after-libya-s-elections-transitional-justice-balance (16 January 2017).

France 24, *Assad Exit not Necessary for Syria Transition, Says Fabius*. http://www.france24.com/en/20151205-assad-exit-not-necessary-syria-transition-france-fabius-islamic-state-group (17 December 2015).

Freeman, M., *Necessary Evils: Amnesties and the Search for Justice* (Cambridge, UK, New York: Cambridge University Press, 2009).

Freeman, M. and Pensky, M., 'The Amnesty Controversy in International Law' in F. Lessa and L. A. Payne (eds.), *Amnesty in the Age of Human Rights Accountability: Comparative and International Perspectives* (Cambridge, New York: Cambridge University Press, 2012), pp. 42–65.

Friedman D., Pactat L. and Weisell A., *Accountability and Impunity: Afghanistan, Kosovo and Argentina*. http://www.gpia.info/files/practicum/28/2008%20Spring%20-%20Human%20Rights%20Watch%20-%20Accountability%20and%20Impunity.pdf (12 June 2012).

Gall, C., 'With Killer's Execution, Karzai Signals Move on Warlords', The New York Times, 03 May 2004.

Gall, C., 'Afghanistan Offers Amnesty to Wanted Taliban Rebels', The New York Times, 09 May 2005.

Gang R., *Community-Based Dispute Resolution Processes in Kabul City*. https://areu.org.af/wp-content/uploads/2016/02/1107E-CBDR-Processes-in-Kabul-City-CS-2011-web.pdf (19 May 2017).

Gaudin A., *IACHR Rules Against Uruguay in Operacion Condor Case*. http://www.thefreelibrary.com/IACHR+rules+against+Uruguay+in+Operacion+Condor+case.-a0254827283 (12 March 2017).

Gavron, J., 'Amnesties in the Light of Developments in International Law and the Establishment of the International Criminal Court', *The International and Comparative Law Quarterly* 51 (2002), 91–117.

Georg, H., 'Kolonialisten kommen zurück – NATO-Staaten inclusive Deutschland setzen auf afghanische Warlords', Neue Rheinische Zeitung, 31 March 2010.

Gerding, M., 'Völkerstrafrecht vor Internationalen Strafgerichten' in H.-H. Kühne, R. Esser and M. Gerding (eds.), *Völkerstrafrecht*, 1st edn. (Osnabrück: Julius Jonscher Verlag, 2007), pp. 251–91.

German Federal Foreign Office, *Nuremberg Declaration on Peace and Justice*, press release. http://www.auswaertiges-amt.de/EN/Infoservice/Presse/Meldungen/2008/080620-Nuernberger-Erklaerung.html (07 February 2017).

Gilbert, J., 'Ex-Military Officers Convicted of Human Rights Crimes During Argentina Dictatorship', The New York Times, 25 August 2016.

Girke P. and Kamp M., *Norduganda: Frieden versus Gerechtigkeit?* http://www.kas.de/wf/doc/kas_18362-1522-1-30.pdf?091209114909 (05 January 2017).

Gossman, P., *The Past as Present: War Crimes, Impunity and the Rule of Law*, State Reconstruction and International Engagement in Afghanistan (2003).

Gossman P., *Transitional Justice and DDR: The Case of Afghanistan*. http://ictj.org/sites/default/files/ICTJ-DDR-Afghanistan-ResearchBrief-2009-English.pdf (12 May 2017).

Gossman, P., 'Kabul's Stealth Attack on Human Rights', The New York Times, 26 December 2011.

Gossman P., *Afghanistan: The Past as a Prologue: Leveraging the Coming Transition to Break the Cycle of Abuse in Afghanistan*. http://ictj.org/sites/default/files/ICTJ-Afghanistan-Briefing-English-%202012.pdf?utm_source=International+Center+for+Transitional+Justice+Newsletter&utm_campaign=98396109c7-PR_Afghanistan_Briefing_24-July-2012&utm_medium=email (19 January 2016).

Gossman P., *Afghanistan War Crimes Suspect Comes Home: Hekmatyar Deal an Affront to Victims of Grave Abuses*. https://www.hrw.org/print/294431 (12 October 2016).

Gossman P. and Kouvo S., *Tell Us How This Ends: Transitional Justice and Prospects for Peace in Afghanistan*. http://www.afghanistan-analysts.org/wp-content/uploads/2013/06/2013-06_AAN_TransitionalJustice2.pdf (26 January 2016).

Government of the Islamic Republic of Afghanistan, *Action Plan on Peace, Reconciliation and Justice in Afghanistan*. http://www.aihrc.org.af/media/files/Reports/Thematic%20reports/Action_Pln_Gov_Af.pdf (22 January 2016).

'Govt's Disregard for Court Order Upsets Victims of Conflict', 16 November 2015.

Graham-Harrison E. and Roth A., *Taliban and Afghan Groups Find Common Ground in Landmark Talks: Insurgents attend Moscow peace summit, but Afghan president is excluded*. https://www.theguardian.com/world/2019/feb/06/taliban-say-they-have-no-plans-to-seize-afghanistan-by-force (07 February 2019).

Greiff P. de, *Transitional Justice, Security, and Development: Security and Justice Thematic Paper*, World Development Report 2011 Background Paper. http://web.worldbank.org/archive/website01306/web/pdf/wdr%20background%20paper_de%20greiff_0.pdf (08 January 2016).

Häberle, P., *Der Sonntag als Verfassungsprinzip*, Schriften zum Öffentlichen Recht, 2. Aufl. (Berlin: Duncker & Humblot, 2006), vol. 551.

Hakimi, A. and Suhrke, A., 'A Poisonous Chalice: The Struggle for Human Rights and Accountability in Afghanistan', *Nordic Journal of Human Rights* 31 (2013), 201–23.

Harris Rimmer S., *Building Democracy and Justice After Conflict: The Afghanistan Independent Human Rights Commission*. http://regnet.anu.edu.au/sites/default/files/BD-WorkingPaper5.pdf (11 June 2012).

Hartmann, M. E., 'Casualties of Myopia' in W. Mason (ed.), *The Rule of Law in Afghanistan* (Cambridge: Cambridge University Press, 2011), pp. 172–204.

Hartmann M. E. and Klonowiecka-Milart A., *Impunity Prevails in Afghanistan*. http://www.rawa.org/temp/runews/2010/12/01/impunity-prevails-in-afghanistan.html (22 January 2016).

Hayner, P. B., *Unspeakable Truths: Facing the Challenge of Truth Commissions* (New York: Routledge Chapman & Hall, 2002).

Hazdra, P., 'Verurteilen – Vergessen – Versöhnen. Die wichtigsten Ansätze zur Konfliktaufarbeitung im Überblick', *Humanitäres Völkerrecht – Informationsschriften / Journal of International Law of Peace and Armed Conflict* (2006), 156–67.

Heintze, H.-J., 'On the Relationship Between Human Rights Law Protection and International Humanitarian Law', *International Review of the Red Cross* 86 (2004), 789–814.

Henckaerts, J.-M. and Doswald-Beck, L. (eds.), *Customary International Humanitarian Law: Volume II: Practice – Part 1 and 2* (Cambridge, UK: Cambridge University Press, 2005).

Henckaerts, J.-M. and Doswald-Beck, L. (eds.), *Customary International Humanitarian Law: Volume I: Rules*, 3rd edn. (Cambridge, UK: Cambridge University Press, 2009).

Henrard, K., 'The Viability of National Amnesties in View of the Increasing Recognition of Individual Criminal Responsibility at International Law', *Michigan State University-DCL Journal of International Law* 8 (1999), 595–649.

Hesse, K., *Grundzüge des Verfassungsrechts der Bundesrepublik Deutschland* (C.F. Müller GmbH, 1999).

Higgins, A. and Mashal, M., 'Taliban Peace Talks in Moscow End With Hope the U.S. Exits, if Not Too Quickly', The New York Times, 06 February 2019.

Nkadimeng and Others v National Director of Public Prosecutions and Others (High Court of South Africa, 12 December 2008).

Hinton, A. L., 'Introduction: Toward an Anthropology of Transitional Justice' in A. L. Hinton (ed.), *Transitional Justice: Global Mechanisms and Local Realities after Genocide and Mass Violence* (New Brunswick: Rutgers University Press, 2011), pp. 1–22.

Hoffman, M. B. and Berring, R. C., *International Legal Research in a Nutshell*, West nutshell series (St. Paul, MN: Thomson/West, 2008).

Hollinder, B. D., *How to Build a Better Truth Commission: Applying Lessons from Past Truth Commissions to the Selection of Commissioners for an Afghanistan Truth Commission* (2006).

Hovell, D., 'The Authority of Universal Jurisdiction', *European Journal of International Law* 29 (2018), 427–56.

Hudson, M. O., 'Working Paper', A/CN.4/16 in United Nations (ed.), *Yearbook of the International Law Commission 1950 Volume II* (1957), pp. 24–33.

Human Rights Watch, *Blood-Stained Hands: Past Atrocities in Kabul and Afghanistan's Legacy of Impunity*. http://www.hrw.org/sites/default/files/reports/afghanistan0605.pdf (21 March 2017).

Human Rights Watch, *Afghanistan: Bring War Criminals to Justice: Special Court Needed for Past Atrocities*. http://www.hrw.org/news/2005/07/07/afghanistan-bring-war-criminals-justice (26 April 2017).

Human Rights Watch, *Afghanistan: Justice for War Criminals Essential to Peace*. https://www.hrw.org/news/2006/12/12/afghanistan-justice-war-criminals-essential-peace (22 January 2016).

Human Rights Watch, *World Report 2008: Algeria*. https://www.hrw.org/world-report/2009/country-chapters/algeria (23 January 2017).

Human Rights Watch, *Selling Justice Short: Why Accountability Matters for Peace*. http://www.hrw.org/sites/default/files/reports/ij0709webwcover_3.pdf (29 February 2016).

Human Rights Watch, *Afghanistan: Repeal Amnesty Law*. http://www.hrw.org/en/news/2010/03/10/afghanistan-repeal-amnesty-law (26 January 2016).

Human Rights Watch, *Seductions of "Sequencing": The Risks of Putting Justice Aside for Peace*. http://www.hrw.org/sites/default/files/related_material/Sequencing%20Paper%2012.7.10.pdf (28 July 2016).

Human Rights Watch, *World Report 2011: Afghanistan*. http://www.hrw.org/world-report-2011/afghanistan (26 January 2016).

Human Rights Watch, *Afghanistan: Little Progress on Rights*. http://www.hrw.org/news/2012/01/23/afghanistan-little-progress-rights (18 January 2016).

Human Rights Watch, *World Report 2012: Afghanistan*. http://www.hrw.org/sites/default/files/related_material/afghanistan_2012.pdf.pdf (08 March 2017).

Human Rights Watch, *Suriname: Revoke Amnesty Legislation*. http://www.hrw.org/news/2012/04/18/suriname-revoke-amnesty-legislation (20 December 2016).

Human Rights Watch, *Death of a Dictator: Bloody Vengeance in Sirte*. https://www.hrw.org/report/2012/10/16/death-dictator/bloody-vengeance-sirte (20 January 2017).

Human Rights Watch, *Afghanistan: ICC Prosecutor Finds Grave Crimes*. http://www.hrw.org/news/2013/12/01/afghanistan-icc-prosecutor-finds-grave-crimes (02 August 2016).

Human Rights Watch, *World Report 2015: Afghanistan*. https://www.hrw.org/world-report/2015/country-chapters/afghanistan (04 August 2016).

Human Rights Watch, *World Report 2016: Afghanistan*. https://www.hrw.org/world-report/2016/country-chapters/afghanistan (28 January 2016).

Human Rights Watch, *Burundi: ICC Withdrawal Major Loss to Victims*. https://www.hrw.org/news/2016/10/27/burundi-icc-withdrawal-major-loss-victims (30 October 2017).

Human Rights Watch, *World Report 2017: Ukraine*. https://www.hrw.org/world-report/2017/country-chapters/ukraine (24 January 2017).

Human Security Network, *Annual Ministerial Meeting: Statement by Ms. Patricia O'Brien, Under-Secretary-General for Legal Affairs, The Legal Counsel*. http://legal.un.org/ola/media/info_from_lc/POB-keynote.pdf (08 January 2016).

Iliopoulos K., *Afghan Amnesty Law a Setback for Peace*. http://www.crimesofwar.org/commentary/afghan-amnesty-law-a-setback-for-peace/ (26 January 2016).

Inazumi, M., *Universal Jurisdiction in Modern International Law: Expansion of National Jurisdiction for Prosecuting Serious Crimes under International Law*, Teilw. zugl.: Utrecht, Univ., Diss., 2004, School of Human Rights research series (Antwerpen: Intersentia, 2005), vol. 19.

Ingelaere, B., 'The Gacaca Courts in Rwanda' in L. Huyse and M. Salter (eds.), *Traditional Justice and Reconciliation after Violent Conflict: Learning from African Experiences* (Stockholm, Sweden, 2008), pp. 25–59.

Inter-American Commission on Human Rights, *Report № 29/92: Cases 10.029, 10.036, 10.145, 10.305, 10.372, 10.373, 10.374 and 10.375 Uruguay*. https://www.cidh.oas.org/annualrep/92eng/Uruguay10.029.htm (04 February 2019).

International Afghanistan Conference in Bonn, 5 December 2011 – Conference Conclusions. http://afghanistan-un.org/wp-content/uploads/2011/12/Konferenzschlussfolgerung_engl.pdf (14 March 2017).

International Center for Transitional Justice (ICTJ), *Afghanistan: Addressing the Past*. http://ictj.org/sites/default/files/ICTJ-Afghanistan-Addressing-Past-2005-English.pdf (19 January 2016).

International Center for Transitional Justice (ICTJ), *Amnesty Must Not Equal Impunity*. http://ictj.org/sites/default/files/ICTJ-DRC-Amnesty-Facts-2009-English.pdf (09 January 2017).

International Center for Transitional Justice (ICTJ), *Challenges to Peace and Justice in Afghanistan*. http://ictj.org/sites/default/files/ICTJ-Afghanistan-Peace-Justice-2009-English.pdf (12 January 2017).

International Center for Transitional Justice (ICTJ), *Stabilizing Afghanistan: Legitimacy and Accountability in Governance*. http://www.ictj.org/sites/default/files/ICTJ-Afghanistan-Stabilizing-Accountability-2010-English.pdf (19 March 2017).

International Center for Transitional Justice (ICTJ), *ICTJ Statement on Afghanistan: Amnesty Law*. http://www.saajs.org/eng/index.php?option=com_content&view=article&id=47:-ictj-statement-on-afghanistan-amnesty-law&catid=42&Itemid=2 (16 October 2012).

International Center for Transitional Justice (ICTJ), *A Year of Change – A Decade of Hope: Annual Report 2011*. http://ictj.org/sites/default/files/ICTJ-Global-Annual-Report-2011-English_0.pdf (24 June 2017).

International Center for Transitional Justice (ICTJ), *Facing a Troubled Past, Yemen Debates Transitional Justice Measures*. https://ictj.org/news/facing-troubled-past-yemen-debates-transitional-justice-measures (15 January 2017).

International Center for Transitional Justice (ICTJ), *Afghanistan Mapping Report Opportunity to Break Cycles of Abuse*. http://www.ictj.org/news/afghanistan-mapping-report-opportunity-break-cycles-abuse (28 July 2016).

International Center for Transitional Justice (ICTJ), *Briefing Note on the Recent Political Developments in Nepal Leading to a Lack of Access to Justice for Victims of Gross Human Rights Violations and International Humanitarian Law*. http://ictj.org/sites/default/files/Briefing%20Note%20to%20the%20SR%20on%20TJ%2023%2008%202012.pdf (20 January 2014).

International Center for Transitional Justice (ICTJ), *No One Above the Law: Vetting the Security Sector in Nepal*. https://ictj.org/news/no-one-above-law-vetting-security-sector-nepal (16 January 2017).

International Center for Transitional Justice (ICTJ), *What is Transitional Justice?* http://ictj.org/about/transitional-justice (07 January 2016).

International Center for Transitional Justice (ICTJ), *Conviction of Ríos Montt on Genocide a Victory for Justice in Guatemala, and Everywhere*. http://www.ictj.org/news/ictj-conviction-rios-montt-genocide-victory-justice-guatemala-and-everywhere (14 December 2016).

International Center for Transitional Justice (ICTJ), *Twenty Years Later, A Chance for Accountability in El Salvador*. http://ictj.org/news/twenty-years-later-chance-accountability-el-salvador (13 December 2016).

International Center for Transitional Justice (ICTJ), *Lawyers for Guatemala's Ixil Community Take Justice Demands to Inter-American Commission*. http://ictj.org/news/lawyers-ixil-justice-demands (14 December 2016).

International Center for Transitional Justice (ICTJ), *ICTJ Urges Nepal to Amend Flawed Bill on Truth Seeking*. http://ictj.org/news/ictj-urges-nepal-amend-flawed-bill-truth-seeking (18 January 2017).

International Center for Transitional Justice (ICTJ), *DRC: Refusal to Pardon Serious Crimes Signals Justice Could Be on the Way*. http://ictj.org/news/drc-refusal-pardon-serious-crimes-signals-justice-could-be-way (11 January 2017).

International Center for Transitional Justice (ICTJ), *Anniversary of Guatemala's Genocide Verdict Marked by Denial and Polarization*. http://ictj.org/multimedia/audio/anniversary-guatemala-genocide-verdict-marked-denial-and-polarization?utm_source=International+Center+for+Transitional+Justice+Newsletter&utm_campaign=5c2da04a39-World_Report_Issue_35_May_2014&utm_medium=email&utm_term=0_2d90950d4d-5c2da04a39-237811229 (14 December 2016).

International Center for Transitional Justice (ICTJ), *ICTJ Program Report: Nepal*. http://ictj.org/news/ictj-program-report-nepal (18 January 2017).

International Center for Transitional Justice (ICTJ), *Experts Gather in Kinshasa to Discuss the National Judicial Response to Serious Crimes in the DRC*. http://www.ictj.org/news/experts-gather-kinshasa-discuss-national-judicial-response-serious-crimes-drc (11 January 2017).

International Center for Transitional Justice (ICTJ), *ICTJ Welcomes the Historic Final Report from Brazil's National Truth Commission*. http://www.ictj.org/news/ictj-welcomes-historic-final-report-brazil%E2%80%99s-national-truth-commission (18 December 2016).

International Center for Transitional Justice (ICTJ), *South Africa*. https://www.ictj.org/our-work/regions-and-countries/south-africa (04 January 2017).

International Center for Transitional Justice (ICTJ), *South Africa: Impunity, Political Interference Emerge Below Veneer of a Celebrated Reconciliation Process*. https://www.ictj.org/multimedia/audio/south-africa-impunity-nokuthula-simelane-justice (05 January 2017).

International Center for Transitional Justice (ICTJ), *With Amnesty Law Overturned in El Salvador, Prosecutors Must Work with Victims to Investigate Civil War Atrocities*. https://www.ictj.org/news/amnesty-el-salvador-civil-war (29 November 2016).

International Center for Transitional Justice (ICTJ), *ICTJ Denounces South African Government's Attempt to Exit the International Criminal Court*. https://www.ictj.org/news/ictj-denounces-south-africa-icc-withdrawl (29 November 2016).

International Center for Transitional Justice (ICTJ), *Sustainable Peace After Mass Atrocities: The Case for Transitional Justice: Recommendations of the Working Group on Transitional Justice and SDG16+*. https://www.ictj.org/news/recommendations-working-group-transitional-justice-and-sdg16 (08 February 2019).

International Commission of Jurists, *Independent Observation Mission to the Trial of President Desiré Delano Bouterse and Others in Relation to Extrajudicial Executions That Took Place in December 1982 at Fort Zeelandia, Paramaribo, Suriname: Statement on the Importance of Resuming the Trial Without Undue Delay*. https://www.icj.org/wp-content/uploads/2017/05/Suriname-Justice-delayed-Bouterse-case-Advocacy-2017-ENG.pdf (04 February 2019).

International Committee of the Red Cross (ICRC), *Practice Relating to Rule 159. Amnesty*. http://www.icrc.org/customary-ihl/eng/docs/v2_rul_rule159 (05 December 2016).

International Committee of the Red Cross (ICRC), *Afghanistan Accedes to Additional Protocols I and II in Historic Step to Limit Wartime Suffering*. https://www.icrc.org/eng/resources/documents/news-release/2009-and-earlier/afganistan-news-240609.htm (11.02.16).

International Committee of the Red Cross (ICRC), *IHL and human rights law*. https://www.icrc.org/en/doc/war-and-law/ihl-other-legal-regmies/ihl-human-rights/overview-ihl-and-human-rights.htm (20 December 2018).

International Criminal Court (ICC), *Preliminary Examination: Afghanistan*. https://www.icc-cpi.int/afghanistan (31 July 2016).

International Criminal Court (ICC), *ICC Judges Reject Opening of an Investigation Regarding Afghanistan Situation*, ICC-CPI-20190412-PR1448. https://www.icc-cpi.int//Pages/item.aspx?name=pr1448 (23 April 2019).

International Criminal Court (ICC) – The Office of the Prosecutor, *Policy Paper on the Interests of Justice*. http://www.icc-cpi.int/nr/rdonlyres/772c95c9-f54d-4321-bf09-73422bb23528/143640/iccotpinterestsofjustice.pdf (03 August 2016).

International Criminal Court (ICC) – The Office of the Prosecutor, *International Seminar on the Imperatives of the Observance of Human Rights and International Humanitarian Law Norms in International Security Operations: Speech of Mrs Fatou Bensouda – Prosecutor of the International Criminal Court*. https://www.icc-cpi.int/iccdocs/otp/SpeechProsecutor-AbujaNigeriaFra.pdf (07 September 2016).

International Criminal Court (ICC) – The Office of the Prosecutor, *Report on Preliminary Examination Activities 2014*. https://www.icc-cpi.int/en_menus/icc/structure%20of%20the%20court/office%20of%20the%20prosecutor/comm%20and%20ref/reports/Pages/default.aspx (02 August 2016).

International Criminal Court (ICC) – The Office of the Prosecutor, *Report on Preliminary Examination Activities 2015*. https://www.icc-cpi.int/en_menus/icc/structure%20of%20the%20court/office%20of%20the%20prosecutor/comm%20and%20ref/reports/Pages/default.aspx (02 August 2016).

International Criminal Court (ICC) – The Office of the Prosecutor, *Report on Preliminary Examination Activities 2016*. https://www.icc-cpi.int/iccdocs/otp/161114-otp-rep-PE_ENG.pdf (16 November 2016).

International Criminal Court (ICC) – The Office of the Prosecutor, *Situation in Afghanistan: Summary of the Prosecutor's Request for Authorisation of an Investigation Pursuant to Article 15*. https://www.icc-cpi.int/itemsDocuments/Afghanistan/171120-afgh-art_15-app-summ_ENG.pdf (05 February 2018).

International Criminal Court (ICC) – The Office of the Prosecutor, *Situation in the Islamic Republic of Afghanistan*, No. ICC – 02/17. https://www.icc-cpi.int/CourtRecords/CR2017_06891.PDF (05 February 2018).

International Criminal Court: Preliminary Examinations, Afghanistan. https://www.icc-cpi.int/pages/preliminary-examinations.aspx?ln=en (02 August 2016).

International Crisis Group, *Afghanistan: Judicial Reform and Transitional Justice*. https://www.crisisgroup.org/asia/south-asia/afghanistan/afghanistan-judicial-reform-and-transitional-justice (11 January 2017).

International Crisis Group, *Talking About Talks: Toward a Political Settlement in Afghanistan*. http://www.crisisgroup.org/~/media/Files/asia/south-asia/afghanistan/221-talking-about-talks-toward-a-political-settlement-in-afghanistan (19 January 2016).

International Crisis Group, *Yemen: Enduring Conflicts, Threatened Transition*, Middle East Report N°125. https://www.crisisgroup.org/middle-east-north-africa/gulf-and-arabian-peninsula/yemen/yemen-enduring-conflicts-threatened-transition (15 January 2017).

International Crisis Group, *Trial by Error: Justice in Post-Qadhafi Libya*, Middle East/North Africa Report N°140. https://www.crisisgroup.org/middle-east-north-africa/north-africa/libya/trial-error-justice-post-qadhafi-libya (16 January 2017).

International Federation for Human Rights (FIDH), *Afghanistan: Victims' Voice Must Be Heard*. http://www.fidh.org/Afghanistan-Victims-voice-must-be (13 March 2017).

'International Guidelines on Post-Conflict Justice: The Chicago Principles' in M. C. Bassiouni (ed.), *The Pursuit of International Criminal Justice: A World Study on Conflicts, Victimization, and Post-Conflict Justice* (Antwerp, Oxford, Portland: Intersentia, 2010), pp. 41–65.

International Justice Resource Center, *DR Congo Parliament Approves New Amnesty Law for Insurgency and Other Crimes, as Part of Agreement with M23 Rebel Group*. http://www.ijrcenter.org/2014/02/10/dr-congo-parliament-approves-new-amnesty-law-for-insurgency-and-other-crimes-as-part-of-agreement-with-m23-rebel-group/ (09 January 2017).

International Law Commission. http://legal.un.org/ilc/ (02 December 2017).

International Law Commission, *Draft Articles on Responsibility of States for Internationally Wrongful Acts, with commentaries – 2001*, UN Doc. A/56/10 (2001). http://legal.un.org/ilc/texts/instruments/english/commentaries/9_6_2001.pdf (05 July 2016).

International Legal Foundation, *The Customary Laws of Afghanistan*. http://www.usip.org/files/file/ilf_customary_law_afghanistan.pdf (06 May 2017).

International Partnership for Human Rights, *Making Amnesty Work: Prospects of Granting Amnesty to the Parties of the Conflict in Eastern Ukraine*. http://iphronline.org/wp-content/uploads/2016/01/ENG-Making-amnesty-work-January-2016.pdf (23 January 2017).

International Peace Academy (IPA), *A Framework for Lasting Disarmament, Demobilization, and Reintegration of Former Combatants in Crisis Situations*. https://www.ipinst.org/wp-content/uploads/publications/framework_for_ddr.pdf (02 May 2017).

Ipsen, K., *Völkerrecht: Ein Studienbuch*, 6th edn. (München: C.H. Beck, 2014).

IRIN – Humanitarian News and Analysis, *ICC Could Suspend Northern Investigations – Spokesman*. http://www.irinnews.org/report/53945/uganda-icc-could-suspend-northern-investigations-spokesman (15 September 2016).

IRIN – Humanitarian News and Analysis, *Uganda: No More Amnesty Certificates for Rebels*. http://www.irinnews.org/report/95569/uganda-no-more-amnesty-certificates-for-rebels (06 January 2017).

Irving S., *Talking With Taliban: A Political Solution to a Political Problem*. http://atlismta.org/online-journals/0809-journal-intervention/talking-with-taliban/ (21 January 2016).

ISAF – International Security Assistance Force, *Afghanistan Peace and Reintegration Program*. http://www.isaf.nato.int/article/focus/afghanistan-peace-and-reconciliation-program.html (18 April 2012).

Islamic Republic of Afghanistan, *Realizing Self-Reliance: Commitments to Reforms and Renewed Partnership*, London Conference on Afghanistan. http://www.afghanistan-un.org/wp-content/uploads/2014/12/REALIZING-FINAL-SELF-RELIANCE-25-November-2014.pdf (12 January 2015).

Jackson A., *The Cost of War: Afghan Experiences of Conflict, 1978 – 2009*. http://www.oxfam.org/sites/www.oxfam.org/files/afghanistan-the-cost-of-war.pdf (18 January 2016).

Jacobs, D., 'Puzzling over Amnesties: Defragmenting the Debate for International Criminal Tribunals' in L. van den Herik and C. Stahn (eds.), *The Diversification and Fragmentation of International Criminal Law*, Leiden studies on the frontiers of international law (Leiden, Boston: Martinus Nijhoff Publishers, 2012), pp. 305–45.

Joint report by the Advisory Council on International Affairs (AIV) and the Advisory Committee on Issues of Public International Law (CAVV), *Transitional Justice: Justice and Peace in Situations of Transition*. http://aiv-advies.nl/6cf/publications/advisory-reports/transitional-justice-justice-and-peace-in-situations-of-transition (07 January 2016).

Jones-Pauly, C. and Nojumi, N., 'Balancing Relations between Society and State: Legal Steps Toward National Reconciliation and Reconstruction of Afghanistan', *The American Journal of Comparative Law* 52 (2004), 825–55.

Josi, C., 'Nach fast 20 Jahren: Gerechtigkeit für die Opfer von Barrios Altos und La Cantuta in Peru', *TRIAL Zeitschrift* (2010), 9–12.

JURIST Legal News & Research, *Suriname Lawmakers Pass Amnesty Bill Ending President's Trial*. http://jurist.org/paperchase/2012/04/suriname-lawmakers-pass-amnesty-bill-ending-presidents-trial.php (20 December 2016).

Kaczorowska, A., *Public International Law*, 4th edn. (Abingdon, Oxon [UK], New York: Routledge, 2010).

Kaleck, W., *Mit zweierlei Maß: Der Westen und das Völkerstrafrecht* (Berlin: Klaus Wagenbach, 2012).

Kasande S., *Kwoyelo and Ongwen Trials Show Progress in Fight Against Impunity*. http://www.monitor.co.ug/OpEd/Commentary/Kwoyelo-and-Ongwen-trials-show-progress-in-fight-againstl/689364-3308688-pl7jgr/index.html (06 January 2017).

Kazim, H., 'Kriegsverbrecher-Studie: Massaker-Berichte belasten afghanische Politiker', SPIEGEL ONLINE, 23 July 2012.

Kersten M., *Rethinking Amnesty and Accountability*. http://justiceinconflict.org/2014/01/14/rethinking-amnesty-and-accountability/ (16 January 2017).

Kersten M., *The ICC in Afghanistan: Peace, Justice and Accountability*. http://justiceinconflict.org/2014/01/21/the-icc-in-afghanistan-peace-justice-and-accountability/ (02 August 2016).

Khan, A. N., 'Afghanistan: War Crimes, ICC and NGOs', *IPRI (Islamabad Policy Research Institute) Journal* XII (2012), 88–118.

Khan, N., 'Justice to the Extent Possible: The Prospects for Accountability in Afghanistan', *Temple Int'l & Comp.L.J.* 23 (2009), 1–34.

Khatiwada N., *SC Annuls Discretionary Powers of TRC*. http://www.myrepublica.com/portal/index.php?action=news_details&news_id=93003 (19 January 2017).

Khatiwada N., *No Support to TRC, CIEDP on Present Status: UNOHCHR*. http://admin.myrepublica.com/feature-article/story/38075/no-support-to-trc-ciedp-on-present-status-unohchr.html (19 January 2017).

Kihika K. S. and Regué Meritxell, *Pursuing Accountability for Serious Crimes in Uganda's Courts: Reflections on the Thomas Kwoyelo Case*. https://www.ictj.org/sites/default/files/ICTJ-Briefing-Uganda-Kwoyelo-2015.pdf (06 January 2017).

Kippen, G., 'The Long Democratic Transition' in A. J. Thier (ed.), *The Future of Aghanistan* (Washington D.C., 2009), pp. 35–44.

Knust Rassekh Afshar M., *Max Planck Manual on Afghan Constitutional Law, Volume Two: Constitutional Practice and Human Rights*. http://www.mpil.de/shared/data/pdf/mpil_hr_engl_1st.pdf (04 October 2012).

Kotzur, M., 'Intertemporal Law' in R. Wolfrum (ed.), *Max Planck Encyclopedia of Public International Law*.

Kotzur, M., '(Internationales) Strafrecht im Dienste des effektiven Menschenrechtsschutzes' in K. Gaede, H. Goerlich, M. Kahlo and B. Zabel (eds.), *Im Zweifel für die Freiheit: Gedächtnisschrift für Manfred Seebode* (Berlin: BWV Berliner Wissenschafts-Verlag, 2015), pp. 287–99.

Kouvo S., *After Two Years in Legal Limbo: A first Glance at the Approved 'Amnesty law'*. http://aan-afghanistan.com/index.asp?id=665 (13 January 2016).

Kress, C., 'Frieden statt Recht?', Süddeutsche Zeitung, 27 August 2016.

Kreß, C. and Grover, L., 'International Criminal Law Restraints in Peace Talks to End Armed Conflicts of a Non-International Character' in M. Bergsmo and P. Kalmanovitz (eds.), *Law in Peace Negotiations*, 2nd edn. (Oslo: Torkel Opsahl Academic EPublisher, 2010), pp. 41–84.

Kritz, N. J., 'Promoting a Formal System of Justice in Post-Taliban Afghanistan', *Conn. J. Int'l L.* 17 (2001-2002), 451–9.

Kritz, N. J., 'Progress and Humility: The Ongoing Search for Post-Conflict Justice' in M. C. Bassiouni (ed.), *Post-Conflict Justice* (Ardsley, New York: Transnational Publishers, 2002), pp. 55–87.

Küntzel M., *Westliches Wunschdenken: Keine Anti-Terror-Allianz mit Assad* (2015). http://www.deutschlandradiokultur.de/westliches-wunschdenken-keine-anti-terror-allianz-mit-assad.1005.de.html?dram:article_id=338520 (17 December 2015).

Laplante, L. J., 'Outlawing Amnesty: The Return of Criminal Justice in Transitional Justice Schemes', *Virginia Journal of International Law* 49 (2009), 915–84.

Laville S., *UK Court Convicts Afghan Warlord: Zardad Found Guilty of Torture after Landmark Old Bailey Retrial*. http://www.guardian.co.uk/uk/2005/jul/19/afghanistan.world (02 May 2017).

Leicht, L. and Baldwin, C., 'In Syrien müssen Kriegsverbrechen geahndet werden', Zeit Online, 03 August 2012.

Leopold J., *Afghanistan Enacts Law That Gives War Criminals Blanket Immunity*. http://globalresearch.ca/index.php?context=va&aid=18216 (25 January 2016).

Lessa, F., 'Barriers to Justice: The Ley de Caducidad and Impunity in Uruguay' in F. Lessa and L. A. Payne (eds.), *Amnesty in the Age of Human Rights Accountability: Comparative and International Perspectives* (Cambridge, New York: Cambridge University Press, 2012), pp. 123–51.

Lessa, F. and Payne, L. A., 'Introduction' in F. Lessa and L. A. Payne (eds.), *Amnesty in the Age of Human Rights Accountability: Comparative and International Perspectives* (Cambridge, New York: Cambridge University Press, 2012), pp. 1–16.

Ludwin King, E. B., 'Amnesties in a Time of Transition', *George Washington International Law Review* 41 (2010), 571–618.

Lutz, E. and Sikkink, K., 'The Justice Cascade: The Evolution and Impact of Foreign Human Rights Trials in Latin America', *Chicago Journal of International Law* 2 (2001).

Maass, C. D., 'National Reconciliation in Afghanistan.: Conflict History and the Search for an Afghan Approach', *Internationales Asienforum* 37 (2006), 5–36.

Macedo, S. (ed.), *Universal Jurisdiction: National Courts and the Prosecution of Serious Crimes under International Law*, Pennsylvania studies in human rights (Philadelphia, Pa.: Univ. of Pennsylvania Press, 2004).

MacLean E., *Guatemala Justice Update, January 2014: Rios Montt Trial Faces Continued Challenges as Guatemala Selects New Slate of Judges and Attorney General*. https://www.ijmonitor.org/2014/01/guatemala-justice-update-january-2014/ (14 December 2016).

Madabish A., *Yemen Legal Affairs Minister: Former President Saleh Could Be Prosecuted*. http://www.aawsat.net/2014/01/article55326833 (15 January 2017).

Mallinder L., *The Amnesty Database*. http://www.incore.ulst.ac.uk/Amnesty/index.html (23 November 2016).

Mallinder, L., *Amnesty, Human Rights and Political Transitions: Bridging the Peace and Justice Divide* (Oxford, Portland, Or: Hart Pub., 2008).

Mallinder, L., 'Amnesties' in M. C. Bassiouni (ed.), *The Pursuit of International Criminal Justice: A World Study on Conflicts, Victimization, and Post-Conflict Justice* (Antwerp, Oxford, Portland: Intersentia, 2010), pp. 793–922.

Mallinder, L., 'Amnesties' in W. A. Schabas and N. Bernaz (eds.), *Routledge Handbook of International Criminal Law* (London and New York: Routledge, 2011), pp. 419–34.

Mallinder, L., 'Amnesties' Challenge to the Global Accountability Norm? Interpreting Regional and International Trends in Amnesty Enactment' in F. Lessa and L. A. Payne (eds.), *Amnesty in the Age of Human Rights Accountability: Comparative and International Perspectives* (Cambridge, New York: Cambridge University Press, 2012), pp. 69–96.

Mallinder, L., 'Power, Pragmatism, and Prisoner Abuse: Amnesty and Accountability in the United States', *Oregon Review of International Law* 14 (2012), 307–76.

Mallinder, L., 'Amnesties in the Pursuit of Reconciliation, Peacebuilding, and Restorative Justice' in J. J. Llewellyn and D. Philpott (eds.), *Restorative Justice, Reconciliation, and Peacebuilding* (Oxford: Oxford University Press, 2014), pp. 138–73.

Mallinder, L., 'The End of Amnesty or Regional Overreach?: Interpreting the Erosion of South America's Amnesty Laws', *International and Comparative Law Quarterly (ICLQ)* 65 (2016), 645–80.

Mani R., *Ending Impunity and Building Justice in Afghanistan*. http://unpan1.un.org/intradoc/groups/public/documents/apcity/unpan016655.pdf (19 March 2017).

Manley L., *Physicians for Human Rights – Afghan Panel on Human Rights and Transitional Justice*. http://physiciansforhumanrights.org/blog/guftegu-afghan-panel-on-human-rights-and-transitional-justice.html (08 March 2017).

Marquis, C., 'U.S. Is Seeking Pledges to Shield Its Peacekeepers From Tribunal', The New York Times, 07 August 2002.

Mashal, M., 'Afghanistan's Electoral Reform Plan Is Met With Skepticism', The New York Times, 31 August 2015.

McGregor, L., 'International Law as a 'Tiered Process': Transitional Justice at the Local, National and International Level' in K. McEvoy and L. McGregor (eds.), *Transitional Justice from Below: Grassroots Activism and the Struggle for Change* (Oxford and Portland, Oregon: Hart Pub., 2008), pp. 47–73.

Meisenberg, S. M., 'Legality of Amnesties in International Humanitarian Law: The Lomé Amnesty Decision of the Special Court for Sierra Leone', *International Review of the Red Cross* 86 (2004), 837–51.

Mendelson, M. H., *The Formation of Customary International Law*, Recueil des cours (Leiden: Martinus Nijhoff Publishers, 1998), vol. 272.

Miazad, O., 'Transitional Justice in Post-War Afghanistan', *Human Rights Brief* 9 (2002), 1–5.

Minder, R., 'Argentine Judge Seeks to Put Franco Officials on Trial', The New York Times, 30 September 2013.

Ministry of Foreign Affairs (Government of Afghanistan), *Security and Defense Co-operation Agreement Between the United States of America and the Islamic Republic of Afghanistan*, Pre-decisional Document as of November 2013. http://mfa.gov.af/Content/files/2013-11-18%20BSA%20TEXT.pdf (01 April 2017).

Mobekk, E., 'Transitional Justice in Post-Conflict Societies – Approaches to Reconciliation' in A. Ebnother and P. Fluri (eds.), *After Intervention: Public Security Management in Post-Conflict Societies – From Intervention to Sustainable Local Ownership* (Geneva, 2005), pp. 261–92.

Moen H. and Mohammadi A. Z., *International Criminal Court (ICC) in Afghanistan: A Report on the Consultative Meeting on Obligations of Afghanistan under ICC.* http://www.operationspaix.net/DATA/DOCUMENT/5012~v~International_Criminal_Court__ICC__in_Afghanistan__A_Report_on_the_Consultative_Meeting_on_Obligations_of_Afghanistan_under_ICC.pdf (31 July 2016).

Mohr, J.*, 'Negotiation, Reconciliation and Outreach: What Are the Options on the Table?' in W. Danspeckgruber (ed.), *Petersberg Papers on Afghanistan and the Region*, Liechtenstein Colloquium Report (2009), pp. 103–15.

Mojumdar A., *Afghanistan: Amnesty Law Fuels Debate on Reconciliation Process.* http://www.eurasianet.org/departments/insight/articles/eav031510.shtml (26 January 2016).

Moreno-Ocampo L., *"Das Recht darf nicht wegverhandelt werden"* (2012).

Morris, M., 'International Guidelines Against Impunity: Facilitating Accountability', *Law and Contemporary Problems* 59 (1996), 29–40.

Mühlmann, S., 'Afghanistan erteilt Massenmördern einen Freibrief', WELT ONLINE, 18 March 2010.

My Republica, *Nepal: Govt Proposes Amnesty to Serious HR Violators.* http://www.myrepublica.com/portal/index.php/thweek/www.cpnm.org/index.php?action=news_details&news_id=40343 (17 January 2017).

Nadery, A. N., 'Afghans Struggle to Restore Justice in their Country: How Can Afghans Redress Past Abuses Without Creating New Injustices?' in *Bonn International Center for Conversion – Confronting Afghanistan's Security Dilemma* brief 28, pp. 49–53.

Nadery A. N., *Peace or Justice?: Transitional Justice in Afghanistan.* https://www.boell.de/sites/default/files/assets/boell.de/images/download_de/worldwide/Peace_or_Justice_Nadery_Oct2007.pdf (28 July 2016).

Nadery, A. N., 'A Human Rights Awakening?' in A. J. Thier (ed.), *The Future of Aghanistan* (Washington D.C., 2009), pp. 55–62.

Nakandha S., *Supreme Court of Uganda Rules on the Application of the Amnesty Act.* http://www.ijmonitor.org/2015/04/supreme-court-of-uganda-rules-on-the-application-of-the-amnesty-act/ (06 January 2017).

Naqvi, Y., 'Amnesty for War Crimes: Defining the Limits of International Recognition', *International Review of the Red Cross* 85 (2003), 583–626.

Naqvi, Y., *Impediments to Exercising Jurisdiction over International Crimes* (The Hague: T.M.C. Asser Press, 2010).

National Prosecuting Authority of South Africa, *Prosecution Policy and Directives Relating to the Prosecution of Criminal Matters Arising from Conflicts of the Past.* http://pmg-assets.s3-website-eu-west-1.amazonaws.com/docs/2005/060117nel.html (05 January 2017).

NDR, *Auswärtiges Amt zeichnet in vertraulichem Bericht düsteres Afghanistan-Lagebild.* https://www.ndr.de/der_ndr/presse/mitteilungen/Auswaertiges-Amt-zeichnet-in-vertraulichem-Bericht-duesteres-Afghanistan-Lagebild-,pressemeldungndr16542.html (15 December 2015).

NDTV, *UN Removes Former Afghan Warlord Gulbuddin Hekmatyar From Blacklist.* http://www.ndtv.com/world-news/un-removes-former-afghan-warlord-gulbuddin-hekmatyar-from-blacklist-1655968 (04 February 2017).

Niland, N., 'Impunity and Insurgency: a Deadly Combination in Afghanistan', *International Review of the Red Cross* 92 (2010), 931–50.

Nordland, R., 'Top Afghans Tied to '90s Carnage, Researchers Say', The New York Times, 22 July 2012.

Nordland, R., 'Old Atrocities, Now Official, Galvanize Afghanistan', The New York Times, 30 September 2013.

Ntoubandi, F. Z., *Amnesty for Crimes against Humanity under International Law* (Leiden, Boston: Martinus Nijhoff Publishers, 2007).

Nuremberg Declaration on Peace and Justice. http://www.auswaertiges-amt.de/cae/servlet/contentblob/491058/publicationFile/3491/080620-NuernbergerErklaerung-EN.pdf (07 February 2017).

Oellers-Frahm, K., 'The Evolving Role of Treaties in International Law' in R. A. Miller and R. M. Bratspies (eds.), *Progress in International Law* (Leiden, Boston: Martinus Nijhoff Publishers, 2008), pp. 173–96.

O'Keefe, R., *International Criminal law*, 1st edn. (Oxford: Oxford University Press, 2015).

Okiror S., *Forgive and Forget? Amnesty Dilemma Haunts Uganda*. http://www.irinnews.org/report/101625/forgive-and-forget-amnesty-dilemma-haunts-uganda (09 January 2017).

Olsen, T. D., Payne, L. A. and Reiter, A. G., *Transitional Justice in Balance: Comparing Processes, Weighing Efficacy* (Washington, D.C: U.S. Institute of Peace Press, 2010).

Olsen, T. D., Payne, L. A. and Reiter, A. G., 'The Justice Balance: When Transitional Justice Improves Human Rights and Democracy', *Human Rights Quarterly* 32 (2010), 980–1007.

Open Society Foundations, *Gomes Lund v. Brazil*. http://www.opensocietyfoundations.org/litigation/gomes-lund-v-brazil (12 February 2014).

Orakhelashvili, A., 'The Acts of the Security Council: Meaning and Standards of Review' in A. v. Bogdandy, R. Wolfrum and C. E. Philipp (eds.), *Max Planck Yearbook of United Nations Law* (Leiden, Biggleswade: Martinus Nijhoff Publishers/Brill Academic, 2007), pp. 143–95.

Ordinance on Investigation of Disappeared Persons, Truth and Reconciliation Commission, Nepal 2013. http://www.simonrobins.com/missing/wp-content/uploads/2013/02/Nepal-TRC-Ordinance.pdf (17 January 2017).

Orentlicher, D. F., 'Settling Accounts: The Duty to Prosecute Human Rights Violations of a Prior Regime', *The Yale Law Journal* 100 (1991), 2537–615.

Osberg C., *Inter-American Court Invalidates Amnesty Law Enacted during Brazil's Military Dictatorship*. http://hrbrief.org/2011/04/inter-american-court-invalidates-amnesty-law-enacted-during-brazil-military-dictatorship/ (12 February 2014).

O'Shea, A., *Amnesty for Crime in International Law and Practice* (The Hague: Kluwer Law International, 2002).

Osiel, M. J., *Making Sense of Mass Atrocity* (Cambridge, UK, New York: Cambridge University Press, 2009).

Osman B., *Peace With Hekmatyar: What Does It Mean for Battlefield and Politics?* https://www.afghanistan-analysts.org/peace-with-hekmatyar-what-does-it-mean-for-battlefield-and-politics/ (10 October 2016).

Otim M. and Kihika K. S., *On the Path to Vindicate Victims' Rights in Uganda: Reflections on the Transitional Justice Process Since Juba*. https://www.ictj.org/sites/default/files/ICTJ-Briefing-Uganda-TJProcess-2015_0.pdf (06.01.17).

Otto A.-K., *Afghanistan: Developmets in Justice & Reconciliation*. http://www.operationspaix.net/DATA/DOCUMENT/6347~v~Afghanistan__Developments_in_Justice___Reconciliation__Analysis_of_Reconciliation_and_Amnesty_Law_Detainee_Issues_March_2010.pdf (01 February 2017).

Oxford Dictionaries: Obiter Dictum. https://en.oxforddictionaries.com/definition/obiter_dictum (21 March 2017).

Peace Agreement between the Governement of Sierra Leone and the RUF (Lomé Peace Agreement). http://peacemaker.un.org/sierraleone-lome-agreement99 (13 February 2017).

Pejic, J., 'The Protective Scope of Common Article 3: More than Meets the Eye', *International Review of the Red Cross* 93 (2011), 189–225.

Perez S., *Guatemalan Court Upholds Top Prosecutor's Ouster*. http://bigstory.ap.org/article/guatemalan-court-upholds-top-prosecutors-ouster (14 December 2016).

Permanent Mission of Afghanistan to the United Nations, *Statement by Dr. Zalmai Rassoul, Minister of Foreign Affairs of the Islamic Republic of Afghanistan at the High-Level Meeting on The Rule of Law at the National and International Levels*. http://afghanistan-un.org/2012/09/statement-of-h-e-dr-zalmai-rassoul-minister-of-foreign-affairs-of-the-islamic-republic-of-afghanistan-at-the-high-level-meeting-on-the-rule-of-law/ (31 July 2016).

Petersen, N., 'Customary Law Without Custom? Rules, Principles, and the Role of State Practice in International Norm Creation', *American University International Law Review* 23 (2007), 275–310.

Petersen N., *The Role of Consent and Uncertainty in the Formation of Customary International Law*. http://www.coll.mpg.de/pdf_dat/2011_04online.pdf (03 November 2016).

Postema, G. J., 'Custom in International Law: A Normative Practice Account' in A. Perreau-Saussine and J. B. Murphy (eds.), *The Nature of Customary Law* (Cambridge: Cambridge University Press, 2009), pp. 279–306.

Program in Law and Public Affairs P. U., *The Princeton Principles on Universal Jurisdiction*. http://lapa.princeton.edu/hosteddocs/unive_jur.pdf (23 March 2016).

Promotion of National Unity and Reconciliation Act: Act 34 of 1995 (1995).

Quinones N., *6,060 Years in Prison for Former Guatemalan Soldier*. http://edition.cnn.com/2012/03/13/world/americas/guatemala-human-rights-trial/index.html (14 December 2016).

Radio Netherlands Worldwide, *Amnesty Not Applicable for KRouge Defendant*. http://www.rnw.nl/international-justice/article/amnesty-not-applicable-krouge-defendant (17 February 2014).

Rafael, P. and Yardley, J., 'No Extradition for Franco-Era Police Inspector', The New York Times, 30 April 2014.

Rai D., *Panel Set to Start TRC Formation*. http://www.ekantipur.com/2014/09/12/top-story/panel-set-to-start-trc-formation/394922.html (07 January 2017).

Rai D., *Transitional Justice Process Hangs in Balance: Victims Worried About Being Left out in Cold*. http://kathmandupost.ekantipur.com/news/2017-01-19/victims-worried-about-being-left-out-in-cold.html (09 February 2017).

Raimondo, F. O., *General Principles of Law in the Decisions of International Criminal Courts and Tribunals*, Zugl.: Amsterdam, Univ., Diss., 2007 (Leiden: Nijhoff, 2008).

Raymond-Jetté M., *Small Gains on Large Crimes in DR Congo*. http://www.insightonconflict.org/2015/07/small-gains-large-crimes-dr-congo/ (11 January 2017).

Razesberger, F., *The International Criminal Court: The Principle of Complementarity*, Völkerrecht, Europarecht und internationales Wirtschaftsrecht (Frankfurt am Main: Peter Lang, 2006), vol. 1.

Recknagel C., *Explainer: Key Points in U.S.-Afghan Bilateral Security Agreement*. http://www.rferl.org/content/explainer-bsa-afghan-us-security-agreement-bsa/26613884.html (09 January 2015).

Renteria N., *El Salvador Top Court Orders Probe of Civil War Massacre*. http://www.reuters.com/article/2014/02/06/us-elsalvador-justice-idUSBREA1506K20140206 (13 December 2016).

Reuters, *UN Rights Office Against Proposed Saleh Immunity*. http://in.reuters.com/article/2011/10/18/idINIndia-59968420111018 (15 January 2017).

Reuters, *Genocide Trial for Guatemala Ex-Dictator Rios Montt Suspended*. http://www.reuters.com/article/us-guatemala-trial-idUSKCN0UP21F20160111 (29 November 2016).

Reuters, *Gambia Withdraws From ICC, Accuses World Body of Bias Against Africans*. http://thewire.in/76049/gambia-withdraws-from-the-icc-accuses-it-of-ignoring-the-war-crimes-of-the-west/ (02 November 2016).

Reydams, L., *Universal Jurisdiction: International and Municipal Legal Perspectives*, Oxford monographs in international law (Oxford: Oxford Univ. Press, 2003).

Richter A., Aguiar V. and Queiroz A., *Supreme Court Halts Proceedings Against Military Accused of Dictatorship Crimes*. http://agenciabrasil.ebc.com.br/en/politica/noticia/2014-09/supreme-court-halts-proceedings-against-military-accused-dictatorship (19 December 2016).

Robinson, D., 'Serving the Interests of Justice: Amnesties, Truth Commissions and the International Criminal Court', *European Journal of International Law* 14 (2003), 481–505.

Röder, T. J., 'Kollisionen zwischen shari'a, Gesetz und Stammestradition in Afghanistan' in M. Kötter and G. F. Schuppert (eds.), *Normative Pluralität ordnen: Rechtsbegriffe, Normenkollisionen und Rule of Law in Kontexten dies- und jenseits des Staates*, 1st edn. (Baden-Baden: Nomos, 2009), pp. 257–301.

Röhl, K. F. (ed.), *Procedural Justice*, Oñati international series in law and society (Aldershot, Hants: Dartmouth, 1997).

Roht-Arriaza, N., 'State Responsibility to Investigate and Prosecute Grave Human Rights Violations in International Law', *California Law Review* 78 (1990), 449–513.

Roht-Arriaza, N., *Transitional Justice and Peace Agreements*, Peace Agreements: The Role of Human Rights in Negotiations (Belfast, 2005).

Roht-Arriaza, N., 'Amnesty Laws in Latin America: Devalued Currency?', *The Canadian Consortium on Human Security* 6 (2008), 13–6.

Roht-Arriaza N., *Uruguay Supreme Court Annuls Amnesty Law, as Accountability Continues in Latin America*. http://www.intlawgrrls.com/2010/11/uruguayan-supreme-court-annuls-amnesty.html (04 February 2019).

Roht-Arriaza, N., 'The Spanish Civil War, Amnesty, and the Trials of Judge Garzón', *The American Society of International Law* 16 (2012).

Roht-Arriaza, N. and Gibson, L., 'The Developing Jurisprudence on Amnesty', *Human Rights Quarterly* 20 (1998), 843–85.

Roht-Arriaza, N. and Mariezcurrena, J. (eds.), *Transitional Justice in the Twenty-First Century: Beyond Truth versus Justice* (Cambridge, UK, New York: Cambridge University Press, 2006).

Rondeaux, C. and Grono, N., 'Prosecuting Taliban War Criminals', The New York Times, 23 March 2010.

Rubin, B. R., 'Transitional Justice and Human Rights in Afghanistan', *International Affairs* 79 (2003), 567–81.

Rubin, B. R., 'The Transformation of the Afghan State' in A. J. Thier (ed.), *The Future of Aghanistan* (Washington D.C., 2009), pp. 13–21.

Ryngaert C., *Another Afghan Case in the Hague District Court: Universal Jurisdiction over Violations of Common Article 3*. http://www.haguejusticeportal.net/Docs/Miscellaneous/Portal%20Ryngaert%20Commentary%20Abdullah%20F%2012-9-2007.pdf (03 May 2017).

Sadat, L. N., 'The Effect of Amnesties Before Domestic and International Tribunals: Morality, Law and Politics' in E. Hughes, W. A. Schabas and R. C. Thakur (eds.), *Atrocities and International Accountability: Beyond Transitional Justice* (New York: United Nations University Press, 2007), pp. 225–45.

Sadat, L. N., 'Individuel Progress in International Law: Considering Amnesty' in R. A. Miller and R. M. Bratspies (eds.), *Progress in International Law* (Leiden, Boston: Martinus Nijhoff Publishers, 2008), pp. 335–56.

Saeed A., *Armed Men Besiege House of Legal Affairs Minister*. http://www.yementimes.com/en/1796/news/4069/Armed-men-besiege-house-of-legal-affairs-minister.htm (16 January 2017).

Sain A. C., *Latin American Amnesty Laws Annulled; the Struggle Against Impunity Continues*. http://www.peacepalacelibrary.nl/2011/01/latin-american-amnesty-laws-annulled-the-struggle-against-impunity-continues/ (09 December 2016).

Sajjad T., *Peace at all Costs: Reintegration and Reconciliation in Afghanistan*. http://www.refworld.org/docid/4cb411692.html (12 April 2017).

Sala de lo Constitucional de la Corte Suprema de Justicia: Incostitucionalidad 44-2013/145-2013, San Salvador, (unofficial translation, footnotes omitted). http://www.jurisprudencia.gob.sv/VisorMLX/PDF/44-2013AC.PDF (04 February 2019).

Salahuddin, S., *Afghanistan Must Not Repeal Amnesty Law* (Kabul: Reuters, 2010).

Sandoval, C., 'The Challenge of Impunity in Peru: The Significance of the Inter-American Court of Human Rights', *Essex Human Rights Review* 5 (2008), 1–20.

Sandoz, Y., Swinarski, C. and Zimmermann, B. (eds.), *Commentary on the Additional Protocols of 8 June 1977 to the Geneva Conventions of 12 August 1949* (Geneva, Norwell, MA, USA: International Committee of the Red Cross; Martinus Nijhoff Publishers; Distributors for the United States and Canada, Kluwer Academic Publishers, 1987).

Schabas, W., *Unimaginable Atrocities: Justice, Politics, and Rights at the War Crimes Tribunals*, 1st edn. (Oxford: Oxford University Press, 2012).

Schabas, W. A., 'National Amnesties, Truth Commissions and International Criminal Tribunals' in B. S. Brown (ed.), *Research Handbook on International Criminal Law*, Research handbooks in international law (Cheltenham, UK, Northampton, MA: Edward Elgar, 2011), pp. 373–90.

Scharf, M., 'The Letter of the Law: The Scope of the International Legal Obligation to Prosecute Human Rights Crimes', *Law and Contemporary Problems* 59 (1996), 41–62.

Scharf, M. P., 'The Amnesty Exception to the Jurisdiction of the International Criminal Court', *Cornell International Law Journal* 32 (1999), 507–27.

Scharf, M. P., 'Justice versus Peace' in S. B. Sewall and C. Kaysen (eds.), *The United States and the International Criminal Court: National Security and International Law* (Lanham, Md, Oxford, England: Rowman & Littlefield Publishers; American Academy of Arts and Sciences, 2000), pp. 179–95.

Scharf, M. P., 'Trading Justice for Peace: The Contemporary Law and Policy Debate' in E. Hughes, W. A. Schabas and R. C. Thakur (eds.), *Atrocities and International Accountability: Beyond Transitional Justice* (New York: United Nations University Press, 2007), pp. 246–74.

Scharf, M. P. and Rodley, N., 'International Law Principles on Accountability' in M. C. Bassiouni (ed.), *Post-Conflict Justice* (Ardsley, New York: Transnational Publishers, 2002), pp. 89–96.

Scheffer, D., 'The Extraordinary Chambers in the Courts of Cambodia' in M. C. Bassiouni (ed.), *International Criminal Law, Volume III: International Enforcement*, 3rd edn. (Leiden: Martinus Nijhoff Publishers/Brill Academic, 2008), pp. 219–55.

Schlütter, B., *Developments in Customary International Law: Theory and the Practice of the International Court of Justice and the International Ad Hoc Criminal Tribunals for Rwanda and Yugoslavia*, Developments in international law (Leiden, Boston: Martinus Nijhoff Publishers, 2010), vol. 62.

Schmeidl, S., 'Engaging Traditional Justice Mechanisms in Afghanistan: State-Building Opportunity or Dangerous Liaison?' in W. Mason (ed.), *The Rule of Law in Afghanistan* (Cambridge: Cambridge University Press, 2011), pp. 149–71.

Schmolze B., *Ein wichtiger Sieg für die Gerechtigkeit: Amnestiepolitik der südafrikanischen Anklagebehörde für verfassungswidrig erklärt*. http://www.gerechtigkeit-heilt.de/texte/suedafrika-amnestiepolitik.html (04 January 2017).

Schoiswohl, M., '"Transitional Justice" in Afghanistan: Vergangenheitsbewältigung der nächsten Generation', *juridikum – zeitschrift im rechtsstaat* (2005), 94–8.

Seibert-Fohr, A., 'The Relevance of the Rome Statute of the International Criminal Court for Amnesties and Truth Commissions', *Max Planck Yearbook of United Nations Law* 7 (2003), 553–90.

Seibert-Fohr, A., 'Human Rights as Guiding Principles in the Context of Post Conflict Justice', *Michigan State Journal of International Law* 13 (2005), 179–96.

Seibert-Fohr, A., *Prosecuting Serious Human Rights Violations* (Oxford, New York: Oxford University Press, 2009).

Seils, P., 'Political Pardons Would Damage the Legacy of South Africa's Truth and Reconciliation Commission', The Huffington Post, 06 March 2015.

Seils P., *In Syria, Little Chance of Justice or Change Without Return of Displaced*. https://www.ictj.org/news/syria-refugees-justice-return-displaced (04 February 2017).

Senier, A., 'Rebuilding the Judicial Sector in Afghanistan: The Role of Customary Law', *The Fletcher School Online Journal for issues related to Southwest Asia and Islamic Civilization* (2006), 1–10.

Sharifzada M. J., *Eide Concerned at Amnesty Law*. http://www.pajhwok.com/ps/node/90839 (20 February 2012).

Shaw, M. N., *International Law*, 5. ed. (Cambridge: Cambridge Univ. Press, 2006).

Shaw, R. and Waldorf, L., 'Introduction: Localizing Transitional Justice' in R. Shaw, L. Waldorf and P. Hazan (eds.), *Localizing Transitional Justice: Interventions and Priorities After Mass Violence* (Stanford, Calif: Stanford University Press, 2010), pp. 3–26.

Shelton, D., 'International Law and 'Relative Normativity'' in M. D. Evans (ed.), *International Law*, 3rd edn. (Oxford, New York: Oxford University Press, 2010), pp. 141–71.

Showaia, K. M., 'Transitional Justice in Libya: Between Current Challenges and Future Prospects', *Macquarie Law Journal* 13 (2014), 61–78.

Shuja A., *Key Afghan Opposition Leader Calls for a Truth Commission, Says Negotiation with Insurgents Possible*. http://www.undispatch.com/key-afghan-opposition-leader-calls-for-truth-commissions-says-negotiation-with-insurgents-possible (16 May 2017).

Sibaja, M., 'Brazil Prosecutors: Judge Takes First Junta Case', The Huffington Post, 31 August 2012.

Sigdel K. R., *War-Era Crimes: UN Report to Sound Alarm Bell against Nepal's Blanket Amnesty*. http://kathmandupost.ekantipur.com/printedition/news/2012-03-18/war-era-crimes-un-report-to-sound-alarm-bell-against-nepals-blanket-amnesty.html (17 February 2017).

Sikkink, K., 'The Age of Accountability: The Global Rise of Individual Criminal Accountability' in F. Lessa and L. A. Payne (eds.), *Amnesty in the Age of Human Rights Accountability: Comparative and International Perspectives* (Cambridge, New York: Cambridge University Press, 2012), pp. 19–41.

Simons, M., 'Investigators in Syria Seek Paper Trails that Could Prove War Crimes', The New York Times, 07 October 2014.

Simons, M., Gladstone, R. and Rosenberg, C., 'Hague Court Abandons Afghanistan War Crimes Inquiry', 12 April 2019.

Skaar, E., *Judicial Independence and Human Rights in Latin America: Violations, Politics, and Prosecution*, 1st edn. (New York: Palgrave Macmillan, 2011).

Slater M., *Uruguay High Court Declares Dictatorship Trials Unconstitutional*. http://jurist.org/paperchase/2013/02/uruguay-high-court-declares-dictatorship-trials-unconstitutional.php (08 December 2016).

Slattery G., *Chile Doubles Down on Prosecutions for Pinochet-era Crimes*. http://www.reuters.com/article/us-chile-dictatorship-trials-idUSKCN0SQ2D120151101 (17.12.15).

Slye, R. C., 'The Legitimacy of Amnesties Under International Law and General Principles of Anglo-American Law: Is a Legitimate Amnesty Possible?', *Virginia Journal of International Law* 43 (2002), 173–247.

Slye, R. C. and van Schaack, B., *International Criminal Law: Essentials*, Essentials (Austin, New York, NY: Wolters Kluwer Law & Business; Aspen Publishers, 2009).

Snow, S., 'Ghani's Deal With the Devil: Hekmatyar and Transitional Justice', The Diplomat, 22 September 2016.

Snyder, J. and Vinjamuri, L., 'Trials and Errors: Principle and Pragmatism in Strategies of International Justice', *International Security* 28 (Winter 2003), 5–44.

Sooka, Y., 'Dealing With the Past and Transitional Justice: Building Peace Through Accountability', *International Review of the Red Cross* 88 (2006), 311–25.

Sooka, Y., 'The Politics of Transitional Justice' in C. L. Sriram and S. Pillay (eds.), *Peace versus Justice? The Dilemma of Transitional Justice in Africa* (Oxford: James Currey, 2010), pp. 21–43.

Spiegel Online, *Bürgerkrieg in Syrien: Cameron befürwortet Exil für Assad*. http://www.spiegel.de/politik/ausland/buergerkrieg-in-syrien-cameron-schlaegt-exil-fuer-assad-vor-a-865704.html (16 January 2017).

Stahl, S., *Schutzpflichten im Völkerrecht – Ansatz einer Dogmatik: Ein Beitrag zu Grund, Inhalt und Grenzen der völkerrechtlichen Schutzpflichtendogmatik im Bereich konventionell geschützter Menschenrechte*, Zugl.: Hamburg, Univ., Diss., 2010, Beiträge zum ausländischen öffentlichen Recht und Völkerrecht (Berlin: Springer, 2012), vol. 232.

Stahn, C., 'United Nations Peace-Building, Amnesties and Alternative Forms of Justice: A Change in Practice?', *International Review of the Red Cross* 84 (2002), 191–206.

Stahn, C., 'Complementarity, Amnesties and Alternative Forms of Justice: Some Interpretative Guidelines for the International Criminal Court', *Journal of International Criminal Justice* 3 (2005), 695–720.

State Library of New South Wales, *Non-International Armed Conflict*. http://www.legalanswers.sl.nsw.gov.au/guides/hot_topics/intnl_humanitarian_law/non_intl_armed_conflict.html (12 February 2016).

Synovitz R., *Afghanistan: Karzai Confirms Amnesty Offer Is for All Willing Afghans*. http://www.rferl.org/content/article/1058802.html (21 January 2016).

Synovitz R., *Afghanistan: Amnesty Law Draws Criticism*. http://www.rferl.org/content/article/1075272.html (18 March 2017).

The Afghanistan Justice Project, *Casting Shadows: War Crimes and Crimes against Humanity:*, 1978-2001. http://reliefweb.int/sites/reliefweb.int/files/resources/B7C09154CD3E144EC12570430049F76A-ajp-afg-18jul.pdf (19 January 2016).

The Afghanistan Justice Project, *Amnesty Would Jeopardize National Reconciliation and Security*. http://www.afghanistanjusticeproject.org/ (10 July 2012).

The Coalition for the International Criminal Court (CICC), *Afghanistan Signs Up for the International Criminal Court: War Crimes in Afghanistan May Now Be Tried Before the ICC*. http://www.iccnow.org/documents/2.10.2003-Afghanistan.pdf (11 February 2016).

The Coalition for the International Criminal Court (CICC), *Updates on Afghanistan (31 Dec 2005)*. http://www.iccnow.org/?mod=newsdetail&news=1 (31 July 2016).

The Coalition for the International Criminal Court (CICC), *U.S. Bilateral Immunity Agreements or So-Called "Article 98" Agreements*. http://www.iccnow.org/documents/FS-BIAs_Q&A_current.pdf (27 January 2017).

The Country of Origin Information Centre (Landinfo), *Afghanistan: Blood Feuds, Traditional Law (Pashtunwali) and Traditional Conflict Resolution*. http://www.landinfo.no/asset/1940/1/1940_1.pdf (17 May 2017).

The European Sting, *Amending Guatemala 'Reconciliation Law' Would Lead to Unjust Amnesty, Warns Bachelet*. https://europeansting.com/2019/01/23/amending-guatemala-reconciliation-law-would-lead-to-unjust-amnesty-warns-bachelet/ (08 February 2019).

the guardian, *Guatemala Overturns Former Dictator's Genocide Conviction*. http://www.theguardian.com/world/2013/may/21/guatemala-efrain-rios-montt-genocide-conviction (14 December 2016).

The Himalayan Times Online, *ICJ Finds Faults in TRC Act, Says Amend It*. http://www.thehimalayantimes.com/fullNews.php?headline=ICJ+finds+faults+in+TRC+Act%26sbquo%3B++says+amend+it+&NewsID=416400&a=3 (01 June 2014).

The Liaison Office, *Linkages between State and Non-State Justice Systems in Eastern Afghanistan: Evidence from Jalalabad, Nangarhar and Ahmad Aba, Paktia*. http://www.tlo-afghanistan.org/sites/default/files/Working-Paper-Series/TLO-Linkages-between-state-and-non-state-justice-systems-in-eastern-Afghanistan.pdf (30 April 2017).

The Liaison Office, *Building Dispute Resolution Institutions in Southern Afghanistan: Lessons from The Liaison Office Justice Shuras in Helmand, Uruzgan, and Nimruz*. http://www.usip.org/sites/default/files/ROL/TLO%20-%20Building%20Dispute%20Resolution%20Institutions%20in%20Southern%20Afghanistan%20%282%29.pdf (16 March 2014).

The London Conference on Afghanistan: Afghanistan and International Community: Commitments to Reforms and Renewed Partnership, Communique. https://www.gov.uk/government/uploads/system/uploads/attachment_data/file/383205/The-London-Conference-on-Afghanistan-Communique.pdf (10 January 2015).

Rabindra Prasad Dhakal v Nepal Government, Ministry of Home Affairs and Others (The Supreme Court of Nepal, 01 June 2007).

The Telegraph, *Minsk Agreement on Ukraine Crisis: Text in Full*. http://www.telegraph.co.uk/news/worldnews/europe/ukraine/11408266/Minsk-agreement-on-Ukraine-crisis-text-in-full.html (23 January 2017).

The World Bank, *Uganda – Emergency Demobilization and Reintegration Project*. http://documents.worldbank.org/curated/en/366461468318292528/pdf/dh0Project0Inf1raisal0Stage1updated.pdf (27 February 2017).

Thielbörger P. and Özdemir Ö., *"Afghanistan" als Risikofall: Machtspiele am IStGH in Den Haag*. https://www.lto.de/recht/justiz/j/istgh-icc021733-afghanistan-usa-kriegsverbrechen-keine-untersuchung/ (23 April 2019).

Thier, A. J., 'Introduction: Building Bridges' in A. J. Thier (ed.), *The Future of Aghanistan* (Washington D.C., 2009), pp. 1–11.

Thirlway, H., 'The Sources of International Law' in M. D. Evans (ed.), *International Law*, 3rd edn. (Oxford, New York: Oxford University Press, 2010), pp. 95–121.

Tico Times, *Human Rights Court Condemns El Salvador for El Mozote Massacre*. http://www.ticotimes.net/More-news/News-Briefs/Human-rights-court-condemns-El-Salvador-for-El-Mozote-massacre_Tuesday-December-11-2012 (12 December 2016).

Tittemore, B. D., 'Ending Impunity in the Americas: The Role of the Inter-American Human Rights System in Advancing Accountability for Serious Crimes under International Law', *Southwestern Journal of Law and Trade in the Americas* 12 (2005-2006), 429–75.

Tolbert D., *Address by David Tolbert to the National Forum on Launching the Dialogue on Transitional Justice in Tunisia*. http://ictj.org/news/address-david-tolbert-national-forum-launching-dialogue-transitional-justice-tunisia (07 January 2016).

Tolbert D., *A Wrong Turn for Human Rights*. http://www.project-syndicate.org/commentary/david-tolbert-warns-that-the-gains-made-since-the-end-of-the-cold-war-are-at-risk (13 January 2016).

Tolbert D., *Much Work Ahead for Spain in Facing the Ghosts of the Past*. http://www.huffingtonpost.com/david-tolbert/much-work-ahead-for-spain_b_5965638.html (07 January 2017).

Tolbert, D. and van Genugten, W. J.M., *International Justice in a Time of Transition*, International Peace Institute (IPI) Policy Forum (The Hague, 2012).

Tondini, M., *Statebuilding and Justice Reform: Post-Conflict Reconstruction in Afghanistan* (London and New York: Routledge, 2010).

Transitional Justice Coordination Group – Afghanistan, *TJCG Statement on the Amnesty Law: Accountability, Not Impunity: Only Victims Have the Right to Forgive*. http://tjcgafghanistan.wordpress.com/2010/03/01/tjcg-statement-on-the-amnesty-law/ (20 March 2017).

Transitional Justice Institute U. o. U., *The Belfast Guidelines on Amnesty and Accountability*. http://www.ulster.ac.uk/__data/assets/pdf_file/0005/57839/TheBelfastGuidelinesFINAL_000.pdf (24 March 2016).

TRIAL, *TRIAL WATCH: Assadullah Sarwari*. http://www.trial-ch.org/en/resources/trial-watch/trial-watch/profiles/profile/452/action/show/controller/Profile.html (01 June 2012).

TRIAL, *TRIAL WATCH: Faryadi Sarwar Zardad*. https://trialinternational.org/latest-post/faryadi-sarwar-zardad/ (01 May 2017).

TRIAL, *TRIAL WATCH: Habibullah Jalalzoy*. https://trialinternational.org/latest-post/habibullah-jalalzoy/ (01 May 2017).

TRIAL, *TRIAL WATCH: Heshamuddin Hesam*. https://trialinternational.org/latest-post/heshamuddin-hesam/ (30 April 2017).

Tribunal Supremo. 'Manos Limpias' and Association Liberty and Identity against Judge Baltasar Garzón for 'Prevaricación' (Criminal Offence of Breach of Judicial Duty): Summary of the Judgment 101/2012, of 27 February. http://www.poderjudicial.es/portal/site/cgpj/menuitem.0cb0942ae6fbda1c1ef62232dc432ea0/?vgnextoid=3dc82a011feb5310VgnVCM1000006f48ac0aRCRD&vgnextlocale=en&perfil=2&vgnextfmt=default&lang_choosen=en&vgnextchannel=6d70f20408619210VgnVCM100000cb34e20aRCRD (20 January 2017).

Trumbull, C. P., 'Giving Amnesties a Second Chance', *Berkeley Journal of International Law* 25 (2007), 283–345.

Tyler, T. R. (ed.), *Procedural Justice*, The international library of essays in law and society (Aldershot: Ashgate, 2005).

UN Committee Against Torture (CAT), *Concluding Observations of the Committee Against Torture: El Salvador: CAT/C/SLV/CO/2*. http://tbinternet.ohchr.org/_layouts/treatybodyexternal/Download.aspx?symbolno=CAT/C/SLV/CO/2&Lang=En (12 December 2016).

UN News Centre, *Nepal: Pillay Welcomes Supreme Court Ruling Against Amnesty for Serious Crimes*. http://www.un.org/apps/news/story.asp?NewsID=46872#.WH9RpH3zz90 (18 January 2017).

UN News Centre, *DR Congo: UN Officials Urge Justice for Grave Crimes Committed by M23*. http://www.globalsecurity.org/military/library/news/2014/10/mil-141009-unnews02.htm (11 January 2017).

UN Office of the High Commissioner for Human Rights, *Rule-of-Law Tools for Post-Conflict States: Prosecution Initiatives*, HR/PUB/06/4. http://www.ohchr.org/Documents/Publications/RuleoflawProsecutionsen.pdf (12 March 2017).

UN Office of the High Commissioner for Human Rights, *Rule-of-Law Tools for Post-Conflict States: Truth Commissions*, HR/PUB/06/1. http://www.ohchr.org/Documents/Publications/RuleoflawTruthCommissionsen.pdf (30 January 2017).

UN Office of the High Commissioner for Human Rights, *Rule-of-Law Tools for Post-Conflict States: Vetting: an Operational Framework*, HR/PUB/06/5. http://www.ohchr.org/Documents/Publications/RuleoflawVettingen.pdf (31 January 2017).

UN Office of the High Commissioner for Human Rights, *Rule-of-Law Tools for Post-Conflict States: Reparations Programmes*, HR/PUB/08/1. http://www.ohchr.org/Documents/Publications/ReparationsProgrammes.pdf (31 January 2013).

UN Office of the High Commissioner for Human Rights, *Rule-of-Law Tools for Post-Conflict States: Amnesties*, HR/PUB/09/1. http://www.ohchr.org/Documents/Publications/Amnesties_en.pdf (07 January 2016).

UN Office of the High Commissioner for Human Rights, *Rule-of-Law Tools for Post-Conflict States: National Consultations on Transitional Justice*, HR/PUB/09/2. http://www.ohchr.org/Documents/Publications/NationalConsultationsTJ_EN.pdf (23 March 2017).

UN Office of the High Commissioner for Human Rights, *OHCHR Comments on the Nepal "Commission on Investigation of Disappeared Persons, Truth and Reconciliation Ordinance – 2069 (2013)"*. http://www.ohchr.org/Documents/Countries/NP/OHCHRComments_TRC_Ordinance.docx (18 January 2017).

UN Office of the High Commissioner for Human Rights, *The Nepal Act on the Commission on Investigation of Disappeared Persons, Truth and Reconciliation, 2071 (2014) – as Gazetted 21 May 2014*. http://www.ohchr.org/Documents/Countries/NP/OHCHRTechnical_Note_Nepal_CIDP_TRC_Act2014.pdf (18 January 2017).

UNDP in Afghanistan, *Afghanistan Peace and Reintegration Programme (APRP)*. http://www.af.undp.org/content/afghanistan/en/home/operations/projects/crisis_prevention_and_recovery/aprp.html (27 January 2016).

UNDP in Afghanistan, *Afghanistan Peace and Reintegration Programme: 2015 Third Quarter Project Progress Report*. http://www.af.undp.org/content/dam/afghanistan/docs/crisisprev/APRP/APRP-3QPR-2015.pdf (02 June 2017).

United Nations, *UN Mapping Report Afghanistan – unpublished*. http://www.flagrancy.net/salvage/UNMappingReportAfghanistan.pdf (20 April 2017).

United Nations, *United Nations Treaty Collection: Glossary of Terms Relating to Treaty Actions*. https://treaties.un.org/Pages/Overview.aspx?path=overview/glossary/page1_en.xml (10 February 2016).

United Nations, *The Work of the International Law Commission*, 6th edn. (New York: United Nations, 2004).

United Nations, *Yearbook of the International Law Commission 2001: Volume II, Part Two*, A/CN.4/SER.A/2001/Add.1 (Part 2). http://legal.un.org/ilc/publications/yearbooks/english/ilc_2001_v2_p2.pdf (09 February 2016).

United Nations, *High Commissioner Expresses Concern Over National Stability Plan Passed by Afghanistan's Lower House*, Press Release (2007).

United Nations, *What is Transitional Justice? A Backgrounder*. https://www.un.org/en/peacebuilding/pdf/doc_wgll/justice_times_transition/26_02_2008_background_note.pdf (07 January 2016).

United Nations, *Guidance Note of the Secretary-General: United Nations Approach to Transitional Justice*. https://www.un.org/ruleoflaw/files/TJ_Guidance_Note_March_2010FINAL.pdf (17 March 2017).

United Nations Assistance Mission in Afghanistan (UNAMA), *Transcript of Press Conference in Kabul by Norah Niland, Representative of the UN High Commissioner for Human Rights in Afghanistan*. https://unama.unmissions.org/norah-niland-representative-un-high-commissioner-human-rights-afghanistan-0 (16 February 2017).

United Nations Assistance Mission in Afghanistan (UNAMA), *Afghanistan Mid Year Report on Protection of Civilians in Armed Conflict 2010*. https://unama.unmissions.org/sites/default/files/August102010_MID-YEAR%20REPORT%202010_Protection%20of%20Civilians%20in%20Armed%20Conflict.pdf (17 February 2017).

United Nations Assistance Mission in Afghanistan (UNAMA), *Afghanistan Midyear Report 2011: Protection of Civilians in Armed Conflict*. https://unama.unmissions.org/sites/default/files/2011_midyear_poc.pdf (11 February 2016).

United Nations Assistance Mission in Afghanistan (UNAMA), *Draft Peace Agreement Between Government and Hezb-i-Islami Gulbuddin*. http://unama.unmissions.org/print/draft-peace-agreement-between-government-and-hezb-i-islami-gulbuddin (11 October 2016).

United Nations Commission on Human Rights, *Independent Study on Best Practices, Including Recommendations, to Assist States in Strengthening Their Domestic Capacity to Combat all Aspects of Impunity, by Professor Diane Orentlicher*, E/CN.4/2004/88. http://www.unhchr.ch/Huridocda/Huridoca.nsf/0/94b45b7493a558cac1256e6e005a6d1d/$FILE/G0411355.pdf (20 March 2017).

United Nations Commission on Human Rights, *Report of the Special Rapporteur on the Independence of Judges and Lawyers, Leandro Despouy*, E/CN.4/2005/60. http://daccess-dds-ny.un.org/doc/UNDOC/GEN/G05/104/13/PDF/G0510413.pdf?OpenElement (23 February 2016).

United Nations Commission on Human Rights, *Report of the Independent Expert to Update the Set of Principles to Combat Impunity, Diane Orentlicher, Addendum: Updated Set of Principles for the Protection and Promotion of Human Rights Through Action to Combat Impunity*, E/CN.4/2005/102/Add.1.

United Nations Commission on Human Rights, *Report of the Independent Expert to Update the Set of Principles to Combat Impunity, Diane Orentlicher*, E/CN.4/2005/102. https://documents-dds-ny.un.org/doc/UNDOC/GEN/G05/111/03/PDF/G0511103.pdf?OpenElement (13 March 2017).

United Nations Development Programme Afghanistan, *Disbandment of Illegal Armed Groups (DIAG): Annual Project Report 2010*. http://www.undp.org.af/Projects/Report2011/diag/2011-03-21-%20Annual%20Progress%20Report%20of%20DIAG.pdf (07 May 2012).

United Nations Development Programme Afghanistan, *Afghanistan's New Beginnings Programme (ANBP)*. http://www.undp.org.af/whoweare/undpinafghanistan/Projects/psl/prj_anbp.htm (07 May 2012).

United Nations Development Programme Afghanistan, *Afghanistan Peace and Reintegration Programme (APRP) – UNDP Support: Third Quarter Report 2011*. http://www.undp.org.af/Projects/Report2011/APRP/3rdQ/APRP_00076674_QPR_Q3_2011.pdf (17 April 2012).

United Nations General Assembly, *Basic Principles and Guidelines on the Right to a Remedy and Reparation for Victims of Gross Violations of International Human Rights Law and Serious Violations of International Humanitarian Law*, A/RES/60/147.

United Nations General Assembly, *International, Impartial and Independent Mechanism to Assist in the Investigation and Prosecution of Those Responsible for the Most Serious Crimes under International Law Committed in the Syrian Arab Republic since March 2011*, A/71/L.48. http://www.un.org/ga/search/view_doc.asp?symbol=A/71/L.48 (24 February 2017).

United Nations General Assembly – Security Council, *The Situation in Afghanistan and Its Implications for International Peace and Security: Report of the Secretary-General*, A/56/681–S/2001/1157. http://www.un.org/en/ga/search/view_doc.asp?symbol=S/2001/1157 (20 February 2017).

United Nations General Assembly – Security Council, *The Situation in Afghanistan and Its Implications for International Peace and Security: Report of the Secretary-General*, A/59/581 – S/2004/925. http://www.securitycouncilreport.org/atf/cf/%7B65BFCF9B-6D27-4E9C-8CD3-CF6E4FF96FF9%7D/Afgh%20S2004%20925.pdf (20 February 2017).

United Nations General Assembly – Security Council, *The Situation in Afghanistan and Its Implications for International Peace and Security: Report of the Secretary-General*, A/64/705–S/2010/127. http://afghanistan-un.org/wp-content/uploads/2010/11/S20101271.pdf (13 February 2017).

United Nations Human Rights Committee, *Concluding Observations of the UN Human Rights Committee: Uruguay: CCPR/C/79/Add.19*. http://tbinternet.ohchr.org/_layouts/treatybodyexternal/Download.aspx?symbolno=CCPR%2FC%2F79%2FAdd.19&Lang=en (07 December 2016).

United Nations Human Rights Committee, *Rodríguez v. Uruguay, Communication No. 322/1988: U.N. Doc. CCPR/C/51/D/322/1988 (1994)*. http://hrlibrary.umn.edu/undocs/html/vws322.htm (07 December 2016).

United Nations Human Rights Committee, *General Comment No. 31: The Nature of the General Legal Obligation Imposed on States Parties to the Covenant*, CCPR/C/21/Rev.1/Add.13. https://www1.umn.edu/humanrts/gencomm/hrcom31.html (29.02.16).

United Nations Human Rights Council, *Analytical Study on Human Rights and Transitional Justice*, A/HRC/12/18. http://www2.ohchr.org/english/bodies/hrcouncil/docs/12session/A-HRC-12-18_E.pdf (24 November 2016).

United Nations Human Rights Council, *Report of the International Commission of Inquiry on Libya: A/HRC/19/68*. http://www.ohchr.org/Documents/HRBodies/HRCouncil/RegularSession/Session19/A.HRC.19.68.pdf (20 January 2017).

United Nations Human Rights Council, *Report of the Special Rapporteur on the Promotion of Truth, Justice, Reparation and Guarantees of Non-Recurrence*, A/HRC/27/56. http://www.ohchr.org/EN/HRBodies/HRC/RegularSessions/Session27/Pages/ListReports.aspx (12 January 2017).

United Nations Security Council, *Sierra Leone*, S/PV.4035. http://www.un.org/en/ga/search/view_doc.asp?symbol=S/PV.4035 (28 February 2017).

United Nations Security Council, *Report of the Secretary-General on the Role of United Nations Peacekeeping in Disarmament, Demobilization and Reintegration*, S/2000/101. http://www.un.org/en/ga/search/view_doc.asp?symbol=S/2000/101 (31 May 2017).

United Nations Security Council, *Report of the Secretary-General on the Establishment of a Special Court for Sierra Leone*, S/2000/915. http://www.rscsl.org/Documents/Establishment/S-2000-915.pdf (16 February 2017).

United Nations Security Council, *Agreement on Provisional Arrangements in Afghanistan Pending the Re-Establishment of Permanent Government Institutions: "Bonn Agreement"*, S/2001/1154. http://www.unhcr.org/refworld/docid/3f48f4754.html (20 January 2016).

United Nations Security Council, *The Rule of Law and Transitional Justice in Conflict and Post-Conflict Societies, Report of the Secretary-General*, S/2004/616. http://daccess-dds-ny.un.org/doc/UNDOC/GEN/N04/395/29/PDF/N0439529.pdf?OpenElement (08 January 2016).

United Nations Security Council, *United Nations Security Council – 5052nd meeting*, S/PV.5052 (Resumption 1). http://www.securitycouncilreport.org/atf/cf/%7B65BFCF9B-6D27-4E9C-8CD3-CF6E4FF96FF9%7D/IJ%20SPV5052%20Res1.pdf (16 February 2017).

United Nations Security Council, *Resolution 1674 (2006)*, S/Res/1674 (2006). https://documents-dds-ny.un.org/doc/UNDOC/GEN/N06/331/99/PDF/N0633199.pdf?OpenElement (16 February 2017).

United Nations Security Council, *Resolution 1757 (2007)*, S/RES/1757 (2007). http://daccess-dds-ny.un.org/doc/UNDOC/GEN/N07/363/57/PDF/N0736357.pdf?OpenElement (12 February 2017).

United Nations Security Council, *The Rule of Law and Transitional Justice in Conflict and Post-Conflict Societies: Report of the Secretary-General*, S/2011/634. http://www.securitycouncilreport.org/atf/cf/%7B65BFCF9B-6D27-4E9C-8CD3-CF6E4FF96FF9%7D/ROL%20S2011%20634.pdf (17 February 2017).

United Nations Security Council, *Resolution 2014 (2011)*, S/RES/2014 (2011). http://www.securitycouncilreport.org/atf/cf/%7B65BFCF9B-6D27-4E9C-8CD3-CF6E4FF96FF9%7D/YEMEN%20S%20RES%202014.pdf (15 January 2017).

United States Agency for International Development (USAID), *Afghanistan Rule of Law Project: Field Study of Informal and Customary Justice in Afghanistan and Recommendations on Improving Access to Justice and Relations Between Formal Courts and Informal Bodies*. http://www.usip.org/files/file/usaid_afghanistan.pdf (15 March 2017).

University of Minnesota – Human Rights Library, *Ratification of International Human Rights Treaties – Afghanistan*. http://www1.umn.edu/humanrts/research/ratification-afghanistan1.html (11 February 2016).

Unofficial Translation of the Comprehensive Peace Agreement concluded between the Government of Nepal and the Communist Party of Nepal (Maoist). http://www.usip.org/sites/default/files/file/resources/collections/peace_agreements/nepal_cpa_20061121_en.pdf (16 January 2017).

'Uruguay: Justice or Democracy?', The Economist, 23 March 2013.

Valinas, M., 'Interpreting Complementarity and Interest of Justice in the Presence of Restorative-Based Alternative Forms of Justice' in C. Stahn and L. van den Herik (eds.), *Future Perspectives on International Criminal Justice* (The Hague: T.M.C. Asser Press, 2010), pp. 267–88.

van der Vyver, J. D., 'The United Nations and International Criminal Law', *The University of Queensland Law Journal* 24 (2005), 317–36.

van Eijl, R., *Dealing with Crimes of the Past: No More Amnesty? An Inquiry into the Lawfulness of Amnesty for Human Rights Atrocities Under International Law* (Utrecht: Kennispunt Recht, Economie, Bestuur en Organisatie, Universiteit Utrecht, 2009).

van Hoecke, M., 'Methodology of Comparative Legal Research', *Law and Method* (2015).

van Schaack, B. and Slye, R. C., *International Criminal Law and Its Enforcement* (New York: Foundation Press, 2007).

Vendrell, F., 'The International Community's Failures in Afghanistan' in W. Mason (ed.), *The Rule of Law in Afghanistan* (Cambridge: Cambridge University Press, 2011), pp. 53–60.

Villiger, M. E., *Customary International Law and Treaties: A Manual on the Theory and Practice of the Interrelation of Sources*, Developments in international law, 2nd edn. (The Hague [u.a.]: Kluwer Law International, 1997), vol. 28.

Vogenauer, S. and Weatherill, S., *General Principles of Law*, Studies of the Oxford Institute of European and Comparative Law (Oxford UK, Portland, Oregon: Hart Publishing, 2017).

Walker, S. and Bowcott, O., 'Russia Withdraws Signature from International Criminal Court Statute', The Guardian, 16 November 2016.

Wardak, A., 'State and Non-State Justice Systems in Afghanistan: the Need for Synergy', *U. Pa. J. Int'l L.* 32 (2011), 1305–24.

Wardak A., Saba D. and Kazem H., *Afghanistan Human Development Report 2007: Bridging Modernity and Tradition: Rule of Law and the Search for Justice*. http://hdr.undp.org/sites/default/files/nhdr2007.pdf (22 January 2016).

Werle, G., 'Transitional Justice – Der juristische Rahmen' in H. E. Müller, G. M. Sander and H. Válková (eds.), *Festschrift für Ulrich Eisenberg zum 70. Geburtstag* (München: Beck, 2009), pp. 791–806.

Werle, G., *Völkerstrafrecht*, 3rd edn. (Tübingen: Mohr Siebeck, 2012).

Werle, G. and Jessberger, F., *Principles of International Criminal Law*, 3rd edn. (Oxford: Oxford University Press, 2014).

Westerwelle Recommends Assad the Passage Into Exile. http://www.zitecode.com/Articles/detail/westerwelle-recommends-assad-the-passage-into-exile.html (21 August 2012).

Wilkinson B., *Court to Soon Rule in Military Executions Trial in Suriname*. http://amsterdamnews.com/news/2018/nov/08/court-soon-rule-military-executions-trial-suriname/ (04 February 2019).

Williams, S., 'Amnesties in International Law: The Experience of the Special Court for Sierra Leone', *Human Rights Law Review* 5 (2005), 271–309.

Winterbotham E., *The State of Transitional Justice in Afghanistan*. http://www.areu.org.af/Uploads/EditionPdfs/1014E-The%20State%20of%20Transitional%20Justice%20in%20Afghanistan%20PN%20April%202010.pdf (12 January 2017).

Winterbotham E., *The State of Transitional Justice in Afghanistan: Actors, Approaches and Challenges*. http://www.areu.org.af/Uploads/EditionPdfs/1009E-The%20State%20of%20Transitional%20Justice%20in%20Afghanistan%20-%20Actors,%20Approaches%20and%20Challenges%20DP%202010%20Final%20Web.pdf (18 January 2016).

Winterbotham E., *Legacies of Conflict: Healing Complexes and Moving Forwards in Ghazni Province*. http://www.refworld.org/docid/4e92ba3a2.html (10 March 2017).

Winterbotham E., *Wartime Suffering: Patterns of Violations in Afghanistan*. http://www.areu.org.af/Uploads/EditionPdfs/1123E%20-%20Legacies%20of%20Conflict%20-%20Wartime%20Suffering%202011.pdf (19 January 2016).

Winterbotham E., *Healing the Legacies of Conflict in Afghanistan: Community Voices on Justice, Peace and Reconciliation*. http://www.areu.org.af/Uploads/EditionPdfs/1201E-Healing%20the%20Legacies%20of%20Conflict%20in%20Afghanistan%20SP%202011.pdf (19 January 2016).

Wisner, D., 'Is Time Ripe for Transitional Justice in Afghanistan?', *The Fletcher School Online Journal for Southwest Asia and Islamic Civilization* (2008), 1–12.

Wolkowa, I., 'Generalpardon für "heilige Krieger": Afghanisches Parlament beschloss Amnestie/Kämpfer der letzten 25 Jahre bleiben straffrei', Neues Deutschland, 03 February 2007.

Worden S. and Steele R., *Telling the Story: Documentation Lessons for Afghanistan from the Cambodian Experience*. http://dspace.cigilibrary.org/jspui/bitstream/123456789/25297/1/Telling%20the%20Story%20-%20Documentation%20Lessons%20for%20Afghanistan%20from%20the%20Cambodian%20Experience.pdf?1 (10 April 2017).

Yemen Times, *Yemen's Immunity Law: Breach of International Obligations*. http://www.yementimes.com/en/1720/report/3013/Yemen%E2%80%99s-immunity-law-Breach-of-international-obligations.html (15 January 2017).

Ynetnews, *113 Countries Sign Pledge Against Sexual Violence*. http://www.ynetnews.com/articles/0,7340,L-4433351,00.html (24 January 2017).

Zegveld, L., 'Dutch Cases on Torture Committed in Afghanistan: The Relevance of the Distinction between Internal and International Armed Conflict', *Journal of International Criminal Justice* (2006), 878–80.

Zulfiqar S. and Calderon H., *Chad and Five Other Central African Countries Pledge to End Use of Children in Armed Conflict: 'N'Djaména Declaration' Adopted*. http://www.unicef.org/infobycountry/chad_53966.html (23 January 2017).

Zumach, A., 'Signal gegen Straflosigkeit', taz, 23 December 2016.

Zupan, N. and Servaes, S., *Transitional Justice & Dealing with the Past*, Guidance Paper Transitional Justice (Bonn, Germany, 2007).